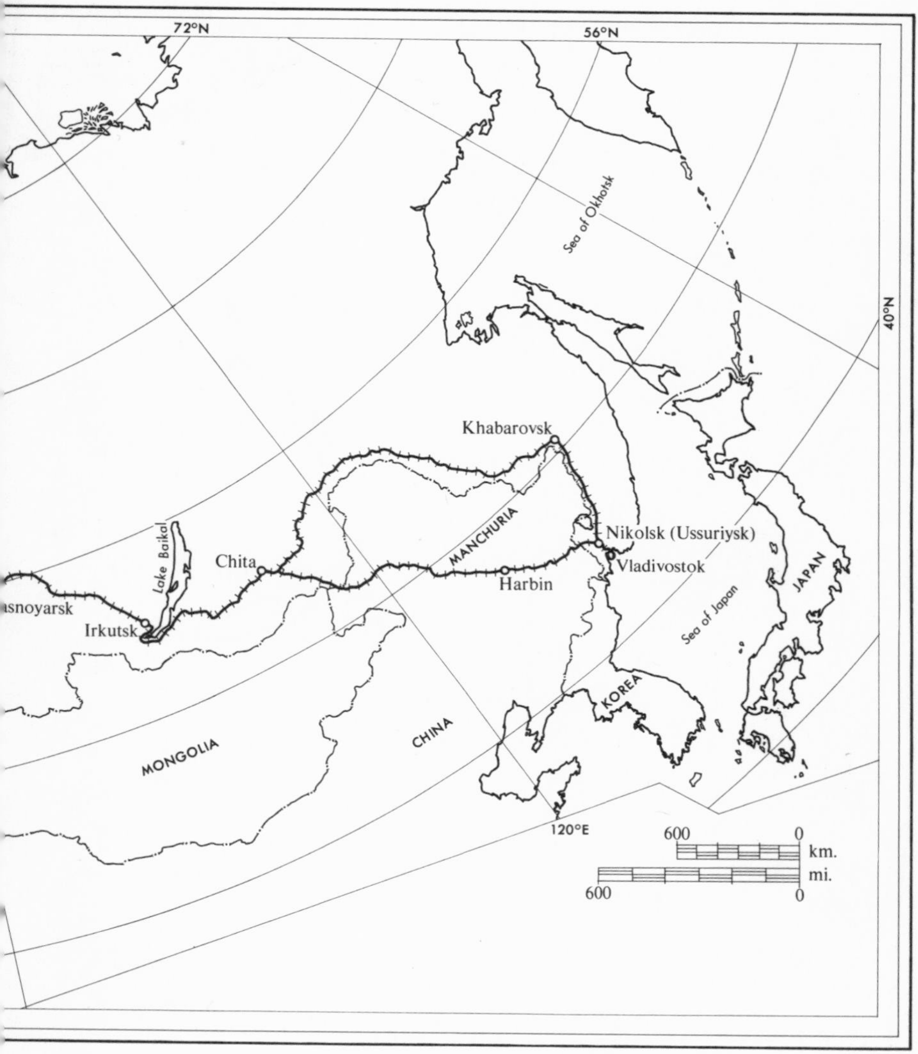

72°N   56°N

Sea of Okhotsk

40°N

Khabarovsk

MANCHURIA

Nikolsk (Ussuriysk)

Lake Baikal   Chita   Vladivostok

Harbin

asnoyarsk

Irkutsk

Sea of Japan   JAPAN

MONGOLIA   CHINA   KOREA

120°E   600   0
km.
mi.
600   0

In Russia to work with the Y.M.C.A. prisoner of war relief program, Edward T. Heald found himself in St. Petersburg at the time of the February Revolution, in Kiev at the time of the Bolshevik take-over, travelling in various parts of Siberia during the first months of the Civil War, and in Vladivostok when the American Expeditionary Force landed. He was an articulate young man, abroad for the first time, and he described all he saw, heard, and did in long letters home. Edited now for publication, they provide a street-corner view of the greatest social upheaval of our time.

Neither an ideologue nor an analyst, not always aware of the significance of what he reported, Heald's greatest contribution to our understanding of the Russian Revolution is human rather than political. With him we see the mobs in the streets and the soldiers in the trenches, we feel the tensions of living by rumor and conflicting reports, we walk the tightropes of dealing with shifting power factions within changing governments. And we are amazed at how much of normal life continues beneath the boiling surface—the usual comings and goings, the vacations, the concerts, the shops and restaurants; indeed, Heald's wife came from the States to join him for a year in 1917–18, although arranging the trip was a stew of confused communications.

Witness to Revolution is both a fascinating story of day-to-day events in the Russian Revolution and a revealing account of life in crisis and change.

Witness to Revolution

LETTERS FROM RUSSIA 1916-1919

Witness to Revolution

LETTERS FROM RUSSIA 1916-1919
BY EDWARD T. HEALD

EDITED BY JAMES B. GIDNEY
KENT STATE UNIVERSITY

The Kent State University Press

The photographs were selected from a large collection Heald deposited with the Stark County Historical Center. They are made available through the courtesy of Gervis Brady, Director of the Stark County Historical Society and are reproduced here for the first time.

Contents

Preface

The First World War presented the western world with a phenomenon unknown in the annals of civilized man, that of prisoners of war in wholly unprecedented numbers confined behind barbed wire for years at a time for no crime other than that of having obeyed their national leaders. By the summer of 1916, there were well over five million such prisoners and, with no end in sight to what so many had expected to be a short war, it could be anticipated that the number would increase. The burden of boredom and idleness lay heavy on the spirits of these men and even exacted a toll of lives.

Of those who were determined to alleviate the suffering of these unhappy victims of what George F. Kennan has called Europe's attempt to commit suicide, none was so active as the Y.M.C.A. It was not at first certain that the efforts of the *Y* would be acceptable to the host governments because of the bitterness of feeling against prisoners of war on the part of local populations—perhaps another unfamiliar phenomenon—but the reciprocal nature of the program induced the governments to allow it. The German government could hardly deny help to French prisoners if it meant that no help could be offered to German prisoners in France. The *Y* was therefore permitted early in the war to organize camps in all belligerent countries except Turkey. This permission allowed a secretary to go into a camp and arrange with those in charge for the loan of a building or, if no such concession could be had, to erect a temporary shed. He would then seek out those prisoners best qualified for leadership and organize them into committees or groups for educational work, handicrafts, music, and other activities, including those of a religious nature. Using this method, a single secretary

could bring new interest, new hope, even new life to from 50,000
to 100,000 unhappy victims of the European convulsion.

The Y.M.C.A. was, of course, in part a religious organization.
A secretary was expected to be conscious that he was performing
a Christian ministry; he might even be reminded that he had
fallen heir to an exceptional opportunity since the bitterness
of war and imprisonment had put men into a mood more receptive to religious teaching than that of civilian life. The charge
of proselytizing intent cannot therefore be entirely rejected. It
should be borne in mind, however, that a large part of the
Y's activities were quite unrelated to sectarian religion, that the
religious "message" was not forced on anyone who didn't want
to receive it, nor was anyone in consequence of such rejection
disqualified from other benefits. Moreover, the stark truth is
that young manpower had been so frightfully drained by the
war that no belligerent could afford to let another five million
disintegrate under the tedium of camp life into a passive vacuity
or destructive bitterness that would have limited their usefulness
when they returned to civilian life.

It was with a view to enlisting an additional secretary in
this work that C. V. Hibbard, Associate Secretary for War Work
of the Y.M.C.A.'s International Committee, wrote in June 1916
from the Committee's New York office to Edward T. Heald,
secretary in Davenport, Iowa. (He called him "Held.") In this
letter Hibbard described in some detail the work, its objective,
and the qualifications desired in those who did it. "If possible,"
he wrote, "we desire men who have a knowledge of European
languages but first and foremost we require men of strong Christian character, of tactful, genial personality, and of strong
optimism who will give a year or more to this unique service to
the manhood of Europe." He concluded by inquiring whether
Edward Heald, who had been recommended to him, would be
interested in becoming a prisoner-of-war secretary.

Whether or not Heald recognized himself in Hibbard's
specifications, anyone carefully reading his letters will feel that
they fit him very well. I have had a hint or two that some of the
tact dropped out of his nature as he grew older, but he certainly
had it in 1916. He was and remained a man of strong character

which was related, though not ostentatiously, to his Christian faith; he was also—no reader of these letters can doubt it— genial, friendly, and incurably optimistic. He even had some German, which he had studied at Oberlin College.

A native of the Hood River Valley in Oregon, Heald had moved with his family to Peoria, Illinois, at an early age. He attended Oberlin and graduated in 1907. Graduating with him was Emily Ainsworth of Moline, Illinois, whom he married three years later. Following a brief stint in business in Peoria, he entered Y.M.C.A. work, becoming student secretary at Colorado College. (He developed there an affection bordering on adulation for the State of Colorado, and in his letters everything of superlative beauty in European Russia or Siberia reminds him of Colorado.) From Colorado Springs he went as secretary to the *Y* in Manhattan, Kansas, thence to Toledo, Ohio, as membership secretary and finally in 1914 to Davenport.

Heald must have accepted the prisoner-of-war assignment very quickly, for Hibbard wrote again only five days later to congratulate him on "the good judgment which has enabled you to appreciate the extraordinary value of this opportunity and on the willingness to sacrifice personal convenience that has led you to offer your services." There is even a reference to Mrs. Heald's sacrifice for it was made clear that wives were not to accompany their husbands to the camps. Mrs. Heald did get to Russia and stayed there from mid-1917 to mid-1918, but only because circumstances, including the February Revolution and America's entry into the war, were such that her husband's work was shifted away from the prisoner-of-war field.*

We cannot know Heald's motives completely, but his immediate acceptance of Hibbard's offer is not surprising. It is possible that at thirty he was still feeling some youthful wanderlust, but his essential reaction—cynical readers will find themselves forced to believe it—was to welcome an opportunity to help

---

* Twenty-six thousand Y.M.C.A. secretaries served in Europe and Asia during the First World War. It is not clear how many of the 26,000 worked in Russia, but the ratio of $6,000,000 spent in Russia to the total budget of of $152,000,000 certainly tells us something.

people in need, particularly to do so in a Christian undertaking and under the aegis of his beloved "Association."

No doubt some young men go overseas for no better reason than a desire to get away from home, but it is impossible to attribute this motive to Heald. The tone of his letters reinforces the testimony of his friends that there was never a more loving couple than the Healds. They were devoted as college kids at Oberlin, they were devoted through changes of fortune and residence and two world wars until they died within three months of each other in their eighties.

Hibbard wrote again on the 27th of June advising that "if you are not a Mason, I think it will be best for you to plan provisionally to go to Russia." In that case, Heald would leave New York on August 17 and travel to Petrograd where his camp assignment would be determined by Y.M.C.A. representatives in consultation with the Russian government. As Heald was not a Mason, he planned to go to Russia, and did in fact leave New York on August 17. He stayed there almost three years, working in European Russia, the Ukraine, and Siberia, and writing a letter to his wife or his parents or her parents virtually every day. It is from those letters, amounting probably to six hundred pages of typescript, that the present volume has been assembled.

Before leaving he visited his family at their farm, Orchardells, near Peoria. From there he wrote Emily a most revealing letter about the state of the farm and his father's management of it. This is mentioned here because the family's difficulties in farming were on Heald's mind constantly throughout his stay in Russia. His father was healthier and happier on the farm than he had been in an office, but he could not seem to make a go of it, and the large mortgage presented a mountainous threat to family solvency. The farm was the cause of disagreement between Edward and Emily virtually throughout his Russian service, since she felt his first duty was to come home and help his family. It is testimony to his strong (and different) conviction of duty that he remained in Russia as long as he did, for in addition to his feeling for his wife and family, he admitted that Orchardells exercized a strong attraction for him. He rather touchingly confessed that Gladstone's simultaneous management of the British government and the family estate at Hawarden represented something of an ideal for him.

He also devoted some time, between packing, getting vaccinated, and visiting his family, to answering a circular letter from the secretary of the *Y* in Hartford, Connecticut, in which secretaries in other parts of the country were queried about their problems. Nothing perhaps better characterizes Edward Heald than his thoughtful and detailed four-page answer. It must have been written on his last day or two in Davenport, yet it betrays no suggestion that he had anything on his mind but a desire to be helpful to a fellow-secretary. It illustrates one of his noteworthy capacities—a capacity without which the present volume would have been impossible. He could write at any time or place, clearly, vividly, and with excellent organization of his thought, and he could do it quickly. Whether written in longhand or punched out on his Corona, his manuscript is always legible and with almost no mistakes, if we except those, to be discussed later, that Heald did not recognize as mistakes.

One other characteristic should be mentioned—although it has probably already been inferred by the reader—Heald's rocklike integrity. This is important not only for a just appreciation of his character but perhaps even more for the assurance it provides of the reliability of the work which follows since, as will appear later, the editor was not in every case able to see the originals. For this integrity the editor relies not only on the assurances of those who knew Heald in Canton, Ohio, nor on that of Professor Warren B. Walsh who prepared some of these letters for publication in *The American Slavic and East European Review* in 1947, but on the evidence of the letters themselves, those which appear here and those which don't. Perhaps the reader will be content with a single illustration.

During Heald's stay at Omsk, he received a letter from his immediate superior in Vladivostok, G. S. Phelps, in which, after discussion of Association problems in the usual tone of their correspondence, Phelps suddenly accused Heald of disloyalty and of attempting to undermine his authority. He protested bitterly that in twenty years as a Y.M.C.A. executive he had never been treated as Heald had treated him. Whatever his exaggeration, a genuine sense of hurt and outrage comes through.

Heald replied that he had been shocked and saddened by Phelps's letter, that he had had no thought of disloyalty but had been merely expressing a difference of opinion on policy. He added that his opinion had been generally that of the men in the field who, not surprisingly, saw things differently from those at headquarters. He added that much of the field criticism of Vladivostok had ended upon receipt of more complete information. He confessed that Phelps would probably be even more hurt when he read another letter which was presumably still on its way, but protested again that no disloyalty or personal reflection had been intended and that, on the basis of information recently received, the men in Western Siberia were now content with Vladivostok's policies. Reading the two letters together, I found Heald's reply convincing; yet the tone of Phelps's complaint lingers and I wonder how many of us would have kept such a wounding communication in open files for half a century.

Heald's work profits also from his being what some would call "objective" but others might call "uninformed." I put it thus bluntly because it's well the reader should know what he can properly expect and what he can't. Although a highly intelligent man and a keen observer, Heald was in no sense a scholar.* This is not intended as denigration; indeed it is one of his advantages. He is not tendentious about many historical questions because he does not know they are questions. Extraordinarily good at reporting what he himself saw and experienced, he is not particularly good at relating it to larger issues and seems singularly incurious about some matters on which we are still arguing. He was obviously delighted to see American troops arrive at Vladivostok—he had the view peculiar to our countrymen at that time that Americans did things better than anyone else—but it never seems to have occurred to him to wonder what they were there for. He appears too little aware of the number of the Czar's subjects who were not Russians and although quite

---

* This judgment characterizes Heald during his stay in Russia and is in no way intended as a reflection on his later work as a historian of Stark County, Ohio.

without malice, he is at times insufficiently sympathetic toward minorities. After his return to the United States, he seems to have had no thought of pursuing the kind of studies which his three-year residence in Russia and his mastery of the language so well fitted him for. Although he spoke and wrote frequently about Russia in later years, it was always from the standpoint of the revolutionary time which he had experienced. Readers, therefore, who are looking for a high-powered analysis will not find it. But we have so many high-powered analyses. What Heald's reader will find is something rarer—the account of a man who was there and could tell about it. Edward Heald is above all a superb *witness*. History always needs analysis but it is fact that must be analyzed and the pearl of greatest price may well be the man or woman who, placed by fortune in a position to know the fact, has also the skill, the patience, and the literacy to set it down intelligibly. Intelligibly and, if not dispassionately, at least accurately.

Such a one was Edward Heald and he seems to have known it. He knew, at least, that he had been in a rare position to observe the Russian Revolution without having a personal stake in any part of it. When he prepared these letters for publication in the 1940s, he wrote that his value consisted in his being neither pro- nor anti-czar, neither pro- nor anti-Provisional Government, neither pro- nor anti-Bolshevik, except to the extent that the Bolsheviks were placing an extra burden on the allies by taking Russia out of the war. Of course a man as committed to Christianity as Heald had to be somewhat anti-Bolshevik, but he tried to be fair even to them. When a person whose judgment he respected assured him that Lenin had struggled selflessly for years to better the lot of the mass of the Russian people, Heald listened thoughtfully and put it down in a letter home. And while he felt, as others had, the charm of the old regime, he never failed to make clear that Russia was in need of sweeping changes to make it habitable for the majority of its people.

Perhaps, too, the characterization of "uninformed" should be subject to some reservations. In the first place, Heald's ignorance was frequently but a reflection of a general ignorance. He

seems never to have really understood what Lenin and Trotsky
were up to, but during the period of the Russian Civil War,
how many outsiders did? Heald was optimistic about a Kolchak
victory early in 1919, but wasn't this the general expectation
of the people with whom he was in contact, not to mention
several supposedly well-informed foreign governments? And on
the other side it must be recorded that Heald well understood
what some didn't, and many still don't, that one of the strengths
of Bolshevism was the wretchedness of life for so many under
the self-satisfied "establishment" the Bolsheviks were seeking to
replace. He seems even to have grasped that Kolchak was
defeated by his supporters.

An even more important qualification of his lack of information is the impossibility of being sure he really lacked it.
Perhaps at times he was manifesting a massive discretion. The
best example—and since every attentive reader is going to
wonder about it, it may as well be discussed here—is his treatment of the Y.M.C.A.'s pullback to Irkutsk in the spring of 1919.
Throughout the preceding weeks Heald, moving from town to
town in the Urals and even as far west as Ufa, radiates optimism.
The *Y* is doing a splendid and indispensable job in the middle
of overwhelming destitution and starvation. Even with allow-
ance for his customary buoyancy and optimism, it can hardly
be accounted anything less than a smashing success. Then on
March 14 he suddenly tells us that activity west of Omsk is to
be terminated and that on April 5 all of Western Siberia is to
be abandoned and headquarters are to be pulled back to Irkutsk.
We know him well enough to be sure he has some strong feelings
about this, but he tells us nothing.

Surely an incurious man! Or is he? A clue is provided in
the account of the American intervention in Siberia by its
commander, General William S. Graves.* Graves, determined
to carry out to the letter his difficult instructions to stay out of
Russia's internal quarrels, tells us that fidelity to his orders
became more difficult with the advent of the Kolchak govern-

* William S. Graves, *America's Siberian Adventure 1918–1920* (New York:
J. Cape and H. Smith, 1931).

ment at Omsk. No organization, he writes, which furnished services of any kind to troops or civilians was to be allowed to
continue except under Kolchak's supervision. In effect, such an
agency was to become an arm of the Kolchak government.
According to General Graves's testimony, the American Red
Cross bent the knee to these demands, but the Y.M.C.A. refused
to do so. May we not deduce from this that the Y pulled
back to Irkutsk (where Kolchak's writ didn't run) because
withdrawal from Western Siberia was the only way to
retain its independence?

If this is indeed the explanation, we can hardly doubt that
Heald, who was in charge of the entire Western Siberian operation, knew it. We can also be sure he resented it. Seen in this
light his silence appears not as ignorance but rather as an
impressive self-mastery. The Y.M.C.A.'s refusal to knuckle under
to Kolchak brought the whole question into a realm of such
international delicacy that he could not mention it even to his
wife or his parents. The only clue we find in the letters is a
negative one—no more favorable references to Kolchak.

Long before Heald reached Siberia the prisoner-of-war work
for which he had been sent to Russia had become impossible.
Prior to America's entry into the war, the American Y had
conducted sixty-two of these operations in Russia. With the
declaration of war it was obliged to turn them over to workers
from the neutral countries. Heald's service, therefore, was
transferred to Russian troops; after the Siberian intervention
began, Czech, American, British, French, and Japanese troops
were added. By the time he reached the interior of Siberia
prisoners of war, usually Germans, Austrians, and Hungarians,
had also to be helped, as did the totally disorganized Russians
returning from the war in which, thanks to the treaty of Brest-
Litovsk, they were no longer involved. Some of these had been
prisoners of the Germans and Austrians who had simply let
them go; others were Russian soldiers who, with their services
no longer required, were left to find their way home.

The rest of the story is in Heald's letters so it remains only
to describe the manuscript as I found it and what I have done
with it. Actually I did not find a manuscript. There were, in

addition to a mass of largely unsorted papers, two manuscripts.
Each of these, prepared by Heald himself in the 1940s, was
contained in three looseleaf notebooks.

The remainder of the collection, treasure trove or rubbish
heap according to the taste of the reader, included some, but not
all, of the original letters, many of them in excellent condition,
a large number of letters to and from Heald that are not part
of the manuscript, as well as a collection of photographs, some
identifiable, some not, and memorabilia of all sorts. There were
also some letters to and from Emily Heald and papers, some
complete but more incomplete, which appeared to be texts of
speeches Heald had delivered, presumably during the years he
lived in Canton, Ohio. In a few cases, however, they appear
not to be speeches but earlier attempts to compile a volume like
this one. My impression is that the desire to publish his letters,
fairly strong with Heald when he returned from Russia, weak-
ened over the ensuing two decades and then became stronger
during the Second World War when he felt, as so many did, that
the future happiness of the world might rest on the ability of
Americans and Russians to understand each other. He therefore
set out again to produce a publishable manuscript and in doing
so used a number of the original letters to fill in his copy. That
is the only way I can account for the absence of some of the
originals, for Heald strikes me as one of those people who saved
everything. The foregoing explanation is offered in an attempt
to appease those who can see no value in a collection of this
kind unless it contains the author's exact words, festooned with
footnotes, and with a pontifical [sic] intervening when the
jostling of a Siberian train induced him to strike a few wrong
keys. I decided rather early in my investigations that such a
scholarly treatment was not at all suited to this material and in any
case would be out of the question because of the condition in
which I found the papers. I couldn't publish all of the originals
just as they were because a number of them weren't there nor
could I even publish the 1945 manuscript as I found it, because
I had found two of them.*

---

* Readers who prefer the full scholarly editing can find it in *The American
Slavic and East European Review* for 1947 (vols. xvi and xvii). There

The two manuscripts are in themselves a bit mystifying, simply because they don't seem different enough to justify the extra effort of producing a second. The only hint I can supply is one offered me by an associate of Heald's who said that "as Ed got older, he tried to acquire a style." Heald had, as I hope the reader will notice, a remarkable natural style, so I regard it as fortunate that he didn't go too far in changing his original manner. In any case, faced with two similar manuscripts I chose the one I liked better, but I can assure the reader the difference would not have been great had I chosen the other.

In short, then, after reading through these manuscripts and such of the originals as I could find, I discovered that Edward Heald had himself done a good job of editing. So far as selection was concerned, I could not hope to do it better, so I accepted his. I have restored only one letter which he took out. That is the one in which he recounts his difficulty in finding a dandruff remedy in wartime Petrograd. I suspect that the aging Heald considered this somewhat undignified. It certainly adds little to our understanding of the Russian Revolution, but I thought it revealing of the problems of life for the young man in a foreign city at a time when his Russian was quite fragmentary. I also thought it funny, which I understand the later Heald was not.

I discovered one other emendation in Heald's editing of which the reader should be aware. He telescoped letters and diary entries of several days into a single letter. Thus a letter dated, for example, May 17 might contain material from every day between May 12 and May 17. Doubtless he felt it would be more agreeable to the reader since it broke up the text less. There was no deception in this, either in purpose or in result. Heald was not capable of it. On the contrary, he retained a certain amount of material which turned out to be egregiously wrong and which he could easily have suppressed.

Having arrived at the decision to use Heald's manuscript as my point of departure, I was determined to let him do what

---

Professor Warren B. Walsh of Syracuse University has edited the letters from March 3/16 to June 19 / July 2, 1917. Professor Walsh, however, started from Heald's reworked manuscript as I did. He shares my impression of Heald's integrity.

he could do so well—tell his own story. I have tried to keep footnotes to a minimum and am, in general, well satisfied with what I have done. My only source of dissatisfaction is that I would have liked to better identify Heald's colleagues, the Y.M.C.A. personnel who shared his hardships, but that hasn't been possible.

What, then, the reader may wonder, does my editing consist of? First, the exigencies of publishing have obliged me to cut about one-third of the text. I enjoyed every page of the 550-page manuscript so cutting wasn't easy, but it was plain that not everything in it was of equal value. Heald's adventures in the art galleries of Petrograd I found full of interest, but, as the publisher said, "You can find that in other books." So I cut some of it. Not all, because I think, among other things, it throws an interesting light on Heald's character. Although Heald himself had removed many purely personal things, there were still some that could go, and they went. Nor did I think we needed *all* the odds and ends of information he offers about his acquaintances. I jettisoned some of this reluctantly but probably no serious loss is involved.

Most difficult was the task of cutting down the detail of Y.M.C.A. activities. Particularly in the Siberian pages there was just too much of it. We believed from the start that the book's primary emphasis was on Russia, not the Y.M.C.A., hence, some of the Y.M.C.A. material had to go. On the other hand, since the Association was Heald's reason for being in Russia, since his travels up and down the Trans-Siberian Railroad were always on *Y* business and could have no meaning outside of it, the *Y* is, so to speak, the skeleton on which the story hangs. If it were cut too much the whole thing would have a tone of unreality. What had to be done, therefore, was to take out enough material to keep the letters from being too exclusively a chronicle of the Y.M.C.A., yet at the same time to leave in enough to keep Heald's adventures in an understandable light. The reader will have to judge the degree of success I have had in this.

Once the cutting was out of the way, the remainder of the editorial work was of the pesky kind that any editor would do for any manuscript that was presented for publication. Heald's work probably needed more of it than most, partly because it consisted of private letters written in haste but even more because he had some real idiosyncracies of his own. The handling of Russian words and names was a vexing problem. I had no desire to crumple Heald's free-wheeling renditions into any standard system of transliteration, but to leave them as he had left them was equally out of the question. I concluded that he could, for all I cared, transliterate Russian any way he wanted to provided: (1) there was at least *some* identifiable relation between the spelling and the Russian sound; (2) the spelling was not so outlandish as to throw off readers who knew Russian; and (3) a word or name was spelled the same way whenever it appeared.

English too was a problem. I have already expressed the opinion that Edward Heald was a natural writer whom it was and is a pleasure to read. This excellence is attended, however, by some personal oddities of no significance at all in personal correspondence but which I deemed quite unsuited to a published volume. Among these is his use of capital letters. He probably capitalized more nouns than anyone since Thomas Carlyle. The editor has therefore been obliged to spend many uncreative hours getting a good many of them into lower case. Heald also appears to have got through Oberlin with no real understanding of the use of the comma. At least three readers have struggled with this and while we don't claim perfection, we have produced a substantial improvement.

Finally, as the reader will note, Heald wrote characteristically in rather long sentences. In general they are very good sentences, and I have preferred to leave them as I found them. Occasionally, however, when I thought it presented a real stumbling block to the reader, I have broken a long sentence into two shorter ones.

There will of course be those who think I should have changed nothing, but I am sure Edward Heald, if he were with us, would not be among them. He had obviously reworked his material to some extent, not to make himself look wiser (he was far too honest for that), but to make the letters more *publishable*. However, for the benefit of those who want to get as close to the original as possible, I am asking the Kent State University

Library to make such of Heald's papers as we have been able to salvage available to scholars who may wish to consult them.

There are, as always, more people who deserve thanks than get them, but among those with leading claims the first is surely Gervis Brady, who succeeded Edward Heald as Director of the Stark County Historical Center. But for Gervis I would still be in ignorance of the letters' existence, and he has been patience itself in accepting extraordinary delays.

I could not allow the book to go to press without expressing my deepest appreciation to Warren B. Walsh who raised no objection to my reprinting the letters from March 3/16 to June 19/July 2, 1917, which he edited earlier for *The American Slavic and East European Review* (now *The Slavic Review*). As Professor Walsh's cuts are not always the same as mine, some scholars might like to read both.

I acknowledge with gratitude clarification on points of Russian language, history, and geography by my colleagues Alexander Kramer, Alfred A. Levin, and Jordan A. Hodgkins. Roxan Rohrich, Staff Cartographer of Kent State's Geography Department, drew the map for the end papers, and Murrow W. Schwinn of Oberlin's Alumni Records Office helped with biographical details.

Finally, I must do my best to acknowledge an obligation I can never fully express to Mrs. Josephine Zuppan, editor of the Kent State University Press, and to Mrs. Joyce Wilson, a former employee of the Press who now lives in Virginia. Between them they took over the final editing when a retinal operation made it extremely difficult for me to do the kind of close examination required at that stage. I feel it no exaggeration to say that without Mrs. Zuppan and Mrs. Wilson the project would have been abandoned.

James B. Gidney

Kent, Ohio
June 1971

Petrograd

Tammerfors, Finland
August 22 / September 4, 1916*

Dear Emily:

This is a beautiful autumn day, more like October in America. There is more color on the trees than in Sweden. We are stopping at a large manufacturing town in Finland, which has more the appearance and atmosphere of an American city than any place I have seen since leaving New York.

I have just visited the lunch counter in the restaurant and had an excellent meal for eighty kopeks (about twenty-five cents). These railroad restaurants are on the self-serve plan and you pay at a National cash register. The trains in Russia† usually stop from twenty to thirty minutes at lunch stations, where the service is, as a rule, better and cheaper than on the diner. We had supper on the diner last night, however, and it was a fine meal, including vegetable soup with sour cream, fried fish, a big bird something like a grouse but larger, potatoes, beans, raspberry shortcake, and coffee. No butter was served. One must get accustomed to eating bread without butter. Grapes cost eighty cents a bunch in Stockholm, and you can't buy fruit for love or money so far in Russia. Of course we avoid unboiled water.

---

* Until after the Bolshevik Revolution Russia was still using the Julian calendar. Heald put both Julian and western dates on his letters. The first is the Russian date, the second the date his correspondents were using in the United States.
† In 1916 Finland was still part of the Russian Empire.

Finland is mostly a flat, swampy land, with evergreen forests and many lakes its chief claim to beauty.

Diary entry for August 22/September 4, 1916

A Russian aviation officer came and sat down in our compartment and tried to engage me in conversation in broken English regarding the iniquities of the Russian bureaucracy and the glories of the democratic movement. I suspected him of being a spy and tried to be as non-committal as possible without offending him. He told of his exploits on the Roumanian front, but also told how they were tired of fighting for bureaucracy. The situation became so uncomfortable that one by one the doctor, the Englishman who swapped stories, and the Englishman engaged in relief work, sidled out of the compartment finally leaving me alone with my talkative friend. I finally made a mad dive and escaped.

Neither could I write of the episode with my German books at Haparanda, the Swedish frontier. Dr. Friese, Secretary of the Stockholm Y.M.C.A. warned us that we should take no books in that could arouse suspicion. When I asked him about the German books I was taking along to study in preparation for my work with the war prisoners, he raised his hands in horror and said that I would surely compromise myself and the Association by trying to take them in. Part of them were in my suitcase and part in my trunk. I could not help about the ones in my trunk until I reached Haparanda, as the trunk was checked to that point. But on the last evening in Sweden, when the sun had finally dropped below the horizon and it was getting dark at ten o'clock, I picked my German books out of my suitcase, and strolled out to the back platform and threw them to the winds.

The next morning, as soon as we rolled into the cold bleak station at Haparanda, and before the customs officials got around, I got hold of my trunk, pulled the German books out and stuck them under the station platform. Later on a Dane with whom I talked said it was all nonsense about having any trouble with the Russians and that I could take the books in as well as not. They would never look inside by baggage. After consulting a number of fellow passengers, I decided to go up to the Russian consul in Haparanda and see what he would advise. So, tucking my German books under my arm, I walked around to the consul, who spoke English. He didn't think I would have any trouble with the books, but wasn't sure. He thought the best thing was to consult the authorities in Petrograd about them when I got there. Take them along anyway. So I placed them back in my trunk. The Dane was right. The Russian officials merely went through the form of opening my trunk, and passed all without question.

As we came into southern Finland where the fortified places are, the curtains on our train were pulled down so we could not see out.

Grand Hotel, Petrograd*
August 23/September 5

Dear Emily:

We arrived at Petrograd at 11:30 last night. No one was at the station to meet us. With the help of a man who spoke Russian, we dickered with two taxi drivers of Ford cars and got transported uptown with our twenty pieces of luggage. We tried the Angleterre Hotel first, on St. Isaac's Square, but it was full. The night clerk couldn't speak English and I couldn't speak Russian. With the aid of a policeman we had our drivers directed to the Grand Hotel, a block away on Gogol Street, and here we found rooms. This is a large, old-fashioned hotel, with enormous rooms and no modern bathrooms nor hot water in the rooms. We are only a block from St. Isaac's Cathedral and directly across the street from Y.M.C.A. headquarters which are at No. 19 Ulitza Gogolya (*ulitza* is the Russian word for "street").

It is now 9:30 in the morning and Dr. Shedd and I have had breakfast and are waiting for the Y.M.C.A. office to open

---

* Petrograd, previously known as St. Petersburg and now as Leningrad, was the capital of the Russian Empire from the time of Peter the Great until after the Bolshevik Revolution. Heald stayed at the Grand Hotel from his arrival in the city until Christmas.

at the customary Russian opening hour of ten. In the reading room at the hotel the latest English paper is August 13 and the latest American, the Paris edition of the New York *Herald,* is for August 17.

We saw little of Petrograd last night as we came up the four or five miles from the station to the hotel. The main impression was the crossing of the Neva with the grand line of lights showing for miles up and down the river. Petrograd is said to have a population of 2,400,000 and to be much overcrowded with refugees.

Judge my surprise this morning when a cheery voice called my name and into my hotel room walked Harlow McConnaughey, Oberlin '08.* I didn't know my old college friend was in Russia. He and Dr. Haggard, head of the Petrograd office, had just received my Stockholm telegram. Harlow has been at work in the war prison camps around Orenburg, but is visiting Petrograd to get an extension on his permit to cover four more provinces adjoining Orenburg.

Dr. Haggard took me over to meet Mr. Artsimovitch, First Secretary of Foreign Affairs. He is a charming gentleman. For a number of years he was Russian consul at San Francisco. He married an American woman and speaks English fluently. He explained that he had wired the officials at Tornio on the Finnish border to see that I got through without delay and expressed his satisfaction that all had gone well with me on the trip from Stockholm.

This morning I joined Dr. Shedd and his party of Persian missionaries in a visit to St. Isaac's Cathedral. We ascended the five hundred stairs to the dome where we had a wonderful view of the city.

August 24 / September 6

Ralph Hollinger was our guide at the depot and customs this morning. He is Mr. Gaylord's assistant at the Mayak, an organization in the Russian Orthodox Church. It is practically a

---

* McConnaughey, with whom Heald spent a good deal of time in Petrograd and later in Minsk, is usually referred to in subsequent letters as "Mack."

Y.M.C.A. except in its name, which means "lighthouse." It
has close relations with the International Committee of the
Y.M.C.A. Ralph is a graduate of Western Reserve University in
Cleveland, and I knew him well when we were fellow student
Y.M.C.A. secretaries in America.

This afternoon we have been sightseeing. We visited two
noted cathedrals, Kazan and the Church of the Resurrection.
Kazan was filled with worshippers. It is popular with the soldiers
and is famous in the patriotic history of Russia. It was from
this church that the troops were led out against Napoleon. The
building has an imposing approach from the Nevsky Prospect,
with two wings of large columns. The most striking cathedral
inside is the Church of the Resurrection, built on the spot
where Emperor Alexander II was mortally wounded by an
assassin in March, 1881. The walls, ceilings, and great pillars
are all covered with marvelous mosaics illustrating Bible scenes
and characters.

We also visited the summer palace of Peter the Great, built
in the Summer Gardens in 1711. We saw the clock which he
made, also the tables, chairs, and cupboard which were his
handicraft. The building is a modest two-story house near the
bank of the Neva River and the Fontanka Canal.

I drank my first kvass this noon. It tastes like sour cider.
I am also learning to like tea. The craving for cold water is
gradually passing.

August 26 / September 8

Dr. Shedd's party and I were over at the Haggards' this evening
for tea. We were served from a steaming samovar, Russian style.

This afternoon we went to the Hermitage and the Alexander
III Art Museums. The Hermitage contains collections from
foreign countries and is rated by Baedeker as the fourth best art
collection in the world. The collections at Alexander III are
by Russian artists. I was more impressed by the Russian than
by the foreign, more colorful. The galleries were thronged by
the rank and file of the people. Peasants were making copies of
the great masterpieces.

This evening we had supper at the Prince Albert Restaurant. All the restaurants might as well be named Prince Albert as I have not seen one yet where the waiters were without their Prince Alberts.

I had my first Russian bath last night and am ready to join the enthusiasts for that famous institution. McConnaughey took Dr. Shedd and me over to show us the ropes. After leaving our clothes in the dressing room we went into the steam room. Even the bottom of the room was the hottest spot I had ever been in. But the bottom was a cool wave compared with the heat of the wooden seats at the top near the ceiling where we spent most of our time. When I opened my mouth, it seemed to scorch my insides. We kept pouring tepid water over our heads to keep them a trifle cooler, while the perspiration rolled off our bodies in streams. We were there about ten minutes, cooling off with showers before leaving. Our Russian companions seemed to enjoy this room immensely, shouting at the tops of their voices as they switched themselves with heavy withes. Then we went into the scrubbing room where we lay on wooden couches while scrubbers lathered us all over and rubbed us with handfuls of rough cloth that would have drawn blood if we hadn't remonstrated. They rubbed every spot of our bodies. After fifteen minutes of this, we were ready for the plunge, but there were no signs of filtration, so I passed it up. We then rinsed off under a shower, were given a big sheet which we wrapped around us, and went into the dressing rooms where we sat on couches for an hour and a half. Then we dressed and left—all for a ruble and twenty kopeks, less than a shampoo would have cost at home.

Yesterday afternoon Dr. Shedd and I visited the Cathedral of St. Peter and St. Paul, within the grounds of the Peter and Paul Fortress. It contains the tombs of the House of Romanov and is dark and gloomy. The golden spire, however, rising four hundred feet, is a bright landmark.

We also visited the little three-room log cabin built by Peter the Great in 1703 on the banks of the Neva. From here he directed the founding of the city. The old log cabin has been enclosed in an outer structure to preserve it. The little dark bedroom, which has been converted into a chapel, contains the wonderworking ikon which he carried with him.

It rained last night; the first rain since I arrived. Otherwise the weather has been delightful and cool, which I am told is exceptional for this time of the year. Usually it is wet and disagreeable.

This evening McConnaughey joined our Persian missionary party in a trip to the Alexander Nevsky Monastery to hear the beautiful Saturday evening vesper service, famous as the finest in Petrograd. The boys' choir was exquisite, and the men's bass something I shall never forget. No musical instruments are used but the voices are as perfect as instruments. Many of the boys must have been only six to eight years of age, but their voices seemed to be perfectly trained.

The Alexander Nevsky Monastery is one of the four most important in Russia, distinguished by the Russian word *lavra*, which is reserved for the most important monasteries. The tomb of Alexander Nevsky, all in silver, is magnificent. The service is impressive, and is attended by a large number of worshippers, as many being men as women. The chimes of bells, which were ringing as we entered the grounds at sunset, were a concert in themselves. The grounds are beautifully laid out on the banks of the Neva. Here also are a number of splendid churches, chapels, shrines, and other buildings artistically landscaped.

Our trip to the monastery gave us the unique experience of riding on the upper deck of a steam train of four tram cars, all chock-full, mostly of working people.

Although the weather has been threatening today, Mack and I took the train to Peterhof, sixteen miles out, one of the summer residences of the Imperial Court. It is on the Gulf of Finland west of Petrograd. The grounds display the most wonderful landscaping I ever saw. Approaching them from the railroad station we passed through large groves of splendid pines.

Peter the Great chose this for his summer residence in 1720 and built the present palace at that time. We went through the palace, which is striking for its exquisite beauty down to the minutest detail. In the central room we had a superb view down the terrace, fountains, and canal out to the gulf shore a quarter of a mile away. In the gardens in the rear of the building we looked down on cascades, lakes, flowers, and trees. All is maintained in perfect condition.

In the front of the palace is a great bronze statue of Samson and the Lion, called the Samson Fountain. This shoots a large column of water up seventy feet. Down the terrace and around the Samson Statue are other statues and fountains. Along the banks of the canal from the fountain to the gulf are more fountains forming an avenue on each side, throwing water as high as the tall evergreens at their sides. Although it is late in the season the fountains were playing. For a thousand feet on each side of the canal the grounds are landscaped in the formal Versailles style, stretching from the high natural terrace down to the shore of the gulf.

Tomorrow I get down to language study in earnest. I have been studying Russian mornings thus far, and sightseeing afternoons. From now on my schedule is eight hours a day in language study.

August 29 / September 11

This afternoon I cut the language study to help Mack pack books for war prisoners. We are packing fifteen boxes of over four thousand books. These were turned over to us with the permission of the Empress's Committee on Prisoner's Aid. They come from the old library of the Lutheran Y.M.C.A. in Petrograd, of which Count Pallen is patron. He was largely instrumental in making this arrangement.

August 30 / September 12

Mack and I went to the station to see the Shedd party off for Persia. They left on the Moscow train. Mack can use enough Russian to be mighty handy for such an occasion. One must deal with innumerable baggagemen, porters, and other officials, in getting started on a journey in Russia. We left the hotel for the depot at eight o'clock for a 9:40 train and had not a minute to spare. A Persian acquaintance and his wife were also down to see Dr. Shedd off.

We are having wonderful weather, clear every day since we came except last Sunday. The sky is the rich Colorado blue, unclouded with factory smoke, although there are large factories here. The moonlight is sharply bright. The weather doesn't keep jumping from hot to cold and vice-versa so often and so suddenly as in America. This is much like Indian summer, except that the trees are still green.

August 31 / September 13

The shortage of my present stock of Russian language was evident today when I tried to locate the English-Russian Hospital to arrange for the second innoculation against typhoid fever. The first hospital that I strayed into on the Nevsky Prospect possessed no English-speaking officials or attendants. I was soon surrounded by a dozen well-intentioned officials, doorkeepers, nurses, and clerks. They seemed to understand what I wanted but they couldn't make me understand what they were trying to tell me. I finally visited an English bookstore and learned that the desired address was further out the Nevsky at the corner of the Fontanka Canal.

This evening Mack and I took a stroll past St. Isaac's through the Admiralty grounds, to the wonderful statue of Peter the Great on the banks of the Neva. As we stood in the bright moonlight while it played on the golden dome of St. Isaac's and then turned to the sight of the magnificent city stretching along that splendid river, we could not help feeling that the whole city of Petrograd was a monument to the genius of a man of energy and practical works whose equal has probably never been produced by any western country.

September 1 / 14

This was an April shower day, and I experienced the combination of a sousing shower and a Petrograd rush hour. After putting in six hours on language study and another on instructions for the secretaries going to the field, I felt ready for an airing. I walked over to the Public Library where I viewed a large reading room in which five hundred men and women were reading and studying. A tremendous painting of the Czar almost filled the end of the room.

It was then about five o'clock so I decided to get on the first streetcar that came along and see where it would take me. It proved to be car number thirteen. It landed me across the Neva River opposite the Alexander Nevsky Monastery. I walked back on the further side of the Neva until I caught a horse-car. That ride soon ended and then I ran into the factory crowd going home. It reminded me of the Willys-Overland crowds in Toledo. The streetcars were too crowded to trust my vaccinated arm so I kept on walking. It poured rain, but cleared off for a beautiful sunset. I finally caught a less crowded car and reached home at seven-thirty for a cup of tea and food bought at the corner grocery store.

The Petrograd rush extends over a long time. People begin going home before three o'clock and the streetcars are still jammed at seven. What New York crowds into an hour, Petrograd extends over four hours, but there are no subways nor elevated railways, and for much of those four hours Petrograd straphangers take a back seat to no other city. The droshkies are the Petrograd jitneys.

September 4 / 17

Mack, Bartholomews, and I went over to the service at St. Isaac's this morning. There must have been three or four thousand people present, and the majority were men. The singing was wonderful and the whole service impressive. The singing of the boys was so perfect that I thought it was musical instruments. Every time I hear the bass of the men I marvel. It is a remarkable combination of nature's gift and church training.

The convenient feature about the Russian church service is that while the service is two hours long both Saturday evening and Sunday morning, the latter being a continuation of the former, you can go in and out during the service at any time and stay as long as you please. And strangely the

coming and going of the people doesn't disturb the reverent
atmosphere of the worship. After spending an hour at the
Russian service, Mack and I left and went over to the British-
American church which begins at eleven.

At noon the Haggards, Mack, Burri, and a correspondent
of *Collier's Weekly* named Arthur Ruhl, and I ate dinner
at the Angleterre. After that Mack and I went to the Alexander
III Museum to further enjoy the Russian paintings. I especially
liked the collection of Vereshchagin which practically filled
one hall. Most of these works were small paintings he had
made while in Japan just before the Russian–Japanese war of
1904–1905.

September 7 / 20

I saw Mack off at the station tonight on his way back to
Orenburg. He had ten big bundles, five of which were books.
I feel that I have lost a helpful prop, but it will throw me
more on my own resources and I shall probably learn Russian
that much quicker.

September 8 / 21

I have just returned from seeing my first Russian grand opera
in company with the Bartholomews. The performance was
Tchaikovsky's *Pikovaya Dama (Queen of Spades)*. All the
heroes and heroines are killed off before the opera ends. There
is an underlying element of melancholy, and the music accom-
panies in a wonderful manner. The singing was an eyeopener
for one new to grand opera, but Bartholomew said that I would
hear better. Marshall said that the Russian opera is departing
from the death and destruction style and depicting the greater
tragedies of everyday life where the victims do not escape
from their misery by death.

Russian operas last a long time. This began promptly at
eight and was not over until twelve. Between every act there was
an intermission of ten to twenty minutes when nearly everybody left their seats and went out for a promenade around
the lobbies.

Although we were at one of the Imperial houses (The Conservatory of Music), there was little dressing up. There were many officers in uniform, and as soon as the lights went on after each act, they would all stand so that no lower officer would be guilty of sitting in the presence of superiors without permission.

This was one of the twelve "big" holidays, but I put in my time as usual on language study, worked a while at the office where none of the Russian help were working, helped Burri move from the hotel to take Mack's place at the Haggards', and went to the American and Danish Embassies with commissions for Dr. Haggard.

September 10 / 23

I went shopping for a showcase this noon. The Russian system of salesmanship seems to be the reverse of ours. They seem to proceed on the psychological principle that the more indifference you show a customer and the less you seem to want to sell, the more eager he will be to buy. At the last place I visited the proprietor stated emphatically, "I have nothing to sell," and turned on his heel and left me. Perhaps my mutilation of the Russian language injured his feelings, though I had been quite proud of my linguistic progress until then. I was surprised today to find that I could read all the signs on the streetcar.

Not finding a walking companion this afternoon I took a streetcar out to the suburban islands and walked around Kammeny Ostrov, meaning Rock Island. These islands are at the mouth of the Neva River on the end of the Finnish Gulf. They are a popular summer resort spot for the wealthy Petrograders. The foliage is at its prettiest, making a beautiful picture with the scatered evergreens, the branches of the river, and the numerous canals.

I was out to the Alexander Nevsky Monastery for the Saturday evening service again this evening. This time the Bartholomews and I stayed through the wonderful anthem. Then we took the droshky and went across the city to the

Narodni Dom, or People's Theater, and heard *Carmen* in Russian. We had ordered tickets for Tolstoi's famous *Anna Karenina*, but there had been a mixup in our tickets. I was not disappointed myself as to my inexperienced view *Carmen* was given magnificently.

The Narodni Dom is a remarkable building, combining in one immense structure theater, opera house, moving picture house, and cafe. Tens of thousands of people throng the place every night. The prices are low and the best things in music and drama are available for the populace. We patronized the Cafe between acts and got the supper which we had not had time to get before the play.

September 11 / 24

Today was misty but that did not stop the Bartholomews and myself from following out our trip to Peterhof. It was the second time for me but well worth it. The foliage is in the climax of autumnal color. The park surrounding the summer palace is a mass of golden glory with enough evergreen to sharpen its beauty. The promenade along the gulf shore was alone worth the trip.

This evening we went around to the Sunday service at the Mayak where Hollinger had reserved seats in the front row for us. It was well that he did for there was a tremendous jam. The Mayak is certainly popular with the Russian young men and is drawing them in great crowds.

The gymnasium is too small for the large membership of over 3,000. Another floor has recently been added, but it is already outgrown. There is a cafe which is always crowded, while games of chess are going on at the tables.

The program tonight included a cornet solo, quartette by Imperial artists, a reader, and a violin solo. It was all high class, and the audience encored as enthusiastically as at a high school affair at home, but oh!, the air. The Russians are afraid of night air. I never remember being in such a close room. Bartholomew says it is the way it will be every night in the prison camps only worse because things will not be so clean. The average Russian seems to thrive on thick air.

Diary entry for September 11 / 24

The fact that the University students and soldiers were not admitted into Mayak membership on account of the government's fear of revolutionary activities was an item I could not write about.

September 12 / 25

Dear Emily:

In half an hour I shall be on the way to the station with Dr. Haggard to meet another secretary, who is due tonight, Fred Goodsell, who will room with me and be one of the field secretaries.

I changed my room at the hotel today, and now have a double room on the third floor. All these rooms have ceilings twice as high as hotel rooms in America. My present room is an inner one that looks out over the hotel court and its woodpiles. Woodcutters frequently awaken us in the mornings. The room is divided into two compartments by big sliding curtains, the inner compartment having no outdoor windows and being the sleeping room. It contains two beds, one wide and one narrow. Other furniture includes a good chiffonier with three drawers, a good writing table in front of the outdoor window, a full-length mirror, a stand that serves as a tea table, a divan, five upholstered chairs, and one study chair. Instead of a closet there is a movable wardrobe, also a washstand. There is no running water in the rooms of this hotel, though there is a fair bathroom on each floor.

September 13 / 26

A Colorado day put fever in my blood for a hike, and when the Bartholomews suggested at noon that we go out to Pavlovsk and Tsarskoe Selo, I quickly fell in with the plan. We took the noon train for the fourteen mile ride to Tsarskoe Selo where the Czar's palace is and arrived at the park surrounding the palace about four o'clock. I believe we saw everything in its most ideal setting for the whole year. The sun was shining brightly with just plenty of light fleecy clouds to give contrast to the beautiful reds and blues, yellows, grays, and greens of the trees and grass. We walked around the old palace, which is now open to the public. The large pond in the middle gave everchanging panoramas of new beauties, with chapels, little palaces, and vistas out to the big palace and other buildings.

Just as we reached the corner of the grounds a regiment of Russian soldiers came swinging to their barracks, singing one of those pounding peasant songs. They were in perfect harmony, their soul seemed to be in their song, and it was as hard to imagine them getting out of tune as it would be surprising to hear a similar body of American soldiers in harmony.

Then we took a long road to Pavlovsk and walked four miles as the sun was setting. We arrived at the Grand Duke's Palace at Pavlovsk just as the sun had set. It is regal in its splendor and taste, resting as it does above ponds and cascades formed by a stream that tumbles through the grounds. We walked the length of the magnificent park adjoining the palace, admiring the marvelous landscape effect. Vistas kept opening up before us, leading to ever new and increasing beauties. The clumps of trees were so disposed that the heavy green color of the evergreens was at the bottom, and the light bright colors of birches, elms, and maples went towering up capping the pines and firs. The foregrounds were bright reds and yellows and the backgrounds dark browns and greens.

The Bartholomews, who have been through all the countries of Europe and through the eastern states of America, living in Maine and Connecticut, declared that they had never seen anything surpassing such landscaping. Everything was kept up perfectly. It is true that we probably saw it within a half hour of the most beautiful time of the whole year. The sunset seemed to linger for our special benefit.

September 14 / 27

This was another of the twelve most important Church holidays, "The Raising of the Cross." My attention was first called to it last night on returning from Pavlovsk when I saw the brilliantly lighted cross showing through the windows of St. Isaac's

Cathedral. Goodsell and I went over to hear some remarkable singing by the choir. We entered just at one of the most impressive moments of the service. There was a tremendous audience, filling the entire floor of the church, which "stands" twelve thousand people.

This evening Goodsell and I went over to the Mayak. The place was humming with activities. Hollinger showed us into a bookkeeping class with one hundred twenty-five members present, into a class in penmanship where the teacher was explaining how Peter the Great had changed the Russian script, into a class of English literature taught by an Irishman, and into some of the music rooms. Music, with three hundred students, is the largest and most important department of the institution. The gymnasium, though small, was crowded much like an American *Y* gym. There is no swimming pool, but there are showers and lockers.

Downstairs was a combination cafe with young fellows all sipping tea and most of them playing chess and checkers. The library has over three thousand volumes, and the large reading room had every seat taken. The hallways were so crowded that it took a line-buck to get through. This was said to be a normal night.

September 17 / 30

The last day of September, American time, brings the first snow flurry of the season; not enough, however, to whiten the ground. There is a frosty feel to the air, and the general atmosphere is that winter is here. All the windows are now sealed up, but that doesn't mean that the rooms are being heated. There is one pane of glass in each window which can be opened for ventilation. Nearly all windows are double-paned, and at the bottom between panes a white filling of moss or cotton, or some substance, is wedged in to prevent the intaking of cold air. The cracks between the frames are all puttied up.

September 18 / October 1

We went over to the Hotel Europe, a larger and more expensive hotel than where we are staying. The roof garden and restaurant are quite luxurious with the glass dome and large palms and striking decorations. The service was good and the change a treat. More English is spoken than at the Angleterre, and more at the latter than at the Grand. A large annex has recently been added to the Europe, which is the finest part of the hotel.

After dinner we took the car out to the Islands and had a fine walk through Kammeny and Yelagin Islands. There we had a splendid view from the *strelka* (Point) out over the Finnish Gulf toward Cronstadt and the setting sun.

The days are getting shorter much more rapidly than they do in America. When we got back to the city, we found the streets white with snow. Ice was a quarter of an inch thick in the streets even in the afternoon.

This evening I visited the Stepans* and carried on my first exclusively Russian conversation. Mr. Stepan knows no English and had always been so silent when I was around that I thought he was tongue-tied. But he warmed up this evening in the Russian language and became quite animated.

September 19 / October 2

You would be interested in our Petrograd office. You enter a substantial stone building and are carried up to the top or sixth floor where the office is located in an American Otis elevator, called *lift* in Russian. The elevator, like most in the city, is the self-serve or dummy type. When you arrive at the office door you do not walk in as we do in America, but you press a button and wait until the doorkeeper inside opens the door. Even the proprietors do not open their own doors. Our door is opened by Alexander, a little boy *(malchick)*, about seven or eight years old, three and a half feet high, who takes your hat and deftly reaches up to help you remove your overcoat.

---

* Mrs. Stepan and her daughter, to whom he sometimes referred as "Miss Vera," instructed Heald in Russian.

With athletic ingenuity he gets hat and coat to a high row of hooks. Being a regular employee, I do not have to be announced. I go in and shake hands with ten or twelve clerks and stenographers and interpreters before proceding to work. No matter if there are a hundred employees it is improper to come to work or leave without shaking hands all the way around.

Diary entry for September 19 / October 2
Press censorship prevented me from giving my impression of the doorkeepers. Alexander, like most boys of his station in Russia, seems underfed and stunted in growth from unfavorable living and working conditions. He has had to give up his schooling, after only one or two years, to help support his family.

Dear Emily:
     Mr. Zemmer, who is a Russian officer, has been transferred from Russian Red Cross duty to assist the Y.M.C.A. He is a good interpreter, legal adviser (having graduated from law school), and an invaluable office man. Mr. Nelson, a colored man from the West Indies, takes dictation at nine o'clock in the morning and at six in the evening and writes most of it after seven at night. He is the only colored man I have seen thus far in Petrograd. He is holding another position and drawing a double salary. There is no racial antagonism to the Negro in Petrograd, even socially. Mr. Nelson is paying attentions to a Russian young lady friend, which seems to be accepted as perfectly proper in this country.
     Aside from the American secretaries all other helpers, of whom there are five, are Russian women. They usually stay through the noon hour having their tea brought up to them by the *malchick*, together with some sandwiches, cake, or candies. The office force comes at ten and leaves at four-thirty.
     Speaking of doorkeepers, they are a great institution in Russia. Every office, hotel, store, apartment house, and other kind of building has its doorkeeper. In the high apartment

houses you can save the climb up six or seven flights of stairs by asking the doorkeeper whether the person you want to see is in. He always knows.

Diary entry for September 20 / October 3
The fact that the situation in government circles was quite muddled and the outlook for permits for secretaries to go out to the prison camps anything but bright, was something I could not write about. From now on the shadows of the gathering storm, the heavy blanket of government spying from which we never felt free, and the atmosphere of gloom, began to oppress us more and more. We became more and more careful of what we wrote and said. We looked for sudden searchings at any time. We were still in the dark as to the government attitude, but we felt that it was strained. We could not account for the change, the officials being as non-committal and as courteous as ever.

September 24 / October 7

Dear Emily:
     A cold rain all day today spoiled our plans for an afternoon excursion and also going to the Alexander Nevsky Monastery this evening. It was a good day to stay inside, though the temperature has ranged down from forty-eight to fifty-seven degrees Fahrenheit in our room all day. We sit around bundled up in sweaters, gloves, and bathrobes. The room will not be heated for a couple of weeks yet.
     After lunch Goodsell and I went to the Imperial Library and had the interesting experience of holding in our hands the Codex Sinaiticus, the oldest copy of the Biblical manuscript known in existence. Goodsell knows how to read the old Greek in which it is written. He saw the apocryphal books of Barnabas and Hermas which were still a part of the canon at the time this was written. Also, the book of Mark closed with the eighth verse of the last chapter. The manuscript is remarkably well preserved. The ink is hardly faded, and there is practically no discoloration of the paper. We were surprised that they allowed

us to handle and turn over the pages of the original, though
we did most of the handling with a photographed copy. The
original is kept locked up in a wooden box and is unlocked only
by the keeper in charge. We were also shown the prayer book
of Mary Queen of Scots, with her autograph in it. The library is
immense. We walked at least a block inside the building from
the office to the room in the basement where the Codex is kept.

September 27 / October 10

Dr. Haggard has recommended a dandruff cure that he says, in
his usual and conclusive fashion, is the *only* cure. It is Eau de
Quinine Tonique and is on sale here in Petrograd. I have
purchased a bottle and am going to make the first application
tonight. My old trouble with this ailment has increased rather
than decreased since I came to Russia, and the Russian baths
do not seem to feaze it. By chance the subject came up while
I was chatting with Dr. Haggard the other morning and he
recommended his remedy. He said, however, that it did not
stop hair from falling out, and his own head is convincing proof
of that statement. Daily applications for three or four days and
then bi-weekly or monthly after that will be the program.

I made quite a hunt before I located a bottle of the tonique.
I first went to a drugstore but nothing doing. They have absolutely nothing but drugs in their *aptekas* here; that doesn't
include perfumery of any kind. Then I tried a grocery store
but nothing there. On inquiring again from Dr. Haggard,
I was told I could get it at a perfumer's. I walked a mile
without locating such an establishment, when a lucky thought
struck me as I passed the window of a *coiffeur* and saw some
bottles of perfume in the windows. Going inside, I found
myself in a barber shop and sure enough they had what I
wanted.

Sunday, October 2 / 15

We went to the Alexander Nevsky Monastery for the morning
service. Afterwards we walked about the cemetery. Many of
the most famous literary and musical men of Russia are buried
here. The cemetery, like others in this country, seems strangely

crowded in comparison with cemeteries in the States. Most
of the stones are simple. Russian cemeteries are interesting and
instructive, rather than sad. In fact they are popular picnic
spots. The people go there for holidays with their children,
take their lunches along and put in the day there.

We had our first lunch in a typical Russian restaurant of
the workingmen's type this noon. It was Dickens-like. The
food was satisfactory. Most of the people seemed to come for
tea, which was served in the customary large *chainik*, and
usually ordered with some black bread to eat with it. Instead
of putting lumps of sugar into their tea, as they do at the
Angleterre, they put the lump between their teeth, and drank
the tea through the lump. A little sugar goes farther this way.
The waiters wore dress suits as usual, but a little the worse
for wear. The dishes were pewter plates, and the knives, forks,
and spoons were old nickle-plated ware instead of the rich
silver used in the better cafes. The furniture looked secondhand
also. An immense music box that filled a quarter of the room
played incessantly and wretchedly.

October 4 / 17

Goodsell and I are just back from the Farce Theater on the
Nevsky. It is evidently one of the best built little playhouses
in the city. The armchairs are more convenient and comfortable
than in the usual American theater, and it is better ventilated.
We could understand perhaps a third of the words spoken,
enough to enjoy it, though we lost most of the jokes.

For the most part, the audience seemed to take the fun
quietly with a placid smile. Only a few times did a part of the
audience liven up to a laugh. In spite of our linguistic handicaps, Goodsell and I were in an uproar compared with our
neighbors.

October 5 / 18

I am acquainting myself with the Réaumur thermometer, as that,
instead of Fahrenheit, is the universal thermometer along
the streets and inside and outside the rooms. It requires quite
a bit of figuring to convert the Réaumur into the familiar

Fahrenheit. The weather is on the average about ten degrees colder daily now than when I came. There are not the sudden changes that we have in Midwest America, except from wet to dry. You never know ten minutes ahead whether it is going to be raining, snowing, or sunshining, though the odds are against the latter. At last we are getting heat in our rooms.

October 7 / 20

A blizzard descended on Petrograd yesterday. It snowed all day and the ground is covered with three or four inches.

I have had to come to a mustache. A young man of my age without one is put down as a boy, too youthful to be taken seriously. This is a real handicap in dealing with officials either here in Petrograd or out in the prison camps.

This evening Goodsell and I saw the moving picture *Kabiria* in Russian. I understand that the pictures were taken in Italy and Tripoli. It is appearing in a splendid movie house on the Nevsky. The entrance is on one side of the house, and the exit on the other. The whole change doesn't take five minutes. The people do not keep filing in at all times but the whole audience changes at scheduled times. The men wear their hats and overcoats while watching the pictures.

October 10 / 23

Goodsell and I are just back from seeing a tragedy, *Vera*, at the Malii Theater. It is one of the latest tragedies, and in contrast with *Pikovaya Dama*, the heroine in this play does not kill herself, but suffers the greater living tragedy. Goodsell and I agree that we have seen all the tragedy we want for a while.

We had an enjoyable visit with Mr. Gaylord this afternoon. He is about sixty years of age and has been secretary of the Mayak for seventeen. He was one of the organizers of the Paris Y.M.C.A. before that. He has spent all of his time in Russia in Petrograd and Moscow. He recommends that we smile at all times as a good way of getting along in this country and being useful to the Russians. "What the Russians need is good cheer," he said. "They are too serious and melancholy." Mr. Gaylord

loves his work and the Russians, and has nothing but deep
appreciation for the way officials, business people, and others
have cooperated and helped in the Mayak enterprise. One of
his pastimes is to write Russian poetry. He has a number of
literary friends among the clergy of the Russian church.

October 13 / 26

Ralph Hollinger was describing the effect of Russia on the
Americans: "They come breezing into Petrograd with that
all-conquering, all-knowing American optimism. Gradually
the weather, the melancholy of the Russians, the seriousness
of everything under the sun [*Diary:* I could not add the omnipresent spy system and danger of thinking out loud.] begin
to get his goat, and five or six months later his breeziness has
vanished, and he is becoming as melancholy and serious and
long-faced as the Russians themselves."

You would be interested in the maid, *malchick*, and waiter
who tend to our meals and room. When we ring the bell at
eight o'clock, first the *malchick* appears. We order the pitcher
of hot water and breakfast. Next the maid appears, dressed
in black, with a white lace cap and collar, and wearing a
smiling face. She raps, asking *"Mozhna?"* (May I?). If Goodsell
is still dressing, I jump forward and relieve her of the pitcher
which she reaches through the door. Otherwise she deposits
it at the washstand in our bedroom. An untalkative Tatar,
wearing a dress suit, brings in our breakfast.

October 14 / 27

We saw *Anna Karenina* at the Narodni Dom tonight. As a play
it didn't make the impression that the novel itself does. The
novel is so long that the dramatized version seems fragmentary.
The parts of Anna Karenina, the boy, and Alexei were well
played. Goodsell asked his Russian teacher yesterday if she had
read the play. "What Russian hasn't read it?" she replied.
Russians take it for granted that all other Russians have read
all the Russian classics. The play received enthusiastic applause
from a crowded house.

The Narodni Dom is certainly a popular place with the masses. You pay a small entrance fee which admits you to the general courts and lobbies. You are greeted by an immense map of field operations of the world war, showing all fronts. The map is two or three stories high. Your entrance ticket also admits you to stand in the fenced off sides along the theater, which is a large area reserved for standing room only. This is on each side of the theater seats. The free area is always crowded with people standing during the entire play.

October 15 / 28

Burri relieved his mind about the Russian girl. He does not regard the girls as pretty, but "Oh, those eyes," he says. The dress has a peculiar peaked effect owing to the universal use of fur. This usually hangs in a sloping fashion from the shoulders, ending with a big ruffle on the wide bottom. Also a peaked fur hat on the head, with a plume sticking out of it, continues the general peaked effect in a striking way. Most women walk with an easy swinging stride despite the universal high heels.

The colder weather is beginning to bring out the galoshes and big felt overshoes that are pulled on over the regular shoes.

Sunday, October 16 / 29

Goodsell has demonstrated his poetic qualities with a poem to the Russian flea. Our hotel room furnishes a large fund of inspiration.

Two new secretaries have arrived, Herbert Gott and Harry Baker. Gott was a boys-work secretary at Boston, and Baker at Richmond. They are both married and both are leaving their families in America. Baker has a little girl and Gott baby twins. After all our worry we find that Gott isn't German but Irish.

October 18 / 31

I celebrated Halloween, which of course is not observed by the Russians, by going to the Marinsky Theater with Gott and Baker. I have been trying for two months to get a ticket. The Bartholomews are constant box guests of their friend Mr.

Coates,* the English director of the orchestra. But most boxes
are taken for the season, and there are seldom any vacancies.
I could get tickets through the hotel clerk for any other play or
opera house in Petrograd, but not for the Marinsky. This
afternoon I went to the joint ticket office on the Nevsky, but
there was a line of three hundred waiting for tickets, so I gave
that up. Finally tonight I decided to go around to the theater
and see whether I could strike an eleventh hour vacancy. Baker
and Gott went along with me. When we got there, we were
told that everything was sold except one box. It happened that
a man and woman were there looking for partners for the box.
We soon struck a bargain and got a front box on the lowest
gallery right over the orchestra.

The opera was *Aida*, in Russian, of course. Baker had
heard it at the Metropolitan in New York. He thought the
Marinsky Theater compared favorably with the Metropolitan
in staging, singing, setting, and general effect, and that the
acting was more true to life. The interior of the theater was
similar to the Metropolitan. Most of the seats are bought up on
the subscription plan years in advance, and even handed
down as heirlooms. That is what makes it so hard for strangers
to get tickets unless they are prepared to pay a lot of money.

October 19 / November 1

I spent the afternoon ordering books for the prison camps. I
went to Wolf's bookstore, one of the busiest in the city. This is
school opening time and there was a rush of uniformed students.
All students wear uniforms. Wolf's store is in the Gostinny
Dvor, where there are 256 shops in one tremendous block, equal
to half a dozen blocks in our cities.

Diary entry for October 19 / November 1
For the next three days I was so buried with book ordering
that all other schedules and letter writing went by the board.
Mr. Artsimovitch was promoted to the Senate. This is a delicate

---

* Albert Coates (1882–1953), who later taught at the Eastman School of
Music in Rochester.

way the Russian Government has of retiring a gentleman whose views might not agree with theirs. It removes one of our best friends in the government circles, and the prospects of getting permits for the new secretaries to go to the prison camps are considerably dimmed.

George Day arrived from Kiev, where he has been conducting a remarkable work for the Czechoslovak war prisoners, who have a large camp there. During the Brussilov drive they came through by the tens of thousands, there being as many as seventy thousand at one time at Camp Darnitza, seven miles from Kiev. George's services attracted the attention of the government, and circles of intrigue began to criticize it. One night just as he was leaving for vacation in the Caucasus, twenty armed horsemen appeared at his door, searched his house, and took his papers. He was released but his work at Kiev had to end.

Sunday, October 23 / November 5

Dear Emily:

Burri called in while we were eating our breakfast this morning and announced the arrival of Claude Nelson and his wife. Claude will be our new office secretary. Mrs. Nelson is a stenographer. He is a Rhodes scholar from Arkansas.

Baker and Gott were my new companions at the Hermitage today. Afterwards we all went to the Malo Yaroslavets for another of those satisfying dinners, while we listened to the Balalaika Orchestra playing *Tipperary*, American ragtime, and classical Russian music.

October 27 / November 9

We are just back from hearing Shaliapin, the wonderful Russian bass, in *Boris Godounov*. He is the greatest bass singer I ever heard, and one of the greatest singers living. He is a big powerfully built man, must be four or five inches over six feet, and has a commanding personality. He overshadows everyone else on the stage. The crowd went wild over him. Reminded me of a football crowd at home. The play itself was

typically Russian, the scenes laid mostly in Moscow. One of
the most striking features was the oriental coloring, especially
in the costumes. The coat of gold which Shaliapin wears in this
opera is very famous and the subject of a full-length painting
in the Alexander III Museum.

This noon I lunched at the Malo Yaroslavets with Goodsell and Mr. and Mrs. Nelson. Nelson timed himself in writing
the Russian alphabet in Russian script last night without
referring to the book and did it in two minutes. At his stage,
in respect to length of time studying the language, I had never
thought of committing the alphabet to writing in Russian,
nor to use any script, much less to time my speed. Nelson's mind
seems to soak up a new word and then clamp it down like a
steel vise.

November 2 / 15

Real winter has set in on schedule time. The streetcar windows
are so frosted that you cannot see through them. The temperature was twenty degrees above zero Fahrenheit this noon with
the sun shining brightly. It was a charming day, and so dry
that the cold was not unpleasant. I am still wearing my light
American overcoat, but all Russians started wearing their heavy
fur coats with the first freezing weather a couple of months
ago. Even at noon the sun appears only a few degrees above
the horizon, looking like sunset time even in the middle of
the day.

November 6 / 19

My interest in the Petrograd art galleries has undergone a
curious evolution since my arrival. My first Sunday I went
through the Hermitage hurriedly and was not much impressed,
partly because it was a dark day and the colors showed up
poorly. The next Sunday I went to the Alexander III Russian
gallery and was carried off my feet by the novelty and brightness of the color effects. The next three Sundays I returned
to the Alexander III, gaining a fair idea of the paintings there.
Then I fell in with Bartholomew, who is a great enthusiast

on the Hermitage. He revealed its value as a representative collection, and following his suggestions I set to work during the following six Sunday afternoons, gaining a better appreciation of art in general by visiting the Hermitage.

By that time I was better prepared to appreciate Russian art. At the same time I ran across a suggestive volume by Rosa Newmarch on *The Russian Arts* in one of the art stores here. Miss Newmarch has been in Russia the past twenty-five years, spending much of her time in collaboration with the famous art critic, Stassov of the Imperial Public Library, where she worked.

Heald then devotes several paragraphs to the Russian painters whose works he has seen, concluding rather apologetically: Well, I guess you think I have become daffy on art. It is one line of interest that is perfectly safe to pursue here, and to write about as freely as one wishes.

Diary entry for November 7 / 20
A. C. Harte, head of the European War Prisoner Aid work of the Y.M.C.A., arrived on the evening train. We are officially informed on the same day that no more permits will be granted for new secretaries to work in the prison camps at present. We finish the book packing at the Danish Book Commission.

Diary entry for November 8 / 21
We have a conference with Mr. Harte. He had no idea that the political situation or the situation of our own work in Russia was so critical until he reached Petrograd. Otherwise he would have come through earlier. We had not been able to write about it.

Diary entry for November 9 / 22

Mr. Harte holds a conference of all secretaries. Dr. Haggard, in view of his poor health, has cabled Dr. Mott* for instructions regarding returning to America. Mr. Harte advises us to cut down all correspondence, both personal and war prisoners work. We are to lie low, keep quiet, and not attract attention.

November 10 / 23

Dear Emily:

Mr. Harte is looking in much better health than when I saw him in New York. He is like a fresh breeze blowing in, with a broad smile that never comes off. Many of us had little time to get personally acquainted with him in America. Here, however, we find him a very sociable man, who loves to have a bunch around, and chatting all the time.

His is a striking personality. He condemns theater going as strenuously as he delights in his cigarette. His supreme gift is social, and he is as much at home in the company of czars and emperors as with office boys and secretaries.

He spent until two o'clock this morning discussing his favorite subjects: precious stones on which he is an authority; the southern aristocracy, to whose traditions he is to the manner born; and missionary experiences in India.

This noon Mack and I joined Mr. Harte in a luncheon group at the Malo Yaroslavets. Mr. Harte prefers the Angleterre and thinks our tastes perverted to like the Malo Yaroslavets better. In characteristic fashion he suggested improvements in how I could trim my moustache.

November 14 / 27

Mr. Harte got started on India, beginning with Viceroy's levee and winding up with pearls and rubies. From this he passed on to the testing of jewels, telling us how to test their hardness by "tasting" them, the tongue being an excellent tester for deter-

* John R. Mott was General Secretary of the International Committee of Y.M.C.A.'s.

mining their relative hardness. He wound up with Russian
jewels. Ekaterinburg* in the Urals, he said, is the greatest jewel
market in the world. He recommends the aquamarine as a
souvenir of Russia.

Diary entry for November 14 / 27
The safe was broken into in our office when we arrived on the
scene this morning, and everything was topsy-turvy. The body
of a dead woman was at the bottom of the court six floors below.
The robbers tried to get from our offices into the Gaston Williams Wigmore office adjoining, where thirty thousand rubles
were on deposit, but failed. We have reported to the police
but have little hopes of catching the thieves.

Thanksgiving Day, November 17 / 30
Dear Emily:
Thanksgiving Day was not forgotten by the Americans in Pet-
rograd. Wednesday afternoon Mr. Harte entertained the secre-
taries at a five o'clock tea in his room. We left that for a real
American Thanksgiving dinner at Mrs. Holy's.

We left about twelve o'clock against the strong protest of
our hostess who said that she wouldn't let us go until at least
two o'clock, as it was improper to go earlier in Russia. She
herself had gone to bed at five-thirty that morning and slept
until seven-thirty. Her servants were ill, and besides going out
and doing all the purchasing, she had to do practically all of the
cooking. I don't see how she managed it. She seemed to be spry
enough in the evening, however, and graced the tables with
her vivacious presence during the later courses. This afternoon
she went over to the reception at the American Embassy looking
as chipper as ever. She is an American who married a Russian
nine years ago. She says that she cannot stay long in Petrograd
on account of the weather. She spends three or four months of
the year here and the rest of the year in some other country.

* Now Sverdlovsk.

Just two weeks ago today we had our last glimpse of the sun. It is now dark by 3:30 in the afternoon, and on a dark day like this it is too dark to read without a light in the middle of the day.

November 21 / December 4

I had a pleasant visit this morning with Mr. Fourman* in his room at the Europe Hotel. He had been out to a dance until five o'clock this Sunday morning. He says that men dance here all night. Most of them were officers from the front. Mr. Fourman had an appointment near the Duma about noon and took me along with him in his droshky to see that part of the city. We walked through the Tavrietsky Gardens at one corner of which the Duma building is located. The Duma was much smaller and less pretentious than I expected. It reminded me of temporary buildings at a World's Fair rather than the parliament building of a great empire. Guards were stationed at various corners approaching the palace and would not permit us to cross the little footbridge over the tiny canals or moats that surround the palace. I haven't had the luck to secure a ticket to see the Duma in session yet.

All around the Tavrietsky Gardens are great apartment houses that remind me of the Morningside Heights part of New York, but without the heights. The brown fronts are mingled with a great variety of colors: reds, greens, yellows, and blues, in accordance with the Russian love of bright colors. The Tavrietsky is the prettiest park in the city.

This evening I went with Mack and Day to a meeting of the Petrograd student Y.M.C.A. In this country the boys and girls meet together, and the majority are girls. The speaker was a likely looking young man from Moscow, a Mr. Schupin, who impressed me much like a successful young *Y* secretary; not preacher-like nor oratorical, but a straightforward, quiet conversationalist.

* Mr. Fourman is never identified except as a Russian who worked for the Y.M.C.A.

The Russian endurance for long meetings is wonderful. He spoke for an hour. By that time Mack and I were almost overcome with the closeness of the air. Everybody seemed hushed with alertness and eagerness to catch every word. Then recess was announced and the windows raised to admit air. Day said that after ten minutes intermission the speaker would continue for another hour. We excused ourselves. Day has become accustomed to such meetings and can stick them out as long as the Russians. The people at the meeting were very earnest young people, and most of them intensely devout. Our progress in Russian is not sufficient to follow the speakers closely.

Baron Nicolai presided. He is President, or Patron, of the Petrograd Association. He is much interested in the student work in Russia. He is middle-aged, slightly built, not physically strong, has a tenor voice, and articulates his Russian very slowly and distinctly so that we could understand him easily. He also speaks English well.

Eric Christensen,* a Dane, has joined our group of secretaries. He is the only non-American in the group.

Yesterday I met Mr. Coates, Bartholomew's friend, who is the director of the orchestra at the Marinsky Theater. He was different than I expected; not a nervous artistic-looking sort of person, but more like a professional or business man.

Later, Monday evening. An important change in my plans came unexpectedly today. Mr. Harte has asked me to take charge of the office work here as Senior Secretary for Russia. This means that I shall stay in Petrograd.

Diary entry for November 28 / December 11
Attended a Russian meeting where Russian prisoners-of-war who had escaped from prison camps in Germany told how they escaped and how conditions were in Germany. Escape seems much more possible and general than I supposed. At certain points on the Danish border there is a regular stream of escaping

---

* *Author's note:* Eric Christensen later headed the war prisoner work in Germany during the Second World War.

prisoners. They all tell of the joy of finding food again, and also bear witness to the order and convenience of conditions in Germany.

December 6 / 19

Dear Emily:

The droshkies have gone and the sleighs have taken their place. I feel as if I am really truly in Russia at last. There is not deep snow, but it is well packed and the temperature never rises above freezing any more. I am still wearing my light overcoat but will have to get a heavy one soon.

Last Sunday Goodsell and I attended the services at the Smolensk Cathedral at the other end of the city, near the Neva. Many beggers lined the approach looking pitiable in the cold snowy wind that was blowing. The cathedral is finished in white inside and is much brighter and more cheerful in atmosphere than most of the other cathedrals we have seen. It is rich in silver balustrades and chandeliers, but the art work is more conventional and less artistic than in some of the more famous cathedrals. The audience evidently came from the poorer classes who live in this part of the city. The music is not so fine as we have heard elsewhere.

Practically all of the secretaries have come in from all parts of the empire for conference with Mr. Harte, and we have been having daily afternoon conferences. Hugh Moran came all the way from Irkutsk. He has a tremendous work going in the prison camps of that district, much of which was started by Bartholomew a year ago. It is remarkable how much one secretary can supervise, owing to the organizing genius of the prisoners, who need simply to be shown the plan and furnished with a few simple materials and tools in order to carry on the work. The American secretary keeps in touch by visits every three or four weeks.

Jerome Davis is up from Turkestan.* He visits thirty-one

* "Turkestan" is not restricted here, as we might suppose today, to the area of the Asiatic republics of the Soviet Union, but includes a substantial part of Siberia as well. Davis's headquarters seem to have been in the Tyumen-Tobolsk district.

camps in a territory sixteen times larger than England. He gets around about once a month, using railroad, auto, and horse. He is another Oberlin man, graduated in 1912. Jerome is an enthusiastic young fellow, still carrying the American breeze while all of us Petrograders lost it long ago. We have gotten in the habit of talking in low tones, whether in our hotel rooms or in the dining room. Jerome swings ahead, talking at the loudest pitch.

Diary entry for December 6 / 19

Count Pallen told us at lunch to be careful what we said, as one out of every four in the dining room where we were eating were spies. The gathering of the secretaries from all parts of the country makes from fourteen to eighteen of us at a time. Police regulations only permit up to eight, but although our meetings are not secret, thus far we have not been disturbed.

Vosnesensky Prospect, Petrograd*
December 12 / 25

Dear Emily:

It hardly seems possible that this is Christmas Day. The Russian celebration is still thirteen days ahead. The season of Christmas shopping is only beginning. The Christmas trees have not yet been brought in. None of the dear home folks are near, and family gatherings are far away. Even most of the Americans here wait and join in the Russian celebration. Our office was at work today as usual, though the employees were asking whether they would have a holiday on our Christmas. We reckon that they get enough holidays without adding any foreign ones.

Our group of secretaries is smaller. Mack and Jordan returned to Orenburg and Kazan on the 15th. Hugh Moran took the Siberian Express for Irkutsk on the 19th. Jerome

---

* The apartment on Vosnesensky Prospect was to be Heald's home from Christmas of 1916 until he left with his wife for a vacation in Finland the following July.

returned to Turkestan the 20th. But none of the new secretaries have received permits, and we are all here. The old secretaries were well supplied with books, musical instruments, school supplies, carpenter and other shop supplies as Christmas presents for the prisoners of war. Christmas is a great occasion in the prison camps, and our men play the part of a real Santa Claus.

We secretaries who remained celebrated Christmas Eve with tea at our apartments last night. Mrs. Nelson and Mrs. Bartholomew joined Mr. Harte and the rest of the secretaries.

I am beginning this evening to put in two evenings a week tutoring in Russian with Ivan Ivanovitch Isopov, who is a Russian student in the Philological Department of Petrograd University. He knows no English. I advertised in the Russian paper for a student tutor and of the number of applicants who responded Ivan Ivanovitch was the only pure-blooded Russian. The others were Jews and Poles. He will give me two hours every Monday and Friday evening and go walking with me for an hour or two Sunday afternoons, visiting museums, churches, galleries, and different parts of the city.

St. Isaac's Cathedral is a fairy temple beyond words. A mild spell of barely freezing weather is following a period of very cold weather, and the near-thaw seems to bring the frost out all over the temple so that it is dazzling white.

We have given all members of the office force (Russian helpers) a month's salary. This is the Christmas custom in Russia. Another month's salary is proper at Easter time. This is one of those things that have to be budgeted at the beginning of the year.

Diary entry for December 16 / 29

The General Staff informs Mr. Harte officially that no permits will be granted to new secretaries, but the old secretaries may stay on where they are. There is no objection to the new secretaries staying in Petrograd or Moscow, but no assurance is held out that the permits will be granted at any time in the future. All right to continue remitting money orders and supplies, but will have to ease up on inquiries.

Diary entry for December 17 / 30

Mr. Harte plans to return to Copenhagen, which is the central clearing place for all war prisoner work that he has charge of in Europe. Rasputin killed. One of the Imperial family involved. Walking home from the Mayak near midnight, the atmosphere of the streets full of terror; people seemed to whisper of terrifying events and to be looking behind for the hand of doom from which they were preparing to rush for safety. A four mile walk of alarm and uneasiness.

December 18 / 31

Dear Emily:

We have been having zero weather all week, though it has fallen but little below zero yet. A little more snow keeps falling every day, until there is close to a foot on the level in the parks. The streets are magnificent for sleighing.

The night that Jerome Davis left for Turkestan I had a fine sleigh ride down the Nevsky. He and I had been shopping for toothbrushes all afternoon, and I had a lot of bundles at the office to get to the train for him. I left the office at 8:15 to catch an 8:30 train. When half way there it was 8:23 and I saw that I would miss the train if my sleigh continued at the same pace. I offered the driver an extra ruble if he would get me there in time. In an instant we were flying down the Prospect leaving everybody else behind. The big gloomy outlines of palaces, theaters, canal, and cathedrals flashed by us as we sped down the broad white way. It was the real Russia of the story books. We reached the station without a moment to spare. Tossing the rubles to the driver and the bundles to the waiting porters, I led the latter a chase to the platform where Jerome was waiting for me. A half minute later Jerome was out of sight with all bundles aboard, and I was counting out the kopeks for the faithful porters.

I debated for some time whether to dispose of my New York sheepskin, which was intended for use in the prison camp work, and buy a fur coat for Petrograd use. At first Mr. Harte thought that I had better do so, then he decided that our sheepskins were all right. We have started out to make sheepskins the style and go parading down the Nevsky with our New York twenty-five dollar imported. I haven't seen a Russian wearing our kind of overcoats yet. One baron* thinks they are common and of doubtful propriety for social occasions. Another baron thinks they are wonderful and goes into raptures over them. In the meantime they are keeping out the cold famously, though they are so heavy that my shoulders ache after walking to the Mayak.

Diary entry for December 19 / January 1, 1916–1917
Much talk and excitement about Rasputin's murder. His body was taken from the Neva yesterday, within a mile of the bridge which I walked over coming back from the Mayak an hour after his body had been thrown in.

Diary entry for December 24 / January 6
Penn Davis (Mr. Harte's private secretary) leaves all of Mr. Harte's papers in the sleigh a few minutes while he runs up to the office. When he returns the sleigh and the grip containing the papers are gone. The matter is reported to the police, but Mr. Harte suspects that he and Penn have been followed by spies and that the papers will never be seen again.† All of the reciprocal agreements between the warring countries were in the grip, and Mr. Harte does not have copies of most of them. He had been promised his passport today by one of the departments of the government, but the General Staff caused it to be withheld. Departure for Stockholm necessarily postponed. Not exactly a Merry Christmas Eve.

---

* "Baron" (*barin*), as used here, is not a grade of the nobility but is an honorary title, more nearly equivalent to "gentleman."
† They never were.

Russian Christmas Day
December 25 / January 7, 1916–1917

Dear Emily:

This is a beautiful clear Christmas Day, but with a cold wind blowing at nineteen above zero Fahrenheit. My Russian student tutor accompanied me on a walk along the Neva through the shipbuilding yards to a workingmen's section of the city known as the Kolomenskaya. I was warm in my heavy sheepskin, but Ivan Ivanovitch looked blue with cold in his half-length oil coat, though he tried to pretend that he wasn't cold. Few people were out in the workingmen's section. Lack of heavy overcoats made the stoves inside look more attractive today. There were no signs of holidaying except the absence of people on the sidewalks.

Back in the main parts of the city, the restaurants were closed, and we ate at the hotel. Even the hotel maids were having a "*prazdnik*" (holiday).

Our office help will have three days off. I expect to be at the office each day, though not much can be done until the Russian assistants are back on the job. Christmas time is not so important a holiday season as Easter, when a week's holiday is observed. The Mayak gym is closed for two weeks while locker room space is being increased to take care of the rapidly growing American class.

We celebrated our second Christmas Eve last night at Madame Stepan's. She had a Christmas tree lighted with tinsel and candles in the usual fashion. The table was loaded with cakes, candies, and other good things to eat with the tea. She presented us three who are renting her apartments with a fine big cake.

During the week I was accompanied by Mr. Harte and Penn Davis on a call on Count Pallen. He lives in a palace on the Fontanka Canal. A maid met us at the street floor when we rang. We went up a broad flight of stairs to the second floor, where the Count was standing to shake hands with us. Stuffed bears and deer prongs greeted us at the landing and at the hat racks. Countess Pallen and three daughters and son were home.

They ushered us into a large living room, which was richly furnished, with a cheerful fire blazing in a grate on one side. The pictures, rugs, books, and curios reflected a high degree of culture. The Countess is English, and the children speak English and French as fluently as they speak Russian. [*Diary:* They could also speak German just as readily, but did not.] Their manners are charming and they know how to make you feel perfectly at home. The Count told of their big estates and of some of the mines in the Altai Mountains in which he is interested. Tea was brought in and one of the daughters served charmingly. The Pallens are Lutherans.

Speaking of Lutherans, one of the largest and most valuable business blocks on the Nevsky is Lutheran-owned and there is a Lutheran Street. The Lutheran Church is required to conduct its services in German despite the fact that there is a fine of three thousand rubles for speaking German. There are three and a half million Lutherans in Russia compared with four thousand Anglicans, says Count Pallen. And the relative influence of the two countries in peace time is probably proportionate to their numbers.

Diary entry for December 26 / January 8
Mr. Harte has an encouraging interview with Minister Protopopov.* The delay in passport is due to confusion between departments, indicating the chaos into which the government has fallen.

Diary entry for December 27 / January 9
Rewrite for Mr. Harte the reports which were lost with the other documents.

---

* An affable but rather unbalanced man appointed Minister of the Interior by the Czar at the insistence of Rasputin.

Diary entry for December 28 / January 10
Prince Golitzin appointed the new Premier. Lots of cabinet
changes. Golitzin has been the chairman of our War Prisoner
Aid Committee and is close to the Empress. An amiable man
but a surprising choice for such a tremendous post in such a
critical time.

Diary entry for December 31 / January 13
Our office boy disappears with four hundred rubles postage
money. Reported to the police but expect no more trace than of
the other loss. No passport for Mr. Harte yet, and Bartholomew
thinks none of us will ever get to the field.

January 1 / 14, 1917

Dear Emily:
        Today Burri and I celebrated New Year's with a walk
through Kammeny Ostrov and Yelagin Ostrov, out to the
Strelka, and added another of those never-to-be-forgotten memory
pictures. The trees are covered with three to six inches of
beautiful, fluffy snow, and the park-like islands are fairylands.
They are popular resorts in the winter as in summer, and we
were busy dodging the dashing sleighs and autos. At the Strelka
itself, from which we had a fine view out over the ice-covered
Gulf of Finland, there was a large crowd.
        The great granite columns and steps of St. Isaac's Cathedral
formed a frosted fairyland again today, with clouds hanging so
low that much of the time the top of the dome and cross were
hidden from view, adding to the mysterious awe and splendor
of the whole.
        The weather was mild today, 30 degrees above zero Fahren-
heit. There have been no terrors in the climate here so far. One
of the secretaries wrote in from Irkutsk in Siberia, however, that
the temperature was 78 below zero Fahrenheit there; he was
hoping the worst was over. It was averaging 30 to 50 below.

Diary entry for January 3 / 16

Mr. Harte advises us to drop our Russian student teachers as being too revolutionary in their sympathies and likely to draw down on the organization the suspicion of the government.

January 8 / 21

Dear Emily:

The National City Bank of New York opened up its Petrograd branch January 2. Burri and I went over and made the first deposit of the day, getting account number one for the Y.M.C.A. We talked with Mr. Stevens who has charge of the branch. Our office force of Russian helpers were mostly laid up as a result of the New Year's celebration.

It was a long and tedious job to get my power of attorney fixed up so that I could have access to the Y.M.C.A. safety box at the Siberian Bank and the papers and documents there during Mr. Harte's absence. The bank furnishings are as complete and up-to-date as a New York bank, and the safety box section downstairs is large and modern.

Day before yesterday was the holiday known as "Blessing the Waters." It is the day that the clergy bless the Neva. A hole is cut in the ice, a canopy erected alongside, and the Archbishop, bishops, and all the clergy go down on the ice for the ceremony, while everybody stands around with bare heads in the zero weather in honor of the sacred occasion. Mr. Harte, Burri, and I went to see the ceremony but saw only the crowd.

January 15 / 28

Monday Mr. Harte and Penn Davis left for Copenhagen, leaving me in charge. Thursday Goodsell and George Day left for Kiev. George had to attend a wedding there but expects to be back in about ten days. Goodsell is planning to go on to Moscow from Kiev and perhaps spend a month in study there. Burri and I have taken in our Danish Secretary, Eric Christensen, as roommate. Eric is a big, good-hearted fellow, whose favorite expression is a deep guttural "Well, well," with a rising inflection on the last part of the word.

I dropped my Russian student teacher this week and am now reading aloud with Madame Stepan and Vera Feodorovna.

Diary entry for January 15 / 28
My Russian teacher has been excited lately regarding the government changes. Says soldiers in the army are getting restless, and that the students are all for revolution. Predicts trouble ahead.

January 18 / 31
Dear Emily:
Yesterday I called at the British Embassy and met Mr. Lindley, the Assistant to the British Ambassador. During Mr. Harte's absence, I have the responsibility for the official relations of the organization here.

Zemmer came to me the other day much disturbed about one of his officer friends who has lost heavily at gambling. He said that unless his friend raised forty thousand rubles by that night he would commit suicide as the honor of the Russians is very high on gambling debts. He succeeded in raising the money.

Zemmer hardly ever gets to the office before eleven o'clock, and I asked him why he couldn't get out earlier. "Well you see, Mr. Heald," he said, "our evening entertainments never close until three or four o'clock in the morning, and I wouldn't get enough sleep if I came earlier."

January 25 / February 7
Last Friday, I received the cablegram from Mr. Hibbard* announcing that you were to sail soon. One whole day I spent in happy visions of how we would meet on Russian soil and enjoy these wonderful experiences together. The next morning it was announced that the submarine campaign was reopened on a more terrific scale than ever and that the Port of New York was closed. Then followed the breaking of diplomatic relations with Germany, the recall of Bernstorff and Gerard, and other

* C. V. Hibbard was Associate Secretary in charge of War Work.

events that put out of my thoughts the possibility of your joining me, at least as soon as planned. I was thankful that you had not started.

Of course we have many new and difficult problems to consider in our work here. Mr. Harte is in Copenhagen. George Day, the other old timer, has not returned from Kiev. Goodsell, the most experienced in foreign work, is in Moscow. I have had to counsel much with Ambassador Francis and Basil Miles, who has charge of government work for prisoners of war. I have found both of them mighty helpful and sympathetic in the consideration of our problems.

The only word I have had from Mr. Harte was the wire received from Copenhagen yesterday, advising the secretaries to continue their work in the field pending further instructions from New York. I have forwarded this wire on to the secretaries without comment. It is more easily said than done. The United States, having broken diplomatic relations with Germany, is at once closing its tremendous aid work for prisoners throughout the empire. We are entirely in the dark as to whether our secretaries are continuing the work for the Russians in the prison camps of the Central Powers.

Zemmer thinks we ought to close up everything at once and get into the war. "The Russians are all talking about it. What excuse do you have for staying out?" he asks. Our contention is that America will not get into the war unless she is sure she has a principle to fight for. He thinks that a strange basis for a country to wait for to go to war and disagrees heartily.

Jordan arrived from Orenburg the same night that we received news about the break in diplomatic relations. He arrived on the coldest night we have yet had at 2:30 in the morning. It was thirteen below zero; our windows were open and the room was down to zero. For two hours we all talked around Burri's bed huddled up shivering in our bathrobes and sheepskin coats over our pajamas. We have had several chat fests with him about the work and life in Orenburg. Jordan has a journalistic training and knows how to describe life picturesquely. The insight he gave into the life and thoughts of the German war prisoners was revealing. The spirit of the prisoners is unbroken, and they are more sure of ultimate German triumph than ever, even if America should enter the war.

Last Thursday Burri, Gott, Baker, Christensen, and myself saw the opera *Efgeni Onyegin* at the Conservatory. I fell in love with the heroine, Tatiana. A lovelier character I cannot imagine. I often marvel that in a country like Russia, where life would often strike us as crude and coarse, the stage has a dignity and idealism that it lacks in America. *Efgeni Onyegin* has its melancholy and tragic aspects—it wouldn't be Russian if it didn't— but its appeal is to the highest instincts and emotions. I left the Conservatory as much inspired as I would be by a fine sermon. The Russians are born actors.

January 29 / February 11

This morning I received another cable from Hibbard reading "Emily says passed doctor." That sounds as if you are still planning to come over. I would give much to know your present plans. After the events of the past week, I had given up any thought of your trying to come. I suppose you are now planning to come by way of the Pacific.

Mr. Harte has wired me from Copenhagen with a message for Premier Golitzin to the effect that Austria and Germany are willing to continue the war prisoner aid work on the same reciprocal basis as before. We have had Zemmer and the office force busy the last two days getting the message and proper documents translated and submitted to the Premier.

The American Embassy has turned over all its war prisoner work in Russia and Siberia to the Swedish Embassy, so that from now on our work will be in closer relation to the Swedish Embassy than to the American Embassy. The Swedish Embassy is beginning its work on a broad scale and energetically. They have engaged one of the hotels here for their expected large corps of workers. I have had next to no news from the secretaries yet and feel much in the dark as to what is happening, or as to what we should do.

Dear Mother Ainsworth:*

This is pancake week (*blini* they call them). All the
restaurants and hotels make a specialty of them this week. It
is an annual festival that comes about our Valentine's Day. The
farmers from Finland come down in their sleighs and jingle
their wares around the street in this zero weather. The pancakes
are served with melted butter and whipped cream. The cream
is sour, such as they serve in the famous national soup, *borsch*.

George Day took us around to see *The Fatal Knot* at the
Alexandrinsky Theater the other night. George thought it was
another play of high-toned character. The laugh was on him
when it turned out to be the cheapest thing we have seen.

February 13 / 26

Living conditions are not as easy now as when I came over. The
stores are not carrying such a full line of articles and provisions.
The restaurants no longer provide the big fine pastries that
they did, owing to the scarcity of sugar, and the confectionery
stores have in some cases closed down and in others reduced
their supply. In many of the restaurants the orchestras no longer
play at the noon meals and at some not at the evening meals.
Railroad transportation is getting crowded owing to a smaller
number of engines and cars. George Day is just back from Kiev
and tells how crowded traveling is in that direction. One of our
office girls went to her Kiev relatives for a week's vacation at
Christmas time, but it took her two weeks to make the trip. This
evening George Day and I have been tramping the city in
search of rooms for Mr. Harte and Penn Davis, who will be
back tomorrow, but no luck at all. Even the bathrooms are full.
We shall have to get Embassy pressure to get rooms anywhere.
We are transferring our funds from the Russian banks to the
National City Bank and to the Russian-English Bank.

* Mrs. C. H. Ainsworth of Moline, Illinois, Heald's mother-in-law. Letters
to his mother-in-law are more numerous at this time than during most of
his stay in Russia because he thought his wife might be already on her
way to Russia.

Down in Turkestan the Russian soldiers, observing our work for the war prisoners, have asked for similar service for themselves. Jerome Davis wired me, asking whether we would authorize him to inaugurate work for the Russian army there. I forwarded his wire to Mr. Harte at Copenhagen, which had to be forwarded to him at Stockholm, and a few days ago the reply came authorizing Jerome to go ahead.

Saturday we saw a Russian Comedy, *Dead Souls*, by Gogol. The aim of the comedy is to hold up to contempt the institution of serfdom, and it was one of the influences that led to its abolition. The hero, Chichikoff, spoke so slowly and distinctly that I was able to understand every word of the humor.

Diary entry for February 14 / 27

Opening of the Duma. Mr. Harte and Penn Davis return from Stockholm. Only three of the American secretaries are left in the Central Powers, two in Berlin and one in Vienna. Neutral secretaries have been lined up to take the places vacated by the Americans. For several days after the break in diplomatic relations, Mr. Harte had no word of what our secretaries were doing in Germany and Austria. Then came the wire that all had left except the three.

Diary entry for February 18 / March 3

Mr. Harte sends letters to Prince Golitzin, General Beliaeff, and Prince Oldenburg, submitting the present situation of war prisoner work in the Central Powers, outlining his plan for Russia, and asking their wishes. These three Russians have been loyal friends of our work.

Diary entry for February 24 / March 9

At a meeting of the Committee of the Empress on war prisoner aid work, held this evening, Mr. Harte's offer to arrange for a shipload of foodstuffs to be sent from America for the war prisoners was favored. Mr. Harte was present and asked for their signatures on the request; they were promised for the following day.

February 25 / March 10

Dearest Wife:

In view of your plans for coming over and the uncertainty that any letters would reach you before you left America, I have been writing your mother instead of you. I have had no letter from you for a month now. The last one I received was written about the middle of January, and here it is almost the middle of March. Except for two cable messages I would feel completely cut off from you, and their indication of your plans still to come over leave me bewildered. The situation is such that I cabled Mr. Hibbard this week as follows: "Advise Emily not to come. Am returning Empress of Russia arriving Vancouver July 21st."*

George Day and I had a great time locating a room for Mr. Harte and Penn Davis but finally landed one on the first floor of the Grand Hotel.

An idea of the way plans keep changing can be had from the fact that the day after Mr. Harte arrived from Stockholm he wired three of the Siberian secretaries, Waldo at Tomsk, Donald Lowrie at Omsk, and Leonard at Krasnoyarsk, to come to Petrograd for conference. Two days later he received a wire from Stockholm informing him that it was very important that he be back there the ninth of March. This would not give time for the Siberian secretaries to get in, so he wired them not to come. Mr. Harte planned to leave for Stockholm Thursday morning this week, following a meeting with the Committee of the Empress Wednesday night, but a strike is on, streetcars are irregular or not running, and train service is discontinued. There is no telling when he will get out now.

One of the interesting Russians I have met is a Mr. Yatseievitch, a Ukrainian from Kiev. He spent three years in university work in America, is married to an English wife, and is connected with one of the government departments that is experimenting with peat for fuel. He is much interested in the rural problems of Russia. He was secretary of an agricultural society in the

---

* At this time Heald still expected to return to the United States after a year's service in Russia, as originally agreed. He was even ready to shorten the year somewhat, perhaps because of the growing likelihood of America's entry into the war.

Ukraine where a short course school was maintained during the winter months for the peasants, and he says the school was very successful. He has made a study of Russia's fuel resources and knows the coal mines of the empire thoroughly. He has worked with George Day and me on a scheme which we want to submit to the International Committee, whereby the graduates of engineering colleges in this country can receive scholarships which will give them opportunities for university work and practical experience with farm machinery in the United States, and then return to this country to put their knowledge at the service of the rural communities.

Mr. Yatseievitch seems to be practical and certainly has lots of enthusiasm for Russia's future. He says, "Russia could lose twenty million men in this great war and make up the loss in five years at the rate she is increasing her population."

After seeing Jordan off on the Trans-Siberian for America Tuesday night, I joined the others at the Narodni Dom where we saw *Khovantschina*, a Russian opera depicting the Old Believers. These were the people who clung to the Russian Church and its customs after the reformation of Peter the Great's time.* Rather than give up their old ways they gave themselves up to the flames when the soldiers of Peter the Great came and burned their church down over their heads.

The weather is beginning to moderate, though it is over a month since the temperature has been above freezing any time during the day, and it has been down to zero each day until the last couple of days when the first breath of spring arrived.

Mr. Harte is now planning to go Tuesday morning. We had him and Penn Davis over for tea at the "chummery" Thursday evening and feasted them on chicken. Chicken is easier to get than bread, as the bakeries are closed by a strike, and we have had no bread for two days.

---

* Heald is either in error or expressing himself unclearly. While it is true that the Old Believers' opposition to Peter is the subject of Moussorgsky's opera, the sect arose earlier, in the reign of Peter's father, Alexis.

I am not sure whether the new regime and the new freedom
which have so suddenly come to this land will give the censor
liberty to allow an American citizen to write to his wife in detail
about the thrilling experiences of the past few days, but by
avoiding military matters that have a bearing on the war, I will
take a chance on getting this detailed account through to you.*

I realize that we are living too near the events to grasp
their real significance, but I feel that they transcend in greatness
any revolution in the world's history, affecting as they do the
lives of a hundred seventy million people. And from all that
we can now see the entire change from one end of the empire
to the other has been completely made in a week's time and
with an order and absence of violence that is a wonderful
revelation of the natural self-restraint and good nature of the
Russian people.

Little did we secretaries realize a week ago today that the
strike, which had started in the shops here, had such a tremendous significance. The government and military officials seemed
to have little more realization of it than we, for the Committee
of the Empress met on Thursday night with Mr. Harte and
laid plans for the war prisoner work as if nothing unusual was
in progress. That the strike was far-reaching, however, speedily
became apparent. Streetcar traffic became irregular Friday and
practically ceased during the afternoon. The sleighs with their
drivers likewise disappeared from the streets, so that when Day
and I had to deliver a letter for Mr. Harte to Premier Golitzin
on the other side of the city, we had to walk. We were informed
at the Palace of the Premier that he was not at home but had
gone out to Tsarskoe Selo that day.

Crowds of unarmed strikers and families gathered on the
Nevsky Prospect during the day and order was preserved by
the Cossacks. We anticipated a repetition of former times of
disturbances when women and children were ridden down by
the Cossacks. This time, however, they used no violence, but

---

* This letter went through unchanged, as did most of those written after
the revolution.

merely rode through the open lanes of the people, while the latter shouted at them "You're ours" and the Cossacks smiled back.

That Friday night six of us attended the performance of Gogol's *Revisor*, greatest of Russian comedies, at the Alexandrinsky Theater. The house was filled and everybody in a lively humor at this satire on the political weaknesses of the mid-nineteenth century. Few of them realized that a greater drama was at that moment unfolding in real life throughout the capital. The Czar's empty box was guarded by two sentries who maintained their inflexible pose and stare during a theater performance for the Czar, for the last time.

Burri did not go to the show with us but continued his walk up the Nevsky. He says that while we were at the play there were volleyings up and down the Nevsky several times, the soldiers firing upon the people.

That day, Friday, a notice was posted by the Chief of Police warning people to stay indoors for the next three days, as order would be preserved even if it required the use of arms. The order further stated that those who were promoting the trouble were playing the enemy's game.

Saturday things became noticeably more unsettled. Streetcar traffic entirely ceased. We learned that the motormen had taken off the grips so that the cars could not be started. We were told that the cordial feeling existing the previous day between the soldiers and the strikers had changed owing to the fact that one of the officers had been killed while protesting against the taking of the grips. Zemmer was called by the Russian Red Cross organization Saturday noon to help protect their stores. One of the office girls was called up at noon by her mother and notified that the police had instructed that she should come home at once as it was getting unsafe to go through the streets in that part of the city (near the American Embassy). The other girls were not long in following suit, all except Miss Golubeva who stayed to get out the mail and telegrams. Nevsky Prospect was closed to traffic except two blocks at the end of our street. When we had to cross the Nevsky on our way to lunch at the Malo Yaroslavets, Saturday noon, the bridges were heavily guarded by soldiers. We could see a dense crowd of the strikers a couple of blocks further up the Prospect in front of Kazan Cathedral, waving a big red flag at their head.

Saturday evening three of us walked down to the Mayak, but the attendance at the gym class was small. Mr. Gaylord was there and I asked him how this compared with the Revolution of 1905, through which he had passed. He said that there had been more excitement on the Nevsky this time, but less in the rest of the city. But on Saturday the real movement had not yet gotten underway. The police still had control of the situation at least in the center of the city. There were reports, however, that there were three hundred thousand armed strikers on the outskirts in the factory districts, and that when they should break through into the center of the city, nothing could stop them. We also heard that the government had brought in quantities of ammunition, machine guns, armored automobiles, and tanks as well as large numbers of Cossacks to meet the emergency.

Sunday was a beautiful sunshiny day. I attended church in the morning, and the English pastor was very much perturbed over the conditions in the city. Then I visited the art gallery, and the attendance was not a quarter of what it had been the preceding Sunday. Many people were obeying the warnings to stay off the streets. Then George Day and I set out from our apartments for dinner at the Malo Yaroslavets about three o'clock. We started in the direction of the Admiralty Building but were stopped, along with many others, at the end of our block by mounted police who ordered us back. We went to the Morskaya and succeeded in crossing the Nevsky on that street. I shall never forget the sight looking up the Nevsky that beautiful afternoon. For the whole length of the Prospect not a person was going along the street, either in the street or on the sidewalks, but people were crossing at each cross street.

After dinner we tried to return by the way we came, but the approach to the Nevsky was blocked by a dense crowd of people and by mounted police, who waved us back. So we had to go back through the arch of the Winter Square and try to reach our apartment by the route that was closed when we started out. As we crossed at the end of the Nevsky at the Admiralty corner, there rounded the Square over five hundred Cossacks armed with lances who started up the Nevsky. You could not imagine a more brilliant and martial sight than the Cossack cavalrymen glittering in the sunlight. Three large prospects radiate out from Admiralty Park like spokes from a hub, the Nevsky being one of the three. There had been volleys up the Nevsky as well as on the other two prospects frequently that day, and everybody ran as they crossed the sidewalk where it commanded a view of the prospects. We reached home all right and found Burri excited over experiences he had at the further end of the Nevsky towards the Siberian Railroad station. He had seen the soldiers form lines across the street and fire upon the unarmed crowd. He saw two dead and a number injured. One of the volleys came into the crowd he was with, and he took to his heels with the others into one of the nearby basements. He said that the crowd kept crying "bread, bread" as they came with outstretched arms towards the soldiers.

Bartholomew and his wife had been on the Nevsky later in the afternoon and had seen one of the workingmen step from the crowd and go up to a policeman and say something that seemed to be insulting. At any rate the policeman struck the man down with the flat of his sword. The workingman jumped up again and began spitting in the face of the policeman while he rapidly crossed himself. This is the way the Russian signifies that he is addressing the devil.

Monday, March 12, was the great day that suddenly sounded the knell of the old regime, though we were slow to realize what was taking place. It was quieter on the Nevsky than the day before. I walked up the Prospect to the Sadovaya at noon and saw nothing exciting though the banks and most of the business places were closed. The center of the action Monday was on the other side of the city, three or four miles from our office, in the region of the American Embassy, the Mayak, the Liteiny, and the Finland Station.

Mr. Harte, who always treated our predictions of a revolution with a smile saying that nothing of the sort would happen, was still planning to go to Sweden the next morning. Penn Davis had to go through the trouble zone this Monday morning to complete passport arrangements and secure documents for Mr. Harte and himself. When he arrived at the Liteiny Prospect, he found barricades and was stopped by the strikers who had some student soldiers with them. After showing his American passport and explaining his business, he was allowed to go on and got back all right.

During the day the sound of firing became louder in our part of the city. Neither Baker nor I understood what was taking place when we started over to the Narodni Dom after tea that evening to hear Shaliapin in *The Roussalka*. There was an atmosphere everywhere of excitement, uncertainty, and danger. Volleys and shots started at every crossing and corner. Around the Winter Palace Square people clung to sides of buildings, and if they came to street intersections where they had to cross, they darted across. The gloomy, somber red buildings seemed to be sitting in judgement on the country's doom.

When we reached the middle of the Nikolaievsky Bridge over the Neva, we stopped on the high middle and looked back over the city. We saw flames rising over the Liteiny region, which we afterwards learned were burning law courts. Machine guns were keeping up an incessant rat-a-tat-tat in a dozen different quarters of the city. It was particularly loud in the direction of the Narodni Dom. At the further end of the bridge was a squad of soldiers forming a line across. I went up to the officer and asked if there was any objection to our proceeding on to the Narodni Dom. He asked for passports and when I showed them he said, "All right." As we neared the bridge over the Little Neva, a little further on, another squad of soldiers stood facing us. When we were about fifty paces off, the crowd of women and working people in front of us broke and ran, and looking ahead we saw the guns raised in our direction. We immediately reversed our direction, and while we didn't run, we never walked faster until we put a building between us and the raised guns. We decided to hear Shaliapin some other evening. Later we learned that no performance was held at the Narodni Dom that night.

We saw no policemen during this walk. It was the first time that they had not been on the streets in the center of the city.

We haven't seen any since. They disappeared from the streets late that afternoon.

The real surprise awaited Baker and me when we got back to Mr. Harte's room at the Grand Hotel. He had given up his trip to Sweden the next morning. But not until he and Day had taken a trip to the station that had been full of thrills. They had loaded the trunks and baggage on one of the high freight-carrying sleds, known as *lomoviye*, to take to the station for checking purposes the night before the train leaves, according to the Russian custom. As their *lomoviye* passed the big square in front of the Winter Palace, they were fired upon. As they continued down the narrow Millionaya Ulitza, they were fired upon again. They ducked their heads, and Mr. Harte prayed while George used his Russian on the driver to speed him up. The driver didn't need any coaxing. They arrived at the Liteiny Bridge only to be surrounded and held up by a crowd of about a hundred fifty strikers, students, and soldiers. The leader was a student. The strikers thought that Harte and Day were trying to take ammunition over the river to the enemy and demanded that the trunks be opened for search. There were these two Americans standing up on the high sled with the crowd of revolutionists thronging around them from every side. What Mr. Harte feared most was that some of the Czar's cavalry or police would suddenly appear on the scene and proceed to fire upon them in which case Mr. Harte and George, standing high above the crowd, would be the best targets.

Another thing was troubling Mr. Harte. He had forgotten to bring one of the trunk keys which he had left with Penn Davis at the hotel. What would the strikers think when he told them that he did not have the key? But he had one of the keys and opened the trunk it fitted. After carefully searching it, the mob was satisfied and did not ask to look in the other trunk. They provided an escort of soldiers to conduct him to the station. As soon as they got their trunks off the *lomoviye* at the station, the driver disappeared with his horses and sled. Then Mr. Harte could find no one to take charge of their baggage. The customary crowd of porters was nowhere in sight. No officials were to be seen. The platform was almost deserted. Finally a lone official appeared who looked at the Americans in wonderment and told them that there would be no train in the morning; that the officials had been disarmed by the strikers; that no one was in authority; and that there was no one to look after their trunks.

It was in vain that Mr. Harte and Day searched for another vehicle of any kind to take them and their baggage back to the hotel. They were almost giving up hope of finding a place to store their baggage when a man appeared who showed them a closet where they could lock their things up. It was characteristic of Mr. Harte that the excitement did not keep him from seeing to it carefully that his wardrobe trunk was set up in the right position, doubtful though it was that he would ever see it again. Then he and Day walked the four miles back to the hotel, arriving there shortly before we returned. Mr. Harte was ready to acknowledge that the situation was serious. Half of the area that he had been through was in the hands of the strikers.

The next big surprise awaited us at ten o'clock when Day and I returned to our apartments. A Russian sailor was there, who was a friend of Madame Stepan. He gave us the astounding news that the old government was overthrown, that a new government had been established with a committee of twelve at its head responsible to the Duma, and that the entire city was in the hands of the revolutionists, excepting the police districts which were all under the fire of the revolutionists. He lived in the Morskaya Police District. Most of the soldiers had already gone over to the strikers, and the people and the others were rapidly following suit. Not until then did we realize that we were in the midst of the great revolution that so many of our friends had talked about and dreaded.

One of the pieces of information which our marine friend gave us, which was later verified, was that the same Monday morning the Czar had appointed Minister Protopopov dictator, ordering the dissolution of the Duma. But the Duma ignored the orders of the Czar and immediately went into executive session, thus defying the Czar and his government. That was the point where the real revolution began.

Our marine friend said that he could not get home on account of the siege against the police district near his home.

He said that most of the firing then going on in the city was at the police districts and also by boys who had secured firearms and were shooting them off in the air for sport. Crowds of soldiers and strikers were holding jubilee meetings over the city, as comrades in a common cause, adopting the red flag of the revolution. Officers who stood by their oath of loyalty to the Czar were being arrested. One of the first efforts of the revolutionists was to clean out the Police Department, and the lives of the police were unsafe if seen on the streets. The wrath of the movement seemed directed chiefly toward this institution, the records of which were dumped out of the windows on to the streets and sidewalks below and burned. Russians with whom we talked called the police system a treacherous German institution that had been foisted upon the people back in the time of Peter the Great and used as an instrument to keep the masses in ignorance and bondage ever since.

The next piece of news came when Burri arrived home at midnight. He and Gott met an officer in the block in which our apartments are located. Across the street is the building of the War Ministry. This officer asked Burri and Gott if they were English. They replied that they were Americans. The officer replied "Good, I also foreigner. I Finnlandsky. Tomorrow that building is ours," pointing to the War Ministry. He spoke in Russian and Burri and Gott knew just enough of the language to guess that he said that they were going to blow up the building. We accordingly wondered as we turned in that night whether we would be awakened by an explosion. The Finn was as happy as a boy. Immediately after talking with Burri and Gott, he went over to the building and passed into the court between lines of soldiers who evidently held the building for the revolutionists.

A half hour after midnight, Eric Christensen came home. Ordinarily he is very calm, but this time he was dancing and shouting with excitement. He had just shaken hands with a couple of men who had been released from the famous Peter and Paul Fortress. Both the prisoners were Finns. They had a thousand rubles each, furnished by some Finnish revolutionary committee, to pay their expenses home. The fortress had been taken by the soldiers that evening, and all the prisoners who were there for political and religious reasons were released, including nineteen soldiers who had been imprisoned during the last few days.

It was hard to shake off enough of the excitement that night to get to sleep.

Tuesday, March 13, dawned a beautiful clear day. We were awakened by volleys and artillery fire at an early hour, which increased in intensity. People hugged the courtways in the street below us, and if they crossed the streets, they did so with a dash. If they began to take to the sidewalks, a sudden volley would send them scattering for shelter. We were told that our *dvornik* (house-porter) had given orders to stay in that day.

At nine o'clock, however, I started out as usual for the office planning to stop at Mr. Harte's room in the Grand Hotel on the way. As I reached the end of the block, at the corner of Gogol Street and Vosnesensky Prospect, an imposing sight was before me. Directly ahead, a block away, the square opposite the Astoria Hotel (headquarters for the officers) was full of soldiers. Down the Morskaya came column after column of soldiers, in martial order, greeted with the rousing shouts of the people assembled in the square in front of St. Isaac's Cathedral. The sun shining on the masses of soldiers made a brilliant spectacle. The soldiers stopped short when they came even with the statue of Nicholas, where they faced the Astoria Hotel.

Suddenly there was a tremendous volley and the sidewalks and squares were emptied of people in the twinkling of an eye. I was half way across Gogol Street when the volleys came, and I had that naked feeling soldiers are said to have when they go over the top. I wasted no time covering the remaining half of the street and was soon in Mr. Harte's room. While we stood at his window looking out on the street, soldiers began to come along the middle of the street leading officers to the Duma to swear allegiance to the new government. These were the officers who surrendered and said they were willing to swear allegiance to the new order. Some of them looked downcast and others happy.

During a lull in the fighting, I crossed the street to our office building and with some of the other secretaries looked down from our sixth floor directly on top of the Astoria Hotel roof at the end of the block, on the opposite side of the street, and on the fighting in the street and square in front of the hotel. We could see the marines lying down on Gogol Street in front of St. Isaac's shooting at the hotel. We saw several men fall, and some of them afterwards crawled off dragging a wounded arm or leg. The Red Cross automobiles came and went rapidly. The famous storming of the officer's headquarters was in full swing. More and more detachments of soldiers came along leading officers to the Duma. Some of the officers offered resistance and were killed on the spot. Others shouted "We're for you," and were allowed to keep their swords and arms and often given commands. At the height of the fighting we noticed a commotion on top of the Astoria Hotel roof. A machine gun had been placed there and the officers had begun firing down on the sidewalk below. It did not take long for the soldiers to spot the mischief and put an end to it with short shrift for the unfortunate officers.

While we were watching this affair from our windows, Burri and Gott had an exciting time down on the street. They were on the Morskaya under the Astoria Hotel when the machine gun began its work from the roof. In the rush for shelter Burri fell and had many a kick and cuff before he regained his feet. He said he got all the excitement he wanted that time.

We saw the soldiers smashing bottles of liquor on the sidewalks, and we saw the contents running down the street. We saw only a few soldiers carrying off or drinking the liquor.

The battle lasted about a half hour. By that time the soldiers had everything in their own hands, and the officers had flung out the white flag. This was the day of the private soldier. They told their officers to go home and stay out of sight until things were quiet again. The officers, having taken their individual oath of allegiance to the Czar, considered themselves more bound to it than the soldiers who took allegiance in groups. For the officers it was a great moral struggle, many of them being in sympathy with the revolution. Caught as they were in a situation where they had to make instant decision, there was a variety of reactions on their part, many paying with their lives for their hesitation.

The way the soldiers took things in their own hands was a revelation. They showed perfect confidence, tackled most difficult tasks with a practical efficiency and did all with a buoyant, smiling assurance and mastery that gave everyone confidence that they knew what they were doing. The "children of the Czar" this day stepped forth as their own men and masters.

Probably the predominant impression that an American received from the events of the day was the self-restraint and order of the soldiers, as well as of the workingmen. There were cases of killing and bloodshed, and during the day many were taken to the hospitals; but considering the size of the revolution and the number of men and soldiers engaged in the struggle, the amount of bloodshed was small. Outside of the destruction of property in the police districts, the officer's quarters, and the homes of the suspected aristocracy, there was little looting. And this order was maintained despite the fact that there was an indiscriminate distribution of firearms to workingmen and boys. This was one time when prohibition was a blessing to Russia. If vodka could have been found in plenty, the revolution could easily have had a terrible ending.

One of the problems of this day were the snipers. The soldiers quickly handled such cases by bringing up an armored car or tank against the building from which the shots came and playing the machine gun upon it. Many of the police were in hiding, concealed often through the connivance of *dvorniks*, who formed a part of the old police system. The Hollingers had an exciting experience in their apartments. Shots were fired into the court from some upper floors. A group of fifty or sixty soldiers immediately came in and made a thorough search of every room at the point of a gun. The *starshy* (head) *dvornik* was almost shot, but was saved at the last moment by one of the captors who had an argument that had an effect upon the other soldiers.

The center of action was transferred from the Liteiny District to the Gogol and Morskaya District. We had the full benefit of it. In the afternoon the magnificent palace of Baron Fredericks, the German sympathizer who was the Czar's personal advisor and chamberlain, was in flames. It was in plain view up to the Gogol from our office and was completely burned out.

Towards evening of this day I picked up on the streets a
news sheet entitled *Izvestia*, Number 1, of the Petrograd Soviet
of Workers' Deputies, dated February 28, 1917, and calling upon
the workingmen of all lands to unite. It announced that the
bourgeois system had been overthrown and the capitalistic class
destroyed, and urged the workingmen and soldiers to elect
deputies for a central labor council or soviet. This was the first
printed matter that had appeared in the capital for several days.
It was also the first announcement of, or by, the Soviet. The
newspapers had all been closed since Friday. We didn't know
what was going on in the rest of the world or empire. The
wildest rumors were afloat. One rumor had the Kaiser overthrown
and a revolution successful in Germany. Another had the Czar's
army on the way from the front to put down the revolution.
The discovery of five hundred machine guns on the roofs of the
buildings in Petrograd, carrying an apparent threat of a St.
Bartholomew's massacre to put down the revolution if necessary,
did not dispel our nervousness. The minister Protopopov had
ordered one thousand machines placed, according to report, but
had only succeeded in getting five hundred up when the plan
was discovered. The plan was for all the machine guns to begin
playing upon the multitudes at the same instant, the signal for
which was to be an airplane that would come over the city from
Tsarskoe Selo. Rumor had it that the Czarina was to give the
fatal order that would start the airplane, but that she lost her
nerve at the last moment. Well, to pick up this red revolutionary
bulletin on top of these rumors did not quiet our nerves. All
restaurants and stores were closed. At night the streets were
pitch dark and the street lamps not being lighted. It was a
disquieting evening.

Wednesday conditions became more normal. At 10:30 I
started afoot for the American Embassy. Cheering on the
Morskaya attracted my attention, and when I arrived on the
street, I found a great parade in progress: all revolutionists
carrying the red flag and the bands playing the *Marseillaise*. I
followed the parade along the Nevsky and shall never forget
the wonderful sight. From the Morskaya to the Liteiny, over a
mile and a half, the great Nevsky Prospect was packed with

people from the buildings on one side to the buildings on the other side.

The parade itself consisted of soldiers, officers, marines, and workingmen all marching in order, and every division hoisting the big red banners. The marching columns stretched from the curbstone to the middle of the broad prospect. The spectators packed the rest of the street, and a continuous deafening cheer greeted the marching columns along the whole route. Now and then armored cars darted along with soldiers armed to the teeth. I never expect to see a more thrilling sight in my life.

During the whole time I saw only one drunken man and heard only two shots fired. The order was wonderful. The people were not so much wild with enthusiasm as they were joyously, freely, intensely, spiritually happy. There was an exhiliration to it that was thrilling and indescribable. One felt that it must be a dream, that it was impossible that such things were happening in Russia. Well dressed people were in evidence and apparently as happy as the bent gray-haired workingmen who looked about with a dazed sort of happiness, while their faces shone with a rapturous glow. There seemed to be the best of feeling between the officers and soldiers.

When I reached the Embassy, I learned that the Czar was expected to be at the Duma that afternoon to proclaim a new constitution. The people at the Embassy thought he could still save his dynasty if he would grant the constitution and appoint new ministers who would represent the people. But the Czar never appeared. He let this last chance slip by. Sixty thousand soldiers at Peterhof this day gave their allegiance to the Duma. This same day Grand Duke Cyril went out to the Duma and tendered his allegiance and the service of the marines under his command to the new government. We also got our first outside telegraph news this day, to the effect that Moscow was also in the hands of the revolutionists. The struggle there had been brief and an easy victory for the revolutionists. The Mayor of the city was a liberal. The police took refuge in the Kremlin but had to surrender speedily.

While I was at the Embassy word came that Protopopov, the former Minister of the Interior, had surrendered. He had

been in hiding with the other ministers of the old regime at the
Admiralty since Monday. At 11:15 Wednesday, he appeared at
the Tauride Palace, where the Duma meets. A student was at
the entrance. Protopopov went up to the student and said, "You
are a student?" "I am," was the reply. "I have always been
interested in the welfare of our country," said Protopopov, "and,
therefore, I come and give myself up voluntarily. I am former
Minister of the Interior Protopopov. Lead me to whatever person
is necessary." The student led him to the Temporary Executive
Committee. On the way the soldiers, recognizing him, gave
vent to their indignation and-threatened him, and when he
arrived at the committee he was pale and tottering. Kerensky,
the new Minister of Justice, pacified the crowd and prevented
violence.

At noon this day the Admiralty passed into the hands of
the revolutionary soldiers, and the ministers who had been in
hiding either fled or gave themselves up.

On my way home from the Embassy, I saw armored cars
racing through the streets filled with armed soldiers who were
scattering bulletins. I picked one up. It was called *Prikaz*(Order)
Number One, was dated March 1, and was signed by the Soviet
of Workers' *and* Soldiers' Deputies, the uniting of these two
groups apparently having taken place during the preceding
twenty-four hours. This order called upon the soliders not to
salute their officers except when on duty. All titles were to be
dropped. Soldiers could no longer be addressed by their officers
with the familiar "Thou" but only by "Sir" and the polite "You."
The day before (Tuesday) there had been no saluting, but
during the big parade Wednesday morning saluting was general.
With the appearance of *Prikaz* Number One, however, saluting
stopped.

Thursday noon Zemmer showed up at the office. All his
enthusiasm for the new regime was gone. "Everybody is out for
what he can get for his own profit," said Zemmer. "There is no
patriotism. Everything was beautiful the first two days, then
differences arose and harmony disappeared." Zemmer had been
at the Duma the preceding day to swear allegiance to the new
government, along with two thousand other officers. He was

worried as to the outcome as out of eight thousand officers in the city only two thousand had shown up at the Duma. It was reported that a large number had gone out to Tsarskoe Selo to the Czar. Others were in hiding. Moreover there was a serious struggle going on between the radical revolutionists who wanted a social revolution and the conservative liberals who wanted a constitutional monarchy. Zemmer was afraid that they might split and give the old regime its opportunity to regain control. It was reported that a large army loyal to the Czar was on the way from the front to put down the revolution. Regarding *Prikaz* Number One, Zemmer said that it had been despatched with haste by the truck-load to the front and that it would ruin the discipline of the whole army.

In the evening we heard that the Czar's army had arrived from the front and was engaging the revolutionists in a great battle at the edge of the city near the Baltsky Station. Burri, Day, and I walked over that way but heard and saw nothing out of the ordinary and concluded that the rumor was false.

Friday morning we were thrilled to see in the windows of the *Novoye Vremya* newspaper a bulletin reading that Nicolai Romanov (all titles removed) had abdicated at three o'clock that morning for himself and his heir, Alexei, in favor of Michael Alexandrovitch, the Czar's brother and next in line for the throne. Alongside it another bulletin read that Michael Alexandrovitch declined to accept the throne, stating that the people wanted a republic, and that he wanted to get back to the front where he belonged. The abdication of the Czar had been written on his special train near Pskov, after it had been shunted back and forth in vain efforts to elude the revolutionists.

With the appearance of the morning bulletins, the new Cabinet was announced. The new Minister of Justice is Kerensky, a socialist, and his first order was that any important papers or documents which were found in the Police Head-quarters and were worthy of saving were to be transferred to the Academy of Science. He seems to know how to attract the atten-tion and seize the imagination of the people. There was also appointed a new Minister, one for Finnish Affairs, to take the place of the old Governor General of Finland, who has been arrested. Also the man who was responsible for the new restrictive and repressive measures in Finland in 1905 is in custody.

In the same bulletins the Cabinet announces that it will be guided by the following principles: 1) full and immediate amnesty in all political and religious affairs; 2) liberty of word, press, assembly, unions, and strikes with extension of political liberty to those in military service within the confines permissible by military technical conditions; 3) abolition of all class, religious, and national limitations; 4) immediate preparations to convoke on the basis of universal, equal, direct, and secret suffrage, a Constitutional Assembly which will establish the form of administration and constitution; 5) substitution of national militia in the place of police, with elected leaders and subject to local administration; 6) elections to local administration on the basis of universal suffrage. On the following day a proclamation was issued removing all restrictions from the Jews.

On Friday the old flag of Russia was replaced by the red flag in all quarters of the city. Soldiers were busy all day pulling down the coats of arms of the old regime, including those on the Winter Palace. The Singer Sewing Machine Building protected the American eagle on its top by having it wrapped in the American flag, but all other eagles in the city came down.

Little Alexander, our office boy, when asked what he thought of the revolution, said "*Czarya ne nado*" (No need of a Czar).

One of Mr. Harte's friends, Count Stackelburg, was killed Monday. Revolutionists came to his palace on the Millionaya, and when he refused to open the doors, he was shot down. Sturmer is reported dead in prison. Count Pallen has not been heard of since Monday. He went down to one of his estates in the country near Moscow just before the revolution, and his life is feared for. The girls in our office are back at work, and all seem happy at the new day.

We now feel that we can draw a full breath, that what we see is no longer a dream but a reality, that a new era has opened with consequences beyond imagination. We are thrilled with the new energy, purpose, and enthusiasm that has taken hold

everywhere. It has been good to be alive these marvelous days.
We can take our hats off to the Russian people; they know
how to put great things across. Their good nature is impressive;
even in the course of the fighting they seemed to retain it. They
don't seem to have the natures that would lead to the excesses
of the French Revolution. They handle the most exciting
emergencies in a cool matter-of-fact way. And I am struck with
their continued loyalty to the Allies. I talked with a number
of the soldiers during the week. "Give us a week to clean this
up," they said, "and then we'll go back and clean up the
Germans so quick no one can stop us."

March 5 / 18

The only thing that people talk about these days is the Great
Revolution. "The Old Order," "the New Order," "the Old
Regime," "the New Regime," are the phrases commonest on
everybody's lips, together with "*Tovarisch,*" the Russian word
for comrade, which is the universal salutation.

The most surprising thing is the ease and suddenness with
which the old order collapsed. It went down like the proverbial
stack of cards. The first breath of revolutionary spring melted
it completely and suddenly.

I hope that the good nature of the censor will endure daily
letters to you, at least during the first days and weeks of the
new regime, so that I can share them with you. It used to be
provoking for an American to walk along Nevsky Prospect
because you had to keep dodging everybody as you passed them.
Now we don't have to pass anybody; they all go as fast as we
want to. There used to be a heavy repressed spirit that weighed
down on us as though from a leaden sky, the natural product of
the omnipresent spy and police system. Now everybody's spirits
seem to well up in a great wave of joyfulness, cheerfulness,
and good nature.

I dropped in at St. Isaac's evening service last night. There
was the same attendance, the same spirit, the same devotion,
and the same number of candles as before. The only difference
was the omission of the names of the Czar's family at the climax

of the prayers. When the priest came to the place in his prayer where the imperial names were sung before the revolution, he pulled a piece of paper out of his vestment and read "For the Russian People." I stopped in at St. Isaac's again this morning, and there was a greater attendance than usual.

When I went over to the British-American Church, I found a great change over the preceding Sunday. Then there were but a handful of worshippers, and everybody had forebodings of terrible happenings. Today all was joyous. The British seem to share the rejoicing over the new day in Russia. The prayers of the pastor, always interesting as a sort of current review of the week's happenings, were especially apt today. His sermon was on Hebrews, chapter nine, the verse, "Except blood be shed there is no remission," his Bible reading the revolution of Jehu against Jezebel.

After church we went over to the Academy of Art to attend the spring art exhibit. It was the first day that the exhibit had been open since the revolution. The big brass-buttoned porters had given way to plain-dressed, pleasant, smaller, quicker serving men, who chatted with you pleasantly and were quick to express their happiness over the new order of things. The placards attached to the various paintings stating that they were the gift or loan of members of the royal family had all such references cut out.

We walked back over the Neva by the new bridge by the Winter Palace. We contrasted the appearance with the preceding Sunday when we had such difficulty getting to and from the Malo Yaroslavets. Today the streets were alive with tremendous crowds enjoying their freedom. Soldiers and people mingled everywhere, all wearing the revolutionary red. Red flags hung from the government buildings, the universities, the art galleries, business houses, and even from the Winter Palace. The large coats of arms in gilded yellow that formerly adorned the great iron fence around the Winter Palace were covered from sight with wrappings of bright red that could be seen a mile away.

The first newspapers since the revolution appeared today. The Social-Democrats appeared again with a paper which was stopped in July 1914. There is a new *Soldiers' and People's* newspaper. Of course there is a complete change in the management and policies of the old government papers.

We have had a heavy snow. Mr. Gaylord says this has been the hardest winter he has known in Petrograd. It is the first winter he remembers when sleighing was continuous until spring.

I drew one hundred and twenty dollars at the Lyonnais Bank yesterday at the same exchange as before the revolution. Business seems to be back to normal everywhere.

I am reading the translation of Gorky's *Comrades,* which gives a keen insight into the propaganda that preceded the revolution, and the background of the word that is on everybody's lips, *"tovarisch."*

March 6 / 19

Goodsell has returned from Moscow. There wasn't so much excitement there as here because, as he expressed it, "there wasn't so much to chew up." Moscow learned nothing of the Petrograd events until Tuesday afternoon, and Moscow was quiet until that time. The city was still in the hands of the police, and the old regime still held peaceful sway after Petrograd had become revolutionary. Immediately upon receiving the news from Petrograd, the police in Moscow were notified that they could remove their uniforms, give up their firearms, and clear out. After Tuesday night policemen no longer appeared on the streets. A number of them, however, disguised as soldiers, made trouble later. Only three soldiers lost their lives in the revolution at Moscow. A tremendous funeral was held for them yesterday.

March 7 / 20

Winter is hanging on surprisingly late. There hasn't been a day this month when the temperature has gotten up to freezing, and for the past two weeks it has been down to zero or two or three degrees above every morning.

The streetcars are running again after ten days without

them. One feels that the new government is pushing things ahead with strong and rapid strides. The graft of the old regime becomes more astounding with every discovery. The new procurator of the Holy Synod seems to be a forceful man who is proceeding to remove some of the handicaps that have clogged the usefulness of the church.

Days are getting longer. The sun now rises before six and sets after six. It seems strange to have such long days while the snow still lies on the ground.

There is much talk and expectation that Russia will soon adopt the western calendar. The main stumbling block in the past has been the large number of church holidays. Six or seven of these drop automatically with the abdication of the Czar.

March 8 / 21

Every evening Mr. Harte has tea in his room at nine o'clock, and it is the gathering spot for the secretaries. The big topic is what to undertake in Russia now. Requests are coming in from officers and soldiers of regiments stationed in the city for libraries and clubs similar to what we have for the prisoners of war. The trouble is that the opportunity is boundless and our force so small that it is no easy problem to decide where to start in.

The new Minister of Agriculture has his office in the same building as our office. I came up the same elevator with him this morning at 9:15. Some of the ministers of the old regime did well to keep their office hours from 1:00 to 4:00 p.m.

We saw the Hollingers off on the Siberian Express last night. They had a splendid coupe on a finely furnished car. There must have been thirty people to see them off. They have been away from America two and a half years. He is the first of our secretaries to return to America from Russia after the revolution.

It is interesting to get reports of how the news of the revolution was received in America and England. It was evidently a great sensation abroad. As the news trickles in from all over the empire, it is astounding how complete the revolution was clear through Siberia to Vladivostok.

Day and I were over at Yatseievitch's apartments in Vassilio-
strov last evening and worked further on our plans for the
agricultural development of Russia. The goal can be reached
much more quickly and directly now.

The Czarina has been arrested, but Kerensky has taken
her under his personal protection to make sure that no mob
violence shall be done to her.

Mr. Harte has had an interview with Mr. Gaylord regarding
the future of Y.M.C.A. plans in Russia. The question is whether
the Mayak or the War Prisoner Aid organization shall take the
lead. Another question is whether the Mayak shall change its
name to Y.M.C.A. now. These questions also involve other
questions as to whether the revolution is permanent or not. We
younger secretaries are all sure it is, while Mr. Harte has his
doubts and thinks we ought to go slow.

The Russian General Staff has given Zemmer his choice as
to whether he wants to go with the army or stay with our organization. Zemmer isn't enthusiastic over the prospects before the
Russian officer in the new Russian army and has decided to
remain with us.

March 10 / 23

"Citizens, please have your fares ready." That is the greeting of
the conductors these days as contrasted with the old dreary,
monotonous, lifeless, "Fares, fares, fares." The innate politeness
of the Russian people at last forces itself into the streetcars. Men
no longer grab seats for which the ladies are waiting, and rough
words have given place to "Please excuse me," and "Pardon me."

The elevator boy at the hotel reflects the new spirit. We
used to salute him with the greeting "Mr. General." He now
speaks up, "I am not a general. I am a citizen soldier," as the
thing to be prouder of.

The great political issue now is between those who want a
republic and those who want a constitutional monarchy. The
idea of republic is the most popular and gaining ground every
day. There are a multitude of newspapers and most of them
are for the republic. One of them has its big headline on every

edition, "Hail to the Republic." The working men are, of course, solid for the republic. One of the problems is how the peasants will vote. There seemed at first to be the general impression that the peasants would be for the monarchy. But one of Day's friends, an engineer who is well acquainted with the habits and thoughts of the peasants, said last night that they would be for the republic. They reason this way: "Well, Nicholas II abdicated; he didn't want it. Michael declined it; he didn't want it. Nobody wants it. Then it mustn't be necessary."

The Grand Duke Cyril, next in line after Michael, was interviewed by a newspaper reporter yesterday. He said that he was doing nothing but reading the papers these days. The papers are all liberal or socialistic. They must make interesting reading for him.

Now the former Czar and Czarina are reported leaving for England. They were accompanied from the palace to the port by the Minister of Justice Kerensky.

Mr. Harte talked with Mr. Shidlovsky, who is one of the Committee of Twelve which selected the present Cabinet. When Mr. Harte saw him ten days after the revolution, Mr. Shidlovsky had just been home for one night since the revolution began. Zemmer worked at the Duma for a week and said that some of the men went without sleep for three or four nights in succession. One of them fell asleep while delivering an address before the Duma. The Duma is now divided up into committees which are working night and day to bring order out of chaos.

March 11 / 24

Mr. Harte has cabled to the National Council of the Y.W.C.A. in New York recommending that they send over a secretary as there is an opening here for work among working girls. Some of the prominent Russians are prepared to sponsor and finance such work. Madame Shidlovsky is particularly interested and alive to the new opportunities. The Shidlovskys were known as among the leading liberals even before the revolution and were acquainted with President Harper of Chicago University and with other Americans who had been in Petrograd. Mr. Shidlovsky is mentioned as the probable next Minister to England.

The Chief of the General Staff has informed Mr. Harte that the General Staff has decided to grant the permits for which our secretaries have been waiting so long and that we can probably be on our way within a week. There has been little change in the personnel of the General Staff since the revolution; only a few of the highest-ups have changed. The men who did the detail work on permits and documents under the old regime are still at their old jobs. Their viewpoint has changed with the revolution; or, in many cases, they can now avow the sympathies which they have always felt.

Goodsell fell in love with Moscow. He wrote in the book which served as his guide book there, "If ever I loved a city, I love Moscow." He was there six weeks. Nelson, who was there a month, says that he considered the month he put in there equivalent to a year's university course.

Yesterday was the first day of spring, but we have yet to see our first thaw for this year. The snow lies two feet deep on the level. Sleighing has been continuous since December first.

I will describe our Russian War Prisoner Aid work, which I was unable to do under the old regime. The Petrograd office is the largest War Prisoner Aid office, though there are more secretaries in Germany and Austria than in Russia. In our office there are at present four American secretaries besides myself, one Dane, one Russian officer (Zemmer), and five young women clerks. When I first came over, there was one full-time stenographer and one part-time, but after Mr. Harte arrived and learned how delicate the political situation was, we got orders to reduce correspondence to a minimum. I dispensed with both stenographers and reduced correspondence ninety per cent and have been pegging out all correspondence on the typewriter myself since that time.

The office is divided into five departments: Financial, Book and Purchasing, Russian, Money Order, and Inquiry. The Financial Department includes handling of all moneys and accounts and is in the charge of Burri. The Book and

Purchasing Departments have charge of purchases of books, clothing, and other supplies requested by the prisoners of war, and George Day has charge. The men in this department know where practically every purchasable book in Petrograd is and have now provided libraries of from one hundred to fifteen hundred books for practically every camp that our secretaries visit. The Russian Department forwards money and food parcels to Russian prisoners of war in Germany, Austria, and Hungary from their friends and relatives in this country. These go to Copenhagen and are forwarded from our office there. The Money Order Department forwards money orders to German, Austrian, and Hungarian prisoners of war in Russia from their relatives and friends in the Central Powers. There is much work in this department as the work of the Y.M.C.A. War Prisoner Aid has been extensively advertised. The Inquiry Department forwards thousands of inquiries monthly both ways. We are permitted to forward greetings and inquiries about addresses, health, desires, etc. We forward millions of kisses.

My work is largely correspondence, the receiving and editing of reports of work from the various secretaries in the field in this country as well as from the Central Powers, and the general supervision of the office arrangements and the various departments.

At present there are seven secretaries in the field in Russia and Siberia; ten in Germany, of whom four are Americans and the others from neutral countries; and fifteen in Austria, Hungary, and Bulgaria. There are five men waiting here for permits who will probably be on their way soon.

March 14 / 27

At last the spring thaw has arrived. Yesterday the temperature went above the freezing point, and the streets are becoming seas of mud and slush. The sleighs are still hanging on but will probably give way to the wheeled droshkies today.

Two days ago Mr. Harte announced plans for immediately opening up Y.M.C.A. work among workingmen and soldiers. The Duma was back of the workingmen's *Y*, and it looked

as if things were opening up big. Today, however, the plans
for this type of work have been given up after Mr. Harte had a
talk with Count Pallen. The Count says that the factories are
hotbeds of socialist and German agitation that would make
Y work impossible now. They are also the centers of agitation
against the government and for extreme revolution.

The Count told of his experiences during the revolution
while on his visit to his estate. He got through safely but with
many rough handlings. Things were worse in the country
districts than in the cities. The peasants were agitating about
taking over the big estates without waiting for government
action and in some cases had already done so. The Count says
that if he had been in Petrograd he would have suffered death
rather than renounce his allegiance to the Czar before the
latter abdicated. After the Czar's abdication, he felt free to
swear allegiance to the Duma. One of his sons is in the Imperial
Horse Guards, a crack cavalry regiment of the old regime, mostly
composed of sons of the nobility. They are much disturbed
about the future. The times do not sit well upon the traditions
of the group.

Bartholomew heard Kerensky deliver a brief speech at
the Marinsky Theater last night. Kerensky came in during the
performance and all eyes were fastened upon him. The performance could not go on until he had responded to the call for
a speech. Bartholomew says he is wonderfully magnetic and
fiery in personality and oratory and concluded his brief appeal
with the words "United for Victory and Freedom." He is the
man of the hour.

Baker has been trying to get a ticket to Kazan but is having
difficulties as the Russian soldiers have all at once taken it into
their heads that freedom means free transportation for all, and
the trains are overtaxed with them and their baggage.

March 15 / 28

Last evening, eight of us secretaries went down to the station to
see Christensen off on the Trans-Siberian for Irkutsk. I went
down with him in the sleigh thinking it would be the last

sleigh ride of the season, but it turned cold again last night, dropping to ten above zero this morning, so the sleighs have a lease of life for a few days yet. We saw Christensen off amid slush and snow flurries that reminded us of the dreary November days.

In the same compartment with Christensen were a French woman and her two little girls who were scheduled to travel with him for six days to Irkutsk. That is the way they travel here, men and women strangers in the same compartment. Such things are taken as a matter of course.

March 17 / 30

Here it is next to the last day of March and as wintry as ever. I wore my light overcoat two days and then had to return to my heavy sheepskin. Zemmer says he never puts aside his heavy overcoat until the ice goes out in the Neva. That happens in May. The river is solid now and the snow a foot deep on the level.

One of our office girls had to go to Kiev with her mother who was ill. She said she would be back in a week. She just got back this morning after three weeks. She asked, "Are you angry with me, Mr. Heald?" Nobody could be angry with her, pretty as she is, young enough still to be wearing her hair in braids. She lived in America two or three years and speaks English remarkably well and four other languages besides Russian. She says traveling is becoming very uncomfortable, so crowded with soldiers. She was not able to leave Petrograd until Thursday of revolution week, and then had to wait ten days in Kiev before she could get a ticket for the return trip. Lines of people, blocks long, wait for tickets at the ticket offices now.

Gott is our *ekonomka*, who takes Christensen's place as purchaser of our provisions for the "chummery" table and to keep accounts and collect our money. Each *ekonomka* tries to outdo the last, and Gott broke all records tonight by placing hot baking-powder biscuits before us, the first time that I have had any kind of bread other than black bread for a month. We have all gotten honestly to like black bread, however. It is more filling and nutritious than white bread and is especially good with jam, a supply of which we always keep on hand.

I met one of the young revolutionists this morning by the name of Nusenberg. He was formerly in the Y.M.C.A. student movement in Russia but was imprisoned in Peter and Paul Fortress on account of revolutionary sympathies at the time of the uprising. He is interested in our plans for a workingmen's Y.M.C.A. but says the workingmen want to know where our money comes from. They are being told by agitators that we are a capitalist organization and that the American capitalists have sent us over here to enslave them. There is a readier opportunity for our work in the army than in the factory.

March 20 / April 2

Yesterday (Sunday) morning, Mr. Harte, Nelson, and I went down to look over the Stackelburg Palace as a possible headquarters for our offices. This palace is on Millionaya Ulitza, one of the most fashionable streets of the city, lined with palaces of Grand Dukes and the nobility. It is only a block from the Hermitage and two blocks from the Winter Palace. It is all furnished with chandeliers, bric-a-brac, paintings, books, and furniture of the Countess to whom it belongs, and who lived there until the death of her husband in the revolution. She is now living in the country.

There is room not only for all the office space we need but also for the living quarters of all the secretaries who will be in Petrograd. The elegantly furnished front rooms have full length mirrors and rich dressers. The servants' quarters in the rear are decidedly less elegant. The office we now have at Gogol was rented to us by Gaston Williams Wigmore, and now they need the space when their contract expires with us.

On the way back from the palace, we found a big review of soldiers going on in the Winter Palace Square. The red banners of the revolution were flying on every side, and the bands were all playing the *Marseillaise*.

In the afternoon Goodsell and I took a walk over to Vassily Ostrov to explore the oldest section of the city. It was a beautiful spring day, the first that has brought out the wheeled droshkies again. The quickly melting snow made rivers of water everywhere, though we walked back across the ice of the Neva with hundreds of others. We walked around the low-lying, one-story structures with heavy iron shutters and great padlocks, some of them still occupied, dating back to the time of Peter the Great.

Saturday evening, Goodsell, Baker, and I went to the Alexandrinsky Theater and saw *Foggy Night*, a modern play. It was an April Fool on George. He had bought tickets for Turgeniev's *A Month in the Country* and didn't wake up to the fact that it was a different play until it was nearly over. Theater life is back to normal with very little change since the revolution. The soldiers no longer stand at salute guarding the Czar's box, and *A Life for a Czar* will not be sung by Shaliapin, or any other artist, very soon again. Soldiers begin to appear in the audiences as well as officers. Otherwise all is as before.

While George and I were at the Longs' for dinner the other evening, Mr. Gaylord came in excited over an alarmist letter he had just received from a royalist friend in the country. All was chaos, the peasants were taking everything into their own hands, the government was doing nothing about it, and everything was going to the dogs. Zemmer takes an equally pessimistic view regarding the future. He says that fifty thousand interned German-Russian civilians, who were in prison under the old regime, were let out at the time of the uprising, and are now working for Germany and helping to throw Russia into the greatest possible chaos.

March 23/ April 5

Today was the great funeral day when the victims of the revolution were buried. The clouds and slush put nature in tune with the occasion. If the parade of Wednesday morning of revolution week was inspiring, the parade today was awful in its solemnity and immensity.

The columns started marching at eight o'clock from six

different sections of the city, all converging on Mars Field,
where the burial service was held. All that part of the city was
blocked off so that the general public could not approach, but
only those in line or those with tickets of admission. The whole
city was given up to this one thing today, and all streetcar and
even cab traffic ceased. We could not even cross the line of march
on foot to reach the American Embassy.

At twelve o'clock only the second of six divisions of the
parade had passed through the field, and the parade was still
passing our corner near the Nevsky after passing that point continuously for over three hours. Day and I were out all morning
seeing what we could. On the raised places where the Nevsky
Prospect crosses the canals on bridges, we could get fine views of
the whole length of the Prospect, which was jammed with
marchers and spectators from one end to the other. I estimated
that I could see a hundred and fifty thousand people at one
time on the Nevsky, and I doubt if there were more than a fifth
or a sixth of the marchers on the Prospect in sight at any one
time. There must have been half a million marchers in line.
And what an impression it made; faces and forms that showed
a lifetime of suffering and for whom a "Free Russia" had real
meaning.

The strains of Chopin's Funeral March were constantly
in the air played by hundreds of bands that were in line. The
singing choruses of marching thousands were marvelous; such
harmony we Americans could not imagine outside of trained
choruses. Every once in a while they would break out in church
music or a prayer or chant and then the spectators would join
in with bowed heads and doffed hats. The *Marseillaise* was
also sung.

The whole Prospect was a sea of flags and banners reading
"Eternal Memory to Our Fallen Brothers," "Heroes Who for
Freedom Fell," and all the changes on "Free Russia" and "Hail
to the Democratic Republic." In the lines were carried the
coffins containing the victims of the revolution, wrapped in red
bunting. The marchers were soldiers, workingmen, students,
women, marines, and some boys and girls. At one place rows of
workingmen alternated with rows of soldiers and above them

waved a big banner with a picture of two hands clasped, and
nearby another picture of a soldier shaking hands with a workingman. The atmosphere of the whole was solemn, spiritual.
The order was perfect and that without a policeman in the
city. There had been rumors that this day was to be the signal
for counter-revolution, that attempts would be made to spread
disorders, and that it wouldn't be safe on the streets. But it was
as quiet as Palm Sunday. I didn't see one sign of disturbance
the whole morning.

We saw Mr. Harte, Penn Davis, and Burri off on the train
for Sweden and Copenhagen early this morning, walking to
the station as all traffic was stopped for the day; no streetcars,
autos, or cabs. We had to get up at five o'clock to catch a 7:40
train, and by the time Day and I had completed the eight-mile
walk to the station and back to our room, we were ready for
breakfast.

And now America is in the war. Over here she just seemed
to slide in. Day before yesterday the Russian papers announced
that America had declared war on Germany, but we had been
so used to such announcements that it failed to make much of
a sensation. Yesterday, however, the Embassy confirmed the
report. It is hard to realize what tremendous changes are going
on all the time.

Mr. Harte had an interview last evening with Minister of
War Gutchkov. He and George Day had been waiting at the
entrance to the general's room a long time when they were
suddenly ushered in before the overworked Minister. Before
Mr. Harte fully realized that he was talking with the Minister
of War, the interview was over. The red tape and long formalities of the old regime are gone, and all business is in a hurry
now. He tried to see Kornilov, the Commandant of the Petrograd
Garrison, but was unable to do so.

The extent to which manufactured articles are vanishing
from the shops was impressed on me the other day when I spent
three hours walking eight miles hunting for galoshes without
success. The Walk Over Shoe Company did a rushing business
before Christmas time. When they got a shipment in, people
formed queues around several blocks waiting for their turn to

buy them. Those standing in line would sell their positions for high amounts.

March 25 / April 7

Baron Nicolai, the friend of the student movement, was in our apartment yesterday. He is up in the air under the new regime and doesn't know what is coming next. He is pessimistic about the outlook. He thinks the way is open, however, for the Y.M.C.A. to do a lot.

At last the first permits have been received. Day and I were over to the General Staff today and received the permits for Christensen, Bartholomew, and Gott. There is nothing but good will and anxiety at the General Staff now to accommodate Americans.

Countess Stackelburg has called off the deal for her palace. Her agent objected to our occupying the place. He has plans that would be more profitable to himself. So I must resume my search for office headquarters.

Later: We found St. Isaac's crowded for the service tonight. The revolution has not decreased the attendance or interest in the Church.

March 30 / April 12

Dear Mother Ainsworth:

Saturday, April 7, I received a letter from Emily and learned that she was still at Columbia University instead of at Moline. Before my reply was mailed, I received a cable from the New York office stating that the Davenport Association approved my staying until December first, and they wanted an answer by cable at once. On the same day, we received official confirmation of war being declared between the United States and Germany. Until men of my age shall be called out for military service, I feel that there is no place I can better serve my country than here. After thinking it over all day, I decided to stay on until December first hoping that Emily can come along over with Mrs. Baker, to whom Baker cabled just the preceding day.

Monday, April 9, I cabled New York agreeing to stay until December and urging Emily to come to Petrograd. On the same day, I got permits from the General Staff for Baker and Leonard. Also received a wire from our Turkestan Secretary, Jerome Davis, and from Mack at Kazan, appealing for authorization and funds to start work among the Russian officers and soldiers who were requesting it. I forwarded these appeals to Mr. Harte at Copenhagen.

Tuesday, April 10, the newspapers were full of accounts of the danger from the western front. A great invasion by the Germans is expected. The tension is growing. The three wives of the Mayak and Y.M.C.A. secretaries who still remain in Petrograd reserved tickets for a return trip to America in May, not that they have finally decided to go, but to be prepared for emergencies. It made me feel queer to have just cabled Emily to come on and then have the last American women preparing to leave. I'll wait a few days before reversing my cable. In the evening we saw Day off for America and Gott for Chita, and now there are only three of us secretaries left in Petrograd, less than at any time since I came. At the same time there are more of them in the field which means more work at headquarters.

Wednesday, April 11, Mr. and Mrs. Nelson moved over from the Grand Hotel to the "chummery." We are the only three in the apartments now. It is the first time that there has been a woman in the apartments. The Easter holidays began today. These call for more celebration than the Christmas holidays. The snow still lies a half foot deep on the parks and in the country, though it has been melting steadily for over a week. The weather during April has been much like March at home.

April 2 / 15

Dear Mother:

This is Easter Day, and a beautiful day it has been with the fascinating spring sunshine. Two of the new secretaries Malcolm Davis and Morgan arrived last night from Stockholm, and Baker and I went down to the station to meet them. The train did not arrive until midnight, and we did not get back to

the hotel until one o'clock this morning After that we conducted the new men over to St. Isaac's Cathedral where an all
night service was still in full swing with the inside of the Cathedral crowded with probably twelve thousand worshipers, and a
big line waiting outside to get in.

On Easter Eve the service begins at the usual time, six
o'clock, and continues without interruption until the break of
dawn, which now comes at 3:30. At 11:30 the bells of all the
churches begin to ring, and by midnight they make a grand
chorus. At the same time the priests and worshipers come out
of all the churches and make a procession with banners and
candles around the church three times. While we were waiting
for the train, the procession of priests from a neighboring church
came through the depot three times, followed by a procession
of singing worshipers. The midnight hour is the time for the
kissing to begin, and all day on Easter men are seen kissing each
other three times, the Easter salutation. Everyone begins to use
the greeting *Christos Voskres* (Christ is Risen) when the dawn
breaks. The service is so timed that the Resurrection comes at
this moment of climax.

At midnight the great torches on the four corners of the
roof of St. Isaac's were ablaze, a landmark for miles around. The
crowd entered by the big doors on one side of the Cathedral
and left through the big doors on the opposite side. These
largest doors are open only a few times in the year, the regular
Sunday crowds being handled through smaller side doors.

April 9 / 22

Dear Home Folks:

The great event this week was the cable from Mr. Hibbard
which read: "Emily sails Vladivostok company Spencer Boies
Womans Association secretaries 26th." That means four days
from now. The same day this cable arrived we received a report
of German submarines appearing off the coast of California.

During the past two weeks spring has come with a rush.
There is not the changing back and forth from frost to warm as
in the spring of the States. There is one steady grind of winter

right up to the break of spring, and then the temperature suddenly slides up over the freezing mark and stays there, crawling up little by little every day. Now it is averaging forty to fifty in the morning and sixty to seventy at noon. The days, which were short but a little while ago, are already longer than the longest days of June back home.

We are now wondering what has become of Mack. We received a wire from him in Kazan two weeks ago that he was leaving for Petrograd. Baker had been in line for a railroad ticket for Kazan for four days and had just worked down to a number low enough to buy one when Mack's wire caused him to wait until Mack arrives. He is still waiting, holding his place in line as number one by going to the station every morning and night and responding with his name when number one is called. If he should miss once, he would have to start all over again and spend four or five days working down to a number that would get called.

Now comes Waldo, our secretary from Omsk, with a wire that it is impracticable for him to remain.

April 16 / 29

Political events are speeding up. Last Monday I attended a Russian-American meeting at the City Duma and heard Ambassador Francis, Ministers Miliukov and Nekrassov, Commercial Attaché Huntington, and Dr. Simonds. Miliukov impressed me as an amiable college professor with much ability. Nekrassov impressed me favorably as an out-from-the-shoulder business fellow who had the facts and figures on the economic situation and realized what a big job he is up against in trying to restore the country's commerce and industry. Dr. Simonds spoke in Russian—a Russian so Americanized that I understood it perfectly. Huntington, who has been here only a few months longer than I, started out to speak in Russian but had to finish by reading. At that, he used the Russian pronunciation and idioms so well that he got a round of applause from the Russians when he finished.

The radicals are for peace at any price, even if it is a

separate peace. The moderates are unwilling that such a blot should be attached to Russia's record, and yet the pressure for peace is so great that they are doing everything in their power to bring about a general peace. That is all the talk now—a general peace. In the meantime the Germans keep coming on, and the Russians are reported to be fraternizing with them on the front instead of fighting, and a new propaganda called Bolshevik propaganda is spreading through the army. The first time I saw the big headlines in a Russian newspaper "Russian Soldiers Fraternizing on the Front," it made me shudder regarding the fate in store for the Allied cause in Russia. Zemmer says, however, that it will take the Germans a long time to reach Petrograd at this time of the year, even without opposition, owing to the mud caused by the spring thaws.

I had another taste of the radical program of propaganda at the formal opening of our first club for Russian soldiers, at the Peter and Paul Fortress, Thursday noon of this week. The soldiers and officers had tastily decorated the three splendid rooms of the Fortress which had been donated to the Association for a club center. One soldier had donated a library consisting of books costing four hundred rubles; we had furnished the dishes and equipment for the tea room, gramophone and records, harmonica, and correspondence materials.

All three rooms were jammed with five or six hundred soldiers and officers for the dedication. The ceremony started off in proper style by having a priest scatter the holy water and invoke the divine blessing upon the undertaking. The soldiers all came forward in file, one by one, while the priest slapped or sprinkled it on each soldier. When this was over, the priest took advantage of the occasion to express his misgivings as to how the men would take it. He was followed by music from a church choir, remarks by officers, and a welcome by Nelson, whose remarks were interpreted by Nusenberg. The program was scheduled to close when two individuals stepped forward and spoke to the officers. They were delegates sent from the Workingmen's Soviet to address the soldiers at the opening. The officers didn't relish having them speak, neither did they have the nerve to oppose the Soviet, so they agreed to let them speak.

The first man made a good revolutionary talk. He belonged to the moderate socialists, the Kerensky kind, and urged the soldiers to be true to the government, to their responsibilities as soldiers, and to the principles of the revolution which they had won. No one could take exception to the sane way in which he talked.

The next speaker was a little, hunch-backed man who represented the radical wing in the Soviet. He spoke for a solid hour and kept repeating remarks that could be summarized as follows: "*Tovarische*, you see all these things which the Americans have brought over here which must have cost at least two thousand rubles. They have been sent over by the American capitalists to keep you in slavery. They wish to poison your minds. They wish to make you their friends, so that you will be friends of the capitalists instead of the workingmen. Don't listen to what these Americans say. This Y.M.C.A. is a capitalist organization. They are the tools of the rich American capitalists whose only interest is to keep the workingman poor and enslaved. Don't have anything to do with this club and these diversions. The Americans want you to continue to fight the Germans. Don't do their bidding. The German working people are your friends. The American capitalists are your enemies. I come as a representative of the workingmen to give this charge to you soldier comrades who helped us win the revolution. The revolution is not yet won. The capitalists still have control. Let us remain banded together until they are overthrown."

The crowd stayed and heard the talk through, the officers very uncomfortable and the soldiers perplexed. After the talks were over, the soldiers seated themselves around the tea tables where we served them and stood discussing the club and the speakers. They all liked the first speaker, but ninety percent of them said that they thought the last speaker was wrong and that it was out of place for him to come and give such a talk at such a time. The officers told us afterwards that the reaction among the soldiers was in our favor rather than otherwise.

The opening of this club was six weeks from the day of the abdication of the Czar. Adjoining our club rooms at the fortress are the famous cells where the Czar kept hundred of political prisoners who had been connected with the Revolution of 1905, and also Finns. At the present time the ministers of the Czar's government who were captured are imprisoned here, as are members of the old police force.

We saw Goodsell and Morgan off for Jassy in Roumania yesterday afternoon. They went with excellent credentials and backing from all the governments interested, as well as with funds from the Rockefeller Foundation to provide food, thanks to our friend Mr. Arnett. They ought to be able to do a big job of relief.

I am still hunting apartments but have a new location in view, Number 9 Mochavaya Ulitza, the home of Madame Olchina. I visited her there a few days ago. She is trying to get away from here to the Caucasus and is trying to convince us that the house would be a gift at the nominal rent of five hundred rubles a month (which is really an outrageous rent), but she would be willing to let it go at that price for the sake of having Americans occupy it. Meanwhile we are willing to wait until she comes down to about a half or a third of that amount. One problem that puzzles her is what our status would be, first, if there should be a violent revolution by the radicals in Petrograd, and second, if the Germans should capture the city. Wouldn't we have a stand in with the Germans on account of our service to their prisoners, and therefore, wouldn't they let us and her property alone if we occupied the house? And then the revolutionists would surely respect Americans, wouldn't they? She wishes to get a guarantee from us about these things, which, of course, we can't give. She dreads the revolution much more than the Germans. In fact she is a great believer in the old regime and would evidently prefer the Germans to the present order.

She told us about her trouble in trying to get a ticket to the Caucasus. How different from the good old days under the Czar. Then all she had to do was to give the faithful gray-haired English-looking butler, who is one of the few remnants of former days to stay by her, a ruble, and presto, the next morning the tickets were delivered to her for first-class compartments, everything arranged through to her destination. A ruble plus the charge for the regular fare was all it cost. Now she had to wait days and weeks on a commissioner who charges anything from a hundred to three hundred rubles, besides the fare, and then she is likely to get an awful second-class ticket. "Democracy means that everybody wants to hold you up," she said.

Mr. Harte has wired from Copenhagen that it is practically impossible to get neutral secretaries and urges that our men remain.

While I have been writing this letter, our Omsk secretary, Waldo, has dropped in, and we have been visiting with him. Omsk is four or five days away on the Siberian Express, so you see what dropping in means. He comes in reply to a wire which he had just received from Mr. Harte, whom he was expecting to find here on his arrival. He thought the wire had been sent from Petrograd. We have not received word from Mr. Harte when to expect him.

Waldo's first comment on life in the capital was "how much faster and fuller of pep the people are now than when I went through a year ago." He said that many former Siberian exiles were constantly passing through Omsk on their way to Petrograd. Here in Petrograd now the exiles have seats of honor in the boxes formerly reserved for the Czar in all the theaters, and they are keeping them well filled. They are continually getting ovations from the audiences.

April 19 / May 2

Yesterday was the great May Day celebration of the Internationale, the Socialist Workingmen's organization. It is Europe's Labor Day and under the old regime was the day when the demonstrations were usually attempted which were so often put down with sword and bayonet. The Russian workingmen have always observed the same day as the other European countries despite the difference of the Russian calendar.

All day long a steady stream of oratory flowed from hundreds of speaker's booths that covered every available free spot in the parks and squares of the city, while thousands of red banners waved from one end of the city to the other from buildings and parades. Restaurants, hotels, and places of business were all closed. Waldo and I spent most of the day studying the demonstration and listening to the speakers.

In the square between St. Isaac's Cathedral and the German Embassy building, which loomed up heavy and massive like a Bismarckian threat behind a row of the speakers' booths, were so many platforms for speakers that we could stand in one spot and hear six different orators going at once from as many platforms. The speakers were mostly workingmen of all grades of intelligence and character. There were lanky, gawky young fellows, little hunch backed men, bitter-faced, wrinkled workers, conspicuously Jewish faces, German types, but few of the typical Great Russian type. They all possessed the Russian gift of oratory, however. Unhesitatingly, soulfully, forcefully, the stream of eloquence flowed hour after hour. As soon as one speaker would tire, after about half an hour, another speaker would be rushed to the platform, hoisted up, and carry on without a second's interruption. Thus for hour after hour the torrent rolled on.

The substance of the propaganda was all cut from the same cloth: "Down with Miliukov, down with the capitalists. End the war. If you wait until one side wins, there will be no end. The capitalists are using you to wage this war. The workingmen of Germany, Austria, and Hungary are your friends. The capitalists of England, France, and America are your enemies. Don't allow them to deceive you. Workingmen of the world, unite." Every speaker in St. Isaac's Square ran true to form to this propaganda.

Over at the Winter Palace, the whole square was fitted up with speakers' booths. Most of the speakers were giving the same line as at St. Isaac's. In some places a general or official was trying to stem the tide by making an appeal to stand by the government and keep faith with the Allies. It was interesting to watch. The simple soldiers, mostly peasant folk, would stand in front of the radicals and cheer and cheer. They would then drift in front of a general or government official and again cheer. I couldn't see any difference in the heartiness of their cheering.

Particularly conspicuous were the Jewish orators, who were all the more striking because they were usually well dressed, even in morning suits, as contrasted with the workingmen's speakers, who wore ragged clothes. There was something crafty about the way some of them smiled as they descended from the platform, and their fellow racial brethren would gather the simple Russian soldiers to the front to shake hands with them. Their smile seemed to say, "Oh, what simple folks. How easy to put it over on them."

Nothing was spared to make the demonstration a success. Bands, barkers, fake rooters, and even fake crowds, were all utilized by the energetic propagandists. My impression early in the day was: "How fine, all this exercise of democracy. Here are speakers for and against the government, and all are allowed equal freedom of speech, assembly, and press." But before the day had progressed far I felt that some tremendous plot was on to take advantage of the new freedom to overthrow the very liberties they were enjoying. Whether it would have been possible to do otherwise than let them thus speak themselves out, was another question.

During the afternoon we ran across knots of Russians of the middle class who were discussing the demonstration thus: "What I can't understand is why these workingmen have so much confidence in the working classes of Germany, Austria, and Hungary, and so little in the working classes of England, France, and America."

Another slogan of the demonstration was "The Land and Power to the People" and "Down with the Landowners."

The sudden burst of radical propaganda, which has developed during the past week, is attributed to a man named Lenin, who has just arrived from Switzerland. He came through Germany, and rumor is that he was banqueted by Emperor William, who is said to be back of his designs here. As he entered the country through Finland, he harangued the soldiers and workingmen along the way with the most revolutionary propaganda. One of the Americans who came through on the same train told us how disheartening it was. Lenin's first words as he got off the train at Petrograd were "Hail to the Civil War." God knows what a task the Provisional Government has on hand without adding the trouble that such a firebrand can create.

Soon after arriving in the city, Lenin gathered four or five hundred of the workingmen together in a street parade with banners that read: "Down With the Government," "Down With the Capitalists," "Down with the War," and down with everything else. "There is the poison that will destroy the democratic revolution," was my comment to one of the secretaries.

Fortunately May first passed without a ripple of violence; a beautiful sunshiny day.

April 23 / May 6

This has been the most intense and exciting week in the capital since the revolution. The May Day celebration was the prelude to chaos. Miliukov's note to the Allies was a storm center. Although the note had received the approval of the Soviet before Miliukov sent it, the radicals in the Soviet objected that it was serving the imperialistic ends of the war under cover, and under their leadership street demonstration began to take place, increasing in size and violence. Thursday the streets were covered with enormous red banners reading, *"Mir bez annexii i contributzii"* (Peace without annexations or indemnities).

Friday the black flags of the anarchists appeared on the Nevsky. The black flag sends the chills down your spine. The anarchists were taking advantage of the situation to plunge everything into disorder. Rumors flew about that the agents of the old order, "the black hundreds," were behind these anarchistic disorders and doing what they could to encourage so much violence and disorder that the people would become tired of it and turn back to the monarchy for relief. A woman and a general were killed during the disorders of the day.

I went over to the American Embassy and had a talk with J. Butler Wright. "On the lid of a powder can" was the way he expressed the situation. I crossed the Liteiny just after the black flag procession had passed, and groups of people were gathered around the soapbox orators on every corner.

In the evening we shook off our dismal forebodings by going to the Narodni Dom to hear Shaliapin in *Don Carlos*. Miss Vera accompanied us. The curtain raiser was not accompanied by the usual playing of the *Marseillaise* by the orchestra.

The audience yelled for it, but the orchestra and opera went on with the performance without the usual song of revolution.

Before the curtain was raised for the second act the large audience of six thousand began shouting for the *Marseillaise* again. The curtain again went up without the playing of the *Marseillaise*. The crowd kept up its yelling longer this time, but Shaliapin went ahead with the performance and the crowd finally subsided. As soon as the second act closed, however, they began again and kept up the demonstration for the *Marseillaise* for ten minutes until the orchestra yielded and played the great French music. The Russians pronounce the word *"Marsiluiza,"* and kept repeating it in a grand chorus. I wondered whether some parties higher up put the orchestra up to this trick to feel the pulse of the people.

The telegram which brought Waldo to Petrograd turns out to be one which Mr. Harte sent from here six weeks ago but which the present inefficiency of the telegraph service had taken five weeks to get into his hands. Waldo says that mail service is now quicker from Petrograd to the Siberian cities than the telegraph service. The Siberian newspapers still get their "telegraph bulletins," but they simply wait for the arrival of the Petrograd newspapers and then copy the news and publish it fresh as new telegrams.

This makes me wonder what will be the fate of the wire I sent for Emily yesterday at Tokyo. I wired the Student Y.M.C.A., "If convenient meet Mrs. Heald company Women's Association secretaries Spencer Boise arriving Yokohama May tenth Empress Japan. Ask her wire me when leaves Vladivostok for Petrograd."

Waldo has been giving an interesting insight into the war prisoner situation in Siberia. He says the conditions are good. They are well supplied with food and clothing and are allowed much liberty. A large part of the prisoners secures permits which allow them to live in the city outside the camps. They secure jobs with the Russians who are held responsible for them. The prisoners as a rule are better educated and trained than the local population and quickly come into demand for all sorts of artisan and professional work, such as carpentry, tailoring, engineering, electrical work, teaching, managing business, etc.

Many of the prisoners are making more money than they ever did before and are saving it up and sending it home. The Russian Government keeps all above a certain amount, but even this leaves them a liberal margin. Many of the prisoners like the life and opportunities in Siberia and plan to stay there even after peace comes. They find larger business opportunities than at home. Many of them marry into the population and are slipping imperceptibly into the status of Russian citizens. The prisoners universally prefer working out to living in the barracks.

The days are longer now than in July at home, but there is no green on the trees. Snow flurries have been frequent the past week, and it is as cold as March at home, though the ice went out in the Neva last Sunday.

April 30 / May 13

Imagine my surprise on receiving yesterday morning a cable from Mr. Hibbard reading: "Wife sails Japan Monday. Awaits you Tokyo." That is all the data I have to go on in planning a round trip of sixteen thousand miles requiring a month or more. I do not know the date the cable was sent from New York, nor the Monday that Emily sailed or is going to sail. Why didn't she sail from Vancouver with the Y.W.C.A. secretaries according to the plan mentioned in the last cable? All I can do now is to get the cable verified and act in accordance.

Nelson and I are working overtime and every night trying to keep abreast of the additional work made by fifteen secretaries in the field, and no one else in the city to help in the office work. Our work keeps growing rapidly despite the increasing unsettlement of conditions. Have received splendid reports from Hugh Moran and Jerome Davis this week. The last letter from Jerome told of having discontinued war prisoner work on the sixteenth of this month so as to devote his whole time to the army work. He had sent a telegram to this effect, but it never reached me. I have wired Conger at Vladivostok to go ahead with the army work there. Baker and Mack have written in from Kazan that things are chaotic there and that transportation and telegraph services are impossible. The parcel orders are constantly growing and taking longer days of my time.

Another job that is taking a lot of time is the revision of the list of books for the Russian war prisoners in Germany and Austria. The books we have been sending have been a hundred books selected by the Holy Synod of the old regime, and many were, of course, very monarchistic and entirely inconsistent with the new regime. Sam Harper* went with us to the new Procurator of the Holy Synod to see what could be done about them. The Procurator is a nervous high-strung man and seemed to feel himself between many fires. He referred us to a certain archbishop, who, he said, was the proper person to solve our problem. This week I have been spending long hours with a Professor Mallak and a Mr. Dubo of the Russian Red Cross, to whom the archbishop passed the buck on the revision job. Maybe some day after the war is over the revision will be completed. The trouble now is that the revision gets out-of-date in two days' time, and new questions come up at every meeting as to what books should be eliminated and what added.

Anarchy raises her finger higher and higher. Leninism is spreading through the army and fraternizing is growing on the front. Business is going to thunder, and the destructive forces are working faster than the constructive. The speeches of the ministers grow more pessimistic daily, and I am pessimistic over the future to say the least.

May 3 / 16

Dearest Wife:†

After all your waiting for me, it is not easy to sit down and write that I've got to give up the trip to Tokyo and must ask you to wait for further instructions. Mrs. Nelson is in very poor health and must return to America at once and is too frail to take the trip across Siberia alone. To delay the trip until I should get back from Tokyo would, I fear, be fatal to her.

---

* Samuel N. Harper of the University of Chicago was probably the outstanding American student of Russia in the years before the revolution.
† This letter never reached Mrs. Heald.

Living conditions get more impossible every day. It is too much to ask Mrs. Nelson to hunt up food to keep us going. Even old timers like Mrs. Long and Mrs. Summerville, who know the language and the ins and outs of things, have to devote all their energies to getting enough food to keep their families going. They spend a fortune doing so. Prices keep soaring while supplies are vanishing. Lunch prices have risen from a ruble and a half to two rubles and seventy-five kopeks since I came.

This afternoon I went over to the Peter and Paul Fortress with Nusenberg, the Lithuanian, who is our key man there. Much change has taken place since we opened up three weeks ago. Then only ten per cent of the soldiers were Bolsheviki. Now ninety percent are. Nusenberg says they all have money which has been shipped in from Germany. Discipline is gone. The drilling which kept up well for the first week or two after the revolution has practically vanished. The officers have no control over the men. There is no schedule for drilling; it takes place only if and when the notion seizes the soldiers. I saw men lying around on the ground doing nothing but enjoying the pleasant spring sunshine. One of the soldiers said, "Well, let's go and drill." There was a chorus of yeas and nays with the majority favorable. So they called an officer and off they started for the drill grounds. I followed. Halfway there they spied an orator holding forth on a crowded corner. One of the soldiers took a fancy to hear the orator and shouted, "Let's shake the drill for the orator." A chorus of approvals and disapprovals gave the democratic decision in favor of continuing to the parade grounds. A streetcar passed by in the opposite direction full of passengers. One of the soldiers suggested that they shake the drill and go streetcar riding, and again democracy voted and decided to go on for the drill. The squad escaped all of the side diversions and reached the drill field. There the soldiers decided what the drills should be and under what conditions the officers should conduct them.

With Nelson's going you can see how impossible it would be for me to leave. I shall be the only secretary left with fifteen secretaries in the field constantly wiring and writing for supplies, money, and instructions. The Embassy informed me today that

Dr. Mott has been appointed a member of the Root Commission,* which is to come at once, reaching here probably before Mr. Harte gets back, and before you could reach here. I shall have to make most of the arrangements so far as they affect our work.

Minister of War Gutchkov resigned on the 13th saying that he was useless in an army without discipline and under a government that was helpless before an undisciplined army.

I am sending this letter by Mr. Golder, who is going to Vladivostok with the Russian Commission to meet the Railroad Commission which America is sending over with an offer to help the Russians restore their transportation. Mr. Golder is a history professor in the state of Washington and will interpret for the Commission.

If this reaches you in time, bring some flour and bacon along.

May 7 / 20

I hope that this letter will get delivered to you somewhere between here and Tokyo by the Nelsons who are leaving Tuesday night.‡ I am writing you today at Tokyo in care of the Student Y.M.C.A. as follows: "May 20. Impossible come Tokyo as I am only secretary remaining in Petrograd. If you can find company for Petrograd urge come ahead. If not can you proceed Vladivostok address care American Consulate and await company there? Wire reply."†

It doesn't seem feasible to connect up with the Commission Dr. Mott is with as we don't know whether he is coming by the Atlantic or Pacific, and if by the Pacific, whether via Japan and Vladivostok or Peking and Harbin.

The situation has cleared somewhat the last few days, and

---

* The commission, headed by former Secretary of State Elihu Root, had been appointed by President Wilson to persuade the Provisional Government to remain in the war.

‡ The Nelsons met Mrs. Heald in Japan and from them she learned for the first time that her husband wanted her to continue her journey to Petrograd.

† Mrs. Heald received the telegram, but it was so garbled that it was unintelligible.

while the inconveniences remain, the dangers seem less. The resignations of Gutchkov and Miliukov produced a crisis. There were forces at work in the Soviet who wanted to overthrow the government and put the Soviet in power, which would mean ending the war and our work in a jiffy. Some big conventions were held. The Soldiers' delegates from the Front held a convention May 10–17. The first All Russian Congress of the Peasants is in session now, having begun May 17. In between these, there was an important meeting of the Workingmen's and Soldiers' Deputies. These conventions have had their effect upon the Soviet.

Gutchkov made a moving appeal to the Soldiers' delegates. He drew a gloomy picture of the awful condition things were in and said that he was asked to sign army orders which he as an officer could not conscientiously do; he knew they would destroy the discipline still further. Kerensky made an eloquent speech and appeal to the same delegates, and they responded with a resolution to carry on the war and approved the introduction of stronger discipline.

The Petrograd Soviet was still in session when the Peasants' Convention opened up. Madame Breshkovskaya, the "Grandmother of the Revolution," who has recently returned from her long exile in Siberia, made a strong appeal for real democracy, and the peasants came back strong for democracy and against the radical Bolsheviki. The latter only got two or three votes out of eight hundred.

In the Petrograd Soviet a radical, who has just arrived from New York, by the name of Trotsky, a German Jew* whose real name is Braunstein, got up and made a demogogic appeal for the overthrow of the Duma and for the putting of the Soviet in power as the government. But the great leaders of the meeting, Kerensky, Tseretelli, and Plekhanov, were against him, and the Soviet voted for participation in the Duma Government and a new cabinet by a large majority.

I hope you can get here in time for the White Nights. They

---

* Trotsky was indeed Jewish but not German. He was born and reared in the Ukraine.

are already nearly here. Last night I walked home from Zemmer's between 12:00 and 12:30. The glow of the dawn was already noticeable when I started home, and by the time I had walked the four miles to our apartment, it was light enough to read large print inside the house, and outside the buildings were bright with the morning glow.

It seemed strange that with the summer light there still hangs on the winter cold. In fact the twentieth day of May is a freezing, snowy day. The ground was white with snow as I came home. It has been cold all week. Everybody is still wearing overcoats. There is hardly a suspicion of green in the trees.

An unexpected boost for our war prisoner kitchens this week, just when we didn't see how they could be maintained any longer. Before America entered the war, the American Government advanced us German Government funds for the maintenance of these kitchens through Siberia for convalescents, undernourished, etc. We were able to provide a good meal three times a day for thirteen to fifteen kopeks or between a penny and two cents a meal. But after America entered the war and the Embassy withdrew from the war prisoner work, we no longer received these funds. This week the Swedish Red Cross Director called upon me and said that we could have ten thousand rubles per month government funds for our kitchens. The American Embassy approves of our continuing the service with this support, and we are naturally happy to be able to continue a work that saves hundreds of lives.

Food parcels keep increasing—three hundred and three in the last order—and it is a full day's job to get out an order of that size.

May 15 / 28

The saddest blow of all came today when the two Y.W.C.A. secretaries arrived with the news of why you didn't come with them. They say that you received a wire from the New York office while you were on the train the day before your boat sailed from Vancouver. The wire had been forwarded as a cable from me telling you not to come as I was returning in July. That was the cable I sent in February, two months before the other cable telling you to come, but it got delivered to you after the first one.

The consequences of this mix-up of cables is sure a mess. There you are down at Tokyo waiting for me to pick you up on my way back to America in July, whereas I'm not going back until December. I have been doing my best to reach you by wire in Japan, but the prospects aren't bright. I don't know when we'll finally get in touch with each other.

Then in New York they are expecting me back in July after all and have probably notified the Davenport Association to that effect. I can now understand a telegram which Mr. Harte received recently from New York stating that Davenport had extended my time and I had agreed to stay, and that then I had suddenly sent an unaccountable cable reversing all plans, but that Emily was en route to Japan to meet me anyhow.

I tried to straighten the whole thing out today by wiring Galen Fisher of the Tokyo Y.M.C.A. suggesting the possibility of connecting with the Root Commission at Vladivostok.* The Embassy has wired the Consulate at Vladivostok asking them to assist you in every way possible when you arrive.

The Y.W.C.A. secretaries arrived at three o'clock this morning when the sun was already up a half hour. None of their telegrams had gotten through so no one was down at the station to meet them. They said that they saw you only a few minutes before their boat left Vancouver. You thought my cable meant new troubles had broken out in Russia and that they had better give their trip up too. But they are the kind that would rather see revolutions than quietness; they are entering into the situation here with enthusiasm and energy.

I can't resist the fascination of these white nights. We are now having the best weather of the year. I donned my spring suit yesterday. I like to stroll along the Neva by the Winter Palace about 10:30 or eleven o'clock in the evening and watch the beautiful sunset glow across the river in the northwest. While the colors gradually fade between 11:30 and midnight, the light of a new day begins to brighten the sky in the northeast. Twilight

* This telegram was received, but it was garbled and unintelligible.

fades into dawn, and the northern sky is really one continuous glow from the sun which has hidden not far below the horizon. One can read the magazines on the streets until 10:30, and by twelve o'clock, when I usually turn in, it is noticeably lighter. Of course there is never any need of lights to go to bed by, and the street lamps are never lighted any more.

The home at 9 Mochavaya is now ours by contract until December. Madame Olchina finally agreed to come down to two hundred rubles and we took it at that.

Miss Vera had a birthday party yesterday at which we association secretaries were guests. There was a Mrs. Katts there with her daughter. Mr. Katts is a mine operator, and she says that he is losing three hundred thousand rubles a month by keeping the mines running now. She doesn't know what will happen when the funds all give out and the miners can draw no more pay. She says the same thing is going on everywhere. She thinks the country is going to ruin as a result of what she calls the sabotage of Lenin and his followers. But the Leninites lay the blame on the Kerensky government for being too weak.

May 21 / June 3

Dear Home Folks:

This is Pentecost Sunday and a beautiful spring day. The trees have leaved out during the week, overcoats have been shed, and we suddenly find ourselves in almost summer weather, though we may still expect snows.

Today is one of the big holidays, and the restaurants and dining rooms were closed after twelve o'clock. The people in the hotels could not get service in their rooms after that hour as all keep the holiday. I couldn't blame them. The weather was so irresistible that I wanted to get out to Pavlovsk or the Islands myself, but instead I had to finish a seventy-eight page report on the war prisoners work for Mr. Harte. It has taken sixty hours to prepare. Meanwhile my correspondence has fallen far behind, and we are moving to our new office at 9 Mochavaya Tuesday.

Last Tuesday the Nelsons left for America, securing their tickets fifteen minutes before the train left by paying the commissionaire the outrageous sum of one hundred and fifty dollars extra for the privilege of buying them. This was more than the fare itself. We didn't have time to see to what the tickets entitled them until they were on the train, and then found that one was first-class and the other second-class, so that to be together one would have to stand. Even so they sighed with relief to get on the train and know they were headed for America. Mrs. Nelson would have collapsed had she missed the train and faced the ordeal of another week's wait.

From Tuesday until Thursday Burri and I were the only association secretaries in the city. Then Mr. Harte and his secretary Penn Davis arrived from Stockholm. Mr. Harte is planning to go down to Roumania Tuesday and return by the middle of the month when Dr. Mott is expected.

Mr. Shidlovsky has been announced as Ambassador to England. Madame says that they have lost practically everything. It was mostly landed estates. They still have their beautiful palace near the Islands, however.

The political situation has taken a turn for the worse this week. After all his pledges for introducing iron discipline in the army, Kerensky has signed a Declaration of Soldiers' Rights which frees the soldier from the duty of saluting except when on duty. It places him on the same social basis as the officer in civil life and in fact places things back where they were put by that fatal Order Number One at the time of the March Revolution.

You feel the reaction in the atmosphere. The soldiers lounge around the streets enjoying their new liberties. It seems impossible to foresee anything but disaster ahead, though Kerensky is straining every nerve to put on an offensive at the front. The new situation makes our opportunity in the army work much more problematical.

May 27 / June 10

On Tuesday Mr. Harte and Penn Davis left for Roumania to confer with Goodsell and Morgan. My new roommate is Arthur Ruhl, whose splendid stories about life in Russia under the title of "The White Nights" have been appearing in *Collier's Weekly*.

Ruhl and I are enjoying our cold showers every morning
and taking in political meetings in the evening. He wants me
along to interpret as his knowledge of Russian is largely confined
to the word *tovarisch* and the first lesson in Bondar's grammar.

The white nights are now at their best. You can read fine
print out-of-doors at midnight. When we came out of a meeting
last night at 10:30, it was almost sunshining, and the glow on the
tall Admiralty and Peter and Paul Church spires, on St. Isaac's
dome and scores of other domes and spires, was fascinating. The
weather has been perfect, the temperature most of the time in
the sixties and seventies day and night, and clear all the time.
The light bothers Ruhl a good deal, and he wears a black eye-
band called the "black night." The people love to promenade
around all night.

We moved our offices Tuesday. Our new apartments are
roomier, and the office force seems pleased with the change. The
only objection they raised was our omission of the dedication of
the new quarters with the sprinkling of the holy water, the bless-
ings of the priests, and lighting of the candles under the icons. This
was the customary thing in Russia under the old regime and
involved an extra holiday. They tried to convince me what a
sacrilege I was committing, but found me unyielding. The rush
of work makes a day precious now, and on this holiday fever I
am what the Russians call *strogii* (severe).

The ballroom is our main office. The house is decorated
with stuffed bears, many full-length mirrors, shining brass cannon, and in the library is quite an arsenal of old firearms, swords,
etc. We are closer to the American Embassy and the Mayak, but
further from our rooms. It is a twenty-five minute walk. At noon
it takes ten minutes each way to the nearest restaurant. We hope
to arrange lunch at the office to save time. Work has increased
greatly of late. I would add a stenographer if I could locate a
typewriter. As it is I am putting in twelve hours a day including
Sunday trying to catch up with the work before Emily and Dr.
Mott arrive.

One woman came in during the week to send food parcels
to two hundred and thirty-three prisoners in Germany. A man
called, accompanied by a Russian officer, representing a new

trade journal. They offer twenty percent of their net profits for war prisoner work and say that they have selected our organization as the one best organized and quickest in getting things through to the prisoners.

While we were having a meeting of our committee at the Peter and Paul Fortress yesterday, Kornilov, the Commander of the Petrograd Military District, arrived to inspect the regiment stationed there, and the way the men whipped into shape was heartening. There is vast respect for the present commander, and though the military discipline that is evoked by his visits is usually short-lived, it is encouraging that anyone can inspire it.

The food situation is getting worse. We haven't been able to get any butter for a week now. Only a half pound of sugar is allowed each ten days. Everything is by card only, except the strawberries which are being peddled around the streets. We are afraid that the street peddlers, however, are carrying cholera in their wares.

June 3 / 16

"Lost, somewhere between Tokyo and Petrograd, one wife. Finder please do something besides wiring."

This morning I made a second trip to the station to meet the Siberian Express and Emily, but she did not come. I haven't had a word from her since she arrived in Japan. During the week, however, Major Washburn, one of the members of the Root Commission, brought me a splendid letter that Emily had written on board the *Empress* May 23. In this letter Emily explained how she received the cable the day before sailing from Vancouver, while she was still on the train in the Canadian Rockies, and how she stayed on at Vancouver three weary weeks after that, and then decided to come on to Japan and do some sight-seeing while waiting for my return to America and the trip back together. I don't know yet whether she even knows that I am expecting her to come on here, and that I am not returning in July.

Mr. Reading, a member of the American Railroad Commission, was also waiting at the station and gave some interesting observations about the condition of the road. There were plenty of locomotives, cars, and sidetracks, he said. Give them more locomotives and they would simply have more out of commission. Give them more cars and they would have more empties. Give them more sidings and they would have more useless cars lined up on them with people living in them. What they needed was organizing brains. They had no way of organizing the facts about their railroad. The American Commission had done more to organize the facts and to show the railroad management where they were at during their two week's trip across the country than the Russians had done in their whole history. The Russians had never made a distinction between passenger and freight traffic; all had been carried as so many poods. The railroad had existed merely as a military system, and no one had attempted to make it pay its way.

While we were spending our several hours waiting for the train, a number of other trains slid into the station crowded with layers of humanity, mostly uniformed men, but also many peasants, women and children. The locomotives were covered with people at every point where a foothold or a handhold was to be obtained. The roofs of the cars were covered thickly just as close as human beings could lie down. The platforms held enough to fill the insides of the cars. Most of these people were riding free, at least all the soldiers, and they smuggled along a lot of women and children as part of the family. The American engineer said that nothing could be done to restore the railroad until someone received the authority to stop this universal joy-riding. Nothing could ruin the road quicker than these ceaseless streams of soldier tramps riding free without order or aim except to buy their pack of articles at one point and sell it at the next at a profit. Most of them were taking advantage of the provision crisis in Petrograd to ransack the country for hundreds of miles around to make use of their free transportation privilege to bring in the precious packs. They all laugh good-naturedly over their fun like children, but the question is when will the spanking come?

Meeting the Siberian Express is great business. It is due at ten o'clock Saturday evening. You can't get service over the

telephone to find out whether it is late or not. I went down the
four miles to the station last evening at train time only to learn
that it wouldn't be in until five o'clock in the morning. I
returned home, turned in, and was waked by an alarm clock
at three. When I reached the station they told me that the train
would be in at seven. It finally arrived at eight-thirty. I shall
have a similar experience each week until Emily arrives.

The walk down the Nevsky at four o'clock on a June morning gives a new picture of Petrograd. The sun is already about
three hours up, a pale sunshine in a pale sky. The sunshine is
not hot at this time of the day, and the temperature is enjoyable.
Along the street come droshkies with returning joyriders or a
few travelers coming from the station on the beginning of a long
hunt for hotel rooms. Street sweepers are out. In front of the
Novoye Vremya newspaper offices a discussion is going on with
a knot of thirty or forty men excitedly talking. Another large
group occupies a side street nearer the station, while on the large
square in front of the station, a couple of hundred civilians and
soldiers are standing around some orators. The Leninite agitators
are at work night and day convincing the people and the soldiers that Kerensky's efforts to put on an offensive at the front
are wrong, and that the army should quit fighting and overthrow
the Duma and the capitalists instead. On the sloping base of
the monstrous monument of Alexander II, soldiers are lying
asleep, huddled close together. The omnipresent droshkies are
already lined up in front of the station, or along the side streets
from the Nevsky, with the drivers fast asleep on their seats
waiting for customers to wake them up.

On Wednesday night the Railroad Commission arrived and I
learned from Mr. Holder that Emily did not reach Vladivostok
in time to come either with it or with the Elihu Root Commission. Mr. Holder and Hugh Moran were both in Vladivostok the
day before the Commission arrived. They looked for Emily and
could learn nothing except that the Consulate was also looking
for her.

On the same day the Root Commission arrived in Petrograd
with Dr. Mott as one of its members. He is, of course, very busy
and has little time to devote to Y.M.C.A. affairs. I have had one

conference with him for about a half hour. He was surprised
that Mr. Harte was not here; the latter is now in Roumania
looking for Goodsell, who is in Odessa. At the close of my conference with Dr. Mott at the Angleterre, he asked me to go along
with him in the droshky to the Winter Palace. On the way he
asked me what I thought of the general situation. I replied that
I feared that the socialist and Leninite agitation on the front
would prevent the Russians from ever fighting again. He said
that he regarded the outlook as "not favorable but not hopeless."

The American Commission is being entertained at the
Winter Palace. This morning Hugh Moran and I accompanied
them on a trip through the Palace. It was my first tour of this
historic place, which seems an interminable building to go
through. Mr. Root headed our little procession and took special
interest in the hundreds of wounded Russian prisoners who
are being taken care of in the Palace hospital, into which a
considerable part of the building had been converted under
the Old Regime. No hospital could be more ideally situated,
with its large airy rooms looking out over the sparkling waters
of the Neva, while the fresh breezes blow in through the large
windows. All was glorious with the June sunshine. Many of
the men are horribly mutilated, making a sad contrast with
their surroundings.

The life in the Winter Palace and on the train of the Czar
will hardly give the American Commission glimpses of the real
life of the people and of revolutionary Russia. I would like to
have taken them along with me on a visit to the tenement district in the factory end of the city which I made this week with
Greschkievsky, who is Madame Shidlovsky's superintendent and
who is much interested in welfare work among the poorer classes.
He took me to a workingmen's tea room on the Zabalkansky
Prospect beyond the Fontanka Canal, where the tea is sipped
through sugar cubes placed between the teeth, and the patrons
bring along their black bread and the more fortunate ones jam
or cheese to eat with their bread and tea.

Then we continued on towards the edge of the city, past
the Obukhov Hospital, and turned over to an immense solidly
built seven-story concrete structure where he had the address of

a man who was out of work. The outside of the building looked respectable but inside a strange contrast faced us. The building itself was well finished inside as well as out, with great broad corridors and stairways and large windows. The broad corridors and stairways were crowded with pigs, chickens, dogs, cats, children, women, soldiers, and everything imaginable. There were no signs of janitor service. The floors were covered with human and animal filth and dirt in which the children were playing and crying as in a dirty back yard. The windows were so covered with dirt that we couldn't see out. We climbed up six long flights of stairs, all covered with the same indescribable filth and crowds. On each floor were a hundred rooms.

We came to the room where the party lived whose address we were looking for and were admitted by a crippled girl who viewed us suspiciously until Greschkievsky disarmed her doubts with his friendly conversation. The room, which was reasonably large, was divided into two parts by a faded, dirty red curtain hanging across part of the middle of the room. An invalid was bedridden in the unwindowed part of the room nearest the door. In the same part of the room another bed was occupied by a sick woman. In the outer part a soldier was making love to a maiden on the window sill, which shared its space also with the family larder of a hunk of black bread. The window served as family refrigerator and pantry. The window was open and unscreened and flies were everywhere. A dog, a cat, and a pig were the other occupants of the rooms, and three other human occupants were not at home, including the man out of work whom Greschkievsky was looking for. We were informed he had obtained work distributing literature for Lenin. The soldier sitting on the window sill was a Leninite. Many soldiers lived in this tenement of seven hundred rooms, and the man in the window said that they were all Leninites. He was friendly in manner, but his tone was that of a man who saw no need of doing more work because the day was approaching when the present order of society was to be overturned and everything would be in the hands of the proletariat. These are the kinds of homes that most of the city soldiers come from. Most of the men from decent homes are officers. No wonder that the Russian army is revolutionary. And yet, much of the wretchedness of these homes is due not to inadequate housing, for in fact the buildings are quite substantial, but more to the lack of education and training in the first laws of cleanliness and sanitation.

If the American Commission could only see this seamy side of life in Peter's capital, they might understand more easily why it is so embarrassing to Minister of War Kerensky to entertain them, and why it is so difficult to make appointments with him. The radical element hates bourgeois America, which they consider the Commission represents, and they bring pressure to bear on the Provisional Government to neglect the Commission. In spite of this, the Commission has been shown great attention and cordiality from the liberal Russian elements who look to America for their salvation. The American Commission has been entertained imperially in the grand suites of the Winter Palace where they have been assigned rooms.

Dr. Mott and the Commission think that two hundred Y.M.C.A. secretaries will be needed in Russia, and one hundred are being wired for at once to help in the task of restoring morale in the Russian army. One new American secretary is, however, the only addition to our force this week. Paul Anderson, who has come direct from China via New York, has been office secretary for the National Y.M.C.A. office in China and was returning to America to complete his college education when the new situation in America showed that there would be nothing doing in the college education line for the duration. Just at that time New York received my February cable, and not knowing of its two month delay in delivery, were puzzling to know whom to send in my place. They decided that Anderson was the man, so my successor is here. Well, there's going to be work and jobs enough for all so I'm not worrying. Paul is a dandy young fellow, very capable in the office, and an expert stenographer. He is acting as Dr. Mott's stenographer while he is here. He has joined our group at the "chummery," which now consists of Burri, Arthur Ruhl, Anderson, and myself.

Rezvoll, a Norwegian secretary, and the second of our neutrals, arrived yesterday. He is a quiet, unassuming, serious-minded fellow who grows upon you as you get acquainted.

Earlier this week Madame Shidlovsky invited me to come out and have dinner with the family and the two Y.W.C.A. secretaries. The latter are planning to center their efforts upon welfare work with working girls and women. Madame Shidlovsky is a marvelous spring of energy; I only fear she will soon wear herself out at the pace she is going in her welfare and uplift work.

This invitation gave me my first experience at a regular dinner with a family of the wealthy upper class. I have been out to teas, but dinners are different. The Y.W.C.A. secretaries and I waited in a beautifully furnished front room before being called into the dining room. There were still some of the members of the family and friends with us although Madame Shidlovsky had excused herself a few moments before. Then our Russian friends who were in the room with us suggested that we might as well go into the dining room. When we entered, we found several members of the family already seated and proceeding with their meal.

After we had been seated a few minutes, Madame Shidlovsky came in. Whenever anybody wanted anything they would get out of their chairs and walk around to the point of the table where they could most easily reach the desired edibles and reach over for them and walk back to their seats. People were constantly getting up and going around to fork a piece of bread, or get some salt, or abstract a piece of butter from the butter dish.

A messenger was announced and Madame Shidlovsky had the boy come in and deposit his package on a chair which she had a servant place next to her. She proceeded to open the package and examine the curtains they contained, holding them up for our comments while the eating continued. Another messenger was announced and dress goods were brought in and opened at the dinner table. Meanwhile a bewildering multitude of orders was being issued to servants, superintendents, schweitzer, and doorkeeper, during the entire meal with a rapidity that kept me dizzy. Yet between all this feverish activity Madame Shidlovsky seemed to have nothing on her mind but our entertainment and entered absorbingly into the discussion of the table. It was an interesting revelation of one type of Russian woman, not very

numerous but extremely influential. They are the opposite of
the society-loving, novel-reading, dancing kind, who sleep all
morning, primp all afternoon, entertain, and are entertained
all night.

After dinner each person walked around to Madame Shidlovsky, kissed her hand, and thanked her for the dinner in
accordance with immemorial Russian custom which has not been
changed by the revolution.

June 11 / 24

I celebrated our seventh wedding anniversary trying to deci-
pher the following telegram which I received on that occasion
from Emily, dated Tokyo, June 19: "Vchetchis pentachord
hopingly America will await you Tokyo sightseeing celulitas
gekanter Heald." The strange words are neither Russian nor
Japanese. This is the only word I have received from Emily in
answer to the seven telegrams I have sent her since she reached
Japan. Four weeks have gone by since the arrival of the Y.W.C.A.
secretaries who started out with her. I made my ninth trip to the
station this morning to meet her. One of the men of the American
Embassy who came this morning from Vladivostok said that
Emily was not there when he left and that she had not been there.

Dr. Mott returned from Moscow and after a busy two days
went on a brief tour to other cities in Russia with the other
members of the Commission. I have seen little of him. He has
been closeted with Mr. Harte much of the time since the latter
returned, formulating plans for work with the Russian army. At
Mr. Harte's request I have drawn up an estimate of the number
of secretaries and money it would take. Such an estimate for an
army variously estimated at between ten and fifteen million is
some job.

During the week the Bolsheviki have advertised big demonstrations for peace, but the Soviet has issued warnings to the
people to have no part in them, as they are designed to betray
the country and its honor. The Bolsheviki are not yet controlling
the Soviet.

Zemmer has a friend who is closely acquainted with Keren-

E.T.H. and Emily the day he got his Japanese-made American uniform.

Emily Heald in center with Mrs. Hollinger, wife of the Mayak secretary from Petrograd, on the left and Mrs. Long, wife of the Mayak physical director, on the right.

In Vladivostok in May. From the top down: Noyes, formerly pastor
in Fifth Avenue, New York Presbyterian Church; Fred Field Goodsell, in
charge of Vladivostok work; Riley, a seminary graduate from America;
Francis, a physical director from New York City; Tom Martin, a history
professor from Harvard; E.T.H.; Peters, a seminary graduate; and
Bunker, a seminary graduate and professor.

Emily Heald in the back seat with U.S. Consul McGowan and Mrs.
Hollinger; Mrs. Long and Griffin, the kino expert from New York, in
the front seat.

Russian peasants.

As Spasskoye, between Vladivostok and Khabarovsk, a typical Russian village street scene.

British troops were first of the Allies to reach Vladivostok to aid the Czechs.

First Americans off for the Czech front from Vladivostok.

The French procession through Vladivostok.

American infantry passing Czech headquarters, Vladivostok.

sky. In a conversation with him Kerensky stated that he had heard that the people questioned whether he was big enough for his responsibility. He replied that he knew that he wasn't big enough, but what the country needed just then wasn't so much big men as men who could talk to the soldiers and he could do that. Kerensky is said to be in a dying condition,* and the wonder is that he still keeps the vitality to come back at the Bolsheviki with the power and magnetism that he has shown in recent debates. He has shown up the collusion between the German military commanders and the Bolsheviki, and how the Lenin and Trotsky peace offensives parallel the peace offensive of the Germans.

Jerome Davis came up from Turkestan in response to Mr. Harte's call. He is a member of the Soviet in Turkestan and as such has a pass to the sessions of the All-Russian Congress here and is attending its sessions. Jerome seems much more enthusiastic about the Soviet movement than the rest of us. The Soviet would seem to be more of a democratic movement and less of a German propaganda down in Turkestan.

This evening I called on Mr. Yatseievitch and found him quite enthusiastic over the Ukraine movement. He has a keen sense of the superiority of the Ukraine culture over that of the Great Russians or Muscovites, as he calls them. If Great Russia is to go the way of the radical revolutionaries, Lenin and Trotsky, he wants to see it keep out of the Ukraine, he says. He doesn't share my misgivings about the disaster that will befall the country as a whole if it splits up in these parts.

I have now seen the white nights at their whitest. I had to go down to the station at midnight last night to meet the Vladivostok train. As the droshky jogged down the Nevsky, I could read ordinary print in the newspapers at twelve o'clock. The glow of the sunset and sunrise never left the skies. The platform lights were on at the station from 11 p.m. until 1 a.m. but were not needed. As the train did not arrive until three, I had a three hour wait and saw the sunrise at two o'clock.

---

* He died fifty-three years later at the age of eighty-nine in Palo Alto, California.

The weather has been hot the past week, the temperature ranging from eighty to eighty-five even at night, and about ninety-five during the day. I am glad to have my Palm Beach suit.

Zemmer has joined the Tsarsky Selsky Regiment. He is confident that a reaction will soon set in, and this regiment would be a natural leader in such a reaction.

June 20 / July 2

The mystery of Emily's whereabouts was finally cleared up by a cable which I received from Mr. Hibbard Saturday morning reading: "Emily leaves Vladivostok enroute Petrograd June 28th." I bounced around all day like a school boy. To know that at the time I received the cable Emily was already the third day out from Vladivostok seemed too good to be true. Yesterday morning another telegram came from Emily, sent from Vladivostok reading: "Letrve VladivostoknTbentyeuftx. Emuly Xeald." You can see that our communications with New York are better than with Vladivostok.

Yesterday and today have been great days in Petrograd. The long-hoped-for offensive is under way. Today's report of the capture of ten thousand prisoners, including one hundred and twenty-three officers, on the southwestern front made the city wild with joy and demonstrations. The atmosphere has changed as by a miracle. Yesterday the Leninists and Trotskyites were holding sway with peace demonstrations in which the banners rang all the changes on "Down with the Bourgeoisie," "Down with the Capitalists," "Down with War," "Down with Kerensky," "Down with the Capitalist Ministers." Now all is for war and victory.

This offensive, of course, gives us new hope that our own work can be more useful, just as we were getting dubious. We are doing our best to get twenty more secretaries into Russia immediately from other countries while waiting for the hundred from America. Our plans require the fullest possible service from every American secretary now in Russia. The present plan, as decided upon in conference with Dr. Mott yesterday, is to

release me from office work to head up an army work demonstration in one of the garrison centers, probably Kiev. I want
to keep away from the north on account of Emily. Mr. Yatseievitch says that the climate of Kiev is much like that of Virginia.
Jerome Davis is taking over the army work in Petrograd.

The Sunday evening conference last evening with Dr. Mott,
in his room at the Winter Palace, will not soon be forgotten.
The sun still shone over the Winter Palace Square, on the
golden spire of the Admiralty Building opposite us, on the
glistening gold dome of St. Isaac's, and over all that part of
the city, as we sat up to eleven o'clock discussing and laying
plans. Mr. Harte and the other secretaries now in Petrograd
were present. Present also were two members of the Root Commission, Cyrus McCormick and Charles R. Crane. While we
sat and conferred, the full moon rose with the pale color it has
while daylight still lasts. It was a dramatic setting for a Y.M.C.A.
conference.

I trust that the cool wave we are now enjoying extends over
Siberia as it will help Emily on her trip.

The American Commission left last night for Moscow. Some
of the party will continue down to the front to view the offensive.

When Jerome and I went out to the fortress this week to
introduce him as my successor in the army work of Petrograd,
we found that the Soviet Committee at the fortress wants to take
over our work. Everywhere through the army now these Soviet
committees exist. They are doing all they can to get all the
power into their hands. They usually include the most intelligent and peppy men in the regiment, those having the greatest
initiative.

The Soviet Congress voted the other day to continue war
on the basis of "Peace without annexation or indemnities." This
and the offensive make the outlook more encouraging than for
a long time.

June 26 / July 9

Here Emily and I are at last in our Petrograd apartments. The
dream that each of us has had for the last six months has at
last come true. The Siberian Express pulled in Sunday after-

noon at four o'clock, eighteen hours late. It seemed to make a point of prolonging our separation as long as possible. It was the eleventh time that I had been down to the station to meet Emily. Neither of us saw the other in the crowd until we were right in front of each other. Then what was my surprise to see, instead of a tired, dusty, worn-out person, as nearly everybody seems to be after that eleven-day trip, Emily standing there as clean, fresh, and cheerful as a daisy. I never saw her looking healthier. I guess it was the happiest moment either of us ever had.

I quickly initiated Emily into the mysteries of engaging an *isvoschik*, and we went up the Nevsky in two droshkies, one carrying the luggage and the other us two.

One of the first things we discussed was the Davenport situation. Emily agreed that my duty lay here for the duration, and so I have sent back by the American Commission a letter to Mr. Yaggy asking them to accept my resignation so that they will be free to make any arrangements they desire.

I have just been over to say good-by to Dr. Mott, who is leaving with the American Commission tonight. He says that the opportunity here is without parallel. The members of the Commission who were down on the southwestern front are quite excited about what they saw. The Czechoslovaks swept the Austrians off their feet, but the Russians failed to come up to their support. Leninist propaganda has spread a lot of disaffection in the ranks which threatens to ruin the advance. In some places the Russian regiments, instead of advancing, opened up for the Germans to advance through them. We're not out of the woods yet by any means. It is a shame that all the outburst of enthusiasm of a week ago has nearly died out.

On the Fourth of July, the American Embassy held a reception. The war enthusiasm was at its height and Ambassador Francis was beaming. Even the *Novaya Jizn* (New Life) came out in favor of the advance. There was a big parade in honor of the advance. A woman's brigade has been organized and is drilling on my route to and from the office where I see them every day. Lots of Cossacks are in the city, and they are strong for carrying on the war.

Since that meeting Jerome Davis has been appointed National Army Work Secretary, and I have turned over the army work to him. Mr. Harte will now be responsible for the *Y* work in Eastern Europe and Western Asia and Siberia.

Burri, Paul Anderson, and Penn Davis have moved into a palace. One of the newly rich Petrograd families, the San Gallis, have a palace in the city and a summer home on the Finnish Gulf where they are now living. They have been looking for American parties who might live in their city palace the better to insure protection in case of violent outbreaks. Some of our Russian friends, hearing of it, suggested our secretaries. I was out at the palace last night. It is located about three quarters of a mile east of the Nikolaievsky Station where the Siberian Railroad enters. It is a finely built three-story house, surrounded by a large yard in one corner of which stands a modest little factory employing about fifty men, which has been the chief source of the San Galli fortune. Their workers have left except a faithful few. The others have been won over by the Bolsheviki. They have also had trouble securing materials.

The house itself is splendidly furnished and finished with large wooden beams in the ceilings. There is an observatory, a good-sized art gallery with many pieces by well-known artists, and upstairs a plunge, shower, baths, and tubs.

In my last conference with Dr. Mott, he told me that I should take a ten-day holiday as soon as Emily arrived. We plan to go to Finland.

June 30 / July 13

Monday evening, the ninth, we said good-by to the American Mission. The following evening Arthur Ruhl accompanied us on a rowing excursion around Kammeny and Yelagin Islands. All Russia is taking a holiday regardless of war or business. The lagoons around the Islands are fascinating, these long bright sunshiny evenings, filled as they are with rowboats and launches and of picnickers and lovers.

Tuesday evening Emily and I were guests at supper with Burri, Paul Anderson, and Penn Davis at the San Gallis' palace.

On the way back we got hold of a drunken *isvoschik,* who careened from one side of the street to the other and nearly spilled us out a dozen times until I hailed a more sober looking outfit. When I paid the drunken driver only for the distance we had ridden instead of to the destination, he began the characteristic altercation that the Russian droshky drivers resort to when they have a foreigner they think they can milk. He got only a few short Russian words from me and we were off with a better driver.

I bought tickets for Viborg, Finland, despite the reports that there was a strike on the Finnish Railroad. I applied for permits to leave Russia for a ten-day holiday trip in Finland. We received the permits today after a two-day wait. It would take a week to get bread tickets, so we are starting without them, taking a chance on getting by.

Yesterday we visited the Hermitage, my first time there since the March Revolution. All is in order as it was under the old regime, and the crowds seem about the same size, and about as much interested as in former days. In the afternoon we saw Mr. Harte and Penn Davis off for Minsk, where they will negotiate with the officials at the headquarters of the Western Russian front regarding the inauguration of our work there. In the evening we had a delightful stroll along my favorite beat around St. Isaac's, the Admiralty grounds, the bank of the Neva, and past the equestrian statue of Peter the Great.

This morning we climbed the five hundred steps up to St. Isaac's dome, only to be told by the guide that it wasn't gold after all, but just gilded. These democratic guides love to take the glory out of the old regime.

In the afternoon we went to Tsarskoe Selo and Pavlovsk. The wonderful grounds around the Palace of the former Czar are not kept up as they were last fall. The grass is not kept cut and the place is running to weeds. Picnic crowds from the city come out and throw their papers around, and there are apparently no caretakers on the job. It is sad to see things thus going to seed where before they were kept so magnificently. We walked through the Chinese city and came out at a corner of the Czar's Palace grounds. A soldier was on guard. He demanded our passports, and when I showed them to him, he stared at them blankly upside down. I explained that we were Americans and that the passports were in English. He was friendly and chatted with us. He said that the former Czar came out for exercise where he could be seen from the corner where we stood. He had a garden in which he enjoyed working. No one was allowed to enter the grounds without a permit from the government.

The grounds at Pavlovsk are being kept up better, though the picnickers were more numerous. We wound up with a lunch at the restaurant and got stung for the round price of seventeen rubles which at present exchange is nearly four dollars. One of the dishes was marked up from five rubles to six and three quarter rubles after we ordered it. I remarked to the waiter that was the fastest raise in price I had yet seen.

Imatra Falls, Finland
July 3 / 16

Ever since we passed the Russo-Finnish border last Saturday morning, we have been in another world. A sense of relief and quiet came over us the moment we dropped revolutionary Russia behind. We did not realize how tumultuous, disorderly, noisy, and dirty Russia was until we crossed into this quiet, orderly, clean land of pines and lakes, peaceful farming communities, and charming, smart, modern-looking little cities.

Viborg was our first stop. It is a fine, clean city of some 50,000 population, much like an up-to-date progressive American city, but with more distinctive architecture in its public buildings, railroad station, bank buildings, and church edifices.

We had a job getting our American money exchanged. Russian money is at such a discount that we didn't want to take the loss, so I went into the leading bank with a ten-dollar gold piece. The bank seemed so up-to-date and western with its modern furniture and shining brass fixtures that I was surprised when the cashier looked at the coin with a puzzled air and said he had never seen that kind of money before and didn't know whether they could exchange it or not. I had to visit several banks and go through a lot of red tape before I got the Finnish marks I was after.

By that time Emily and I were getting hungry and went

up to an inviting-looking coffee-house for lunch. We couldn't get bread because we didn't have our Russian permit for it. There was nothing else on the bill of fare except chocolate and coffee and crackers. Wherever we went we could get no bread without the permit. No meat was to be had on this day. The Finns are up against the provision problem and have a lot of meatless days.

After lunch we took a little boat to go up the 38-mile Saima Canal. These little Finnish steamers are most attractive; clean and every thing in miniature, down to the neat little cabins. The boat trip up the Saima Canal to Rattijarvel was beautiful. We coasted along between the fields and forests. There are 28 locks with a rise of 253 feet. At Rattijarvel we got out and found an auto waiting to take our boat party overland twenty miles to Imatra Falls. It was my first auto trip since the Ford driver hauled our party up from the Petrograd station to the hotel the preceding September, and we enjoyed to the full the glorious scenery as we sped down the road between the pines, birches, and firs.

One of the Finns on the boat kept warning us not to go to the Cascade Hotel. "Go to a pension instead," he said in his broken English. "The Cascade Hotel charges too much, and they don't know how to cook," he kept saying. But we couldn't help ourselves. The auto dumped us all out in front of the big government hotel, and we couldn't have escaped without creating a scene. We were given a room facing out over the river with the sound of the falls right below us.

After supper we strolled down beside the superb falls. They are more a whirlpool rapids than a falls, and in one way are more effective than Niagara because you can walk along right beside them all the way down. I am not surprised that Imatra is such a popular resort with Finns and Russians alike. It is not a bad trip from Petrograd as we were here before sundown, leaving Petrograd about eight o'clock in the morning.

Villmanstrand, Finland

July 7 / 20

For the past two days we have been having a fascinating trip on
one of the little Lake Saima steamers. We left Imatra Falls early
Tuesday morning in a droshky which carried us up to the lake
on a gray morning with sprinkles of rain. We arrived there just
too late to catch the little steamer for Nyslott, so we walked out
on the isthmus between Lake Saima and the Vuoksen River.
It was like Wisconsin scenery around Lake Delavan. We picked
wild strawberries and again hunted for bread but again had to
content ourselves with *limonaad* and crackers at the village
grocery store and soup and meat at the place where we engaged
a room for the night.

And some night it was. Mice, bugs, flies, and neighbors
kept us awake all night. As soon as it was dark, which was late
enough in this far north region, the village musicians began
to get busy, and violins and band instruments began a long
concert. Our bedroom was a double affair. We were placed in
the inner section with no escape except through the front section
which was to be occupied by two other couples. They arrived
about midnight, after we had decided that the floor was a safer
resting place than the bed. Sleep was no concern of our neighbors. They had to have their midnight lunch first, and it was
well on in the morning before the bottles ceased popping. We
had to be up and down at the dock at five o'clock, so we were
ready to take things easy when we finally got on our little steamer
bound for Villmanstrand. Villmanstrand made a charming
picture in the morning sunshine as we steamed up to it about
six o'clock. It is a town of about 3,000, and we arrived just at
the right time to see the morning market in full swing. Bare-
footed women with baskets were everywhere. Eggs and a doughy
flapjack containing most anything, reminding us of "hot tomalis"
in the States, were the most conspicuous articles for sale. Some
Russian soldiers were selling sugar cubes at a mark a cube. These
are the sugar rations which they receive from the army. The
Finnish army is made up of Russians who are financed by the
Finns, so that it is with no love that the Finns see these Russian

tovarische coining money out of supplies which they themselves lack, at the same time that they are taxed to supply the Russian soldiers with them.

We decided to take a two-day trip north of Lake Saima, and left Villmanstrand on a little steamer at 11:15. It has been a beautiful trip. Wednesday afternoon the scenery was much like the upper Mississippi, and then we would run onto broad views of Saima Lake. The sunset view was marvelous. We passed the musically sounding Finnish towns of Ruokoletti and Puumaala.

We arrived at Nyslott early in the morning, just in time to catch another little steamer over to Punkaharja, a resort center for this region. It was a beautiful, sunshiny day, and the long tongue of sandy beach at Punkaharja with its row of slender pines, branchless for a long ways up, was low enough to permit us to view the flashing waters of the lake on the other side. Summer houses lined the shore, and people were waiting at every landing to greet new arrivals from our boat or to get on to the boat themselves. It was a reminder of the boat trip on Lake George in New York, except that there were no mountains.

We returned to Nyslott and were disappointed to find that our schedule would not leave us enough time to take the boat on to Kuokio, which would have been two days further north, and the most beautiful part of the trip, all on Lake Saima. In fact we could have spent our whole ten days travelling on Lake Saima without crossing our tracks or doubling our course. It is a long chain of lakes, rivers, and canals.

We had time enough at Nyslott to go through the fine old medieval castle, which is on a tiny island at the edge of town. We climbed the winding stairs of the tower, looked out over the blue waters of the lake, gazed through the turret holes, and had our imagination stirred back to the times when the barons fought against robbers and enemies from these strongholds. A good-sized tourist trade is conducted to these castles even in these revolutionary times. The Nyslott castle is one of the best pre-served in Finland. These medieval strongholds suggest how much closer Finland's tie is to Scandinavia and the other Baltic states than to Russia. They themselves feel it, as we were to realize

increasingly the better we got acquainted in Finland. They are
a part of the Baltic Brotherhood.

The trip back from Nyslott Thursday afternoon and evening
was most beautiful. Great lumber piles lined the shores. Before
the war much lumber was shipped to England, but this trade is
now stopped. The timber has been cut faster than it grows, but
the resources of the country have hardly been touched. At one
place we took on cows, which are selling for 500 to 600 marks,
three times as much as a few months ago.

We have gotten well acquainted with our captain, who is
a mine of information and philosophy. He made no bones about
the Finns wanting independence and having no love for the
Russians. He said that most of the Finns in America were from
the west and southwest of Finland and were of Swedish descent.

We were surprised to learn from him how little the Russian
language is used in Finland. In fact, it is the fifth language in
point of usage: Finnish, Swedish, German, and English preceding it in the order named. English is one of the subjects all
captains are required to learn according to the navigation laws
of Finland before they receive their captain's certificates, while
Russian is not required.

Finland has taken 350,000,000 rubles of the Russian Liberty
Loan, under pressure, of course, and this does not add to their
love of the Russians.

We had news of a new revolution in Petrograd while cruis-
ing along Wednesday. Not many details were given, but it seems
that Lenin and his followers have tried to overturn the Kerensky
government by force of arms, and that the streets are barricaded.
Doesn't make us feel like hastening back. The Finns take occasion to express themselves about the Bolsheviki for whom they
have no love. They have a keen sense of superior culture and
fear that if the Bolsheviki come into Finland they will destroy
the higher culture there and bring everything down to the
Muscovite level.

We arrived back here at Villmanstrand this morning and
have spent the morning strolling around and reading here in
the little park. The Russian soldiers are everywhere, and doing
everything except drilling. Selling sugar in the market place

at exorbitant prices seems to be one of their favorite occupations.

At the edge of the city is a large unfinished church, which indicates that building operations suffered in Finland, as they did in Russia, when the war broke out.

This afternoon we will take the boat back through the Saima Canal to Viborg where we will have another day or two before returning to the land of revolutions.

Viborg, Finland
July 9 / 22

We enjoyed the trip back down the Saima Canal yesterday afternoon to the full. The weather was perfect. The captain was as friendly as our captain of the Lake Saima boat and volunteered a running commentary on everything we saw.

Boats were taking on the last loads of wood for Petrograd for this summer. The navigation season is short in Finland, only five and a half to six months. But labor shortage is cutting down transportation and woodcutting this summer. The piles of wood which we saw further north on the lake the past two days will stay there all winter for lack of labor, while the Petrograders will freeze with the smallest supply of wood the city has known within the memory of men now living.

The captain relieved his mind on the labor question. The farm wages are now 250 marks per month (about $40) and board and room, where before the war they were 30 marks. "It is the result of the socialist agitation," he said. "The Finnish Socialists are not Bolshevik but Scheidemann socialists, but that is bad enough. The Finnish Senate is socialist. Thieving is growing. We used to keep our doors unlocked in Finland; now there are thieves everywhere and we have to lock them. Most of the thieves are Russian soldiers, it is true, but the effect upon the Finns has been bad. They are losing their habits of hard work. The Finn used to love hard work and long hours. Now he listens to his socialist comrade. The Finn used to save; now he spends all he gets."

We came to a village where a fine-looking Lutheran church stood on the highest point for miles around. The captain relieved his mind about church conditions: "The pastors are just businessmen. They are the most prosperous men in every community. They build their churches on the highest and most valuable land and get all the privileges of place and position for themselves they can. Meanwhile the young people are not going to church but are flirting and lovemaking instead."

We came to a landing place where a group of Russian *tovarische* were loafing. The captain expressed himself on the Russian soldiers: "Finland has to pay for the Russian army in Finland. There are 800,000 Russian soldiers quartered down on a poor population of 3,000,000 Finns. They commandeer whatever they please from us. There are only 500 Finnish volunteers at the front. The Russians are afraid to allow any more Finns in the army, for fear they will start a revolution. There are no Finnish soldiers in Finland. They would be mobbed by the people if seen in company with the Russians. The way the Russian soldiers are carrying on is a scandal. There are none of them working or drilling or obeying orders. The officers are helpless. All the soldiers do is to keep company with Finnish girls and thieves. Any Finnish girl who keeps company with a Russian soldier is a disgrace to her country. We tell her to go along and stay with the Russian. We don't want her to come back."

As we neared Viborg, a large building stood out on the hillside. "See that building," said the captain, "That is the new Russian seminary. It is closed now. That was where Russia was going to train Russian teachers who could teach Russian to the Finns in the common schools. The ordinary Finns do not know the Russian language. Only the well educated Finns know it. The other Finns don't want to learn it. But the Russians were going to force it on us. As soon as the Revolution occurred, we closed the doors of that building, and they won't be opened again without a fight."

The captain was proud of his little nation. He extolled the national architect, Saarinen, some of whose buildings we had admired at Viborg. He sang the praises of the Finnish sculptor Vallgren, the novelist Aho, and the Finnish epic, *Kalevala*. When we stepped off the little steamer at Viborg, we felt that our captains had revealed to us the heart of Finland. They had been more than kind to us. They had shared their own bread with us, which had real significance as it was the only bread we had in Finland.

We found a place to stay here at the Y.M.C.A. Hospitz. The Hospitz in Finland rents rooms to both men and women as the ordinary hotel does. The service is very good, the prices low, and there is more of the homelike atmosphere. The rooms here are attractively decorated and the furnishings to match. All shows taste and culture.

Yesterday we "did" Viborg. We visited the old castle built by Torkel Knutsen in 1293, which was for a long time the center of the Swedish power and of the Christian religion in Finland. We visited the Viborg Museum, which was full of arms, costumes, and paintings of yesterday. Then we took the streetcar out to the statue of Peter the Great. There stood the gigantic likeness on a high point and looking down over the city with a contemptuous smile. A postal card which we had purchased in town showed the base of the statue surrounded by a well-kept grass plot. What we actually found, however, was a scrap heap of bottles, cans, matches, and cigarette stubs, which the incensed Finns had evidently thrown at the statue since the March revolution to give expression to their hate. The plot of green grass had disappeared.

In the evening we crossed over the Papula Bridge northeast of the city to Mount Papula, where high observatory towers at the top of pine-covered hills gave a splendid view back over the city.

The Russian calendar is not used in Finland. The Russian Church is hardly to be found; the Lutheran Church is everywhere. Everything Russian is taboo "since the revolution."

We have been devouring the newspaper accounts of the uprising in Petrograd. Prince Lvov has resigned as Prime Minister. Kerensky is slated to take his place. Orders are out to arrest Lenin. To quit this quiet, peaceful, orderly Finland for Russia's uncertainties is not so alluring, but Emily is game and is ready for whatever duty brings us. We take the train back to Petrograd this afternoon.

6 Vosnesensky Prospect, Petrograd
July 10 / 23

We got back at twilight last evening to find the revolution over, but the streets still barricaded, and the cab driver took us on a long detour as the region around the Winter Palace is still unsafe.

Burri has been telling us about their experiences during the days just past. For two or three days a wild mob held control of the center of the city. The Bolsheviki started the affair by suddenly turning their armored cars and machine guns into the peaceful men and women walking along the Nevsky near the Sadovaya, and many were killed.

For three days it was unsafe for any person to appear in a uniform or a white collar. Burri was out with Sam Harper along the Nevsky when no other respectable persons were to be seen, and they said it was exciting enough.

Cossacks were called in from the front and saved the day. Things seem to be adjusting themselves again, but as Zemmer says, the experience that Russia seems to be going through is that of winding up and running down, and each time the winding up is a harder process and the running down comes quicker, and pretty soon the clock will stop running for good.

On the way back from Finland yesterday afternoon, we had for our seatmates a fat, jolly Russian merchant, a Russian officer, a little student, and a cripple. They all engaged in a ceaseless discussion of this last revolution and expressed themselves as hopeless about Russia's future unless Lenin and Trotsky can be disposed of.

Minsk

Hotel Europe, Minsk, Russia
July 15 / 28

Dear Home Folks:

On returning to Petrograd we found that plans for my work had been completely changed. The work at Kiev was not ready to be opened up, and Mr. Harte wished to begin with a demonstration of our work at Minsk, forty miles from the German front, before opening up in other centers. Within three days we were on our way to Minsk, where I am to be associated with my old college and Literary Society friend, Harlow McConnaughey.

Minsk is an interesting, busy city of something over 100,000 normal population and 250,000 war population, with many of the brisk business ways about it that remind one of America. In the windows are displayed Faber pencils, Gillette razors, Colgate's shaving soap, and even Corona typewriters. The town is largely Jewish and nearly everybody has friends or relatives in America. This perhaps helps to explain the American touches.

Minsk is in White Russia. There is more poverty and dirt than in Petrograd. The Russians are not so heavy in build and seem to be of poorer stock. They regard themselves as of the purest Russian stock, but there would seem to be something of the same relation to the other Russians as our mountain whites bear to the rest of our race. And as our mountain whites seem economically worsted in their battle with nature, so these White Russians seem economically worsted, but from another cause, their economic battle with the Jews. This is the Jewish Pale, and Jews are everywhere.

As we came west from the junction at Orsha, we seemed to

be entering deeper strata of dirt and shiftless station crowds and Jews with every station. The platforms became more and more crowded with peanut-eating, sunflower-seed-eating Russian soldiers in their unwashed uniforms. When we finally reached Minsk, it required a football rush to get through the jostling crowd and find our way to the rickety droshky. We had no sooner started to rattle along over the cobblestone pavements at a wild rate than Mack gave a shout from the sidewalk. He had come on the previous day and engaged a room for us at the Hotel Europe.

On the way down on the train yesterday in our second-class compartment, we had as seatmates a sister of the Russian Red Cross and a Russian officer. The officer said that the officers of the army had practically all been for the revolution because they had become convinced that the army would never fight again under the Czar. They had not foreseen this radical Bolshevik propaganda, however, and now they were up a tree.

Our present job is to locate a site for our hut. Colonel Vinogradov of the Staff Headquarters has taken us all over the city in his handsome auto viewing possible sites. Our present choice is a lot near the depot on the main street. But we find that the owner lives in Moscow. For one of us to go to Moscow would mean losing a week, so we are considering another lot nearby. It is owned by a big, burly, long-whiskered Father Abraham who takes you back to the times of the patriarchs. We tried to get an interview with him yesterday, but it was Saturday and his lumber yard was closed. The stores all over town are closed on Saturday. I used to think that Petrograd had enough holidays, but Minsk just coolly adds another fifty or so to the year's schedule and thinks nothing of it.

Our first visit was to the Chief of Staff. He is an elderly Russian of the old school, very courteous, polished, cultured, dignified. He it was who gave the orders that assigned Colonel Vinogradov and the auto to us. When we entered the Staff Headquarters and the rooms of his associates, we felt as if we had stepped out of the hurricane of revolutionary tumult into a haven of quiet, an oasis of the old regime. There is a very sharp line drawn by the army officials here against the Soviet. We are advised to have nothing to do with it. Our plans are to be approved by the General Staff, and no steps taken without consulting them. They had a favorable attitude towards our work as a result of their interview with Mr. Harte. The main question now is whether the present situation warrants our proceeding with building plans when things are so uncertain.

To help settle this matter of building more clearly in our own minds, we called on one of the officials at the Zem Gorod, to whom we had a letter of introduction. The Zem Gorod (or Soyuz Gorodov—Union of Cities) is one of the three great popular institutions which have sprung to the front in Russia to assist the government in carrying on the war, the other two being the Zemsky Soyuz and the Red Cross. The Zem Gorod has chiefly engineering problems, the Zemsky Soyuz has more to do with supplies and such welfare undertakings as baths, etc. Our man at the Zem Gorod gave us a courteous reception and passed the buck by advising us to consult the *Nachalnik* or Town Commandant. So we visited the latter and obtained the characteristically Russian advice to wait and see how things turned out; perhaps a week, perhaps a month—meanwhile we should get ready.

Just now the outlook is dubious as there is bad news from the southwest front. During the last seven days there has been a retreat 50 to 75 miles deep on a 200-verst front. It gives a nervous feel to know that the Germans are east of us at a point not so many miles to the south. Mack and I have been figuring out what to do in case the Germans should cut our communications in the rear, and we should wake up some fine morning to find ourselves their prisoners. Mack thought that our credentials as war prisoner aid secretaries would help us, and that we would fare as well if not better than in Russia. There are plenty of individuals we know whom we could call on, with whom we have come in contact through the prisoner aid work. I am willing to avoid the experiment, however.

Possibly these cogitations had something to do with an experience the other night, where the laugh was on me. I was waked up in the middle of the night with a great noise below the hotel. I jumped to the window and there was a great procession coming down the street, big, heavy wagons, helmeted soldiers, torches flaring, and all coming on with the grim steady sureness of the German army. To my dazed mind no other alternative suggested itself. The Germans had sprung a surprise on the Russians while the latter slept, and here was the advance guard of the German army itself. At the edge of the city, flames were flashing skyward; doubtless the Germans were starting to burn the city. I called Emily and Mack, and we stood there with over-coats thrown about our night clothes gazing at this spectacle, while we figured on ways and means of escaping. But where were the Russians? Why weren't they fighting the Germans and trying to keep them out of the city? And where was the rest of the German army? Were these advance guards? For the procession soon passed and nothing followed.

The next morning we learned that the Minsk fire depart-ment had been out during the night. It will be a long time before I hear the last of it.

Emily is the only American woman in Minsk. She creates a sensation whenever she goes out shopping. Sometimes she gets her shopping done so quickly by merely pointing at what she wants that the shopkeepers do not realize that she doesn't speak Russian. When she gets up stump for the right word for "eggs" or "tomatoes" or some other commodity and has to explain that she is an Amerikanitza, everybody stops to stare.

Yesterday being Sunday, we visited the Russian Orthodox and Catholic churches. The beggars are impartial in their selec-tion of faiths and line up at the entrances inside and outside of all churches. The largest crowd of worshippers was at the Roman Catholic Church, and a large part of the congregation seemed to have their beads and prayer books. The presence of a large Polish population in Minsk explains the size of the Catholic church. There are probably as many Poles as Russians and more Jews than both put together. The Jews have a splendid, large synagogue.

The city is flooded with dirty-uniformed soldiers drifting back from the front. We were down at the Governor's Park this afternoon, and a Bolshevik orator was holding forth before a large crowd of these soldiers and appealing to them to stay away

from the front and have nothing to do with the government.
The Soviet is strong and energetic in Minsk, and these orators
have enough of their support so that the army officials have to
go easy in handling such affairs. The orator found plenty of
enthusiastic applause from these "dark minds," as the Russians
call the ignorant peasants.

July 24 / August 5

Short office hours are even more of a problem in getting things
done here than in Petrograd. The regular office hours are 10 a.m.
to 1 p.m. and from 3 p.m. to 7 p.m. Most men are not in before
11 a.m., however, and most professional and official men do not
return for the evening hours. So two hours is about all the
effective time we have for interviewing, and the Russian whom
you can interview in less than that time, including time waiting
in the entrance and time warming up to the subject, is a rare one.

The location of a building site is still our main problem.
Monday we found the owner of the lot near the railroad track
on whose premises stands a big pile of wood. He has rented the
place out for a year on contract, and the renter is in the Crimea.
Communications to the Crimea require weeks instead of days,
so unless he can be persuaded that circumstances require a disregard of the contract that site will be abandoned.

We went around to see the mayor, to see if he could
requisition any town property sites for us. He was a business-like,
clean-cut man with lots of energy and push to him. He expressed
his sympathy in our plans but said Minsk was likely to be
evacuated at any time, and we had better hold up on our building plans. The retreat on the southwest front is a great scandal.
He told us how the Russian soldiers had fled before the Germans,
and the outrages that the civilians, men and women, had suffered from them. He said that the Russians had less to fear from
the Germans themselves than from these "devil-possessed Bolshevik fanatics." This retreat on the southwestern front has raised
the question of evacuating Minsk. The mayor said that it was
quite probable. This held up our building plans again.

Tuesday we had further negotiations with our Jewish

patriarch at his home. We were ushered up from the dusty street through a tangle of dark, gloomy pantries, kitchens, junk shops, and stairways until we arrived at the upper room, a large, attractive, well-furnished room which served as dining-room and living-room for the big family. There was much of culture and art and refinement in the decorations in sharp contrast with the lower floors. Abraham finally agreed that we could rent his property on two conditions: first that the city would postpone its order to move his stores until after the war, and second, that the Zemsky Soyuz would allow the transfer of his wood to their property which adjoined.

So we saw the city officials again and they agreed to observe the condition that affected them if the Zemsky Soyuz would do their part. That depended on Tsevinsky, the president. So we called at the large building occupied by the Zemsky Soyuz, but the President was out of the city and everything had to wait until he returned.

Wednesday, the city architect, who is an up and coming modern engineering school graduate, gave us official confirmation that the city would not have the shops moved until after the war. The Chief of Staff sent an officer around to say that the situation had changed on the front sufficiently to warrant our going ahead. The good news is from the Roumanian front. So all of Emily's packing in preparation for evacuation was unnecessary after all. The evening papers announced that Brusilov had been changed from the southwestern front to the disposition of the Provisional Government.

Thursday we at last found the Zemsky Soyuz president. He gave us precedence over a long list of waiting interviewers, and we entered his office to find a handsome, finely dressed, bustling, business-like young man, who spoke slowly and distinctly, while you felt that his mind was working ten times as fast as his lips. We stated our problem and he immediately dropped all other business, called for his luxurious high-powered automobile, and took us along to the *Sacharny* (Sugar) Corner where the Zemsky property was, to see whether the wood could be transferred there. There was not space enough, so that plan falls through and we have to begin all over again.

Friday we returned to the mayor's office for a fresh start. We found that the president of the Zemsky Soyuz had sent word for us to see their battalion engineer. The latter had figured out that there would be a place for our hut on their premises near the main railroad depot, which was going to be a big feeding point for soldiers passing through. We were taken down to look over this site, and it looked fine. Saturday morning, we made another visit with the battalion engineer, but again our hopes were dashed, as there would be room only for the building and no suitable spot for sports and athletics for several blocks in any direction. So another week has rolled around and we are no further along on a building site than we were when we came, except that some have been eliminated.

In the course of our searches, we came across the Jewish playground on a level stretch next to the Berezina River in the city. It was well fitted out with swings, ladders, parallel bars, jumping standards, slides, and all the regular apparatus of a modern playground. There were a director and assistants in charge, and the grounds were full of children and parents and young men and women all having the time of their lives. It would have done credit to any American city of the same size and seemed as strange in contrast with the surroundings as the costumes of the participants seemed strange. The young ladies were bare-armed, low-necked, and wore bloomers, some with and some without stockings, and were engaging in all sorts of games that seemed to call for the freest display of their limbs. It was apparently exclusively a Jewish affair as I saw no one on the grounds who seemed to be of any other race.

A young Jew called on us last evening. His name is Sammy. He went to America when he was a baby and got a public school education, returning here three years ago after thirteen years in the States. He came around to brush up on his English. After stammering around for a while he espied the Red Triangle on a piece of our literature, with the letters Y.M.C.A. "Oh, I know the Y.M.C.A.," he said. "It is in every city in America. There is a Y.M.C.A. song, 'I'm afraid to go home in the dark,'" and forthwith he began to sing it, and then one ragtime song after another that came to his mind from his school days. It seemed strange to have this American flash out of the cosmopolitan jumble of everything else except English which one finds in this city.

Our language teacher is a young Polish fellow, Youshkevitch, whose name was given me by Jerome Davis, and whom I found at the telegraph office here, where he is connected with the wireless service. He performs the double service of improving our Russian and keeping us in touch with advance information of the doings of the outside world. The local papers are very unsatisfactory, being very meagre in their news of the world outside of Minsk. As for mail, we have had only one letter during the ten days since we arrived, and that was a ten-word request from the Petrograd office to return our Baedeker guide book.

Youshkevitch is a college student and has an officer's rank in the Russian army. He has high ideals for himself and his people and is a shrewd and rather sharp critic of others. He is well educated, knows five languages, and is an omnivorous reader. He says English is the fifth language in the order which he has mastered them. He could hardly understand me when I introduced myself to him, my accent being so different from the English which he learned from a Britisher. He is up on all social etiquette, and Emily was surprised when he took her hand the first day he called and kissed it. That is the custom when men meet and take leave of married women.

We have been enjoying the most wonderful sunsets from our window which faces west. We can see miles into the country beyond the trees and church buildings of the square below us, the edge of the city beyond, and the beautiful meadows and fields still further. The characteristic Lombardy poplars, which are so common in the Ukraine, are to the south of us. Particularly beautiful are the moonlight scenes over the square, when all the roughness and dirt of daytime is lost in the soft moonglow.

You have to get permits for nearly all kinds of supplies. In order to get alcohol for our spirit lamp, I had to go to the *Gorodskoi Nachalnik* (town commandant) and get a permit. Also had to get tickets for sugar, white bread, flour, and a number of other articles. Each ticket allows only so much per month per head. The ticket office was jammed with people waiting to go through the red tape to get their tickets. We were accorded foreigner's privilege of being taken care of ahead of our order, or we should have been waiting there all day. I don't blame the Russians, however, for disliking the way foreigners are shown preference over themselves in such things.

This morning we visited an old Orthodox Russian church, the quaint old tower and dome of which have attracted our attention from our hotel window. A close up and inside view of the church during services dispelled the romance and charm. The priests were woefully old, crippled, and poverty-stricken. Five or six still more beggarly old people made up the audience. Instead of the beautiful music that characterizes the usual Russian church the voices were cracked and squeaky and faltering. As soon as we appeared the collection plates came out, and I could not help feeling how inadequate any such collection method could be to answer the pitiful need. It was probably maintained under the old regime with just sufficient state grant to keep the priests from starving, and now that little support has been withdrawn, and nothing has taken its place. We could not stand to stay long but left for a stroll through the market in the old part of Minsk.

In this old Jewish quarter the streets are so narrow that you can hardly pass a cab without touching; you can almost reach from the buildings on one side to those on the other with your outstretched hands. And all is wretchedly dirty. The sidewalks are full of dirty and lousy people and beggars, probably many of them refugees. The squalor is overwhelming. Our Sunday morning ventures were not inspiring.

In the afternoon we had a more stimulating time down at the Governor's Park. It is Minsk's chief claim to beauty and compares favorably with parks in American cities.

July 30 / August 12

Nothing but delays, postponements, and disappointments all week. We have looked over new sites every day, but every one that is available is unsuitable and every one that is suitable is unavailable. Our Jewish friend, Sammy, is a constant visitor

and bright as a dollar. One of his favorite tunes is "My Wife
has gone to the Country." He has introduced us to the Jewish
bread which they call "*kalatch*," a sweet cakish bread which we
like very well. The Jews make a specialty of it on their holidays.

Our tutor Youshkevitch took us around to his home the
other evening, and we had tea with his mother. They have a
modest, rather poorly furnished home, rather typical, I should
judge, of the poorer middle classes. One of Youshkevitch's
brothers was home, quite different from the studious tutor. He
is a cadet in the army training camp near Moscow and home
for a holiday. His little sister was just starting to learn English
in the common schools of Minsk. She had her primer and read
aloud to show her progress. The way the Poles and Russians can
pick up a new language is remarkable. The Jewish children of
Minsk also are great students. You see the girls and boys constantly reading in the windows as you pass along the street. One
of the tragedies under the old regime was the way these Jewish
children were handicapped in their desires for education, and
now they have the same chance as others.

This morning Emily and I attended the services at the
cathedral, where the mixed choir sang beautifully. The interior
of this cathedral is unusually beautiful even compared with
Petrograd churches, and the whole service most inspiring.

The town is in the midst of its first election under the new
regime. For weeks there has been energetic campaigning. There
were candidates to burn for each of the ten different political
parties. Each party had its circulars, bands, and automobiles.
The campaign wound up yesterday and today with a tremendous burst of activity that would have done credit to a national
election in America. You can judge of the amount of interest
taken when you know that out of a war population of 250,000
there were over 70,000 votes, the women voting as well as the men.

August 6 / 19

At last our long hunt for a site for an army hut has ended. A
splendid spot on the heights of the town on the other side of the
Berezina, close to large barracks, has been assigned to us. The

place is known as the Horse Market, and every week there is a gathering of horses from all this region for barter and trade.

Monday, we were notified that the General Staff had appointed Colonel Vinogradov as our counsellor and staff representative. We had an interview with the Colonel the same day, and Tuesday he took us for another automobile tour of the city, in the course of which we hit upon this inspiring location of the Horse Market, which gives a fine view down over the Berezina valley and part of the city.

In the meantime the building plans arrived from Petrograd, and we took them around to the Zemsky Soyuz. They will get busy on them at once and promise us the specifications within a week and the building up within two weeks after that. We can't believe our luck.

On Wednesday we completed arrangements at the city hall or *Uprava* as they call it. The mayor gave his OK for the site which is town property. Colonel Vinogradov agreed to our sport program and said he would invite the president of the Zemsky Soyuz to act on our committee. In order to get the final papers from the city hall giving us written authority, I had to draw up a *doklad* (report) requesting permission to use the property. The Russians are great on these *doklads*. Nothing is official without them. "Put it in writing" is much more their rule than "Do it now." Every office has shelves full of these *doklads* which have never been acted upon. Writing out this *doklad* and then getting it properly translated took all of Wednesday.

Then Thursday Mack and I went out to the lot and mapped out the place for sports, figuring on a couple of fields for football, a couple more for baseball, four tennis courts, volleyball and handball courts, and several stretches for horseshoes. We took this down to the *Uprava* for their O.K. only to find that all the space they thought we wanted was for the building. There would be difficulties in the way of getting the space for athletics because it would interfere with the weekly Horse Market. Nevertheless we could go ahead and make out a new *doklad* stating what our desires were for athletic fields. Thus another day's work of *doklading* and translating. They, furthermore, added an architect from the city to work with the architectural force from the Zemsky Soyuz in preparing estimates so that no mistakes should occur which might hold us up later.

Friday the papers were all ready for us to sign at the *Uprava.* We could have the athletic fields with the understanding that we would not play baseball too close to the horses on market day. They, on their part, would try to use only part of the field and avoid damaging the tennis courts and baseball diamonds if we would place them far enough from the market side. Saturday we received the certificates from the *Uprava* authorizing us to go ahead on building and athletic fields. It is sure good to have the period of waiting over and be able to move ahead.

Emily's weakening enthusiasm for Russia received a new jolt this week in the shape of cooties in her hair. We each now have our favorite pet. Mack always has a new breakfast story about bedbug experiences; I specialize in fleas; Emily in cooties. I began attacking the cooties Monday with petroleum. But it never feazed them. They came back Tuesday more numerous than ever. Just as building plans began to rush me, I had to begin giving long hours each day to picking those cooties and their progeny out of Emily's long black hair. A desperate shampoo on Friday failed to have any effect on them. I have consulted the local drugstores and been recommended to Vigitalis, which I have purchased and am now trying out. Emily says she is going home December first.

August 13 / 26

We have been having plenty of experiences in getting a start on the first hut to be built for Russian soldiers on the Russian front. The specifications, which were promised for this week, are not ready and will probably not be ready for another two weeks. The building which was to be up a week from now will be doing well to be up two months from now. This is not a country which has specialized on executing according to promises or intentions.

In the meantime, while waiting for the architects, we are doing the best we can to get the athletic grounds into shape. The first job was to get a fence up. The Zemsky Soyuz promised to

have an engineer and gang of workmen on the field Monday
morning. We were on the field at the specified time, but neither
gang nor engineer were in sight. After we had waited an hour,
a droshky rushed up and a young officer stepped out and greeted
us cordially. He was not the engineer but the engineer's assistant, sent out to reconnoiter the job and report recommendations
to the engineer. We decided that the case required special
attention from us and so went back to the city and had an
earnest session with the engineer. The next morning a gang
of twenty Polish workers was on the field calmly sitting and
smoking their pipes when we arrived. They were enjoying those
smokes on the Americans. They were waiting for the spades
to dig the holes for the fence posts. Another trip back to town
and another earnest session with architect and Zemsky Soyuz
officials resulted in the proper tools being on hand the next
morning. Friday morning, the holes, which ought to have been
finished by twenty laborers by Monday night, were at last finished, but the gang was again waiting around, this time for the
fence posts. We had included these fence posts in every earnest
session we had had during the week, but we had to return for
another session this rainy Friday. In fact all the rain for the
summer seems to have held off for this first week's work on the
grounds, as it has rained every day since we started. I was lucky
enough to get next to a sale of rubbers an hour after the stock
arrived and less than an hour before it was exhausted—at the
only store in the city to have had rubbers this season.

While waiting for the fence to get finished, Mack and I have
been lining up athletic supplies for the opening of the field. No
supplies can be expected from America for months. There are
no athletic supplies of any description in the stores here. All the
games we are contemplating are new to the people here except
soccer, which is fairly well known.

So we are in the business of manufacturing athletic supplies.
We hunted up a wood turning establishment and have them
turning out very satisfactory baseball bats. We went to a black-
smith and have him turning out the right kind of horseshoes.
Our next job will be to make baseballs. We plan to make a
baseball about midway between the hard and the soft indoor

variety. We have bought out the stores of the only hard rubber balls we could find and they will be the core of our balls. In the meantime we are lining up supplies of glue, twine, and a melting pot, and plan to give a demonstration of how to make baseballs out on the field sometime next week. I don't know anything about it, but Mack is confident that he can put the stunt across.

We have been looking up what literature we can buy in town for the completed hut. We can find no books whatever, simply scads of paperbound propaganda leaflets of a dozen different socialist parties. Real literature has disappeared. A great banner across the main street corner in town reminds us that the Minsk soldiers have their turn holding down the trenches next week, and the people are urged to contribute books and literature from their private possessions to be forwarded to the front. Russian soldiers are in the trenches for a week and then in the rear for ten weeks. That is one reason that it takes so many Russian soldiers to hold the front.

A problem we have been struggling with is a temporary structure to hold the tools of the workingmen while they erect the hut, and where they can be served with tea and purchase other necessities such as cigarettes and tobacco without going to the nearest stores which are over a mile away. At first we were told that there were no spare tents and that the temporary structure must be wooden, so we put in a *trebovania* (request) to the *Nachalnik* for it, and for a man to guard it and permission to buy sugar to go with the tea. An important question was raised whether we should serve sugar free with the tea or not. The tea ought to be served free, because that was the custom of all business concerns, but free tea for "common laborers" would be an unwise precedent. The problem was that we were a foreign organization and perhaps might be permitted to do this. The best part of a day was spent in threshing over this vital question with a dozen different officials each with a radically different idea about it, and the conferences ended with a decision to postpone action on the matter until "*zavtra*" (tomorrow). We hope the matter will be forgotten.

After considering our *trebovania* requesting a temporary structure and guard, the *Nachalnik*, after two days, asked us to take the matter up with the Chief of *Snabjenia* (Provisions) as the proper official for handling the matter. This we accordingly did, with the result that the latter gentleman agreed to a temporary structure, three men for guards, and a pood of sugar for the tea.

The question of what to do with the Horse Market has arisen afresh this week, and the city engineer wants us to move our football fields down on an adjacent stretch which adjoins and belongs to the tramway station. This has involved further conferences with the Electrical Department of the city and a visit to the electric plant, which is a neat up-to-date brick building with modern equipment. We have satisfied them that no damage will be done to their building and have received permission to go ahead and grade down the lots and erect the goal posts.

If I am not an adept at passing the buck when I finish this job, it will not be for lack of teachers who are past masters.

A People's University is one of the popular ideas of the day before the townspeople here, as it is all over the country. The promoter called on me at the hotel the other day and invited me to contribute Y.M.C.A. funds towards financing the project. The Americans are always the first people the Russians turn to when they face the problem of raising money here. I was sorry to disappoint the promoter in his enthusiastic plans but responded to his invitation to attend a lecture at the university that evening and a long meeting of the executive committee of the university afterwards. The lecture was historical and socialistic, but not Bolshevistic. There was a large audience which listened with close attention. I tried to remain hidden in the rear but became all the more conspicuous for so doing by being called up, and then led up to the front platform to be placed in a chair along with thirty other university promoters and patrons and then to receive very special attention in the announcements of the speaker who heralded me as their brother from America who was seeking to help them in their plans.

The chairman of the committee, a big hearty, talkative man by the name of Berg, led us after the lecture down through the pitch-dark streets to another building where some fifty or sixty men, women, and students were waiting for the executive committee meeting. The ambitious projects which were then laid before us were as bewildering in their extent as the means of carrying them to execution were scanty. One of the main issues was whether the classes were to be free or charged for. They called on me for my opinion and were much interested to know of the Y.M.C.A. system of night schools in the States where a small fee was charged to cover all or part of the expense. I was struck with the similarity of their plans with the Y.M.C.A. system of night schools. The meeting ended without anything definite being decided.

After the meeting I met a little Russian, or Ukrainian, enthusiast. He buttonholed me to invite me to come around and visit him at his room. He said that all over the empire the Ukrainians were drawing their countrymen out of the Russian army to form separate Ukrainian units; that there was a large party of organizers on this front.

During the week Mack and I visited the big baths of the Zemsky Soyuz for the Russian soldiers. They were eye openers. Three or four thousand soldiers a day were getting their baths in the house we visited. There were great steam rooms, drying rooms, and dressing rooms where hundreds could be accomodated at one time. There was a tremendous laundry where the soldiers left their dirty uniforms and received fresh ones, all except their heavy overcoats. Even the toilets were fairly adequate and clean. The proprietor pointed with pride to a big automatic washer which was run by electricity and which had been invented by one of the Zemsky inventors since the war began. He showed how much more efficient it was than other electric washers which they had imported. Big drying rooms for the clothes were shown us. There must have been a force of a hundred women in the laundry. We were shown the modern book-keeping department where young men were keeping records of the number of baths daily, the number of pieces laundered, and exact cost accounts.

This is simply one of a great system of baths which the Zemsky Soyuz has established along the entire front, so extensive that every one of the ten million soldiers can have a bath every week if he will.

We had been considering shower baths or steam baths in our hut, but after this examination of what they have actually in operation so near at hand we consider it unnecessary.

Yesterday morning two German aeroplanes passed over Minsk, and the town air guns got busy so that we could follow the trail of the aeroplane by the puffs of white smoke from the 100 shots fired by the guns.

Today we were again down spending Sunday afternoon at our favorite place in the park. Sunday is the great day for Minsk people to promenade. The promenade is to the Russian what the baseball diamond is to the American. The promenade in the Minsk square takes place on a broad cinder path running diagonally the length of the square, bordered by trees. There is room for about ten people abreast. The usual stunt is for the promenaders to walk from one end of the walk to the other, turn around and walk back, and to keep this up for hours at a time, all the time moving with or against a crowd so dense that you have to gasp for breath. At night there are no lights except the flicker of matches lighting cigarettes, which reminds one of fireflies, and the lights at the soft drink stands at each end of the walk, and here the lights are shaded so as to show no light to anyone who might be going in an aeroplane over the city. The promenade continues until midnight or later.

We are still expecting to be sent to Kiev a little later on, according to the last letters received from Petrograd.

August 20 / September 2

After a week of arduous and patient toil, we opened our athletic field last night with football, baseball, and quoits. Colonel Vinogradov and the chairman of the Athletic Committee, Zavinsky, were on hand, between fifty and sixty fellows got into the games, and there were a couple of hundred spectators. The most popular game was football. The most ludicrous was baseball. The hardest thing for the Russian soldiers to develop is an idea of speed. The officers are quick at football, into which they joined with the soldiers with zest. In fact, the sight of officers and soldiers playing together was as big a sensation as the novelty of the games. One of our big handball courts was ready and attracted attention with its high board back showing conspicuously clear across the field.

Obstacles continued during the week. The Chief of *Snabjenia* decided that a tent was better than a wooden structure for our temporary affair after all, and up the tent went Monday. The Horse Market was in full swing at the other end of the field and kept us off the baseball diamonds and horse shoe spots. Then in the course of the morning we were notified that the city architect wanted to change the location of our building.

The next day, Tuesday, was the holiday celebrated as "The Ascent of the Holy Virgin." No one worked anywhere. The rain poured down. Bright and early Wednesday morning, Mack and I went out with our glue, glue pots, twine, and rubber balls, and manufactured the first baseballs made in Minsk, while a gaping crowd of boys, soldiers in uniform, women, and idle workmen looked on. Our aim was to work some of them into the process so that they could make them themselves, and in this we succeeded fairly well.

The evening Mack and I put in working out a pattern for a baseball cover that would fit our balls. The next morning we took this pattern down to a garmentmaker's, where the scenes made us think we were looking at the original sweat shop. After they had eyed us as the original crazy men for a sufficient time, they agreed to do the sewing if we got the leather, which we proceeded to locate in an adjoining shop.

Work at the field proceeded with deathly slowness. Forty Polish laborers were receiving 285 rubles per day, or 2,010 rubles per week, for an amount of work which Mack and I felt we could do ourselves if we could have gotten the tools.

We spent most of Thursday at the Zemsky Soyuz going through the interminable red tape necessary to get supplies. Earlier in the war the supplies were plentiful and the red tape small. But as the supplies diminished the red tape increased, which was a convenient way of delaying and postponing demand. We got our first baseball covered Thursday and were as hilarious as if we had received a box of Spaulding goods.

Friday Mack spent another day at the Zemsky Soyuz trying

to buy musical instruments and dishes, etc., for the hut of our dreams, while I strained patience to the breaking point with some of the laborers as we dug a trench around the tennis courts and made a box for the tools. The wonder was that we got as much ready for the opening as we did.

Local conditions got unsettled during the week. Sammy turned up Thursday with a bullet in his leg from some robbers whom he and other members of the police force captured in a daring feat of arms, if Sammy's report was entirely to be believed. The affair took place in the city not far from our field, and near the tramway station. Robberies are taking place almost nightly in town. The woods surrounding the city are full of robber soldiers from the front who are on the lookout for lonely travelers. No one thinks of going into the country alone. Sammy told of a party of friends who went out for a picnic. There were twenty-two in the party, and they were well supplied with firearms to meet emergencies. Emily and I have had to deny ourselves the luxury of country hikes in spite of the appeal of the charming natural scenery of the surroundings.

The day after Sammy was wounded there was so much disorder in the city that no newspapers were published, and we had no news from the outside world. Yesterday we received the English news sheet from Petrograd announcing that all English women were leaving the capital. It looks like Emily will be going home December first.

August 27 / September 9

Just as we had our athletic field nicely opened up and had finally broken ground for the hut, which according to schedule ought to have had its roof on a week ago, comes word of the German advance on Riga and rumors that Minsk is to be evacuated.

Tuesday everybody was talking about Riga and evacuation. Colonel Vinogradov, however, was reassuring and told us to go ahead, though he admitted that Minsk might have to be evacuated before long. However, we have heard evacuation talk before and are adopting as our policy to keep going ahead until we are absolutely stopped, as you can never tell what is going to turn up next. We got the foundation posts for the building in Tuesday, finished the handball courts, and made guard nets for the volleyball courts. Our persistence in going ahead with these preparations when all the talk is about the German advance has caused speculation to start among the soldiers that we are German agents getting things ready for the comfort of the Germans when they arrive. The fact that we are Americans and at war with Germany doesn't remove this suspicion.

On Wednesday the report that Riga had been captured by the Germans was confirmed, and they were reported advancing on Dvinsk and Pskov. Emily began packing again. I visited the hospitals this day and found them full of deserters, many of whom were feigning sickness, so the officers in charge asserted. Their slinking, spineless, spiritless faces, and carriage bore out in my mind the charges.

Friday Emily was saying she would like to go through the experience of an evacuation when Mack came in to announce that the evacuation was taking place. Then Emily was anxious to leave at once, ahead of the evacuation. Colonel Vinogradov, however, said later in the day the evacuation had not been decided on. One of our *praporschik** friends, however, has gone to Vitebsk to look over new sites to which to evacuate. The colonel thought it a good thing for women to leave, so we bought tickets for Moscow on the Sunday noon train. The same Friday evening Jerome blew in from Moscow with kino outfit complete, films and everything, to begin picture shows at our field. He agreed to our planning to leave, all except Mack, who is to stay on to the last.

Saturday we exchanged our Moscow tickets for Kiev tickets according to the new plans Jerome has marked out for us, and we will leave Monday midnight.

We put in Saturday getting a rush order for electricity through for the kino shows on the hill. Jerome, Mack, and I were a three-ringed circus, with the city officials giving the stage setting and the town of Minsk our audience. I guess there is no

* Lowest officer rank in the czarist army.

one in the city who doesn't know about the crazy Americans and their plans for free movies out at the Horse Market grounds. The city officials got waked up to real enthusiasm for the stunt, and orders for wiring, poles, and other necessary equipment sped into action with surprising speed.

Meanwhile I put in half the day down at the Zemsky Soyuz getting more cups, spoons, tumblers, pans, sugar, and other things necessary to serve with the tea. Red tape was never longer nor harder to cut. The buck was passed from one department to another, and then when I had finally assembled all my articles and thought at last the job was done, I had to begin the long and weary task of getting the statements properly made out and finding someone who would take my money. The Zemsky Soyuz warehouses cover an immense plot of ground at the edge of the city, half a dozen blocks long and nearly as wide. I had a cab, and we drove miles from building to building in the course of getting these few articles. My Russian cab driver, noticing how exasperated I was getting with the delays and difficulties, finally said, "Well, baron, business will be better a week from now when the Germans come in. They know how to do things better."

According to proclamations dropped from German aeroplanes everything was scheduled for the Germans to be in Minsk within six days. They told the inhabitants not to be alarmed as they would not harm any civilians. The Jewish shops are all preparing for the German occupation by stocking up with a new line of attractive wares and converting their rubles into other currencies that will be more acceptable to the Germans. They have hounded Mack and me to get hold of some American money which they think the Germans will like better. No sign of Russian patriotism outside of the General Staff headquarters. The very Yiddish which you hear everywhere on the streets makes you feel as if you were already an intruder in German territory.

Our regular Sunday program was put aside today while we went to the station in the morning to get our movie outfit and took it out to the field and unpacked it. We stole time out at noon to go with Emily to the park where we four had an

Oberlin Alumni banquet on the veranda. Then we returned to set up the apparatus only to find that the man who did the packing in Moscow had left half the necessary parts behind, so it will be another week yet before Jerome can get back to Moscow, send a courier down with the parts, and be ready for the first exhibition.

Kiev

Imperial Hotel, Kiev

August 31 / September 13

Dear Home Folks:

We arrived in Kiev last night after two days and nights direct travel from Minsk. It will be a long time before we forget our get away from Minsk. We left the hotel at eleven o'clock at night, with the streets pitch dark, no street lamps being lighted. Our luggage was in one droshky, Mack and Jerome in another, and we in a third. In this time of disorder and nightly robberies, we were relieved when we got to the station and found that the luggage was all intact in its cab.

The inside of the station was densely crowded with soldiers and civilians, and the air was indescribably bad. It was so packed that it was too much for Emily to try to push through from one side of the room to the other. You had to look out not to be stepping on some mother sleeping on the floor with a babe in her arms. Most of the soldiers were waiting for the train to Molodechno, the last station before the front, about forty miles away. After two hours of waiting, we were able to get on our train and found that there had been a mistake in our railroad tickets, and other people who had tickets to the same compartment were there first. In an eleventh hour of desperation Jerome, Mack, and I were able to deal with the commandant at the station so effectively that we got another compartment, our bunkmates being a Colonel and two underofficers. Such a mixture of higher and lower officers in the same compartment would have been impossible under the old regime.

There was much excitement about the break between

Kerensky and Kornilov, and nobody seemed to know who was in real authority on this front. The solution of the problem that seemed to strike everybody, soldier, officer, and civilian, as the proper one, was to go down to the station and take the next train out, whether to the front or rear made little difference.

When we woke up the next morning near Bobruisk, along the Berezina River shortly before it enters the Dnieper, we were passing miles and miles of gun carriages, piles of ammunition, cannon, trucks, and other military supplies. The lines of it seemed endless. We were not yet in the Ukraine, but the landscape outlines were softer and gentler than in the north. The houses began to display the attractive thatched-roof style of Southern Russia. The land was richer, the fields beautiful, and an atmosphere of repose, tranquillity, and peace seemed to prevail. The towns were neater and cleaner than we had seen in White Russia. Cattle were plentiful.

Early in the day we arrived at Zlobin, where the line runs north through Mogilev to Petrograd. We had to change trains here and wait for the Petrograd train to Kiev, which meant an all-day wait. The station officials were very uncommunicative about Kornilov's movements, though there were rumors that he was marching on Petrograd, and that there was a strike on the railroad, and no one knew when trains would begin running again. One old railroad conductor, with whom I struck up an acquaintance, shook his head and said things were in a bad way in Russia.

However clean the countryside and towns looked in the early morning sunshine, Zlobin proved on closer acquaintance to have a dirty platform with the usual crowd of soldiers spitting sunflower seeds and Chinese peddlers who sold peanuts (called *kitaisky* or Chinese nuts) which were in turn cracked and littered all over the place.

We tried to take refuge from the station dirt by taking a stroll through the village, but what looked clean and inviting from the railroad station turned out to be dirty and dusty close at hand. Zlobin, like other villages we observed, had a single road leading between fences and through gates to the railroad station which stood on one side of the village. The main street of the village consisted of a string of frail-looking little wooden shops with their wares advertised by pictures. The architecture reminded one of summer cottages at a seaside or lakeside resort in the States. There was a tiny playhouse, and stands of vegetables, fruits, and meats along the dusty street.

Back from the main street the houses were more substantial and surrounded by gardens and enclosed by fences and gates. The dirt and dust, as well as the rough-looking character of the soldiers we passed, discouraged us from going beyond the edge of the village. At one side of town was the headquarters of the Soviet, which seemed to be running things in the village and taking an active part in the civil war between Kerensky and Kornilov. They were bitterly against Kornilov.

At last the train arrived from Petrograd, and we got on to find as our traveling mates this time Little Russians. One of the men was talkative and gave us enthusiastic pictures of the Ukraine. He spoke proudly of how much higher their culture was than that of the Muscovites, as he called the Great Russians. He frowned upon the Bolshevik movement, and said it would ruin their culture if it won out in the Ukraine. That was why he was strong for the Ukraine movement, as a movement of defense to preserve their culture, art, and literature from a lower kind of civilization.

Our Ukrainian fellow traveler was proud of Kiev and of his native land, proud of its art and literature. He said the Muscovite language was the official language of the Ukraine, but that the peasants still spoke the Ukrainian language. The language of the Ukraine movement, however, was not pure Ukrainian, but a professor's Ukrainian, fostered in Austria. The peasants wouldn't understand it any better than they would Great Russian. He said that the Ukrainian peasants were more industrious and skillful than the peasants in the rest of Russia.

The second day of our trip brought us to Bachmatsch, another junction, where we had to wait for another Petrograd train that would take us on to Kiev, while the train we were on proceeded toward Ekaterinoslav. All day we were passing through the beautiful plains of southern Russia on the border of the Ukraine. We were in the region of the black earth, and such crops as were grown here! A mere scratching of the soil produced the most wonderful crops. This helped to explain the very backwardness of the peasants, who didn't have to resort to modern machinery in order to get wonderful results. Sugar beet factories with their neat brick structures and high slender smokestacks began to be conspicuous features of the landscape. We had arrived in the greatest beet sugar center of the world, the place where the modern beet sugar industry started.

Towards the end of the day we came to Darnitza, the famous camp for Czechoslovak prisoners of war. The neat little barracks looked picturesque in between the trim groves of pine trees. Blue-coated Czechoslovaks were everywhere, looking contented and well fed.

Just beyond Darnitza we came out to the broad-sweeping, muddy Dnieper with the high hills of the Kiev Monastery or Lavra opposite, with the golden domes and cupolas of the monastery buildings glowing in the setting sun. The rest of the hills were beautifully wooded. It was a magnificent scene.

After winding around behind the hills, we came in view of the rear side of the city furthest from the Dnieper River. The sight that met us was a surprise. Instead of a provincial, old-fashioned, rambling city such as I had always pictured Kiev, we saw rows upon rows of great apartment houses, miles after miles of splendid handsome homes and business blocks. One cathedral stood out magnificently above its surroundings. We learned that this was the famous Vladimir Cathedral.

It was eight o'clock when we reached the station. A half hour later we were in a cab, which was twice as large as the Petrograd cabs and big enough to hold us and all our luggage except our trunk which we left at the station. We started our quest for rooms. We visited the three hotels whose names I had before leaving Minsk. They were all full. Tips were of no avail. From these hotels, I learned the names of several others, all of which were visited with the same results.

By this time we decided to make use of the only introduction I had to anyone in the city and called upon the Thomases, friends of George Day. Their daughter was the wife of our Ukrainian friend Yatseievitch. We had a greatly appreciated welcome from these dear old people, and they told us that if we still failed in the half-dozen new names of hotels they gave us we should come back and share their house with them. An hour later, after visiting our eleventh hotel, we gave up the search and returned to our English friends. Bedding was spread on the floor, and we were thankful not to have to share the fate of hundreds of others who were spending the night on the floor of the crowded station.

The next morning I was out early and finally landed a double room in the Imperial Hotel, from which we are now writing. But deliver us from a long residence here. It is a Jewish hotel and second-rate in spite of its great size. There are no private baths or toilets, and the public toilet is unspeakable, plumbing out of order and drainage not working.

Kiev has certainly been a revelation to us. Its population now exceeds a million, perhaps half of it being war refugees. The modernness of the city impresses you on every hand; great broad boulevards stretching for miles in a perfectly straight line over hills and valleys; handsome business blocks, broad streets and sidewalks, well paved streets, and an air of progressiveness and hustle that remind one of Detroit or Cleveland. But its hills make you compare it with Kansas City.

The city is rich in historical interest. Right near the center of the city are the famous Golden Gates which have stood nine hundred years since the first of the Russian rulers reigned here. Close by is the old Church of St. Sophia of nearly the same age, inspired by St. Sophia of Constantinople which was still in the hands of the Christians when Kiev was founded. Golden domes of other old churches greet you in every direction. The mixture of the old and the new is delightful, and Kiev immediately increases one's love for Russia.

Settling in leaves little time for sightseeing, however. I have called on Mr. Douglas, the British consul, today and learned that he is a son of a Polish mother and an English father. He has always lived in Kiev and impresses you as more Polish than English. Dear old Mr. Thomas is the assistant at the consul's office.

I called at the Berlitz School this morning to see if they

could put me next to a good interpreter, as I don't feel at home enough in the language yet to go it alone with the important official calls, nor can I do anything with exact translation work from English into Russian in documents. The director of the school, Mr. Spaul, suggested the name of a Mr. Carpenter, who called at our rooms at the hotel this evening and accepted my offer to engage him for ten days.

Carpenter is a Britisher, whose father came over to Russia for business and the son has lived in Russia almost all his life. He talks Russian perfectly and seems to think and work more as a Russian than as a Britisher. He is engaged in supervising the installation of plumbing and fixtures in the new cadet corps building which is being erected on the edge of the city but can handle the work there before and after his interpreting and translating for me.

The atmosphere of Kiev is beautiful, stimulating, uplifting after the Minsk nightmare of dirt and noise. We cannot tell what is coming from one day to the next, but everything points to our being happy if we can only find some decent rooms in exchange for this hotel.

September 2 / 15

This afternoon we walked over to the highest point of the bluffs on the west side of the Dnieper, where the river makes a great bend. The river is about as wide and muddy as the Mississippi at Davenport. The view is superb. Below us lay the Podol, or Jewish quarter. Here have been the scenes of the infamous pogroms. Beyond the Podol and across the river are broad level plains stretching for miles eastward. The bluffs are only on the west side of the river. The other side lies flat, mostly field and plain, with forests in the blue distance. Over all is a sparkling blue sky unclouded with smoke and an atmosphere like Colorado. Around us and along the bluffs glittered the domes and spires of dozens of famous old churches.

My chief occupation at present is to locate decent rooms to live in and quarters for the *Y* work. The main qualification needed is bluff. I should say that Y.M.C.A. secretaries in Russia at present need three qualifications: the first is bluff; the second is bluff; the third is more bluff.

In order to make any headway with any proposition I must first establish my relations with the military officials. And this I have to do with practically no documents except a ragged piece of cheap note paper signed by a clerk in the Minsk Post Office certifying that I delivered to him my American passport on the second day of August to be sent in to Moscow for renewal.

In order to lend dignity to my first call upon His Excellency the Commander of the Armies, Oberutchev, I invited Consul Douglas to go with me, which he kindly did. We did not get to the commander himself but to the next in rank, who asked me to put my requests for quarters into writing. In other words, fill out a *trebovania*. So I have Carpenter busy making out the necessary documents.

In the meantime I have been going about the city deciding which building would be most suitable for our work. I looked at the *Technichesky Institut*, but it is cut up into too small rooms, and besides the Ukrainian movement has hammers on it, and I don't care to compete with them for quarters until I know them better. The next best bet seems to be the Maxime Theater, on Nikolaievsky Street near the famous Kreschyatik (the street of baptizing), in the center of the city. It has a tremendous big hall for picture performances or shows, a big cafe, and plenty of promenade space around the edges; just right for a swell club for officers and soldiers. So I have asked Carpenter to make his request for this building. It all looks too suspiciously easy; however, I'll keep following the leads as far as they go. The bluff will make a favorable impression even if it doesn't land the building.

The proposition of landing rooms for living quarters also seems to have reached the point where nothing but official pressure will avail. The first day I was here I called upon a French family where I was told there might be a room. I was dressed in my morning coat and it seemed to make a favorable impression. Unfortunately the room has just been rented to a French officer who was still there when I called. The lady of the house said she had friends, however, who might be willing to give up their front rooms for us if our mission was as important as I represented it to be.

My next step was to call on Madame Velinsky, to whom the French lady gave me the note of introduction. The Velinsky apartments are in a fine, six-story apartment house on the Nikolaievsky Ploschad, next to a theater, and facing a pretty little square, and standing just below a very steep hill, at the top of which runs another street with large handsome palaces and apartment houses. Madame Velinsky thought they might be able to rent us two of the front rooms which her husband had used as office and bedroom. Fortune seemed to be favoring us. Emily liked the rooms and Madame seemed satisfied with us. But today she called on us at the hotel to inform us that they had been unable to find a bed for less than 325 rubles ($65) and she couldn't rent the room at the price she agreed to (300 rubles or $50 per month) if she had to pay that much for a bed. And then there would be the mattresses and bedding and sheets to think about.

I consulted our friend Consul Douglas again. "Don't judge the Poles," he said. "I know them. I'm partly one myself. The trouble isn't about the bed. She could get one easily enough if she wanted to. The trouble is about your credentials. You haven't convinced her yet that your Mission has enough social prestige about it to make her renting a room to you a social advantage to her. You must get those official papers from Kerensky and then all will sail along smoothly." So I have wired Jerome to rush the permissions.

Who should drop in on us today but Leonard. It was the first time I had met him, though I had corresponded with him when he was located at Krasnoyarsk and I was at Petrograd on the war prisoner work. His present assignment is with the Imperial Horse Guards. They are stationed not a great distance from Kiev on the beautiful 100,000 acre estate of Count Potofsky. The palace is luxurious. Count Pallen's boy is one of the Guards and quite a friend of Leonard's. Leonard said the burdens of a Y.M.C.A. secretary with this group of men are anything but worrisome; they are the most companionable bunch in the world, well bred, highly cultured, most of them speaking English, and adept at tennis and other outdoor sports, at which Leonard spends much of his time with them.

Leonard said the Guards didn't know what would develop next. The regiment still preserves much of the morale and esprit de corps of the old regime, though democracy is creeping in, and the new commander of the troop is a young fellow who is socially inferior to most of them according to their way of thinking, and the spirit of the group is beginning to show some unsettling.

September 4 / 17

Yesterday Leonard joined the Mogilevskys, Emily, and me in a visit to the St. Vladimir, St. Sophia, and St. Michael churches. The Vladimir Church is a marvel of beauty and art, inside and out. It celebrates the thousandth year since Vladimir, the first of the Russian rulers to be baptized to Christianity. The great Virgin of the Snows above the altar by Vasnyetsov is truly Russian in its strength and snowy atmosphere. And how the eyes of St. Olga, the mother of Vladimir, blaze at you from the *ikonostas*. The pagan fires seem not yet to have died in them. The greatest artists of Russia have done wonders with the old Byzantine art forms, without transgressing the art rules laid down by the Church. The Byzantine is here, but also the greatest of modern art.

St. Sophia is a fascinating contrast. Here is the old church in reality. The old frescoes are still on the old walls. The plaster with which they were covered over during the Tatar invasion still shows in spots though it has mostly been removed. The inside of the church is dim, dark, and sombre while the interior of St. Vladimir is a miracle of brightness and light.

St. Michael is another old church on the brow of the bluff overlooking the Dnieper. St. Vladimir and St. Sophia were crowded and had beautiful choirs, while St. Michael had poorer music and smaller crowds.

Between Vladimir and Sophia we visited the famous Golden Gates in the square of that name. Only parts of the gates still stand, and these portions are cased over with masonry to prevent weathering and crumbling.

This morning Leonard and I called on the president of the Zemsky Soyuz. He is a regular American business type of man, clean-cut, brisk, decisive. He spoke English fluently. Leonard has started me with some funds until my ship comes in by transferring 17,500 rubles, with which I am to purchase buildings and supplies for his work with the Horse Guards. We tackled the Zemsky Soyuz on the proposition that they furnish the "knock-down" types of huts, and they have some which they can sell us.

Carpenter had his *trebovania* for the Maxime Theater ready today, and I delivered it to the *Nachalnik Shtaba* (Chief of Staff). Madame Velinsky and Madame Gembitsky called at our hotel quarters during the day to inform us that we could have the rooms after all.

4 Nikolaievsky Ploschad, Kiev
September 10 / 23

This has been a week of getting acquainted. Starting with a name which Mr. Thomas gave me, I called upon Prof. Cholodine of Kiev University. I found him at home, but he was unable to act as an authority on the Ukrainian movement and gave me the name of Steschenko at the Ukrainian Rada.* I found the Rada occupying the beautiful museum building. All was bustle and activity. The broad winding corridors were crowded with tables where various committees were sitting. I finally got hold of Steschenko, but a long line of people were waiting to get at him, and I felt fortunate to get as much as a note of introduction from him to Petlura, the commander of the prospective Ukrainian army. As for seeing Vinichenko, the head of the Ukrainian movement, he was afraid that he would be too busy to see me.

Tuesday morning I presented my note of introduction to General Petlura at the Ukrainian Staff headquarters, across the street from the museum. He was seated behind a plain desk in a plain room, and there was no fuss nor feathers about the place. He received me politely and simply. He appeared to be a

* The Ukrainian legislature.

hardworking sort of man, but more the kind who would be good at details than in conceiving big plans or inspiring large bodies of men. My aim in these interviews with the Ukrainian representatives was to learn how extensive their movement was, how far they would welcome Y.M.C.A. work, and whether their relations with the Provisional Government or Kerensky forces were friendly. Petlura said they would welcome our service but that as yet their army had not been formed. Only one or two Ukrainian regiments had actually been separated from the Russian army, though Ukrainian representatives were working in every regiment of the Russian army where there were Ukrainian soldiers, forming them into separate units for the prospective Ukrainian army.

On the same day I called on Ryabzov, the mayor of Kiev, to enlist his support in helping us secure a building for our work. He has one hour a day for receiving, between twelve and one o'clock. A long line of people were waiting to see him—mostly poor people and refugees. But "American" was again the open sesame, and I was called ahead of turn and ushered into a large room, where the mayor stood disposing of the last visitor. The mayor was a tall, handsome man, dressed in a morning suit after the fashion of the old school, but he was quite democratic in his manner, and everything about him pointed to efficiency and despatch. He heard my story and promised to put in a word with General Oberutchev.

The next day I called at the General Staff to learn the fate of the *trebovania*, but I called after two o'clock and the office was closed. The following day, Friday, was one of the big holidays and nothing could be done at the Staff. I thought I would try the soldiers' and workingmens' deputies instead. Their headquarters were at the Governor's Palace. They were evidently much stronger here than in Minsk, for the idea of their taking over the Governor's Palace at Minsk would have been out of the question. But the deputies were taking a holiday as well as the bourgeoisie this time and very few were about.

I finally connected up, during Friday, with Mr. Trussov, to whom Leonard had left me a note of introduction. On the following day he went with me to look over the Merchant's Park on Bolshaya Vassilkovskaya Street. We found here an amusement park with bandstand, restaurant, motion picture hall, stage, etc., but closed up for the season, it being a summer establishment only. There were no heating arrangements, and the wooden partitions had big cracks, so we quickly abandoned the thought of this outfit for a winter club. On the same day we went out to look over the Ukraine Theater near the Chaussée des Fleurs, the great military road that leads from the end of Bibikovsky Boulevard to Brest-Litovsk. But this was likewise impossible for winter use.

Mr. Trussov spoke no English, so for the first time I was thrown entirely upon my knowledge of Russian in my relations to an associate in the work. With characteristic Russian readiness he has agreed to see General Oberutchev and the president of the Workingmens' Deputies, to both of whom he has leads. He will see them Monday and expects to have our building landed immediately. At the Monday interviews he will arrange appointments for me.

We celebrated my thirty-second birthday Thursday by visiting the famous Lavra, or Monastery. It is certainly a unique and beautiful place. Priests and pilgrims are everywhere, and the atmosphere takes you back to the middle ages. We went through the famous catacombs. Over eighty of the earliest monks and workers of the Russian church, who built these catacombs about 1000 A.D., lay in open coffins placed in niches. They are mummified, of course. We were preceded in our tour by pious pilgrims who stopped to kiss the coffin or mummy at every niche, and drop a kopek or two.* The way is long, dark, and gloomy. Emily began to think we would never reach the end and was beginning to urge that we try to wedge our way back the way we came, when light showed ahead, and we were back where we started.

---

* Mrs. Heald commented on this in a letter to her mother-in-law: "It is weird enough and one has visions of germs."

Sunday, September 17 / 30

Tuesday Mr. Trussov and I called on the *Nachalnik Shtaba*
again to see what progress had been made on our *trebovania* for
the Maxime Theater. We were informed that our request had
been favorably considered but that the Maxime Theater had
already been assigned to another organization—a polite way of
rejecting our request.

The next day Colonel Voschinsky, president of the Republican Club, accompanied Mr. Trussov and me on a visit to General Oberutchev. His headquarters were in a splendid private
residence on Alexandrovskaya Street nearly opposite the Governor's Palace. All was quiet and in order. The place seemed to
have suffered little from its military occupation. Those who were
waiting were in morning coats or uniforms, and I was reminded,
while waiting in the hallway, of the old regime atmosphere of
the Winter Palace or of the army headquarters at Minsk.

After some time, we were ushered into the general's room.
He greeted us warmly, speaking English better than I could
speak Russian. He was a large, powerfully built man with a
heavy beard. He had been in America, knew the Y.M.C.A., and
was very favorable to our plans. But he advised us to consult the
Soviet authorities and be guided by their wishes. In matters of
committees, sites, the kinds of periodicals to have in our reading
rooms, and all other questions, whatever the Soviet authorities
favored he would O.K. As for the Maxime Theater or any other
building for the work, we should go to the Citizens' Committee
of the Staff, and he would instruct them to do everything possible
for us.

We were thus confronted with an entirely different situation
than in Minsk. There we were told to keep clear of the Soviet
authorites. There is a difference, however, in the Soviet. At
Minsk it was intensely Bolshevik and Jewish. In Kiev it is
Russian and Menshevik. The head of the Soviet here is a moderate Socialist, Grigoriev, who is much respected by all groups.

General Oberutchev's position here is complicated by the
three-cornered struggle going on between the Ukrainians, Bolsheviki, and Kerensky forces for control. It means that we have

a peculiarly delicate mission to serve any without compromising ourselves.

Following General Oberutchev's suggestions, we went to the Citizens' Committee at the Staff. Our last hope that a building would be commandeered for our purposes free were dashed in this interview. They advised us to see the owner first, and see whether we can come to reasonable terms with him. If not, they would try to bring him to terms.

So Mr. Trussov and I went back to the theater and found the agent, only to learn that the owner was an Italian living in Italy and that the building, therefore, cannot be requisitioned. Upon learning that the owner wanted to rent the building for a quarter of a million rubles annually, we dropped that site from our list.

In the evening we went to the Chanclera Moving Picture House to see if we could make a dicker with the owner, Mr. Chanclera. We found a fine up-to-date movie house that was doing a big business. Mr. Chanclera would consider nothing at all reasonable in the rent line. It was becoming evident that the government announcements that all places of amusement would be requisitioned for military purposes were not being taken seriously by the owners of these places.

Thursday was another big holiday and all stores and offices were closed. The following day we tried our luck with the museum, having learned that the Ukrainians were going to transfer their headquarters to the *Technichesky Institut*, but again we were disappointed and told that the Ukrainians would continue to hold the museum as well as their new quarters. They seem to be growing.

Our next try was the famous Kontraktny Dom in the Podol, or Jewish Quarter. This was an interesting visit, taking us down the tremendously long incline of Kidilovskaya Street, one of the few streets that connect the upper city with this flat low city by the river. Down in the Podol we were in Jewry. Old Testament-looking characters were plying their characteristic trades and walking and standing and begging all about us. Only the numerous Russian churches reminded us that we were in Russia.

The Kontraktny Dom reflects little of its former glory. The

fair and trading features have sunk into insignificance. A few estate owners and sugar kings assemble annually, but there is little stir commercially or socially. The interior is a series of big, bare rooms. The former famous restaurant is now fitted up with rude tables and benches and chairs and cheap lunch service. There was room galore in the building, but even for the rough comforts of a soldiers' club it seemed too huge and barrack-like. Besides, it was not convenient to the largest garrisons of the city.

We employed the short business hours of Saturday morning visiting the *Nachalnik Shtaba* again to see what progress had been made regarding the general's orders, but the letters and papers which he had promised to turn over to them had not been received.

Another inspiration struck us. Why not try the *Dvoryanstvo Club* (Club of the Nobility)? This is one of the prominent institutions in every city in Russia. It is a sort of country club, usually located in the heart of the city and minus the outdoor features. Perhaps better to compare it to the Union League Club but it is a social center for both men and women. We went to look it over. It was located at an excellent situation at the end of the Kreschyatik, just before the long descent to the Podol. It had just the rooms and facilities we were looking for. It was too late in the day to find the club agent, Uvarov, however, and that is left over to next week.

On Thursday, the holiday making work impossible, Emily and I started out for one of the popular resorts. But when we arrived at the end of the tramway line we found hundreds of people waiting for the cars. All stand in line waiting their turn. You can figure out the length of time you would have to stand in line by calculating the load each car would hold normally, multiply that by three or four, then divide that figure into the lines ahead of you, and the frequency of the car will give you x. We saw no chance under two hours' time. That doesn't feaze our Russian friends. The streetcar waiting lines are just as convenient for conversation as anywhere else, and Russians don't mind standing.

We decided to give up the trip and take a country stroll instead. We crossed the great Brest-Litovsk highway, which kept

straight on its broad, paved course from the end of Bibikovsky
Boulevard past the engineering and polytechnic buildings, which
we could see a couple of miles beyond the city limits where we
stood, over hill and down valley straight on to Brest-Litovsk and
Warsaw hundreds of miles away.

We followed along the edge of the city over a little creek
to the Kadetsky Grove, which surrounded the Kadetsky Korpus.
The target practice grounds were vacant. The drill grounds
were vacant, the school buildings were practically vacant except
for a few students in uniform who appeared in hallways and on
sidewalks. The place didn't have much of the air of a going
concern.

Farther on, handsome, new college buildings were being
erected. These were the ones Carpenter was employed on. A high,
ugly board fence barred us from a most attractive grove that
extended from the first buildings to the new ones. The road
became muddy. There were no sidewalks. The further we got
from the city the rougher became the characters who passed us
and the more embarrassed Emily felt with her good-looking coat
and hat. We began to realize that the country region about Kiev
was flooded with deserters, ruffians, and bandits as surely as was
the region closer to the front about Minsk. We felt relieved to
complete a shortcut back through meadows and pastures to the
edge of the city and find ourselves safely on the high viaduct
over the railroad tracks near the station.

Our old Petrograd friend, Yatseievitch, the Ukrainian,
showed up unexpectedly in the midst of a streetcar strike today.
His enthusiasm for the Ukrainian movement has undergone an
eclipse. He is a sadder and older man. He has found nothing but
disorders all the way down from Petrograd. He is disappointed
in the leaders. "Men with insane ideas have gotten control," he
said, "and are leading the masses astray. God knows to what they
are leading. Things are getting more impossible every day." He
admitted that he thought the leaders of the Ukrainian movement
were playing an Austrian game. The leaders were playing to
the mob and making extravagant promises that could not be
fulfilled.

Wednesday evening I had a call from Kirichenko, the president of the Soldiers' Christian Society here. He is a tall light-haired Baptist, very devout and earnest, and came to learn what our organization was, and whether we were a truly Christian organization or not. All our welfare plans and broad lines of work gave him misgivings and made him wonder whether we were orthodox enough. He wanted to know what my Christian experience was, and how I was baptized, and what the rules and regulations of the Y.M.C.A. were along these lines. It was my first experience with the Russian Baptists, and I began to realize the difficulties of enjoying their confidence and cooperation and at the same time cooperating with the Russian Orthodox Church. No love is lost between these two Christian communions. But Kirichenko, if his religious outlook lacked breadth, had a fine, sincere, big-hearted spirit himself, and seemed disposed to give the *Y* a chance. He spoke no English and so all our conversation was in Russian. While his name was Ukrainian, as are all names ending in "enko," he had little use for the Ukrainian movement. He invited me to attend one of his soldier meetings which are held in the university buildings.

Yesterday afternoon Emily and I went out to Mariensky Park and Tsarsky Park, adjoining the palace grounds on the bluffs overlooking the Dnieper. The fascination of these views from the hills of the sacred city, out over the sunlit plains across the broad Dnieper, increases and now begins to be added the glory of the autumn foliage.

September 24 / October 7

The weary task of locating a site has dragged on fruitlessly all week in this, verily, most crowded city in the world. Monday Trussov and I saw the mayor again, and he gave us a letter to the Department on Sites. We went to the Department on Sites, and they promised us a *reply* on Wednesday. We visited the department on Wednesday, but no one was in. We returned on Friday, but no one was in. Finally, Saturday, we found them in, but nothing doing.

Anticipating this outcome with our city department, we pursued a parallel effort with the General Staff again regarding the Maxime Cafe, with the hope that official pressure might bring a fairer figure from the owner. Kirichenko, whom we saw Monday, also promised to have a reply by Wednesday. It happened that the papers which the Staff had been waiting for General Oberutchev to turn over came to them Tuesday, so Trussov and I were back there that day, and our Wednesday promise was postponed to Thursday. When we returned Thursday, we were asked to come back Saturday, which we did, with the same result that we had secured from the city—nothing could be done.

Anticipating nothing from the city, we have been improving our opportunities with the Soviet. We called at the headquarters Monday, but Grigoriev, the president of the Soldiers' Deputies, was not in. Thursday we found him in. He is a fine, sensible fellow. He assured us that the Soldiers' Deputies would cooperate with us in locating a site. We are to return there next week.

Trussov got a lead on a hall opposite the Duma. We visited the place and found a fine suite of rooms for our purpose, one of them being fitted up with a stage and suited for entertainments, and another for a tearoom, while other rooms could be used for reading rooms, classrooms, etc. None of the rooms were being used, but a labor union of metal workers had asked for the place, and their officers were on hand to keep others out. I had an interview with the secretary of the union. He was a Jew, spoke English, knew all about the Y.M.C.A. in America, and took the familiar attitude of the Bolsheviki, which he took no pains to conceal as being his party—the attitude namely of calling us a capitalist organization which would find no sympathy from him or the union he represented. We decided to leave the problem of these quarters to the Soviet.

The following day Trussov and I interviewed Uvarov, the agent for the *Dvoryantsvo Club*. Uvarov agreed that we could have the upper two floors for a rental of 24,000 rubles (about $6,000) per year if we could find other quarters for the present inmates. This is better than the Italian's quarter of a million but far from our rent-free goal.

Our week's efforts on site hunting wound up Saturday with a return to the town *Uprava*, the General Staff, and the City

Requisition Department, with the usual fruitless results. Trussov would have given the job up as hopeless long ago and thinks I am crazy for persisting in the face of these conditions. But I have learned never to take "No" as final in Russia.

I have come to the conclusion, however, that I shall have to get pressure politically to secure my site. The puzzle is which to bank on, Soviet, Kerensky, or Ukrainian influence. It is hard to tell which is the stronger, or how far I can go with one without getting in bad with the others. I am following leads with the Ukrainians at present. Jerome has sent me the addresses of two Ukrainian workers, Chaikovsky and Praporschik Dietrichs. I have called at each address, but neither was in. From what the landlady said, they are apparently working eighteen hours a day helping to organize the new Ukrainian army.

Yesterday Emily and I took an afternoon off, when it was too late to get any more turndowns at town *Upravas*, city requisition headquarters, or trade union headquarters, and went out to visit the Carpenters at the edge of the city. We got a refreshing whiff of the countryside, sipped tea, gazed with curiosity at the Russian household belongings of his Russian wife, and then went to a neighbor who had an orchard.

Here we had an illustration of the way values have gone up in Russia. This orchard had been bought for 400 rubles twenty years earlier. This year the owners cleared 18,000 rubles on the fruit alone. The owners were simple folk from the peasant class, but their children have had the advantage of a college education and are demonstrating that capacity for practical success which is characteristic of the peasant class wherever they have the opportunity.

Last evening I attended a meeting of the Soldiers' Christian Society of which Kirichenko is president. I found the gathering in a large classroom in the university buildings. Four hundred soldiers were crowded into all the standing and sitting space the room afforded. Kirichenko was on the platform expounding the scriptures in a magnetic, capable way that gave me a new conception of his power and force. There was an atmosphere of intense devotion and worship in that hot, suffocating room. Perspiring in their heavy army overcoats, the soldiers sat there

motionless, hanging on to every word that Kirichenko spoke.
You could hear a pin drop anywhere in the room. Scripture reading was followed by prayer, in which many of the soliders joined.
It was like a Methodist prayer meeting. I was being shown the
soil on which the Baptist missions have thrived and grown in
Russia. It was a revelation of the heart of the Russian peasant
class, for most of these soldiers were from the country.

The trip out to Kirilov Monastery this morning was a rare
treat. These churches bring back all the charm of the old regime,
for there was a charm about the old regime which the revolution
has destroyed. That charm is hard to define. Your head tells you
of the wickedness in high places, of the corruption, of the selfish
privileges of the upper classes, and of the sufferings of the lower
classes. But your heart feels the allure of the mystery of it all—
the mystery of the religion, the churches, the art, the music,
the Slav character. There was charm in the simple customs of
everyday life, in the crossing before the shrines, ikons, and
churches. It may have been foolish, but there was a charm, irresistible, heart-pulling, indescribable. But all that has been swept
away by the revolution as by a mighty, angry, dirty, savage
flood, and only in these islets of churches and monasteries does
the old charm linger.

September 30 / October 13

At last a site is landed. But it is not the handsome downtown site
we have been working for. It is four miles west of the center of
the city, where the 759th Infantry Regiment is located in barracks. It is just one of the little barrack buildings, a frame shed,
stuck off down a side road which is called a street. A short way
beyond is a deep gully, and right in back of the building is
another sharp gully, and beyond that the remains of an immense
amphitheatre or race course, now minus the seats, where an
Imperial velocipede contest was held in 1905. The hillside has
been levelled off here for an area large enough to stage several
football and baseball games simultaneously.

The building is without electricity, and we are now arranging for the connections. We have to connect to the wires at the
Woman's Monastery across the street from our barracks. We were

in there yesterday and revelled in the beauty of the large, quiet grounds and stately buildings and in the charming and inspiring presence of the Mother Superior, or *igumen* as she is called in the Russian church. Shielded from revolutionary and Bolshevik agitation, life goes on in these secluded grounds as it has for hundreds of years in the past.

This goal of our site-hunting efforts was achieved with the aid of Poslavsky, the president of the Republican Club. He is a lightning actor. I called on him at his room the other morning before he had had breakfast. He had been out to doings until four or five o'clock. It was then nine o'clock in the morning. He already had a half dozen political visitors, and he was keeping up a running fire of conversation with all of them while shaving and finishing his morning's toilet. Meanwhile he was preparing his breakfast of coffee and toast. Slashing through his breakfast and business with the other callers, he pulled Trussov and me out to an auto and whisked us out to the headquarters of the 759th Infantry Regiment. With American briskness he whirled us into the Lieutenant's room past the line of waiting soldiers and civilians and had our case explained with a revolutionary disregard of usual Russian formalities and red tape. The Lieutenant and soldiers were delighted with the idea of our organization, and in no time the vacant barracks building was at our disposal.

We did not give up the downtown location until a number of new efforts fell down because General Oberutchev has gone to Petrograd, and it seems that it is the man who is out of the city that everybody agrees is the one with the authority to act in a case of commandeering a building.

When Trussov, Plemyannikov, and I visited the Soviet headquarters Monday, they announced plans for closing five or six theaters including the Maxime Theater. We could pick our choice, and it would be reserved for us. We selected the Maxime as first choice and the Intime as second. On the following day we called for the papers but were informed that the Soviet had changed its plans and they were going to requisition only two theaters now, and neither of these would suit our purpose at all. We would have to wait until General Oberutchev returned.

We returned to the General Staff once more, but there was no *doklad* and nothing could be done until General Oberutchev returned. We called upon the city officials again, but likewise nothing further could be done until General Oberutchev returned.

The latter people also said in reply to our query about getting hold of some barracks to work in that there were no vacant barracks and that if we wanted to work in the barracks we would have to put up our own buildings. We even went to the Zemsky Soyuz to get current prices on their knockdown army huts, and learned that they would cost 3650 rubles each (including heating equipment) before our Republican friend came to our rescue and put us on to our free site.

October 7 / 20

The opening of our club with the 759th Infantry Regiment has been the event of the week. The city provided the lumber for the furniture free, the soldiers have been digging the holes for the football and volleyball posts, soldier committees for the various activities have been formed, and the soldiers have shown their Russian artistic taste in the curtain and stage setting they have fixed up. The city electrical company completed their connections for 443 instead of 3,000 rubles, and our first kino show took place this evening. Everything was all right except the pictures, and they were punker even than the average of the Russian pictures. The rooms were crowded and the novelty of the occasion was sufficient to prevent the enthusiasm of the soldiers suffering on account of poor pictures.

As soon as we got the electricity connected, the building attracted the attention of the Bolsheviki who were living down in the gully separate from the rest of the regiment. They showed up the second evening in a big body and explained that they were going to hold a meeting. The officers and soldiers who were non-Bolsheviki shrugged their shoulders in answer to my query what to do about it, and said "*nichevo.*" The Bolsheviki comprised about one third of the regiment, but they seemed to be the more enterprising and energetic, the natural leaders.

They went ahead with their meeting. It consisted of denunciations of the Kerensky regime and appeals to the other soldiers to join them in overthrowing the capitalists and securing peace and bread and money. They denounced the war with Germany. When a soldier in the crowd had nerve enough to ask them whether it was true they were receiving German money, the reply was "Well, we haven't had any money from Kerensky for three months. We've got to have money from somewhere."

The Bolsheviki were largely the forward, pushing, city type, while the non-Bolsheviki were largely the slow-moving, slow-thinking, good-natured, easy-going, country type. The Bolsheviki were the leaders, the non-Bolsheviki the followers. The non-Bolsheviki were on the defensive. They felt no conviction about any cause. They were not hostile to Bolshevism but simply kind of uneasy in their consciences about it. The Bolsheviki seemed to sense that fact and directed their attack to overcome that uneasiness. Everything favored their appeals. The Kerensky government had no agitators or orators present. No one answered the attacks which the Bolsheviki made upon the existing Provisional Government. It is no wonder that the persuasive powers of the Bolsheviki won converts. You would see a soldier here and another there visibly yielding to the arguments of the Bolsheviki. Perhaps a half dozen or so were won over by this evening's meeting.

The game of the Bolsheviki was readily apparent. They were separating themselves from the rest of the regiment and building up their forces biding their time until things were ripe to strike. Doubtless similar campaigning and separation is going on in every regiment throughout the Russian army. The day I visited the Soviet I saw the Bolshevik headquarters where their agents were drilled and trained in this game of building up Bolshevik sections in the regiments throughout the army. And no power existed with the nerve to say them nay or oppose them.

At the request of the officers and with the concurrence of the soldiers, we have worked out a check system in connection with our tearoom to control deserters. Every soldier has to turn in his certificate of identification when he receives his tumbler of tea and sugar, and this is returned when he returns the glass.

We serve only bona fide soldiers in this way. Plenty of deserters show up every day, but they accept the regulations as a matter of course, in a good natured way. The deserter has a recognized and respectable status, so large has his tribe become, but he usually avoids scenes that would draw overmuch attention upon himself.

I am having my difficulties locating an assistant who can relieve me of the details at the barracks so that I can continue my search for a downtown site. Tuesday I thought I had my man, in a clean cut, efficient-appearing, middle-aged man with the suspiciously un-Russian name of Kruze, a Cossack *Stabs-Kapitan*. Upon Trussov's discovery, however, that he had been a former member of the Czar's police system, I had to dismiss him, as that record is about as useful to a man in revolutionary Russia as a penitentiary record would be to a pastor in the States.

October 15 / 28

The Bolsheviki are ruling the roost at Druzhina 759. The hut is crowded every night, and when the Bolsheviki leave us alone the kino pictures go through to the delight of the soldiers, the chess and checker tables are in constant use, the tea service is taxed to its capacity, our writing materials are going out in a constant flow, and the little pantry that serves as our library draws a constant line of readers.

But about every other night the Bolsheviki decide to put on a meeting. Then it is all off with the kino show. The soldiers gather around and the Bolsheviki continue their bombardment of denunciation and the familiar old appeals of peace, bread, and land. No government defenders or agitators appear. I don't see how such a situation can have any other ending but a bad smash up one of these days.

I have to confess that I have not the art to deal with the Bolshevik committee. They know how little sympathy I have with their cause. In fact, I believe my presence in the meetings is all that keeps a lot of the soldiers from joining the Bolsheviki, though I have made it a policy to avoid political controversy myself.

I have finally signed up another young Russian as assistant at the Druzhina, Constantine Vladimirovitch K———. He is a Caucasian, a graduate of Moscow University, and remembers John R. Mott when he addressed the students there. He is full of all kinds of pep, dresses like a dandy, but has so keen a wit that I think he can handle even the Bolshevik committee. He was for several years a secretary for the Zemsky Soyuz.

Meanwhile a building exceeding in size my wildest dreams has been turned over to us rent free. It is one of the barracks in the Petchersky garrison, where 20,000 soldiers are quartered, less than a mile from the Petchersky Monastery and the catacombs. The building itself is a block long, low and narrow (450 x 60 feet), but with room enough for tea rooms, classrooms, libraries, kino theater, gymnasium, and the like. It is turned over to us by the Polkovnik (Colonel) of the Zapassny Pontony Battalion, and he has promised us every cooperation in furnishing the materials and engineering help and labor necessary for getting it equipped and ready for use in the shortest space of time. Needless to say we are happy over our good luck and feel repaid for all the waiting and searching.

Monday we had a surprise visit from Anthony Chez and wife. He is an Oberlin graduate like ourselves; played on the Oberlin football team back in '98 that defeated Michigan. He has been in the war service of the Association in France and is one of the new recruits for our work in Russia, having come around by way of Norway and Sweden. He is going on to Odessa where Lowrie is down with diphtheria. After a good day's visit, we saw them off to Odessa, accompanying him out to the railroad yards to board the train, that being the only way you can get a seat these days. By the time the train arrives at the depot every seat and available foot of standing room is taken. Even at the yards, it required all the impressive dignity of his 250 pounds, American flag, and camouflage of "Amerikansky Konsul" and a liberal display of rubles to get the coveted coupe which spelled disappointment to scores of others.

October 22 / November 4

Constantine Vladimirovitch has been delivering the goods. The day after he began work at Druzhina 759, he had turned the tide and won over the Bolsheviki to at least not interfere with our program. I was with him in the final session with the Bolshevik committee when they agreed to respect our work. Their committee was made up of unusually intelligent fellows, several of whom spoke English. The line we put up to them was that if they wanted the goodwill of America, they could not afford to monkey with our organization and that point of view got across with them.

So the Druzhina 759 hut is going full blast, jammed to the guards every night. After putting in most of the evenings this week out there with Constantine Vladimirovitch, I feel that the work is well enough organized to leave with him, except for frequent visiting.

Meanwhile the equipping of our immense Petchersky barracks is proceeding with *"po-Amerikansky"* speed, as the Russians term it. Engineer Ivanov and a gang of soldiers as workmen began operations Wednesday and promised that the building would be ready in ten days. Engineer Ivanov is a clever man: thinks, speaks, and executes with the precision, speed, and absence of waste motion of a high-grade American engineer. It is a pleasure to be with him as he reasons out and puts into operation his plans. His brain is like a keen thinking apparatus. And withal he has a winning personality and is full of practical philosophy and liberal culture. He speaks no English but uses Russian of such clearness and simplicity that Russian conversation with him is a joy instead of the usual hard work I find it with most Russians.

Rumors begin to circulate of another Bolshevik rising. The Soviet official organs openly announce November 7 as the date set for the uprising all over Russia. Here in the Ukraine the Rada has issued a *prikaz* announcing the separation of the Ukraine from Russia. This is evidently a step to forestall Bolshevik trouble here. No one can tell what's coming.

🔖 *With the coming of the Bolshevik Revolution Heald apparently dropped the practice of double-dating his letters. The new government very soon adopted the Gregorian calendar, making Russian dates the same as those of the western world.*

November 11

Dear Ones All:

Since Thursday we have been cut off from telegraphic communication with the outside world. The Bolsheviki began another uprising in Petrograd on that day and we hardly know what's doing. Rumors are that Petrograd is in the hands of the Soviet and that fierce fighting is going on in Moscow.

Here, as yet, matters are comparatively quiet, though the Ukrainians took the arsenal from the Bolsheviki yesterday and have come out in a declaration against the Bolsheviki.

Kenneth Miller arrived from Petrograd Friday. He had been three days and nights on the trip that normally takes 36 hours. He had left Petrograd before the fighting began there. He came with the first party of secretaries from America. A second party of 25 secretaries almost caught up with the first party. They are bringing movies, phonographs, films, and records.

Yesterday I went with Miller to visit Professor Maxa, who is the leader of the Czechs here. Miller spent a year in Bohemia before the war, learned the Czech language, and got acquainted with many of the leading Czechs who are now here in Russia. He brought over letters of introduction from the American Czechs to the key men here in Russia. Miller has been in charge of a Czech settlement in New York known as the John Hus House and so is right at home among the men here.

Professor Maxa is a young man in the early thirties, who was the Czech representative in the Austro-Hungarian Parliament before the war. He is a very democratic fellow, fine mixer, and likes nothing better than to be the center of a room full of good companions and story tellers, amidst clouds of smoke. At the same time he is very energetic, and boys and young officers are busy coming and going with all sorts of commissions.

This morning the Russian general in local command was at Professor Maxa's headquarters when we called there. The Kerensky government is trying to prevail upon the Czechs to support them in the armed conflict which everybody is expecting here, but the Czechs are trying to preserve non-partisanship in Russian politics, that being the policy of their great leader Professor Masaryk.

This Czech movement for independence is a great revelation to me. To have been able to build such a compact, strong, spirited little army out of war prisoners in a technically enemy territory is a monument to the genius of Professor Masaryk. The undaunted, confident, enthusiastic spirit of the Czechs, their disdain of danger, and their wonderful morale strike you with admiration from the first. When Miller first said he was going to work with the Czechs, I was disappointed that such a good man was not going to be with our Russian work. But after becoming acquainted with the Czechs, I am glad he will be with them. The Czechs take Miller right in as one of them, show great enthusiasm for our program, and I would not be surprised if, with the cooperation they will give him, Miller will soon have a larger work going with the Czechs than we will with the Russians.

November 12

The rat-a-tat-tat of the machine guns has been busy in Kiev today. Banks and stores are closed on account of the fighting. I tried to get out to Petchersky this morning but was stopped by Ukrainian guards who stated that the Zapassny Pontony Battalion is on the side of the Bolsheviki.

Shooting was going on along the Kreschyatik intermittently all day. It reminded me of the March days in Petrograd. Tonight there are no street lights. Petrograd is reported to be again in the hands of the Kerensky forces.

November 13

Constantine Vladimirovitch was in this morning to report no pictures at Druzhina 759 last night. The Bolsheviki were on hand and held a meeting. They talked of taking over the hut and the movie equipment, but Constantine bluffed them off once more.

The restaurants, banks, and stores were all closed again today, and the tramways not running. The morning *Kievlyanin* was the only paper appearing all day. The Bolsheviki have muzzled the press by calling a strike of the printers on the other two papers.

We went out for lunch at the cafe and were entertained by neighboring volleys. The sidewalks were not crowded.

November 14

The Ukrainians and Bolsheviki have control of Kiev. The Kerensky forces have surrendered. There are no newspapers or trams yet, the banks are still closed, but the fighting seems to be over with very little bloodshed, and the stores are beginning one by one to open up again. The General Staff headquarters of the Provisional Government have been vacated.

The Germans are reported to be marching on Minsk.

Miller and I went around to consult the British officers at the British headquarters this evening. They are flocking in from the front and Roumania and are going on to Kursk tonight. We were nearly tempted to accept their invitation to pack along with them, but in the absence of telegraphic or other advice from Moscow, we decided to chance it remaining here.

Madame Velinsky has asked me to put up the sign of our organization on the hallway door that is the common entrance to both our apartments. America is regarded as the best protection anyone can have under the circumstances.

Miller lunched with us at the Prague Hotel this evening. This skyscraper of a building, with its glassed-in roof garden, built on the highest point in Kiev, is a Czech enterprise named after their capital city. Miller has a room there and has already become well known to the Czech community of Kiev, which is numerous, and more important and influential than their numbers would suggest.

November 15

Today brought out the first newspapers, and a resumption of the trams, but no telegraph or mail service with the outside world. I am arranging for a courier to go through to Moscow. This is where Kirichenko and his trusty Baptists come in handy. They make absolutely reliable servants who are willing to do and die for the Christian cause.

I have written Jerome at length telling him why I think it useless to try to continue Y.M.C.A. work under the Bolshevik regime. My point is that the avowed purpose of the Bolsheviki being a proletarian revolution and peace with Germany, they can have absolutely no interest in the cause of the Allies and we cannot expect to have any influence in changing their attitude by our organization unaided by the presence of Allied armies. I am convinced that the presence of Allied armies alone, and especially that of America, would rally the patriotic elements of Russia together and give those groups who are loyal to the cause of democracy and the Allies a chance to assert themselves and find leadership in this time of chaos and turmoil.

The Ukraine now offers the most hopeful field for the Allies in Russia, the only part of Russia not flat-footed for peace with Germany. The Ukrainians have the power in their hands and have refused to share it with the Bolsheviki. So it has turned out that, after joining with the Bolsheviki to overturn the Kerensky government, they have kicked the Bolsheviki out.

November 16

I went out to our Petchersky plant this morning and found nothing disturbed. A few of the soldier workmen were around, loafing, and said that Engineer Ivanov had not shown up since the trouble began. They also wanted double the pay they had been receiving. They were supposed to be commandeered to us without pay, but we had offered them a couple of rubles a day as additional incentive. It looks as if it will take a lot of rubles to furnish any incentive now.

The adjoining barracks are full of soldiers who have lost all discipline. The Bolshevik ideas are in the air. They lie asleep all morning and then appear in a wildly dishevelled state when food time comes, chasing around madly after each other in all sorts of pranks like school children, shouting and singing at the tops of their voices. It is rowdyism run mad. It makes the progress of work on our "hut" look doubtful, and the good it can accomplish looks doubtful too. But the only thing I can see to do is to carry on as long as possible unless ordered to do otherwise, and live in hopes of change.

Kirichenko came around today bringing Mr. Chapkovsky, a Ukrainian, who is in a rather influential position with the Ukrainian Government and thinks he can secure from them all the recognition and privileges that we enjoyed from the Kerensky Government, and more.

Carpenter also called in today. The Artillery School suffered during the troubles, naturally, being an important military spot. His plans are all shot to pieces, as he is up against the same problem we are of not being able to keep men on the job at the old wages. He has got to establish relations with the Ukrainian Government just as we have.

November 18

Restaurants and banks are still closed. A few stores are open, but food is scarce. Lack of telegraph service still leaves us in the dark as to what is happening in the outside world.

Emily and I watched the Bolshevik funeral procession this afternoon. There were about fourteen coffins—the extent of the fatalities during the recent fighting. Here in Kiev it was not the tremendous event that the March procession was in Petrograd last spring by any means, but in some ways it was more darksome and threatening. It was more distinctly a class threat. The banners are more threatening. The workers look more bitter and desperate. They show more boldness. The Bolshevik ideas have sunk into their system, and there is no restraining force to check their mad course.

Trouble is undoubtedly brewing between the Ukrainians and the Bolsheviki. The latter have withdrawn to the edge of the city where they have formed an encampment under arms. Meanwhile we can be sure they are doing everything possible to establish connections with the Bolshevik world on the outside.

I have to begin all over again the long weary grind of procuring proper governmental status and permissions and have been writing out the requisition requests to be submitted to the Ukrainian Government. Will have to move fast to hold the two huts we already possess, let alone securing new sites. I have hopes that now that there is only one government and one power in Kiev, we shall not have so many complications in getting things done as in the past.

November 23

A new secretary arrived from America today, Mr. Atherton, fresh from the horrors of Moscow. Their whole party arrived in Moscow just in time to go through the terrible Bolshevik uprising, and Atherton rushed into the story at once. For hours we have been listening to tales that would make your hair stand on end.

From the first rousing march of the 10,000 Bolshevik soldiers down the streets of Moscow, singing their wonderful Russian songs, to the fall of the Kremlin and the surrender and execution of the last remnants of the White Guard, the whole tragedy was one succession of excitement.

Atherton said that Bolsheviki stood in plain view on street corners shooting down every white-collared person who came into view. It was death for persons of bourgeois appearance to show themselves. The house where the secretaries were staying was in the center of fighting, and windows, doors, walls, and ceilings were smashed by cannon, machine-gun, and rifle firing. Luckily none of the secretaries were killed, but there were plenty of narrow escapes.

Scores of buildings about the city were gutted by fire and nothing but the brick or stone skeletons left standing. The Hotel Metropole was a dismal ruin. All along the main streets the outsides of the buildings were peppered full of holes from the machine-gun fire. The streets were full of broken glass and ruins. Four or five thousand people were killed during the fighting, many of them peaceable citizens, women and children.

Looting and rioting became terrible during the fight. Wine-cellars were broken into and the streets were full of drunken people, madly using their firearms at anybody and anything. The anarchists took advantage of the situation to proceed their

own sweet way with as much looting and killing as they wished.
Kiev was as quiet as a Methodist Sunday in comparison.

Already the rift between the Bolsheviki and the Ukrainians
is taking form here. To begin with, the Ukrainians have always
depended for the supply of rubles upon Petrograd. No more
rubles will be sent from Petrograd until the Ukrainians come to
terms with Lenin and Trotsky. Our splendid Russian-Asiatic
Bank, with all its modern paraphernalia and pneumatic tubes,
has already announced that it cannot cash checks. I have some
twenty-five thousand rubles of Association money there on
deposit but can only draw up to 1,000 rubles on any one day.
It takes two or three hours to go through the process even when
given special privileges by the cashier and served out of turn.
But believe me, I'll be on the job every day until the money is
all out. The trouble is, the banks are taking to declaring extra
holidays whenever they please to conserve cash. Yesterday was a
holiday in celebration of the Ukrainian Republic.

A large parade was held, and the new Ukrainian army made
its bow to the public. It is a husky, well-drilled army, making a
much more respectable appearance than the regular Russian
army, and showing much more pep and enthusiasm. In fact the
spirit was more like the March days of the revolution than
anything I have seen since.

The same day that we were celebrating the Ukrainian
Republic, we got news that Lenin and Trotsky had issued an
"armistice" or *"peremiriye"* with Germany and her Allies.

I forgot to mention that the banks offer to pay with Loan
of Freedom bonds in place of rubles, but nothing doing. I have
one 300 ruble bond which I personally subscribed in the early
days of revolutionary fervor, paying 83 perfectly good American
dollars for it. It is resting in the vaults of the Siberian Bank at
Petrograd. According to the newspapers just received, the Bolsheviki announce that that money doesn't belong to the capitalists but to the people. They have already sent one guard
around to the bank and withdrawn 10,000,000 rubles.

The newspapers announce that Ambassador Francis is
arranging for transportation for the 200 Americans to return
to America. Emily naturally doesn't care to pass up such a

chance, and we are planning to attach ourselves to the procession. Meanwhile we don't know when it will occur or any other details and will sit tight until we hear further.

The work on the big Petchersky hut has been sadly demoralized. I had to make several trips out there before finding Engineer Ivanov. The procuring of such necessary supplies as nails, iron, pipe, electrical supplies, furniture, dishes, etc., is becoming a terrific task. You have to search the city, picking up a bit here and a bit there at the most outrageous prices, and never getting enough. And the labor problem has become ridiculous. They want as much per hour now as they did per day before the Bolshevik revolution. Soldiers can no longer be commandeered without pay. They want more pay than anybody else, whether they know the kind of work they are expected to do or not. With their greatly increased wages they do not work half the hours nor produce half so much per hour as before. If we get the hut ready by Christmas, we'll do well.

Leonard is back again. Every time he makes the trip he shows up with a heavier layer of dirt. Traveling is becoming impossible. This time he came by boat, which is not quite so crowded as the train. But everything is more crowded than a while back. Soldiers everywhere, drifting back from the front, without order, without leaders, without money, without any aim except to get back to their homes. Floods of those brownish gray uniforms keep ebbing through the city, through the railroad yards, through the streets, backwashing into the stores, the theaters, into the streetcars, but most of all do the trains suffer. The railroads are the channels, the center of the stream, where they pour like an ever increasing resistless torrent. The current sweeps all before it. Ordinary citizens have ceased to travel. On the railroads, law and order have vanished. Authority is not recognized. The mob rule of the soldiers is supreme.

November 25

The Russian situation keeps developing at a dizzy pace. Lenin and Trotsky have notified the Commander in Chief of the Russian armies, Dukhonin, that he is dismissed and that he is to turn over his post to the new Commander, Krilenko, whom the Bolsheviki have raised from the ranks to head the Russian armies.

All this means, of course, that Lenin and Trotsky are bent on just one thing, to smash the old Russian army just as speedily as possible, and the more rapidly they can destroy all basis of discipline and authority, the quicker will their aim be accomplished.

General Dukhonin has received a note from the Allied powers urging him to stand firm, keep the armies to their task, and resist the orders of the Bolsheviki. He is stationed at Mogilev, half way between here and Petrograd, east of Minsk.

Meanwhile the Ukraine looms up as the one semi-quiet place in all the Russian Empire; the one place of comparative law and order; the one section of the land that remains true to the cause of the Allies. The Ukrainian Rada has declared its refusal to submit to the orders of the Soviet. All Ukrainian soldiers have been ordered to remain in the fight regardless of what orders are issued by the Soviet authorities.

Meanwhile there is one sure spot of safety to which we can tie, and that is the Czechoslovak army. We feel safer with them nearby than we could feel anywhere else in Russia. They are absolutely solid for the Allies and are ready to stand together to the last man.

Today Miller and Leonard were with us at the Sophiesky and Vladimir Churches. The charm of these sacred spots is all the greater by contrast with the political upheavals and chaos abroad in the land. The mysterious beauty of this sacred Kiev in these beautiful sunlit autumn days draws added glory from the very blackness of the background. Yet Kiev was ever thus. In the very times when these oldest churches were in the building, the history of Kiev was one succession of uprisings and alarms, usurpations and changing rulers. It seems to be in the blood of these vivacious southern Russians to be capable of great artistic expression in the midst of wars and rumors of wars.

Thanksgiving Day, November 29

Day before yesterday we connected up with a young Russian Jew who has returned to Kiev from America. He left Russia a good many years ago—though he is still a young man—a red hot revolutionist against the Czar's government. He was a dyed-in-the-wool socialist when he went to America. After the March revolution he returned to Russia still a socialist, though a milder one, to enjoy the revolutionist's paradise. Now all of his socialism is gone. He has no use for these Bolshevik theories. He is sick at heart to see Russia falling into chaos and ruin at the mercy of her Bolshevik leaders. He longs to be back in America. But there is no chance to get out of the country. He has used up most of the savings he laid up in America. He can find no occupation in which to use his engineering talents except in the army, and of course there is no place in the army now except for Bolsheviki.

Krizhanovsky—that is his name—has one passion now, and that is gratitude to America. He has offered his services free in doing night work at our hut at Druzhina 759 as an expression of this gratitude. His offer comes at a handy time, as I had to let Constantine Vladimirovitch go Monday. Constantine was a brilliant genius, but he had the unfortunate habit of mixing personal and Association funds. Rather, I think, he had no personal funds and used Association funds in their absence. At last the climax came when he lost 1,000 rubles of Association money at cards. Of course, he did not admit this, but he could neither produce nor account for the sum, though he was confident and assured me that the money would turn up. I had to notify him that when he brought in the money, I would be ready to talk with him again, but until then, his services were no longer necessary. I suppose he thinks he is abused by the Y.M.C.A. and not treated leniently enough, as too often in his circles the only money obligations that are matters of high honor are gambling debts.

The work at the Druzhina has suffered since the local revolution, partly because Constantine had lost his interest in it, and partly because of the greatly increased confusion in the army. This regiment has, of course, become a Ukrainian regiment, and the Bolsheviki in the gully have packed up and joined their brethren in the camp outside of the city. The same soldiers who belonged to the regiment before, when it was a Russian regiment upholding the Kerensky regime, are now enrolled as Ukrainian soldiers in the Ukrainian regiment. Those soldiers who objected were given permission to go home. But to most of the soldiers it is a matter of indifference whether they are fighting for Kerensky or for the Ukraine. The only soldiers who know what they are fighting for and feel a cause are the Bolsheviki and the real Ukrainian soldiers. Most of the men in the 759th Regiment are Russian peasants.

Work at the Petchersky hut languishes. It is rumored that the Ukrainians are going to occupy it. I have been following up my effort to establish relations with the Ukrainian Government but so far without further results than that Petlura has referred our case to the Ukrainian Educational-Cultural Committee and the Staff. Trussov is of course out of luck now, as he has no use for the Ukrainians or the Ukrainian movement, and they have no use for him. "I could weep for my country, Mr. Heald," says Mr. Trussov, and I fear that is all that many well-born Russians are doing these days. Instead of getting together and laying definite practical plans, and fighting, they resign themselves to the situation as an act of Divine Providence—which no doubt it is—but which is really a challenge to them to forsake the old ways and adopt new ways.

I met Professor Masaryk today at the Czech headquarters. You feel the wonderful spirit of the man from the first moment you meet him, quiet, refined, cultured, kindly, but with a reserve force which conceals untold power and determination. He speaks English with a beautiful fluency. I don't know when I have been more impressed with a man. I have no fears for the Czechoslovak nation as long as he lives.

December 2

I called upon Professor Masaryk Friday afternoon for an interview regarding the general situation. He was staying with Czech friends at modest apartments in an out-of-the-way part of the

city. I was surprised how readily he remembered my name and
organization from the brief introduction of the preceding day
when he had been meeting so many.

For a half hour we chatted alone. Professor Masaryk is
master of the art of making you feel that you and your problems
are the only concern in the world for him while you are with
him. I have no doubt but that hundreds of other matters were
pressing him for action and decision, but not a sign of it appeared
during that half hour.

I asked Professor Masaryk what he thought of the outlook
in the Ukraine. He regarded it as quite desperate. Germany and
Austria were doing everything in their power to line up the
Ukrainian Government on their side. The Allies were doing very
little to meet the situation. Most of those in the Ukrainian Government sympathized with the Central Powers, though they were
still keeping the appearance of neutrality or even faithfulness
to the Allies. Several members of the Ukrainian Rada and
Cabinet were loyal Allied supporters, among them being Petlura,
the Commander of the Army. As long as there was any possibility of the Allies turning their attention to the Ukraine and
rendering assistance, it was worthwhile to nurse the situation
along. The greatest need was to offset the widespread enemy
propaganda with some healthy propaganda for the Allies.

This interview with Professor Masaryk confirmed me in the
pessimism with which I have viewed the Ukrainian situation
if left to itself, as it has been so far, without more active help
financially and militarily from the Allies. I have written to the
Moscow office today giving my conviction that the outlook is
hopeless.

I have been busy packing goods for Miller and Atherton the
past two days helping them get their outfits ready for their first
huts with the Czechoslovak soldiers. Miller has ransacked the
city for books and gotten a really good library together. I was
lucky enough to run onto a dozen folding cot outfits at the shop
of a German near the Imperial Hotel. These will come in handy
for our secretaries as they can be easily carried around like a
handgrip.

We visited the Mogilevskys this afternoon. Mogilevsky, an

artillery officer, was visiting from the front. He said that three-fourths of the soldiers on his section of the front were now Bolsheviki. All order was gone. The officers were helpless. There was no fodder for the horses which were dying in masses daily. Horses could not be given away. The soldiers were flooding back from the front, and soon no front would be left except the Bolsheviki, who will then be in a position to have their own way—peace with Germany. Their aim now is to get all the loyal soldiers and officers away from the front.

The Siberians have come out with a declaration of independence. Siberian troops have passed through Kiev fluttering their green and white flags. The Siberian soldiers are husky, fine-looking fellows, with a more intelligent bearing and peppier walk than the other Russians.

December 3

I was fortunate enough to get an interview with V. V. Schulgin, editor of the *Kievlyanin*, today. The *Kievlyanin* is the independent newspaper of Kiev. It speaks its opinions boldly, attacking Bolsheviki and Ukrainians with equal impartiality. Schulgin has already been arrested a time or two, the newspaper plant has been closed more than once, copies of various issues have been confiscated, but still the paper comes out and has a prestige that the popularity-seeking *Novosti* and *Misl* do not enjoy.

Schulgin was one of the three members of the Duma who stayed with the Czar on that last night when he abdicated on his train. While utterly opposed to extreme revolutionary tendencies, such as rule at present, Schulgin is liberal and progressive in his political views.

With this background of knowledge of the man, I was surprised by his appearance when I was ushered into his room. I had expected to find a rugged, long-bearded, heavy-framed, fighting style of person. Instead I met a tall, elegantly dressed, beautifully manicured, poetic kind of personality. I could not get over the feeling that I was talking with Mr. Schulgin's secretary rather than with Mr. Schulgin himself.

When he talked with me, I had the feeling he had America

in mind and that he was trying to interpret the situation to me as he would have interpreted it to America.

First he pulled out a volume from his large library entitled *The Hapsburg Empire in 1918*. The maps accompanying the volume showed the Austro-Hungarian Empire stretching all over the Ukraine to the Black Sea. Kiev and Odessa were cities in the Hapsburg Empire. The book had been written just before the war. Schulgin pointed out how clearly this book convicted the Central Powers of aims of conquest in bringing on the war. The book had been published in Vienna. The Ukraine had always been a pet dream of conquest on the part of Vienna. There was a certain kinship between Kiev and Vienna. They were similar kinds of cities with similar kinds of peoples. A part of the Ukrainian people lived in the Austro-Hungarian Empire. The present Ukrainian Republic was simply a clever Vienna plan for bringing this union into accomplishment. Vinichenko and the other leaders in the Ukrainian movement were Austrian agents, pure and simple, who had lived in Vienna before the war and who had much more in common with Austria than with Russia.

From the Hapsburg Empire in 1918, Mr. Schulgin turned to the new Russia on the Don, the Russia of Kaledin. Kaledin* was now the hope of Russia. The Ukraine, even if a miracle should keep it loyal to Russia, was too weak to stand alone. Kaledin was strong. The Ukraine would stand or fall for Russia according to the fate of Kaledin. Negotiations were underway now looking to a union of the Don Basin movement and the Ukraine. If Kaledin proved successful, it might hold the Ukrainian movement to Russia. If Kaledin failed, all would be for Austria in the Ukraine.

The new Don movement was the most important link in a chain of new transportation routes from Vladivostok to the southwestern front. If the Ukraine was to remain true to the Allies, then this line of communications through the Don country, the Orenburg Cossacks, and the Siberian Cossacks to Vladivostok was the only line through which Allied supplies could be brought to the southwestern and Roumanian fronts. A deadline

---

* Ataman of the Don Cossacks.

was being established beyond which no bread, fuel, or supplies would be allowed to go to the aid of the Bolsheviki. Southern Russia was the granary, workshop, and fuel basin of Russia. The north could not survive if the south were cut off from them. Thousands would undoubtedly die in the north and the suffering would be terrible. But it was war, and hard things must be done in war. "A million patriots who would preserve Russia's honor are even now under arms to preserve this new front," said Mr. Schulgin.

Mr. Schulgin turned his attention for a moment to the relations of Russia with the rest of the Allies. "The Allies have announced that Russia will be at war with them if Russia concludes peace with Germany. There is already a partial truce on the front. The Bolsheviki are arresting the delegates elected to the Constituent Assembly. Russia's only hope is in overthrowing the Bolsheviki."

On my inquiring as to what he thought our organization could do, he advised me to see General Dragomirov, to whom he gave me a card of introduction, and who was the chief leader of the Great Russian party in Kiev. Mr. Schulgin thought the best thing was for our secretaries to go to the Don country and help with the Kaledin forces, which were the only dependable Allied forces left in Russia. Thus were my own feelings of the uselessness of our work in the Ukraine and especially in Bolshevik Russia confirmed.

I had another session with the Cultural-Educational Committee of the Ukrainian Rada today, and our work is ready for presentation to the secretariat of the Rada. What the Cultural-Educational Committee want of us is to act as a Ukrainizing agency. They want us to act as one of the bureaus of their department, carrying out their orders, helping with their propaganda, all of which, of course, I have had to tell them we could not do.

December 4

The commandant of the fortress informed me today that we cannot hold our Petchersky plant. My permissions from the Kerensky Government and General Oberutchev were no longer valid. Only Ukrainian permissions counted. They needed all barrack space in the city for additional garrison forces which would be stationed in Kiev during the winter. There would be 60,000 soldiers quartered here, and there were only accommodations for 40,000.

When I returned to the apartments figuring out that our job was ended here, I found a visitor by the good American name of "Pershing"—an odd little man, with a very brotherly and sympathetic manner, and a master of many languages. He was an artist. He was head of the Art Bureau of the Cultural-Educational Committee of the new Ukrainian Government. One of his commissions was to draw up designs for the new spring uniforms for the "wonderful Ukrainian army which was springing to arms out of the ruins of the old Russian army and would go marching triumphantly to the Black Sea and to Constantinople in the spring, and bring back the City of the Czars (Constantinople) to its proper place as the Mother City of Russia."

Mr. Pershing—and he delighted to repeat this name, and to dwell upon its appropriateness, since the commander of the American army bore the same name—had come around to help develop stronger ties between the Americans and the Ukrainians. I, as the American representative in Kiev, had an unusual opportunity to improve those relationships. The Ukraine was very receptive to American ideas. I could be of service in helping them to adopt approved democratic ideas. I could inform them about America, America's customs, and American traditions. And it would be a great thing if America would send an army and money over to the Ukraine. That would help to clinch the Ukraine for the Allies.

I replied that I couldn't enthuse very much about American assistance for the Ukraine when the Ukrainian Government was thrusting us out of barracks which we had fitted up at much expense to serve their soldiers. Mr. Pershing expressed great surprise that such action had been taken and said it would be the easiest thing in the world to fix that matter up and hold the barracks for our use. He was a close friend of the commander of the Ukrainian army, Pavlenko, and if I would go along with him, we could get the matter straightened out immediately.

While puzzled as to the standing of Pershing with Commander Pavlenko, I was in the mood that I didn't care much what happened. We went out to the same quarters where I had interviewed General Oberutchev a couple of months earlier. There was even more style, paging, and waiting than before. Mr. Pershing's introduction worked, and we were ushered in to where General Pavlenko sat behind his big elegant table. He was a splendidly built, handsome man in the prime of life, immaculately dressed, and manicured. He was very cordial and affable in his greeting. Within a few moments he had issued an order holding the Petchersky hut as ours. So Pershing had turned the trick.

On the way back to the apartments, Pershing informed me that before the revolution he had been a tutor in the Czar's household for years under an entirely different name, of course. He was with the Czar's family until just a few weeks ago. But he was now a devoted Ukrainian and democrat and republican and, if need be, a socialist. And he went on to tell anecdotes by the yard about the Czar's family. He had a special sympathy for the young Czarevitch. Meanwhile I marvelled at this Alice-in-Wonderland time in Russia when the artist-tutor of the Czar's household was seeking a berth with the Y.M.C.A. to better finance himself in his honorable post as Official Artist of the Republic of the Ukraine until the Republic should be able to make enough of its own money to pay its public servants. For this new Republic, cut off from Petrograd, threatened with war by Lenin and Trotsky, had no funds at its disposal, and it would still be a few weeks before the new government money printing presses would begin to turn out the new Ukrainian currency.

This evening brings reports that the Bolsheviki are moving an army on Kiev. It is also reported that General Dukhonin has been killed while defending the headquarters from the Bolshevik forces under Krilenko.

December 5

Today I had an interview with General Dragomirov, to whom Editor Schulgin had given me an introduction. I found him in splendid apartments on Tereschenskaya Street overlooking an attractive park on the opposite side of the street. There was the air of repose, refinement, culture, and beauty that I had found in Petrograd palaces before the revolution, but which one so seldom meets with in these turbulent times.

General Dragomirov bounced into the room with a smiling, optimistic, energetic, enthusiastic personality that was housed in a short, square, but flexible, little body. I liked him from the start. He drew an enthusiastic picture of the Kaledin Cossacks on the Don. He made no bones about being a monarchist, but a constitutional monarchist. The Kaledinites were constitutional monarchists. Nothing but monarchy and a strong hand could save Russia. "We are trying to negotiate with the Ukrainian Government, though we mistrust their aims," said the general. "We are trying to bring them and the Don country into union. The *Kievlyanin* is the only paper in Kiev that will print the truth. Keep some of your secretaries here in Kiev but send most of them to Rostov. We will give them every introduction and permission they need among the forces there."

Artist Pershing was on hand again today with further details of the Ukrainian plans for a big army and their plans for capturing Constantinople in the spring. He brought along his designs for the uniforms to add to my conviction concerning the conquests this army had in store. He said they were too strong already to have any more fear of the Bolsheviki. "You know, Mr. Heald, that the Ukrainians are a very crafty people," he said.

December 9

We have been having an official merry-go-round with the Petchersky plant. After securing the order from Commander Pavlenko commandeering it to us, Commandant Zizinovitch, who is a Great Russian and not a Ukrainian, rose on his dignity and refused to let us have it. Upon that, General Pavlenko, deciding that discretion was the better part of valor, backed water.

I tried to get an interview with Petlura regarding the matter, but he has his own worries with the advancing Bolsheviki, and I could not get to him. I consulted Professor Maxa, the Czech leader, and he thought Schulgin would be the best man to help us out with Zizinovitch.

On the following day, Friday, I met with the Ukrainian Cultural-Educational Committee and informed them that we would proceed no further until we had Zizinovitch's O.K. I have stopped all work on the Petchersky plant pending the solution of the problem. Zizinovitch was around yesterday as if nothing had happened and asked us if we could build beds for the soldiers in our Petchersky plant. I had to admire his nerve but replied that the equipment of army barracks lay outside our province.

Leonard is back from the front, dirtier than ever this trip. He says, disgustedly, that it is his last trip. Things are getting worse daily. His huts and equipment are scattered all around the country, owing to the shifting movements of the troops. He would no sooner order his equipment moved to one point, than the troops would be on the move to some other point before the equipment arrived. It was a hopeless case of trying to catch the army.

Outside events keep moving ever more swiftly to some unknown goal. After a couple of days of reports that Trotsky had called off negotiations for a truce, recalling the Russian delegates from Brest-Litovsk because the Germans would not discuss peace terms, but military measures only, and were demanding that Russia withdraw from all occupied territories, today the report is that Trotsky has concluded an armistice with the Germans to last from December 7 to December 30, and capable of being terminated after that on a three-day notice. Trotsky tried to get the Germans to agree not to send any of their army from the Russian front to the French front, but they refused to agree to it. In fact, the truce is all one-sided for Germany, they adopting the attitude of conquerors.

December 14

Last night the Bolsheviki, who have been staying encamped on the outskirts of the city, were disarmed as they slept by the forces of the Ukrainian Government, and hustled bag and baggage out of the vicinity. Not a person was killed.

Today the Bolshevik workingmen who are left in the city are threatening a general strike by way of retaliation. Nothing but war can be expected from Lenin and Trotsky now. A front already exists between here and Moscow. We can no longer depend upon the trusty Kirichenko Baptists as couriers as they would be suspected of being spies in Bolshevik territory, wearing as they do the Ukrainian uniform. So we will have to depend upon Americans, British, or other chance foreigners, to act as couriers until this trouble ends. Leonard left tonight for Moscow to discuss plans and get money.

Before this new complication arose, our Petchersky hut was returned to us. Our engineer and workingmen are again on the job, and we hope to open next week.

The American film, "Battle Cry of Peace," is showing in the Kiev movie houses. It has been widely advertised and is certainly fine propaganda. It gave us a thrill to go down and see this first glimpse of America in the war.

Artist Pershing has brought around one of his Russian friends, Maievsky, a publisher, who wants to bring out a book about America and offers the Y.M.C.A. the privilege of paying the cost of publishing the book. Much of my time seems to be occupied these days in politely declining similar opportunities. This Maievsky lived in America nine years.

December 16

The Bolsheviki called off their general strike last night. It was a fizzle. The different socialist and workingmen's factions could not agree among themselves. The Rada has won out. We can breathe easily again after only one day of no newspapers (except the *Kievlyanin*), no tram service, no waiters at the restaurants and dining halls.

The Bolsheviki are now to be ousted from the local Soviet.

The Kiev Soviet has been largely Menshevik. The president has been Menshevik. Now it will become entirely Menshevik or anti-Bolshevik.

The banks have drawn in tighter than ever on their reserves, with the prospects of money from Petrograd growing less, and the date when the new Ukraine currency will appear gradually postponed. I could only draw 100 rubles from my account today. At this rate I can not draw nearly enough to meet the expenses of getting the hut into readiness. The *Gosudarst-venny Bank* (State Bank) had to quit cashing checks at all, and a big line of depositors was turned away disappointed.

Dr. Alois B. Koukol, Secretary of the Slavonic Immigrant Society of New York and representative of the Bohemian National Alliance of the United States, arrived in the city yesterday. We had dinner with him and Dr. Goutchov at the Grand today. Through Dr. Koukol's assistance I am negotiating a loan from the Czech headquarters here in Kiev which will give me a few thousand rubles to tide me over temporarily.

December 20

Mr. Jenkins, formerly American Consul at Riga, arrived today to investigate and report. Emily and I lunched with him this noon, and he had tea with us this evening. He explained why America could not move as fast as England, France, and other countries in recognizing the Ukrainian Republic. Congress had to do too much talking. It will place Mr. Jenkins in an embarrassing position as the chief interest of the Ukrainians in America now is to secure our recognition and financial support.

He has come just in time to relieve me of increasing diplomatic embarrassments by virtue of being the only American in Kiev. Monday I received a visit at our apartments from a member of the Ukrainian Rada. He was a *chinovnik* (official) of the old regime who now had a berth with his socialistic and democratic fellows in the new republic. He was a sleek, smooth, oily-tongued, young man dressed in black. His proposition was that it would be timely for America to begin a counter-propaganda program to offset the propaganda of the Central Powers. He seemed to be afraid to go into details at our apartments, fearing that there might be eavesdroppers among the Polish people living there, the Poles being hostile to the Ukrainians. I told him that his proposition had no interest to me or to our organization, but he wanted to give me more information, and so I made an appointment to meet him in the Cafe Maxime the following night.

We met there as agreed and sat at one of the little tables where we talked while we sipped tea and chocolate. The large cafe was crowded with people, many of whom were evidently businessmen or politicians meeting for business like ourselves; others were simply couples meeting before the theater or after the movies for a social tea. I suppose my *chinovnik* friend would derive some political advantage from being seen by his friends in company with an American. It would lend color to any schemes he might be going to them with.

Proceeding to the subject he said that perhaps not more than five or ten percent of the members of the Little Rada were actually in Austrian pay, but this five or ten percent were the ablest and most intelligent members and able to swing the rest. In the Central Rada, or cabinet, all except two of the members were favorable to the Central Powers. The two exceptions were Petlura, the Minister of War, and Schulgin, the Minister of Foreign Affairs. Vinichenko, the President, and Grushevsky, the Vice-President, were in the regular employ of Vienna, who paid their salaries.

He explained the German-Austrian propaganda in the newspapers, showing how much of the space was filled with simply this propaganda, and explained how it came from Berlin, Department "E." He told of the close connection between the members of the Central Rada and the German-Austrian delegation at Brest-Litovsk, which was at that time negotiating with the Bolsheviki. As an instance of the German-Austrian spy work, he cited one military commission which was ostensibly an Allied commission but which was made up, he said, ninety percent of German and Austrian spies.

He said that the only reason the Ukrainian Government

leaned Austria's way was that Austria was financing it. If America would offer higher financing than Austria, then the Ukraine would be pro-American. Every month or so Austria was sending ten or fifteen million rubles to keep the Ukrainian ship of state going. Let America bid this up a little and the Ukraine would be a strong Allied supporter. Naturally I thought this the limit in nation-building, and whatever faith I had previously had in the integrity of the Ukrainian Government disappeared. I had wondered at the apparent prosperity of the Ukrainian headquarters, at the mass of clerks and typewriters, and at the rich furnishing of rooms and automobiles. The *chinovnik's* explanation seemed plausible.

The information of the *chinovnik* agreed with an interview I had again with General Dragomirov, the President of the Great Russian Party yesterday. He said that Petlura could be depended upon by the Allies, and that if the Allies could bring sufficient pressure to bear, in the way of financial assistance and armed forces, he was convinced that the Ukrainian movement could be changed from one dominated by Austrian and German influences to one in favor of the Allies. He was expecting an internal revolution in the Ukrainian movement and hoping that Vinichenko and Grushevsky would be forced out by anti-German and anti-Austrian influences.

General Dragomirov is himself holding regular public meetings to encourage the anti-German-Austrian party among the Ukrainians. Professor Masaryk has also been holding such meetings. At a time when Kiev is flooded with German and Austrian spies, he has the courage to come out in the open and flatly announce that the Czechs are going to keep up the fight with the Allies until the Hapsburgs are overthrown. His meetings have drawn increasing crowds, and the public support of the Allies seems to be growing.

Our courier returned from Moscow Monday with my over-coat and 15,000 rubles. The money comes in handy as the banks are getting tighter every day and 500 rubles is the most I can draw any one day. The courier said he had trouble getting past the frontier and didn't care to try to repeat the attempt.

A money crisis is on. The bank made a special exception in my case again and let me have 250 rubles. Russians are only drawing 100 rubles daily. Of course I did not deposit the last 17,000 rubles which I received from Moscow. Before it came I was having my troubles with the carpenters, electricians, and other workingmen at the Petchersky hut, as I was unable to draw enough money at the bank to meet the weekly payroll. I had just reached the end of my rope with them when the Moscow money saved the day.

Meanwhile the hut at Druzhina 759 keeps open right along, serving 400 or 500 men nightly. Our Russian-Jewish-American friend, Krizhanovsky, found it impossible to make the hut regularly on account of the long distance clear across this widespread city. I am accordingly engaging Tcherkassky, a young fellow who saw service on the Belgian front in the early part of the war and received wounds there which incapacitated him for further active military duty.

In addition to our Petchersky troubles, we are having a mix-up on the shipment of equipment out to Miller for the Czechs. He completed his tour quickly and found everything ripe to begin Association work at once. We have been working day and night to get ready 24 boxes of stuff to send out to him. The biggest job is to land an empty freight car to send it out in. One of the Czechs, Sokol, who has an inside track on such matters, after reconnoitering for several days along the railroad tracks and following up leads with the switchmen, engineers, and officials higher up, assured us that he had a car spotted. He designated the spot to which we were to haul the boxes in the railroad yards. So yesterday morning off we started with three wagon loads of the stuff, five miles across the city to the spot agreed upon. Sokol didn't show up. In no way could we get a line on an empty car. I finally had to leave the 24 boxes lying in the snow, arranging for two Czechs to stand guard, armed to the teeth. Otherwise the ceaseless flow of starving, desperate soldiers and deserters flooding back from the front would have made away with every stick of the stuff within a few hours.

Sokol showed up today, and we now have things lined up for getting the things off tomorrow. They ought to reach Miller Christmas Eve if all goes well.

I talked with a captain of the Death Battalion, whom I met at the home of a dealer in movie outfits with whom I have become acquainted. He was direct from the Minsk front. He had come by foot the whole 500 miles. He and all the other members of the Death Battalion were being hunted down by the Bolsheviki like wild beasts and instantly put to death whenever detected. His officer's epaulets had been snatched from his shoulders by the soldiers. The front was gone. The soldiers were without leaders and converted into bands of pillagers and murderers. The Germans were 100 versts in the rear of where the front had been, selling their wares in Russian territory. Minsk was in German hands, and their forces were moving in. Soon Kiev would be in their hands. The one hope this Death Battalion man had for Russia was that America would still respond and send over an army. It is the only hope I have had, but I fear it is too late.

The German hand looms ever larger. The spy atmosphere in Kiev grows ever darker and more oppressive. It begins to feel like the days of the old regime in Petrograd with all the charm of music, art, literature, and beautiful clean things left out. Meanwhile the iron ring of the Bolsheviki draws nearer.

🦾 *Unfortunately, Heald's diary and his letters covering the period from January 1 to May 6, 1918 were lost. During this interval we have only three rather uninformative letters, one from Edward to his father-in-law, devoted chiefly to thanking him for a Christmas present, and two from Emily to her brother and sister. There are several written to Edward by other Y.M.C.A. secretaries in Russia.*

On February 1 Crawford Wheeler, in charge of the Y.M.C.A. program in Moscow, wrote to Heald instructing him to stay in Kiev as long as possible but to use his own judgment as to what was possible in an emergency. Wheeler's tone was surprisingly optimistic. The Association, he wrote, had "attained an entirely satisfactory standing with the present Bolshevik Government in

Petrograd" and was getting what it needed more quickly than under the old government. At this time fighting was taking place in Kiev. On February 5 Mrs. Heald wrote to her brother Charles Ainsworth describing some of the "excitement" and privations ("no bread, water, or electric light for two days"), but adding that "we are really very comfortably located." However, following the twelve-day battle for the city, which ended in victory for the Bolsheviki, Heald became convinced that his work could no longer be carried on in Kiev and that there would be no security for person or property there. Consul Jenkins and several Russian friends urged this view on him. In his report to the International Committee of the Y.M.C.A. he wrote: "To have attempted to place things on a wagon and take them from the hut to the town would simply have invited an attack from robbers." The ability of the Bolsheviki to restore order was questionable. Moreover, even if the situation could be brought under control, it was expected—correctly, as it proved—that the Germans, supported by Poles and Ukrainians, would attempt to drive out the Bolsheviki.

Since he could not remove the Y.M.C.A.'s property nor continue to administer it, Heald decided to turn it over to the Russian Baptist, Kirichenko, who would keep it operating as long as possible. The Healds left Kiev in mid-February, taking four days to reach Moscow. There they attended a Washington's Birthday party with a number of Y.M.C.A. people. They then spent two days with some of the other secretaries in Samara* and from there proceded by special train across Siberia to Vladivostok.† This journey, which should have taken eleven days by express or fifteen by "post," required twenty-six days.

They arrived on March 17. Exhausted though he must have been, Heald immediately began to write a report of events during the last days in Kiev. Written with his usual lucidity and excellent organization, it was completed the following day at

* Now Kuibyshev.
† The train was chartered by the International Harvester Company to get its employees out of Russia. Other Americans were invited to avail themselves of the opportunity to leave.

Vladivostok and submitted to Admiral Knight, who commanded the American naval forces there.

Extracts from Memorandum Submitted to Admiral Knight at Vladivostok, March 18, 1918
[Regarding conditions in the Ukraine]

The turning point of the situation came about December 20. Petlura resigned and his place was taken by Porsch, reputedly an Austrian agent. The Petchersky garrison with which we worked suddenly disappeared. The great majority of the soldiers received permits to go home for the holidays, and most of them never came back. There were normally 20,000 soldiers in the Petchersky garrison. When the Christmas holidays came, this dropped to 1,000.

The center of the Bolshevik efforts was at the arsenal. Looting and fights became more and more frequent, especially at night. The streets became increasingly unsafe after dark. Raiding of stores increased rapidly.

At one time the Rada forestalled a rising of the Bolsheviki by disarming the workers in the arsenal and certain Bolshevik troops. Meanwhile the Bolshevik armies from Great Russia were drawing near the city. At the end of January the arsenal workers succeeded in capturing arms from a neighboring regiment and started an uprising against the Rada. This began a twelve-day fight which ended with the capture of Kiev by the Bolsheviki.

During this fight the number killed is estimated at between two and nine thousand—I believe 5,000 would be conservative. The property damage was terrific, especially in the regions surrounding the arsenal for about a mile in every direction, which included the finest residence districts of the city. Following the battle I walked three miles through this region. Not only were all windows smashed, but practically every building had its walls and roofs smashed with shells, and in the region nearer the arsenal the destruction was so great that only the shells of the buildings were left standing. As I walked along the sidewalk I could look through to the back walls of the buildings. All wires were down. The bodies of dead Ukrainian soldiers and officers were still lying about the streets in advanced stages of decomposition, and the streets were piled with bricks, glass, mortar, empty shells, and cartridges.

One of the worst features of the whole affair was the shooting down of officers in cold blood by the Bolsheviki, during the two days following the fight. The morning that I made my tour of the city following the fight, two officers, gray-haired old men, who had come out of their quarters to see the ruins, were shot down just before I reached the spot.

The horror raised by these proceedings so incited the Mensheviki and the less radical socialist groups that these entered an energetic protest against the Bolsheviki in the Soviet meeting, accusing the Bolsheviki of being responsible for all these murders and demanding restoration of discipline. Their protests seemed to impress the Bolsheviki who immediately began to introduce discipline with an iron hand, shooting without trial any soldiers or civilians who shot officers without authority from the Soviet or even requisitioned automobiles or committed lootings without authority.

The Bolshevik army that captured Kiev was variously estimated at from 10,000 to 20,000 soldiers, most of whom came from Poltava and Kharkov. They were well equipped with ammunition, machine guns, and cannon. During the first week of the struggle, the Bolsheviki evidently underestimated the strength of the little remnant of a Ukrainian garrison and attempted to take the city with a small force of Red Guards. The Ukrainians succeeded in driving these out of the city after a week of stubborn fighting, the turning point coming when the Red Guards had progressed by hand-to-hand fighting through the city to the money printing plant where the Ukrainians were printing their new issue. At this point the Ukrainians took a stand and gradually drove them back out of the city.

Everybody thought that the battle was over and that the Ukrainians were victorious. Ukrainian processions, headed by bands and orchestras, marched through the streets celebrating the victory. Only a handful of Red Guards remained stationed at the depot with cannon, continuing to pepper the city, and refusing the entreaties of their Bolshevik brothers who had been captured by the Ukrainians to desist from the fight.

Suddenly the Bolsheviki reappeared with reinforcements and began a terrific cannonade of the city from four different quarters. The last two days the cannonading was constant, and the nights were wild nightmares. On the last night nobody in our house took off his clothes. The black night was lighted up with the flare of fires burning in many different quarters. Among the houses set on fire was the one occupied by Grushevsky, the Vice-President of the Ukrainian Republic.

The Ukrainians had been expecting reinforcements of Poles to aid them against the Bolsheviki. Reinforcements did not arrive until the last night of the fight, when the Ukrainians withdrew from the city in company with the Poles. Up to this time, the Polish elements in the city had been hostile to the Ukrainians, as they both claimed the same Galician territory as belonging to their respective nationalities.

The two main leaders of the Bolsheviki were General Muraviev and the commandant of the city. The commandant impressed me, in spite of his Russian name which I suspected of being assumed, as not being a real Russian, but as perhaps a German or Austrian prisoner of war who spoke Russian accurately, but still unlike the Russians. He was a man of unusual ability, firmness, and he exercised unlimited authority over the soldiers. I was in his office for three-quarters of an hour with the American Consul and four other consular representatives. We were all impressed with the strict measures of discipline which he was taking. The higher officials of the Bolsheviki seemed to take a friendly attitude towards the representatives of the Allies despite the fact that the British and French military authorities had been working in cooperation with the Ukrainian army preceding the hostilities.

The struggle between the Bolsheviki and the Ukrainians left this region of the country terribly disorganized. Ever since the Bolsheviki had declared war against the Ukraine, late in November, there had been no shipments of money from Petrograd or Moscow to the Ukraine. Provisions were plentiful up until the time of the fight. They completely disappeared from all markets and stores during the twelve days of fighting. Then the new orders of the Bolsheviki, reducing prices from 70 to 90 percent on milk, eggs, bread and butter, had the effect of discouraging the peasants from bringing anything into the city

On top of this, the Bolsheviki introduced thirty different orders affecting all sides of life—financial, domestic, political, and industrial—within the space of a couple of days. All of the revolutionary measures which they had had two or three months to introduce in Petrograd and Moscow, they sprang in a couple of days at Kiev. It simply turned things topsy-turvy, and no one knew where he stood.

A tax of ten million rubles was levied upon the capitalist class. The Ukrainian money, which had been issued to the extent of 47,000,000 rubles during the last three weeks, was declared null and void by the first financial order. The second financial order stated that all workingmen who had received the Ukrainian money and could produce factory certificates showing that it had been received by them for hard manual labor, could redeem it for the same amount in Russian rubles. Then all at once the Jews began buying up the Ukrainian money right and left, paying 400 to 500 rubles for every 1,000. The next day a new order was issued from Bolshevik head-quarters announcing that all Ukrainian money would be redeemed at its face value for Russian rubles. A few days later a further order levied a contribution of 47,000,000 rubles on the capitalist class to meet the expenses of this redemption.

The method of assessing the contribution was simple. The capitalists were divided into about fifteen main groups, such as bankers, streetcar companies, movie houses, railroads, merchants, manufacturers, etc. To each group was assigned a portion of the whole amount, with the threat that if the money was not delivered at Soviet headquarters by the date set, each and every member of that capitalist group would be under orders of arrest, his rooms would be searched, and he was liable to execution. The threat worked like a charm. The money was all delivered on the date set. There were twenty-five wealthy

Polish families living in the apartment house where we stayed. They sweat blood but came across.

Railroad transportation was terribly disorganized. No passenger service had been resumed with Moscow until we left. In order to get a place on the train, Mrs. Heald and I had to go out to the yards, seven miles from the station, where the train made up, and get on eighteen hours before it was due to start. Every window in the car was smashed, except one. The dirt had not been swept out for weeks. There was no heat, though the temperature was down close to zero.

We had six in our coupe meant for two. The corridor was so crowded with *tovarische* that my wife was unable to leave our coupe a single time during the four days and four nights between Kiev and Moscow. I was able to get out once and to get outdoors by going through the side window. The corridor was so filled with soldiers' luggage that the soldiers sitting on top of the baggage had to bend over in order to keep their heads from hitting the ceiling.

The conductor was not able to get to our coupe once during the whole trip, and the only time we even saw him was one time when he tapped on our window from the station platform and asked where we were going. So the fourth-class tickets which I had purchased in Kiev were unnecessary after all. I I believe no one else on the train had any tickets. I had purchased fourth-class because the Kiev newspapers had told of the Bolsheviki arresting the railroad commandant at Moscow for selling first- and second-class tickets. There was no longer to be any aristocracy of travel. All were to be served and treated alike hereafter, with the Red Guards having the privilege of ousting anybody who might be occupying seats they desired.

We met only one train proceeding in the direction of Kiev during the first three days on our way from Kiev to Moscow. The station agents in Kiev said that they had lost all control and that every train that came into the station was immediately seized by the soldiers who were returning from the front. The roofs of the cars of our train and the locomotive itself were covered with soldiers who clung to every inch of space even in that zero weather. Very few engines were in working order. The yards were full of broken-down locomotives and cars. The Russians call them "sick" cars and locomotives, and the sidetrack they occupy is the "hospital."

I have found the respect for Americans among all these people of the Ukraine practically universal. There is also a friendly feeling towards Germany and Austria among the rank and file of the people. Their real desire is to live at peace with Germany, America, and the Allies. If America were as close to the Ukraine as Germany, I believe that it would be more popular than Germany and would have greater influence, but Germany, being closer, so far commanded the situation.

The majority of the population has been looking for and desiring intervention by the Allies, especially by America, since the Bolshevik uprising last October. They have all along taken the position that the Ukraine, as well as other parts of Russia, was too weak itself to restore order without intervention and that intervention would have to come from the Allies or the Germans. If the Allies did not do it quick enough, the Germans and Austrians would.

🐾 *The memorandum of March 18 to Admiral Knight fills a part of the gap between January 1 and May 6, 1918. The "recollections" which follow provide additional information for this period. Although he wrote them twenty-five years later, Heald was not relying entirely on memory; his notes make clear that at least part of the material was supplied by a description of the Czechs at Vladivostok which he wrote in 1919.*

My wife and I took four days and four nights traveling from Kiev to Moscow, a trip that in normal times required but thirty-six hours. We had expected to continue out through Finland but were notified that the frontier was closed in that direction due to the German advance and the only way out was by way of Vladivostok. We learned that the Germans entered Kiev within a week after we left.

The International Harvester Company had arranged for

a train to take out their American representatives, and the
Y.M.C.A was invited to send out its representatives on the same
train. Mrs. Heald and I took advantage of this opportunity,
which left us a couple of days in Moscow. We did not have a
chance to visit the inside of the Kremlin, but saw it from the
outside and visited the Tretiakov Gallery which was open
and normal under the Bolshevik regime. We had a Washington's
Birthday party in Moscow on February 22 with secretaries
and a number of Russians present, among the latter being
Countess Tolstoy.

We had another two days at Samara, where there was quite
a gathering of Y.M.C.A. secretaries. A number of them went
out on the International Harvester train with us.

It took us 26 days of traveling from Kiev to Vladivostok,
which would take eleven days by express or fifteen by post under
normal conditions.

The entire country was under Bolshevik rule, except the
extreme eastern part of Siberia. Russian soldiers were flooding
back to their homes seizing any transportation they could.
Our engineer was helpless to carry out any orders except what
the soldiers gave him. At every sidetrack strings of freight
cars loaded with soldiers would be waiting. They would order
the engineer to attach their cars until the train was overloaded
and stopped from lack of engine power. Then there would
be some unhooking, the train would get going only to have the
experience repeated at the next siding.

At one station, in Russia, when night had fallen, there
was a sharp gun fight between the Red Guards and the peasant
soldiers, when the former tried to disarm the latter. We had to
lie on the floor of the train while the bullets whizzed through
the windows.

At another station, in Siberia, we were awakened with a
bump and crash as the train ground to a stop. Hurriedly dressing and going outside I overheard rough-looking Russian workingmen regretting that the plans to wreck the "Boorjwee"
hadn't succeeded. We were in the eastern part of Siberia where
some fierce civil war battles had been going on just previous to
our arrival. At Blagoveschensk the bitterest fight had taken

place, and the battle was barely over when we arrived. We felt the bitter spirit of the class struggle.

We saw many of the German prisoners of war. A considerable number of officers were taking advantage of the chaotic times to travel westward toward their homeland, but the great majority were staying put. Some prisoners with whom we talked didn't believe us when we told them America was in the war; they could believe in nothing but German victory.

On account of fighting between the civil war factions in Manchuria, we had to take the long new route around the Amur River way. The single-tracked railroad was so poorly ballasted that the swinging motion of the car made us seasick. After we had been traveling five days from Samara on the same car, we happened to look up at the head of our bed one morning to see it covered with bed bugs. By that time we had become accustomed to such experiences and the slaughter of the insects that followed was simply routine performance.

We arrived at Vladivostok on St. Patrick's Day and rejoiced to see the American flag flying over the U. S. Flagship *Brooklyn*, commanded by Admiral Knight. As soon as we could, we took a boat to Japan, arriving at Tsuruga after a 36-hour trip.

We were in Japan five weeks while I waited for instructions from our New York office. We improved the opportunity to see Japan in cherry blossom season from one end to the other. After the turmoil, dirt, noise, and disorder of Russia, we revelled in the quiet, beautiful, clean, orderly charm of Japan.

Finally I got my orders to return to Vladivostok and take charge of the army work for the Czechoslovak troops, who were speeding through from Kiev. They had made a treaty with the Bolsheviki at Penza allowing them to have transportation across Siberia on freight cars. They were to wait at Vladivostok until the Allies sent warships to take them to France where they were to join the Allied fighting forces. One of the conditions of the treaty with the Bolsheviki was that the Czechs had to surrender all their arms except thirty rifles to a battalion. Their request that an American Y.M.C.A. secretary accompany each regiment with a club car at his disposal was agreed to. The Y.M.C.A. arrangements were handled by Kenneth Miller, who was coming with the rear regiments and had already reached Cheliabinsk in western Siberia, where he had established a large supply depot with Czech helpers.

Emily did not go back to Vladivostok with me at first, but followed a few weeks later, and stayed until her boat sailed from Vladivostok, which happened to be our wedding anniversary, June 21.

Thus began the third phase of my experience in Russia and Siberia, the most thrilling, exhilarating, and rewarding phase of all, which gave me an undying admiration, respect, and affection for the heroic, hardy, and sturdy Czechoslovaks.

Vladivostok

Vladivostok
May 6, 1918

Dearest Emily*:

Here I am writing this letter in the home of your boat-acquaintances of a year ago, the Brynners. It is the beautiful stately mansion on Aleutskaya Street between the depot and Svyetlanskaya, the main street of Vladivostok, and looks right down over the bay. The Y.M.C.A. has two rooms reserved on the main floor, one large front room used at present for conferences and a smaller, but good, rear room for beds. The Brynners live downstairs. Our floor is occupied during the winter by the Maslinakovs, but they are at their *dacha*, or summer home, during this season of the year, and the apartments are rented to the Rassuschins, an Irkutsk family who took refuge here last winter when the Bolsheviki had their rumpus there. The Rassuschins were evidently prominent people in Irkutsk as their home there is now occupied by the French and Japanese Consulates. I had tea with them this afternoon, and they are pleasant people to meet.

Story† has gone to Harbin. He has come east as Colton's representative for Siberia, while Mr. Colton will continue for the present at Samara. We are in telegraphic communication with the latter. I found a letter from Story asking me to take charge of the work for the Czechs until Kenneth Miller arrives.

---

* All the letters to Mrs. Heald during the month of May were addressed to her in Japan.
† Professor Russell Story of Pomona College and E. T. Colton who had taken charge of Y.M.C.A. work in Russia.

Kenneth is coming along with the main body of the Czech troops. There are about 6,000 here already, and anywhere from 40,000 to 60,000 more are expected. They are coming through at passenger schedule speed, far more rapidly than anyone had anticipated. There are four other secretaries here already working with the Czechs: Noyes, Dewey, Bunker and Riley. Riley has had charge up until now, and I am asking him to keep charge of the field work.

Goodsell is in charge of the city Y.M.C.A. work here; and Long and Somerville, both of the Petrograd Mayak, are associated with him, as well as several Russian helpers who have come along with the general refugee movement.

May 8

The Czech soldiers are everywhere about the streets, their barracks being outside of the city at various points from a mile to four miles out. They wear the same uniforms as the Russians but are distinguished by the snappy way they salute and by the red and white ribbon on their hats, these being the Czech national colors. The Russian soldiers are scarce around here, and what few there are don't salute. The city of Vladivostok is the only city in the former Russian Empire not now in the possession of the Bolsheviki, unless you count Manchuria where the troops of Horvat and Semyenov* have cleared out the Bolsheviki. The Allied battleships standing in the bay here keep the Bolshevik element awed.

May 10

After being here a few days, I am convinced that you would find it pleasant to come over from Japan to spend a little time at Vladivostok. There couldn't be a safer place so far as life and property are concerned so long as the large force of Czech troops remain here as well as the Allied battleships. The matter of finding rooms would be easy, as Goodsell has reserved quite a number for American refugees who keep coming out of Russia.

* Cossack commanders.

May 11

We have had our conference with the Czechoslovak division commanders. The Chief of Staff and Colonel Lofitchky, the Russian commander of the Second Division, and the regiment quartermasters are all in back of our work. They say we can have anything we want.

The Czechs keep piling in, new trains of them daily. When I arrived here from Japan, there were already 6,000. Now there are 8,000. Riley made a trip out to Pt. Ulis yesterday. The big zeppelin hangar is part way out, and 1,200 Czechs from the artillery are already located there. Eight hundred more are at Pt. Ulis, belonging to the Fourth Battalion of the Eighth Regiment —or rather they are forming a fourth battalion out of them. They are the Czechs who have been in the Siberian prison camps for the past three and four years and are in wretched shape. They are without uniforms, their faces are sunken and haggard, they have seen the worst of prison camp life and are nothing more than wrecks of humanity. But the Czechs are planning to make them a part of their army and are anxious to have the help of the *Y* in remaking the men. It is a task that appeals to us mightily, and we are sorry to have to delay a day in placing a secretary out there.

Vladivostok and vicinity is a far different sort of a place now than when we were here in March. The ice and snow have all gone. The barren hills are now covered with green and the beautiful rhododendrons are thick on the hills on the opposite side of the bay from town.

May 16

The work among the Czech soldiers is most satisfactory and they are most appreciative. Bill Francis is bubbling over. He says he is having the greatest days of his Association experience. He is certainly popular among his soldiers. Little Russian and no Czech that he speaks, he gets along with no interpreter. You would enjoy seeing the spirit of his men at their volleyball, baseball, and football games.

We moved our office for the Czech army branch of the work

today. We have been in the same office with the Vladivostok city work of which Goodsell has charge. That has become too crowded. Our new office is at No. 12 Aleutskaya Street, across the street from the Brynner house.

Griffin is having his jolts setting up his kino workshop running into *seichassing* (*seichass* is the Russian word meaning "immediately" according to the dictionary, but "any old time" actually), and *nichevoing* (the Russian word that is equivalent to a shrug of the shoulders, signifying "I should worry" or "Ishkabibble"), but he is working hard and has a group of carpenters and workers with him who don't *seichass* and *nichevo*.

May 19

Yesterday the Longs, Mrs. Hollinger, and I were out to the track meet between the boys from the *Brooklyn* and from the British cruiser *Suffolk*. The *Brooklyn* boys walked away with the meet, taking nearly every point. After the meet, we visited our clubs with the Czech troops, which are scattered around the hills and valleys, and I wished you had been along to enjoy the beautiful sunset and the gathering of the cowslips and the last of the beautiful rhododendrons.

Well, it is after eleven o'clock and it is not right to keep the people of the house awake later with this Corona. The Rassuschins had fifteen servants in their beautiful home at Irkutsk. Now they have no servants, as their last maid left them this week because the work caused by us secretaries was getting too hard. So the Rassuschins have buckled down themselves and are doing all the housework, making our beds, serving us the samovar, and doing all their own cooking and cleaning. They seem to be enjoying it too. The fifteen-year-old boy wants to go to America for school.

Dr. C. R. Watson*
124 East 28th St.
New York City

July 2

Dear Sir:

When the compact, high-spirited, well-disciplined Czecho-slovak Army occupied the city of Vladivostok on June 30 amidst the cheers of a joyous populace, I thought of its contrast with the closing days of March when the vanguard of the same little army was fighting its way out of the Ukraine and beginning its seven-thousand-mile trek across Siberia in search of an opportunity to fight for liberty in France. By the middle of June there were already sixteen thousand Czechs in Vladivostok. The other forty-odd thousand extended along the Siberian railroad from Penza west of Samara to near Irkutsk. Finally this forty thousand were forced into open hostilities with the Soviets and with the prisoners of war in order to save themselves from death or the prison camp, the upshot being that the Germans and Bolsheviki were placed under Czech guards in the same prison camps in which the Soviets had ordered the Czechs imprisoned. The efforts of the Soviet at Vladivostok to aid the Germans and Bolsheviki at Irkutsk against the Czechs, and the appeal of the latter to the Czechs at Vladivostok to come to their aid brought about the occupation of Vladivostok by the Czechs on June 30 and the complete abandonment for the present of the contemplated voyage by transport to France.

Communication between Vladivostok and the First Division was always uncertain and, after the Irkutsk conflict, completely broken. Miller and three other secretaries were "somewhere along the Trans-Siberian," and their April instructions as to the voyage to France were reaching Vladivostok the end of June when the trip back into Siberia had taken the place of the voyage to France in the plans of all.

Three impressions have gained strength with me in my

---

* Charles R. Watson had become associated with the International Committee in November 1917 and had assumed responsibility for Y.M.C.A. operations in Russia as well as Italy, Egypt, Mesopotamia, and India.

work with the Czechoslovaks. First is the wonderful recognition which our work and our secretaries receive from them. Secondly, the Association has as much to learn as to teach in its relations with the Czechoslovaks. The wonderful Sokol exhibition held at Vladivostok the first part of June revealed a knowledge and organization in athletics far beyond the Association's scope. The concert which was given by the Fifth Regiment in the city during June by a chorus of over one hundred voices and two orchestras, one of which appeared in public for the first time, would have done credit to any large American city. In decorating and arranging the club rooms, remarkable artistic and organizing talent has been shown by the Czechs. In the third place, the Czechoslovak National Sokol organization deserves careful study with reference to the future relationship of the Y.M.C.A. to it. It evidently holds a central and vital place in the lives of the Bohemians.

We have had new reasons for humility, personally and nationally, since becoming acquainted with the Czechs. We feel that it is an honor to be associated with them and to see the American flag waving with the Czech flag. We are impressed more and more with the essentially democratic and Christian character of their spirit.

July 3

Dear Emily:

I was planning to get a letter off to you on last Saturday's boat, but the Czechs took possession of the city that day and things were too much upset. I was starting from the office into the city a little after ten o'clock in the morning when I suddenly noticed the people on the sidewalks shouting to each other and dancing about for joy. They said the Czechs had seized the Soviet headquarters. I haven't seen such a joyous time since the March revolution in Petrograd. Soon there were parades going about town with Russians shouting for the Czechs and against the Soviet. Everything went off peaceably until four o'clock in the afternoon when the Czechs went to take possession of the fortress headquarters opposite the depot. The Bolsheviki put up a fight there which lasted about two hours. I watched it from the Longs' apartments which gave a splendid view. It was a small affair, but brisk and interesting while it lasted. Several wounded Bolsheviki were led past on the street below us. Three Czechs were killed, several wounded, and the rooms of the fortress pretty well shot up. I walked over to the fortress, after the fight was over, and went through the rooms then guarded by Czech soldiers.

The Czechs moved in from their camps early in the morning, starting from the Gornitzai barracks as early as four o'clock. Our secretaries in the camps could not get into the city until late in the afternoon. We took Chez out to the camp at Pervaya Retchka at noon time, one of the *Brooklyn* officers going along with us. When we went through the railroad shops at Pervaya Retchka, all was quiet, the Bolsheviki having retired towards Nikolsk, followed by one of the Czech regiments. We saw little of the Czech movements until we got back into town and found Svyetlanskaya converted into a Czech camp almost its entire length. They all gave us the glad sign as we came in. They are happy to be busy and have the long suspense at an end.

This event makes a big change in our plans, as the Czechs are evacuating their barracks at Vladivostok and moving inland. This means that we can no longer operate our clubs here, but must devise means of keeping with the troops. Two hours after the Czechs had seized the Soviet headquarters, we had a committee meeting at luncheon Saturday noon to make plans. We decided to try to get hold of American freight cars and transfer our clubs on to them. I went around to the Czech headquarters in the afternoon regarding this matter. They sent me down to the Czech commandant at the station, for now there is a Czech commandant who has precedence over the Russian commandant in all that pertains to military operations. I told him what I wanted, and he said we could have them. The next morning the eight cars were on the siding below the depot, reserved for us. Monday morning Riley had a gang of twenty-five Chinese carpenters and coolies at work putting windows, benches, and tables into the cars and fitting them up as clubs. Today the first car will be ready, and Noyes is scheduled out with the Fifth Regiment train tonight. Only one regiment has gone out so far, the

Eighth, and we aim to have secretaries and club cars with every regiment from now on, as well as to get them out to the Eighth within a couple of days.

July 6

Red Cross circles are whirling into action as a result of a trainload of 200 Czech wounded brought in from Nikolsk yesterday. Nikolsk was taken by the Czechs yesterday afternoon. The bringing of the wounded has caused a sensation, as you can imagine. I was at the depot when the train arrived. The Czech spirit was exhibited when the Czech orchestra stood on the station platform and played some of the stirring national airs while the wounded pulled themselves to the windows and doors of the freight cars, their faces lighting up with joy. As there was no room at the hospital, about 150 of them are quartered on the *Brooklyn*, the *Suffolk*, and in the *Brooklyn* shed.

Dr. Teussler, representing the American Red Cross from Japan, arrived day before yesterday. I was interpreter while he and Dr. Dunn made the rounds of the hospitals yesterday. You would have been amused to see the high officials working up a long telegram for hospital supplies only to learn from us, incidentally after it was all framed, that we had ordered practically everything in the list two weeks previously. Of course, we are tickled that the Red Cross is coming to take this off our hands because we have more of our own work than we can take care of.

Bill Francis left with club car number 2 yesterday. Dr. Teussler went out on the same car to survey Red Cross needs on the front. The 200 wounded were brought in while he was on his survey.

On July fourth the Bolsheviki held a big demonstration opposite the depot. The Czechs allowed them to have a funeral parade for the Bolsheviki who were killed in the action of June 29 on condition that they did not use it for political purposes. As soon as the funeral service was over they converted it into a big political demonstration. I ran into it coming up from an examination of our club cars in the yards. One of the speakers pointed down at the Stars and Stripes which were flying on the *Brooklyn* (in honor of the 4th) and said to the crowd, "Do you know why the *Brooklyn* is flying the Stars and Stripes today? I'll tell you. It is because America is sending an army over to overthrow the Czechs and restore the Bolsheviki to power." The only visible evidence the Czech soldiers have of the falseness of this propaganda is the sight of the American flag flying over the Y.M.C.A. club cars attached to their trains and the Y.M.C.A. "uncles" accompanying them to the front.

I was impressed with the evident lack of sympathy which most of the crowd showed the Bolsheviki orators. Many Czechs were standing in the crowd, and most of the remarks which I heard from the Russians were derogatory to the Bolsheviki. At one time one of the speakers said, "We have been condemned for associating with the Hungarian war prisoners. We ought not to be condemned for that. The Hungarians are fine people. To prove it I am going to show you a fine crowd of them today. Will the Hungarians who are present please hurrah?" And a big section of the crowd in front of the speaker, the section which had been doing most of the noisy applauding, broke loose with a loud hurrah, waving their hats in the air. Sukhanov, the leader of the local Soviet, had been released from prison to attend the funeral and spoke at the demonstration. He affected great emotional distress at the fate of the Soviet. He was rather guarded in his statements regarding the Czechs, stating that they did not realize how they were being used as a tool by the capitalists to overturn the liberties of the peoples. The Czechs who were standing about smiled at these statements as if they were not very much worried as to whether they were pursuing the right course.

These are stirring times. The spirit of the Czechs is wonderful. The Nikolsk battle has simply added pep to them.

July 9

Five of the secretaries have now left on the club cars for the Czech front. We are getting in daily reports from most of them, and they are exceedingly interesting.

All the secretaries agree that the trip is considerably different than anticipated. Instead of being an easy march against a rapidly retreating enemy, they are meeting with the stiffest kind of resistance. The battle at Nikolsk was a ghastly affair, with many atrocities against the Czechs, dum-dum bullets being used by the Bolsheviki. Many of the Czech wounded at the Navy Hospital are horribly mutilated. I was out there this morning; there is the atmosphere of death all about. Matchak, who is back from the front, reports that the Czechs say this is the bloodiest fighting they have seen during the war. This afternoon I attended the funeral of fourteen Czechs from the Navy Hospital, who were killed in the Nikolsk battle. Admiral Knight and the *Brooklyn* boys attended the funeral as well as the officers and marines from the Japanese, British, and Chinese ships.

July 13

The first eight big American cars which we received are all in service. Yesterday I went to the Czech commandant again and asked him whether we could have sixteen more. He said we could, and this morning the sixteen new cars were on the siding where the other eight had been. We are planning to have enough cars ready to serve the Czechs in the interior as soon as the way opens up, and they are united. Fifty Chinese carpenters and coolies are at work on the new cars.

Story and I had conferences with the captain of the Port today with a view to making a big Y.M.C.A. hut and warehouse out of the godown next to the *Brooklyn*, the end of which is now occupied by the *Brooklyn* shed and serving as a hospital for the Czechs. In making these plans, we are assuming Allied intervention. The military officials of course won't tell us whether there will be intervention, and Story thinks we ought not to intervene, but if we wait until the matter is settled, it will be too late to have a hut ready when the Allied troops land. Story and I have a nightly discussion on this intervention question.

July 16

I was in Nikolsk Sunday. Outside of the city I saw the bridge which the Bolsheviki had blown up with dynamite. I saw the fields on which the fight took place, where so many wounded and dead were picked up. The first day the Czechs were at a disadvantage as they had to attack the Bolshevik cars with hand grenades. The cars stood high on a dike through the meadows, while the Czechs had to fight from below. They had to withdraw, but afterwards came back with reinforcements and took the city after a brisk fight. One Czech battalion tried to get around the city and cut off the retreat of the Bolsheviki, but after walking two days and nights, they got to the cutoff just after the Bolsheviki had passed by.

I had a good visit with Noyes and Simmons. Noyes has a club at the barracks and a kino establishment in an unfinished Russian church. Part of the time he shows pictures to the civilians, especially the railroad workers, as well as to the Czechs. The railroad workers asked permission to pay admission fees, and then asked that the funds be turned over for the use of the Czech wounded. Later the Czechs requested that further proceeds be turned over to civilians who had lost relatives in the fighting. Noyes and Simmons report that the Czechs are regarded by the local people as saviours from tyranny. Peasants take pride in scouring the countryside for Bolsheviki in hiding, and capturing them and delivering their arms over to the Czechs. They also come with food and milk for the Czechs and refuse to take pay.

Both Noyes and Simmons have club cars at the station, as many Czechs are still located here. The popularity of the cars has exceeded all our expectations. When I saw Captain Hommaryk, of the Eighth Regiment, at Nikolsk, he said, "All know you now."

I wrote you that we sent Matchak to Harbin on one of our club cars last week. Railroad communications not yet being open beyond Nikolsk, they hitched up a special engine to his one Y.M.C.A. car and he left Nikolsk with flags waving, colors flying, and all the pomp of a railroad president. The next news I got was a telegram yesterday that he was held up on the boundary of Manchuria at Grodekovo by Horvat's forces and they wouldn't let him through. We wired back for him to wait there until communications were opened and meanwhile to open his club. Today one of the members of the Czech National Council, Dr.

Spacek, told me that he and Consul McGowan were going over to Grodekovo and see that Matchak got on to Harbin. Matchak is getting quite an international education.

July 19

We have added an international courier to our service, a Mr. Evans, a middle-aged American who has lived in Russia the past eight years. Our business with China, Japan, and the Philippines promises to be large as we cannot wait for supplies to arrive from America. One of Evans' first jobs will be to bring up nearly a million rubles which we have purchased in Shanghai.

Fred Scherer arrived here from Harbin yesterday. This was his first time on Russian soil, though he has been in Harbin since February. When he reached the boundary at Pogranitchnaya, he found Matchak still there. The next morning General Dietrichs arrived on the scene and arranged for Matchak to go to Harbin. We expect Scherer to start off shortly on another club car destined for Irkutsk. At present the eastern Czechs are a long way from Irkutsk, or even Khabarovsk, as they are only something like 230 versts (180 miles) from Vladivostok, but they are progressing. Much fighting is going on. Yesterday's report was thirty Czechs killed and thirty more wounded.

Day before yesterday we received 500 poods (20,000 pounds) of sugar from the Czechs to use in making biscuits and chocolate for the soldiers. We have contracted with one biscuit company and two chocolate companies to sell us practically their entire output for the Czechs. Sugar is a scarce and dear article here, and we furnish the sugar on condition that all of the product they make from it comes to us. The sugar we received from the Czechs is from the stores they took over from the Bolsheviki, which I visited in their great warehouses at Pervaya Retchka. Most of it is fine cube sugar stored since 1905 and 1906, and of prime quality. The Czechs have put the German and Hungarian prisoners of war at work in these warehouses, and they seem glad to have something to do again.

The working classes are agitating against the Y.M.C.A. as a captialist and bourgeois institution. The *Rabotchie* (Workingmen) newspaper, a Bolshevik paper which appears in spite of the Czech censorship, says that the Y.M.C.A. is a White Guard (as contrasted with a Red Guard) organization, and that the Czechs mutilated the bodies of their own dead for propaganda purposes against the Bolsheviki.

I have signed up three more Czech invalids for our staff, and visited the Czech Home for Invalids today to canvass for still more. We are getting a great aggregation of one-legged, one-eyed, one-armed, and shell-shocked victims. It is pathetic how eager they all are to prove that they are well and strong enough to do a day's work. As soon as the Czechs began their campaign, we notified all the able-bodied Czechs in our employ that we did not wish to hold them from military service in case they were physically fit. The Czechs particularly appreciate the use we are making of the invalids, not only because of the happiness it gives the invalids to feel useful, but because of the decrease of this burden on the scanty resources of the Czechs. Practically every invalid has a trade and can keep accounts.

July 23

I went up to the Czechoslovak front Saturday night and got back this morning (Tuesday). I have been sleeping on the boards of bouncing *teplushkas* (freight cars) and our *sklad* (warehouse) cars for the past three nights. One bowl of soup, 200 versts from Vladivostok, was the nearest to a full meal I got between Saturday noon and this noon. The rest of my diet consisted of biscuits, sweet chocolate, candy, and bread. I found enough boiled water to brush my teeth twice, and to wash once, and to shave once. But I come back refreshed and with new inspiration for our work after seeing it in actual operation up to the last man.

When I reached Nikolsk, I found that Noyes had left for the front. In fact he had left Nikolsk by five hours before I left Vladivostok and was expected back at any time. I left Nikolsk at noon, on one of our *sklad* cars which I found loaded up with supplies. Lewis, the Czech in charge of it, said he has just come back with it from the front and delivered everything that was wanted. I couldn't understand why it wasn't emptied as it had the cigarettes, tobacco, chocolate, candy, and biscuits which everybody had been clamoring for. So I decided to take it on.

I reached Muchnaya about 4 p.m. One of our couriers was there. He had left Nikolsk with Noyes. They couldn't go further than Muchnaya as passenger service went no further. We passed through the country where fierce fighting had taken place between the Czechs and the Germans-Magyars-Bolsheviki. I saw the wrecked armored cars and engines by the side of the railroad which the Bolsheviki had run off the tracks when forced to retreat. I saw the hill on which Captain Yano of the Fifth Regiment had sat for fifty hours and General Dietrichs for eight hours directing the fighting. I saw the admirable Bolshevik trenches which had been made by unquestionable German talent; not simple Russian trenches, but artistic, scientific trenches with trap doors and hidden passages. The fields were covered with holes dug by exploding shells.

I arrived at Evgenevsky about eight o'clock. Found Peters and Simmons there. We had a Sunday evening conference on a pile of logs near the railroad tracks with mosquitoes keeping at us in lively fashion. Simmons' club car was at the station. It was jammed full. He said his canteen business was running as high as 600 rubles daily. He was happy over his new work. Peters' and Francis' clubs were a couple of versts away on a side track where their regiments were located.

I learned that a provision train for the Seventh Regiment (Riley's) was likely to pull out from Evgenevsky that night. They agreed to put my *sklad* car on to the train. We stayed in the yards all night and pulled out early Monday morning. As there was no passenger service beyond Muchnaya we had to take our chance on connections. About nine o'clock we arrived at Sviagino, and I found Bill and Riley still trying to sleep after fighting the mosquitoes all night. Riley had a new scheme for carrying provisions to the men on the front by putting packs on horses loaned by the regiment and going out to the men. Bill and Riley were tickled to see the provisions which I had brought and said they had seen nothing of Lewis and the *sklad* car on its former trip. I learned that the only Czechs who had gone ahead of this point were the engineers who had gone to repair three bridges over the Ussuri River. There was no fighting now except artillery fire, and they didn't expect much more fighting until they started on the third bridge. I had a pleasant chat with Captain Hoblech. This Seventh Regiment seemed happy to be the vanguard. They were the ones in the Irkutsk fight and the rest of their regiment is still on the other side of Irkutsk, the only regiment which got separated. They say they want to be the first ones back to Irkutsk.

Within an hour we had delivered the stuff and were hitched up to an engine returning to Evgenevsky. When we reached there, we learned that we could attach to a train of war prisoners which would be the first train back to Vladivostok. There were 800 German prisoners and 600 Turks assigned for the train. It was an interesting sight to see them moving out of their barracks to the railroad tracks. There were still 800 Magyars left for a later trip. These men did not take part in the recent fighting. The Russian commandant said that only 120 Magyars, 30 Germans, and one Turk joined the Bolsheviki from this camp of 2,500 prisoners of war. These men had been at Nikolsk until December and then transferred to Evgenevsky. It was the famous Spasskoye Camp. A couple of years earlier there were 10,000 prisoners at this camp. Most of the prisoners had been in Siberia three to three and a half years. Many of them had married Russian women in these villages. In fact they relate that there are 800 German-Russian babies whose fathers are prisoners of war. Many of the prisoners spoke English. They all seemed to want to go to America. The Germans still thought there could be only one possible outcome to the war. It was *selbst verständlich*. The Y.M.C.A. car was as popular with the prisoners of war as with the Czech soldiers and Russian railway workers. I snapped a picture showing an interesting assemblage of Turks, Germans, Austrians, Czechs, and Russians, all after the cigarettes, tobacco, biscuits, and chocolate which we had for sale. We soon had to set limits to the amount we could sell the prisoners and when that was gone we told them we were sold out.

There were 51 cars of prisoners of war on our train. One Czech soldier sat as guard in each car.

All was quiet on the front. I neither saw nor heard any

fighting the whole trip. It was a lull between fights.

We got into Vladivostok at 10:30 this morning. I have been on the go all day, and it is now 12:30 midnight, so goodnight and goodmorning.

July 26

I got back yesterday morning from my third trip to the front, the most interesting one yet. Riley was furthest from Vladivostok, 303 versts out, at Kaul. This is the last station before the Ussuri River. The furthest Czech echelons were stationed there, only the armored car squad and engineers being further ahead. That afternoon they had attached Riley's club car to the armored car and run it out to the actual firing line about 10 versts further, where Riley served the armored car squad and engineers with tea and other eatables. The entire country along there is stripped of food; the soldiers are glad of every piece of chocolate and biscuit that we can get to them to relieve the monotony of their black bread, soup, and *kasha*. That evening Riley and I sat on top of the club car and fought the mosquitoes while we watched the flashes of artillery firing at Ussuri about 20 versts ahead. It was not very violent, being too far away for us to hear the reports, and had nothing of the Kiev atmosphere about it. With Riley's field glasses we could see the church of Ussuri in the afternoon. As the Czech patrols came back from scouting duty through the swamps, the first place they hit for was the Y.M.C.A. car, where they stacked their arms alongside while they went inside and sipped tea and ate biscuits.

Simmons and Scherer were at the next point furthest out, Shmakovka. This is where passenger service from Vladivostok now ends. Simmons has become a new man and is measuring up as one of the strongest and most capable secretaries we have. He has the biggest plant going of all. When I was at Kaul, I learned that supplies intended for Riley had gotten stranded on Sim's car with no way of sending them on out. I got back to Shmakovka from Kaul at one o'clock in the morning, slept until five, then went and woke Sim up for those supplies. He had worked until 2:30 that morning, the Czechs crowding his car until midnight and then two hours of accounts before he turned in. But he got up without a groan and turned over the supplies for Riley, while I arranged with a Czech guard bound for Kaul to deliver them to Riley.

By this time it was seven o'clock, and my *sklad* car was attached to the Vladivostok train a couple of miles down the track. I walked down in a blinding rain and had not more than stepped on the car before the train pulled out.

I found that we must triple, if not quadruple, our canteen supplies, as the soldiers can buy nothing at any of the stations after Spasskoye and are depending entirely on our canteen service. I wired ahead to Noyes at Nikolsk on my way back to have 1,000 loaves of white bread and 4,000 pounds of biscuits ready for the *sklad* car when we arrived there. He had most of it ready, and we sent the car right back to the front in charge of the Czech assistants while I came on to Vladivostok in a third-class car. This morning I doubled the biscuit, candy, and chocolate orders and we are preparing to triple the cigarette and tobacco orders.

I had a chat with Bill Francis on the way back, in the pouring rain. He is still at Spasskoye. He was sore because some Russian railway workers had bought cigarette papers from our cars at 2 kopeks a sheet and then sold them in town at 16 kopeks a sheet. Speculation is, of course, one of the problems we have to contend with. We try to confine our service with the railroad workers to such men as have an actual part in the military operations.

During my ride in on the third-class car, I chatted with a Russian peasant. He said that the peasants did not want the Bolsheviki or the Czar back. What they wanted was good business conditions and the development of the cooperatives. He thought America could help the cooperatives. The peasants were willing that the landowners should have their land, or at least part of it, if they didn't compel the peasants to work for them. They wanted to be free to work their own lands.

As a piece of cooperation with the Red Cross, I spent yesterday investigating the refugee situation around Vladivostok. There are 2,030 refugees in Vladivostok and vicinity and 3,500 in the Primorskaya region, of which Vladivostok is the center.

Of the 2,030 around Vladivostok, 475 are classified as needy, most of them living in barracks on the edge of the city near where the Czech Fifth Regiment was located. The barracks are wretchedly dirty, men are hanging around idle, and there is a hopeless and dejected air about the whole place. I learned from the refugees themselves that they received practically no help from the Soviet when it was in power. They were in danger of dying from starvation when the Czechs began to arrive at Vladivostok. The Czech Fifth Regiment provided enough out of their own small rations to feed the refugees. No one knew that the Czechs were doing this until they left Vladivostok, when the refugee problem forced itself upon the city again, and ways and means had to be devised for feeding them. The American Red Cross will probably take over this problem. We had a conference with the Red Cross at Dom Brynner this evening.

One thing that makes my trips to the front possible is the remarkable way in which my Czech assistant, Kabrna, has developed as my right-hand man. He has entire charge of the Czech part of our organization, which takes care of the supply service to the front, ordering the cars, and buying. He is a regular speed demon for detail and can turn out two or three times as much in a day of detail work as I can. He has not seen his wife for over four years. When he was brought to Siberia, he was left freezing outside the camp for a week, and this brought on a skin trouble which is very painful to him during the cold season. He puffs up noticeably in size, and finds it hard to catch his breath. He learned English as a table waiter in London before the war.

August 7

The British landed Saturday morning, the same day that I started on my trip to the front. They are the first Allies to appear. They had a parade through town, but it was so early that there was not a large crowd out. Learning that they brought no Y.M.C.A. secretaries or equipment with them, I went around to their headquarters the same morning to offer our services. We met the British troops at Nikolsk on our way back this morning. They were on their way to the front, and Czech and Russian bands and officials were at the station platform to greet them.

There being no trains scheduled immediately from Nikolsk to Vladivostok, they provided a special locomotive to get our lone car into Vladivostok on time.

After a long discussion, I have agreed with Story to offer to extend the services of our handful of Czech secretaries and our Czech organization to the other Allied units which may come in without Y.M.C.A. secretaries. It will be a bad strain on us until the new secretaries begin to arrive but is likely to lead to dissatisfaction if we don't.

On our way back from the front a Russian railroad engineer boarded our car and rode with us part of the way. He had just escaped, along with fifteen other Russian railway workers, from the Bolsheviki at Ussuri. He said that the Bolsheviki were trying to compel the railway workers to take up arms and fight with them, though most of the railway workers were in sympathy neither with the Bolsheviki nor with fighting. They had escaped around into China, then back into Russian territory. He said that the Bolsheviki had called 300 of the railway workers to a meeting the day before he escaped, giving them an ultimatum of fighting or being arrested.

This man's home was in Shmakovka, which is now in the hands of the Bolsheviki. He said it was lucky his wife couldn't write as the Bolsheviki would probably carry her off for clerical work if she could. And it was lucky he didn't have any grown daughters, because they would carry them off too, just as they had at other villages along the line as the Czechs advanced. He said the Bolsheviki warn the people that the Czechs will kill everybody and that they are calling in the Allies to massacre the Russians and to steal their land. But the peasants know that the Czechs are their real friends. He said the Czechs always treat the Russian women with respect.

August 9

The first British Y.M.C.A. car goes out tomorrow with the chaplain in charge. A French car will go out in another day or two. The French arrived yesterday, and a French captain and Chap-

lain Roberts were out this afternoon with me to inspect our cars
and make arrangements.

When the British troops got out on the front and found that
they could get money changed nowhere except at the Y.M.C.A.
cars and could buy no smokes or anything else except at our
cars, they wanted a *Y* car also. It was their requests that brought
the British chaplain around to our office in Vladivostok with a
request for our service. In view of our shortage of secretaries, he
is willing to act as secretary on their car.

The Czech quartermaster has informed us that there will
be no objection to our using for other Allied forces some of the
supplies which we have bought from the Czech quartermaster
department for work with the Czechs.

August 14

I had an interesting and profitable trip to the front with war
correspondent Donald Thompson. We got nineteen dozen photos
of the Czechs, British, and French on the front, including many
good ones of the *Y*, and he says he will send in a story about the
Czechs that will let the Americans know who they really are.

The Czechs are now at Kraevskaya. The meaning of the
word is "edge" or "limit." It sure is the limit. There is one home
and the station, nothing but sidings, all surrounded by marsh.
It is an unhealthy spot—hot and mosquito-ridden. Czech guards
will go out healthy at night and return in the morning stagger-
ing with sickness. The water is bad even for Russia, the dirtiest
sort of swamp water. This is the point to which the Czechs
retreated after their defeat at Kaul; it is about eighty versts nearer
Vladivostok. The sidings are full of Czech trains, of which there
are some seven or eight concentrated there. There is not room
enough on the sidings for all, so they extend along the main
track both ways from the sidings, blocking the road. If one train
must switch or move, the whole seven trains must switch. Every
morning the trains spend about four hours maneuvering so as
to let each locomotive come up to the water station for a drink.
When we come in with a car of supplies, we usually wait our
chance to unload when they haul the train to which we are

attached up closer to the other trains. Then the secretaries on our club cars send down and fetch the goods to their respective cars, often changing their location a mile or two during the operation.

You might think that tea service would not be the most popular thing for hot weather. But our tea cars are doing a land-office business, and it is a lifesaver where there is nothing else that is safe to drink. We are planning, however, to introduce a new feature this coming week, and that is a refrigerator car. Donald Thompson has helped me to work out the details. He saw them in operation on the French front.

A big part of the British force fell sick the first thing after they struck this god-forsaken region. The British chaplain accompanied us to the front in charge of his car. He was delighted and kept saying, "This is a priceless life." He went to the front Sunday afternoon with chocolate, cigarettes, biscuits, etc., and held an auction with the British troops who are in camp there. "The first Sunday afternoon auction I ever held," he said. He followed it up with an Anglican church service at which he had a full attendance.

Thompson and I visited the Czech trenches at Kraevskaya with Scherer. The Bolsheviki have better artillery than the Czechs and British and have been pounding them every night for some time. It is a frequent thing for the Czechs at night suddenly to get the orders, "Quiet and all lights out," and the long freight trains, which have been scenes of activity and candle-light, suddenly become dark and still, while the enemy artillery begins to play on them.

The British and Czech soldiers are rapidly getting acquainted. The Czechs are teaching the British some Czech words and also learning more English. Many Czechs already have a good start with English as a result of our English classes. The English impress the Czechs as "living like gentlemen." The Czech black bread, soup, and *kasha* rations suffer by comparison with the liberal rations which the British soldiers receive. The Czechs say of the British, "They eat well."

At Spasskoye I went over to a restaurant to order some extra bread. I found a couple of British in the restaurant trying to draw a cow, while the Russian restaurant keeper was trying to understand their English explanation of the cow. As soon as they saw me and heard me begin to talk Russian with the proprietor they heaved a sigh of relief. They said they were trying to buy sterilized milk and had drawn the cow to illustrate milk, but were up against it to indicate the sterilization. The British have only one interpreter. Part of the troops are at the front and part in barracks at Spasskoye. When the interpreter is at the front, the troops in the rear have to get along without one.

August 16

You ought to have heard the American boys cheer when they arrived on their transports here. Such a difference from the others that have arrived. Nothing solemn or funereal, but wholesome, wholehearted, peppy enthusiasm that changed the atmosphere of the whole community overnight. If nobody else was going to cheer their arrival, they would furnish the hurrahs themselves. It was worth two years of Russian and Siberian gloom to get that whiff of American spirit.

The Philippine mules are a feature of the American outfit which excites much interest among the Russians. The mules stood the trip well, and they unloaded them as soon as the boats arrived. All the vacant space along the wharf near where the *Brooklyn* stands is occupied by these mules. There are a number of American soldiers who sleep on shore next to the mules while others keep watch. The only way the Russian street women could be kept from coming and sleeping there also, was to set a guard against them and drive them away. These women have been collecting in Vladivostok from all parts of the Orient ever since it was known that the various armies were coming in.

Quite a number of the American soldiers speak Russian, some of them having been born in Russia. None of the English soldiers speak Russian, and practically none of the other armies except the Czechs.

As soon as the Americans arrived, the dock hands struck, partly as a result of Bolshevik propaganda and partly out of cupidity for the American dollar with which the American soldier is reported to be so well supplied. Well, the Americans didn't worry much about the strike. It saved them delay and bargaining and poor work, for they went ahead at once and organized their unloading with their own men and the job was finished with a rush.

We met the boats the day they landed, offering the service of the Association. We found the chaplain, Captain Webb, well provided with reading and writing matter, and even kino service, but our exchange service was welcomed. We are arranging for a Y.M.C.A. car to go with the first American train to the front.

The Japanese troops have also arrived.* When we got back from the last trip to the front, we found them marching endlessly through the streets in that prepared and precise, German way. Noyes has written that an avalanche of Japanese have descended upon him at Nikolsk. They have occupied the barracks formerly used by the Czechs there. He went around to the Japanese officer the first evening they arrived offering our service. A few minutes later the Japanese soldiers flocked in on him and swamped his facilities.

The Japanese had already reached Nikolsk when we passed through there on our way back from the front. I overheard a Czech trying to talk with a Japanese on one of their cars at Nikolsk. The Japanese already understood the Russian words for soldier and officer. He pulled out a Japanese-Russian dictionary, with the aid of which he made out a reply in Russian to the Czech inquirer. The Czech was so impressed with this exhibition that he exclaimed "*Na vsyo gotov*" (Prepared for everything).

The Port authorities gave their permission a couple of weeks ago for us to rent the *Brooklyn* warehouse. We are transferring our supplies from the freight cars, which have served as our warehouse up to the present time. The main part of the building will be a big International Army hut. Goodsell is busy

---

* According to the Allied Intervention Agreement, Japan was to send in the same number of troops as the United States, 7,500. However, they sent 72,000 to Siberia and an additional 12,000 to the area of the Chinese Eastern Railway in Manchuria. See George F. Kennan: *The Decision to Intervene* (New York: Atheneum, 1967), p. 415.

planning the details and starting the work on it. When the
Brooklyn goes, they have promised to turn over the part they
now use to us, so that the whole building will be in our charge.

August 23

The Czechoslovak secretaries are no longer purely Czechoslovak
secretaries, but Allied secretaries. On my last trip to the front,
I was accompanied by Mr. Saito, one of the National Y.M.C.A.
secretaries from Japan. We found Francis' and Simmons' cars
beseiged with French, English, Russians, Cossacks, Indo-Chinese,
Czechs, and Japanese. It kept us busy as we passed along the
trains sorting out our salutations to fit. *Nazdar, Zdravtsvuite,
Bon jour, Ohayo, Hello*, etc. .

We reached Sviagino just after a general retreat of the British and Czechs from Kraevskaya. The British had a close call
from a Bolshevik ambush, and the marvel is that they escaped.
The front is now back to the point where it was over a month
ago. It has been hard on Czech morale.

Today Saito and I called on Admiral Cato and General
Otani. Admiral Cato received us on his flagship. He was high
in his praises of America for giving her all in the cause of world
civilization. He is a Christian. General Otani received us at the
Japanese General Staff headquarters, thanked us for the service
we had already rendered the Japanese soldiers on the Ussuri
front and hoped that we could rapidly extend our service for
them. General Otani impressed me as a refined, cultured, and
courtly gentleman.

The part that our cars are playing on the front in encouraging friendly relations between the soldiers of the different
nationalities has impressed the Japanese. On every Y.M.C.A.
car you go, you find it crowded with representatives of half a
dozen different armies, with the Japanese usually as many as all
the rest put together.

We roped Saito in to help make exchange and talk with
the Japanese along the way. He was swept off his feet by the
bigness of the job. There was an amusing incident at Sviagino.
Simmons and Francis had both been bothered with the disap-

pearance of spoons from the tea service since the Japanese
appeared. They had tried serving the Japanese with wooden
spoons, but the latter objected to being discriminated against in
this fashion. It seemed too delicate a matter to take up with
the officers at this early stage when we were just establishing our
service for their troops. Simmons thought the whole trouble
arose over not being able to speak their language and the Japanese soldiers thought the aluminum tea spoons were thrown in
with the tea for their five cents. Well, we told Saito our problem,
and he went right over to the Japanese officers who were reclin-
ing under their tents, I accompanying him. The Japanese
officers listened courteously, then conferred briefly by themselves.
The next moment forty Japanese soldiers drew up with a click
in company formation before me, each one with an aluminum
spoon in his hand held out for my inspection. I was nonplussed
but concealing my embarrassment suggested that they show
their spoons to Simmons and see if he could identify them.
Instantly the Japanese officers gave the word of command, the
bunch right about-faced and marched in brisk and perfect order
down to Sim's car, with the forty spoons flashing in the burning
sun at an absolutely similar angle in front of each soldier. I
summoned Sim to the door, and he came out and gave a sober
inspection to the spoons. But they were all new ones, which
meant that they had been purchased from us, and had not been
taken from the tea, as those were old and worn. Therefore, they
were honorably absolved, while we had accomplished our object
of bringing the matter to the officers in such a way that they
explained to their men that the spoons were for sale and not
gifts with the tea.

We have been informed that the Japanese soldiers in this
expedition are from the country districts of the island of Kiushu,
which explains their crudeness of manners and lack of acquaintance with the ways of modern civilization.

August 24

There was another revolution last night. Some of Horvat's troops
dropped in unexpectedly and occupied the fortress opposite

the depot. When I was down at the depot this morning, I saw a train of his Cossacks standing there. They said they had come to take possession of Vladivostok and that the Czechs would have to give up the power. It seems that the movement of the Czechs to the west has raised the question of what Russian authority would take control here after they leave, and this move of Horvat was calculated to be beforehand.

The Allies are busy with negotiations today, as this revolution seems to have been a surprise to everybody. It is announced that the Czechs will continue in military charge of the city, even after the main body of the Czech troops withdraw. In this capacity, they will continue to act under Allied orders which is necessary in view of the large quantities of Allied supplies here and the danger of allowing any local factions getting control of them. The first train of Americans departed for the Ussuri front this morning with a Y.M.C.A. car attached and Chaplain Webb in charge of it.

August 27

Every week our work expands more rapidly than the previous week. We are taking on twenty more assistants this week in addition to any new secretaries who may show up. The army department now far overshadows all other departments of the Siberian work put together. Every week we are ordering cigarettes by the million, biscuits by the tens of thousands of pounds, bread by the fives of thousands of loaves, chocolate by the ton. And we have never met the demand yet.

One thing we have been fortunate in, and that is transportation. That comes from being here from the start and knowing the ropes. Nearly every passenger train that leaves Vladivostok has one of our freight supply cars attached to the end of the train. It is usually the only nonpassenger car. It always has one or two Czechs in charge and usually an American. The *Y* is open for business at every station night and day and is doing the biggest business of any concern in Siberia. The railroad engineers and conductors often come around to watch our business at these stops, and frequently delay their signal to start the train until

they think we have finished serving the local soldiers. Its supplies are exclusively for soldiers and officers, and everything that
is sold is sold for cost. It keeps our various clubs and their can-
teens supplied over fifteen hundred miles of railroad. It is the
most widely advertised institution in Siberia. It is the magnet
that draws the crowd at every stop, it is known to the boy
and the woman and the girl and peasant who call around in the
hope of somehow getting something, as well as to the soldier. To
the great majority it is a mystery. They can't understand why
the supplies should be sold at such low prices. There must
be some deep ulterior purpose. To most it symbolizes America
in generosity, efficiency, and the spectacular. To others it stands
as the forerunner of America's commercial conquest of Siberia,
a sort of bait to win the people's friendship.

August 28

At last we have suitable office quarters commandeered to us by
Colonel Tolstov, the Russian commandant of the city. Or rather
quarters have again been commandeered to us, for this is the
third or fourth place that has been thus commandeered, only to
have the order countermanded the following day. He has commandeered the fourth floor of the new Churin department store
building. The Red Cross is to have another floor of the same
building. This is a handsome building, across from the Czech
military headquarters. It is an up-to-date, substantial building
that would do credit to any American city. The building is just
completed, and the department store has not yet moved into it
from their old quarters which adjoin. The fourth floor gives a
beautiful view out over the bay. Neither Story nor I have much
idea that this is the end of the tale yet. Mr. Churin has not yet
had his say.

There has been a big battle on the Ussuri front. As I wrote
you in my letter describing the trip to the front with Saito, the
Czechs, British, and French had retreated from Kraevskaya to
Sviagino before the Japanese came up. For a few days we got
alarming reports of the situation there. The Japanese got there
just in the nick of time. Before the forward movement began,

the Czechs, French, and British were almost surrounded at Sviagino, and Bill Francis gives a vivid account of the night battle when they were surrounded by the Bolsheviki on three sides. Then the Japanese got busy, the tide turned, and there was no stopping. The Japanese lost a hundred or so. The boys said they plowed ahead as if they enjoyed getting killed, but I guess they enjoyed killing the Bolsheviki more, as Bill Francis says at least four thousand Bolsheviki were killed. He saw enough dead men to last him a long time. The Americans arrived after the battle was about ended and joined in the pursuit which seems to be headed rapidly towards Khabarovsk. This means an extension of our work in that direction before we have the new recruits to handle it. Bill Francis came in from the front worn out today to go to the hospital.

En route Harbin to Valdivostok

September 5

My visit to Harbin was timed opportunely. Chez, Scherer, Matchak, Noyes, and Riley were all there for a conference. While the conference was in progress, word came that the road to Irkutsk had been opened up. Matchak was so happy that he wept. Scherer and Riley departed the following noon on the general's train for Irkutsk—first train out. I was able to arrange matters as to Riley's and Miller's relations when they should meet, which would have been impossible without much loss of time if I had been in Vladivostok.

I had to leave Harbin yesterday without suitcase or razor strap. I was with Gott on the building problem until seven minutes before train time. I had asked Moran to leave my suitcase with the American engineers at the telegraph office. He did so, but the engineers were all away to lunch and the things locked up. I debated a moment whether to miss the train or not, but decided better put up with inconvenience and save time. I'll have a regular Moscow beard on me before I reach Vladivostok. I had planned to return to Vladivostok on our *sklad* car the way I went, but there was a strike on in Harbin; they were only running passenger trains and wouldn't switch our *sklad* car on to the train.

A Czech outpost looking across no man's land at the Bolshevik advanced
lines fifteen miles away, about 200 miles from Vladivostok in August.

Bolshevik demonstration against the Allies at Vladivostok on July 4th.

Coming across Siberia with the Czechs,
American secretaries carried the U.S. flag.

A view of a locomotive wrecked by Bolsheviks fleeing from the Czechs,
taken from a moving train, about 150 miles from Vladivostok.

E.T.H. in a Y.M.C.A. club car with unidentified assistants.

The Y.M.C.A. car was attached to a special prisoner-of-war train of
51 cars carrying 1400 German, Hungarian, and Turkish prisoners back to
Vladivostok from Spasskoye after the Czechs captured the city in July.

Unloading Y.M.C.A. supply cars at the end of the line. At this station
the tracks were full of troop trains, and three of the Y.M.C.A. clubs were
in operation. Dr. Story is carrying out his pile of goods.

E.T.H. distributing cigarettes to Czechs in a front-line trench in Siberia.

E.T.H. with Czech soldiers in a front-line trench in Siberia.

E.T.H. and Emily at Dom Bryner Vladivostok the day she sailed for America.

The scenery through Manchuria to Harbin was a new sort—
a succession of broad rolling plains, deep fertile valleys, bare
mountains, and forests. The forested mountains were beautiful.
The railroad works up and down the tremendous grades with
serpentines and switchbacks.

Vladivostok

September 13

Riley came in from the Manchurian front Tuesday with
Matchak. They are expecting to leave tomorrow night with a
train of supplies for the First Division of the Czechs, from whom
we have been separated all this time. This is the first train of
supplies to go. It is a Y.M.C.A. train of twelve cars, carrying
sugar, chocolate, cigarettes, tobacco, kerosene, and 101 other
articles which the Czechs are calling for. We have received a
letter from Scherer since he reached Irkutsk, reporting that the
work was progressing there though they were out of funds and
in need of supplies. Have also received a telegram from Kenneth
Miller at Cheliabinsk calling for secretaries and supplies.

The *Y* has not been behind over here. We had the first car
through to Harbin, even before communications were re-estab-
lished. Scherer was the first passenger through to Irkutsk from
Harbin. His telegram was the first received by the Consulate
here from Irkutsk after wire communications were opened up,
and the same was true of Miller's telegram from Cheliabinsk.

Diary entry for September 13

The Americans are exercised by the way the Japanese are buying
up the coal mines. They reported that Mr. Rassuschin was
negotiating for the sale of his coal properties to the Japanese.
He has very extensive interests. He tells me that the only reason
he wants to sell is that he is helpless to operate them because
of the Bolsheviki, and he is selling only to save what he can out
of the wreck. He would rather sell to the Americans if they
would buy.

Khabarovsk

October 4

Dearest Emily:

I have been up here a week tomorrow. Khabarovsk is an attractive city, though the streets are wretched, practically impossible for autos. The weather is noticeably colder here than in Vladivostok. We are all living on a fourth-class car at the railroad station, Simmons' "Palace Car." It is dining room, bedroom, office, and social room, all combined.

The foliage was beautiful coming up from Vladivostok. As we got up into this cooler weather, we felt the cold when waked up at five o'clock in the morning to respond, dressed only in our pajamas, to the Japanese pounding on our car doors to sell them supplies. The Japanese were at every station, and all wanted sugar.

Transportation is now open all the 600 versts from here to Vladivostok, and all the way on west by the Amur River route. There are 4,000 Americans here, and 1,000 further on at Blagoveschensk, where they had just had that deadly Bolshevik battle when you and I came through in March. One of our cars is operating with the Americans at Blagoveschensk, and Czechs are operating it in the absence of American secretaries.

October 5

This is the town where you and I drove in the sleigh, when coming through Siberia last March, but were unable to find furs as the places were closed up owing to a holiday. I priced furs yesterday, but prices have gone up so outrageously that even my hardened attitude toward the value of the ruble was feazed.

The wintry blasts of the first three days here have turned to glorious Indian summer. You remember the inspiring views out over the valley of the sweeping Amur at this place. I am reminded of the beautiful views over the Dnieper which we enjoyed together a year ago at Kiev, only we are not so high up and there are fewer trees around.

Sim and I stayed up till 1:30 this morning trying to wind up his accounts so as to turn them over to Hildreth and allow me to get off on the two o'clock morning train back to Vladivostok. But we couldn't make it.

Sim was off before eight to give directions on getting the Cossack club ready for opening tomorrow. At eleven o'clock I had an hour with Gosse, a Russian who has been helping in our purchasing work at Vladivostok, but who is now going to Blagoveschensk where he will resume his work as secretary inspector and teacher in the Polytechnic Institute. He will give his spare time to *Y* work. He is a splendid, dependable, trustworthy Russian, a credit to the country, one who gives you hope in Russia's future.

En route Khabarovsk to Vladivostok

October 6

After one of those rushing windup days, I am on my way back to Vladivostok. Was up till midnight with accounts again with Sim and Hildreth. Woke up again this morning about six and Sim was already up and brushing his shoes. He has me skinned when it comes to short sleeping hours. Without taking time for lunch we worked right through until 25 minutes after train time on his accounts taking our chances on the Russian timetable. Made it perfectly. Second bell had already rung before I reached the train.

On our *sklad* car is Gleason, also returning to Vladivostok, Webster, one of the railroad servicemen in charge of this car, Lopata, and Roharcek, Czechs, and a middle aged Russian who fixes the samovars and keeps the car swept out. They form a representative picture of contemporaneous Russia. Webster was a ranch man in the States before taking up railroad work. Now he makes the weekly run on this car; has fixed up a little room at one end for himself and Czech Lopata—knows every railroad worker (Russian) along the line and is a friend to all. Says the great need in Russia is to introduce a system which makes work and not graft the basis of reward.

Lopata was a table waiter before the war, belonged to the Austrian army when war broke out, got captured by the Russians, was a member of the new Czech army, was wounded by cannon concussion, invalided out of the service, and taken into our work from the Czech Invalid Home near Vladivostok. He is one of our best five Czech assistants and has been granted the Y.M.C.A. triangle.

Roharcek is still in the active Czech army but has been loaned to our organization to make the run on our *sklad* car along this line. He speaks English, spent a year in England, and has visited America. He was a miller in Bohemia before the war, was in the Austrian army for two weeks after war was declared, then was captured by the Russians. He was among the 2,000 Czechs who were immediately freed from the prisoner-of-war camps through the Czech Committee and for two years served as miller in an English mill in southern Russia. All that time he was also assisting in organizing the new Czech army, which has appeared on the scenes, and last August joined its service.

Prosvirkin, the Russian, is typical of the straits the Russian intelligentsia often find themselves in now. Before the war, he was the head of an important department of a big cooperative concern. He had his assistants, good salary, privileges, and was an important man. All of his world has been swept away, and he cannot adjust himself to the new. His chief concern now seems to be to have shelter and food. He is tidy and useful but without initiative. Instead of trying to qualify for advancement by more effective service, he thinks that pull will yield the higher easier job.

Well, we all have our beds made. I am writing this with the Corona on my bouncing lap beside a Standard Oil railroad lantern which rests on the bed of Prosvirkin, while he sits patiently by with folded arms and a contented, well satisfied look after tea. Lopata is smoking a cigarette in bed talking to Webster who is sitting half undressed with pipe in hand at the edge of his bed. Gleason is putting the finishing touch on his cot after writing his diary, and I have my bed which consists of a 15-ruble mattress, or pad, and two blankets, spread on the shelf. The car is not fitted up with double floors or walls or doors or windows for winter and I shall not undress more than my coat and shoes.

October 7

Another glorious day along the road, with the wonderful possibilities of this immense land growing more and more upon one as he passes hour after hour of harvested crops and other hours of undeveloped but fertile land. At every station the soldiers of all nationalities make a beeline for our cars. Czechs, Japanese, Americans, and Cossacks all patronize us. The big hearty smile of the wholesome Czech still remains the great reward of the trip. The car is also besieged with civilians of all classes, from the poverty-stricken peasants and laboring classes, to the aristocrats traveling on the first-class cars. We have to turn them all down as our goods are for soldiers only, and the Russian railroad workers who are having their part to play in the military operations.

The car is shaking so badly that it shakes the light out and I cannot see to write.

Vladivostok

October 12

I couldn't settle down until I saw Rodney.* A broken auto starter prevented me from getting out to him until Tuesday night. Then I chauffered the Y.M.C.A. auto out to the barracks and found Rodney, who, of course, had been expecting me. He is certainly looking well. We went back to the room at Dom Brynner and spent an evening chatting. I had been thinking of the possibility of his coming over on my way back from Khabarovsk, and it really doesn't seem nearly so strange to see him here as it would have seemed a couple of years ago. He chauffered me back to the barracks and said it was a treat to be driving an auto in Siberia. "Who would ever have thought it?" The next evening he came down on the Bay boat and had tea with Gleason, Story, Griffin, and myself. We spent a couple of hours reminiscing. Story is now living in the back room with me, and Gleason puts his cot out in the middle of the same room. We had to give up the big front room the first of October.

* Sergeant Rodney Ainsworth, Mrs. Heald's brother, who came over with American troops from San Diego and arrived at Vladivostok while Heald was on his trip to Khabarovsk.

October 14

We moved office today. Our old quarters had gotten too cramped. The new place at 26 Fontanaya gives more room and brings together departments which had been separated. The big event, today, however, was the receipt of a cable from Colton at New York announcing that he had charge of the New York end of the Russian and Siberian work, and that he wanted to know what we wanted and was prepared to back us up to the limit.

The big hut is becoming a great soldier's center. Rodney said that it was a godsend to the American soldiers who made a beeline for the place nearly every time they came to town.

The Rassuschins left Dom Brynner today. The owner is returning tomorrow, or rather the landlady. They wouldn't give the Rassuschins time to arrange for transportation or find other quarters, so the latter are living on a car in the station yards belonging to Horvat. They may go west with Bunker tomorrow night on Bunker's special third Y.M.C.A. supply train. Lila, the daughter, went to Japan Saturday.

October 18

Noyes is taking the next special supply train out west. That will make train number 4. We have already sent supplies worth over a million and a half rubles. This will bring it up over two millions. You can judge how things are booming at the western end of the line from the last telegram from Kenneth Miller calling for a force of thirty secretaries immediately. Our service now extends in an unbroken line to the Volga front 5,500 miles away.

The Rassuschins got permission to go along on our last special train to Irkutsk where their home is. The only car we could get for them was a fourth-class car, on which rode about half a dozen of our other secretaries and eight Czech guards. It was probably a novel experience for these members of the upper class of the old regime who had been accustomed to every luxury and their fifteen servants. I spent the last hour before the train left, between one and two o'clock in the morning, chasing up mattresses for the family, so that they wouldn't have to sleep on the hard boards.

October 24

This morning we had our first breakfast with our new landlady. Her governess and three children are the other members at the table. I don't know where her husband is. Have not seen or heard of him yet. We had oatmeal, toast, coffee, and it sure tasted good after nothing but restaurant coffee and rolls the past two weeks.

After a month of beautiful weather, it has turned wintry, 15 to 20 above today, with ice forming on swift creeks, and even in the glasses at the hut.

On October 29 Heald wrote his wife that he had decided to return to America "to stay" the following summer.

November 8

Noyes has not gone out with supply train number 4 yet. This is the first time we have arranged simply to attach to a Czech provision train, and the waiting has been longer than when we have run our trains independently. The shortage of locomotives is the reason for the new move, which is causing us serious loss. You see we have a limited canteen capital of a million and a half rubles per month. That is, we have been allowed that as new capital for the two months of September and October. That makes three millions. In addition, there is a half million which represented our canteen capital September first, making a total of three and a half million to date (about $350,000).

The last advices from the International Committee indicates that that will be all we can have to operate on. They have not been over-enthusiastic about their canteen experiences in France and look at the proposition over here in the same light. The truth is that that situation is entirely different, and they don't have the information about our work here. They seem to think our only canteen work over here is with the American troops. The fact is, that is a very incidental part of our canteen service. By far the largest part, I should say three-fourths, is with the Czechs. The Czechs are operating in a country that has been Bolsheviked dry of everything except dairy products, meat, and bread. They have depended on outside shipments for everything else. The Red Cross is handling hospital and medical supplies.

We are handling practically everything else except what the army management itself provides. They look to us for (just to quote from the last invoice): chocolate, caramels, hard candy, table spoons, matches, cigars, cigarettes, tea cups, tea biscuits, jam, honey, tea, coffee, soap, both laundry and toilet, cigarette papers, lead pencils, condensed milk, shoe polish, thread, cigar lighters, tooth paste, tooth brushes, candles, tobacco, brushes, undershirts, underdrawers, blankets, magazines, chewing gum, sugar, hard tack, samovars, charcoal, wrapping twine, tea trays, razor blades, shaving brushes, shaving powder, shoe laces, Czech, Russian, and other Allied flags, primus stoves, newspapers, knives and forks, dominoes, high boots, cash boxes, Bibles, violins, hair clippers, ink, footballs, boxing gloves, volleyballs, basketballs, baseballs, pens, checkers, scales, mattresses, and cocoa. Some of these things are Association equipment, but most are for sale in the club cars and barrack clubs which are operated by our widely scattered secretaries all along the line and all over the Ural-Volga front with the Czechs and Russians. Not a thing has been sent but what has been repeatedly requested by the secretaries in the interior as not to be had there.

Our problem now is to get the money back from the supplies that have been already sent. We haven't received a cent back except about fifty thousand rubles which Peters brought in from his car, which covers only the first train load that went through. We know that Phelps is bringing back between a quarter and a half million with him. Meanwhile, our whole purchasing machinery is held up until the money comes. We tried to get it transferred by the banks, but the demands to settle accounts abroad, especially in Japan, are so great now that it keeps the Vladivostok market drained of money, and though the bank branches in the interior are ready to receive our funds, the Vladivostok bank cannot turn funds over to us until the money arrives here. Our invoices now go out with the up-to-dateness of a commercial concern. The trains are managed with real business technique. The warehouse system has been highly developed there, and we now have branch warehouses with a correlated system at Khabarovsk, Irkutsk, Omsk, and probably at Cheliabinsk.

November 15

The war has ended. We have had quick and complete news service on recent events. By Tuesday we knew that the Kaiser had fled to Holland and that the armistice was to be signed Monday noon. By Wednesday we had the President's speech containing the articles of the armistice. The peace parade occurred today, all Allies taking part.

Omsk

En route Vladivostok to Nikolsk
November 20

Dear Emily:

After wonderful luck getting a private car (*sluzhebny*) for four people assigned to us to take us on our westward trip, I had my first experience in missing a train. Hooper and I had packed the *sluzhebny* with the food we would need for the trip and with part of our baggage. The last hours were hectic, trying to finish a week's work in a few hours. We took a chance on the train leaving late as usual, and when we arrived at the station in the cabs, at ten o'clock at night with suit case,‡ all the rest of our clothing, luggage, and mattresses, we found two trains there, the post train on one side and the big military train on the other. Both were on the point of leaving and we didn't know to which our *sluzhebny* was attached. So I inquired of the train despatcher, and he said it was on the end of the military train. So along we started, with the porters helping us lug our baggage down the length of those nineteen military cars, French, British, Italian, Czech, Russian, Japanese, and American cars for every country operating in Siberia. But no *sluzhebny* in sight. We lugged the baggage around to the post train on the other side of the station just in time to see the red light of the rear car—our *sluzhebny*—disappearing up the track. We had not allowed for the improved efficiency of the train schedule due to the American engineers. We were surely

---

‡ *Author's note.* In a suitcase with a lock out of repair, I carried 500,000 rubles ($50,000) for the needs of Western Siberia.

247

out of luck. We pictured our precious car and food traveling clear out to Omsk without us.

Then we bethought ourselves of getting on the military train, which would soon pass the post train, and having our *sluzhebny* dropped off the post train in Nikolsk, where we could pick it up on the military train as it came by, and beat the post train at that.

The station agent accepted our order to drop the *sluzhebny* at Nikolsk, but it took no end of negotiating to get space on the military train for us and our outrageous pack of luggage and mattresses, the latter, of course, taking up unnecessary space on the luxurious *wagon-lits* of the military train. We finally got space and had just turned in, about midnight, when word came that the train wouldn't leave in the morning, and perhaps not for some days. So we decided to take the morning post train instead, and we dressed and got out and notified the station agent to that effect. In the morning we had to use high pressure tactics to get any space on the post train, as all seats were at a premium and had been sold out for days ahead. But we finally worked it, and left Vladivostok at 10:20.

Diary entry for November 20

It was at Nikolsk that I saw the notorious "Death Train" which left Samara with 2,100 Bolshevik prisoners of war, and now there are only 1,300 left. I saw these wretched fluttering pale shadows of humanity, some of them too weak to lift a hand to carry bread to their mouths. The strongest staggered out to beg bread, which they brought back to their starving comrades. I couldn't learn much about the history of the car, who started it or who was responsible for its continued shifting around. One thing is certain: it left the Ural region and Omsk before the present Kolchak government took charge, so that the reports that are being circulated that Kolchak is responsible for the Death Car are false.

En route to Harbin, between Nikolsk and Pogranitchnaya
November 20

Dear Emily:

We connected with our little *sluzhebny* O.K. at Nikolsk
and are rambling along with all our luggage together now. We
had baked beans, sardines, roast beef hash, bread, apples,
oranges, and tea for supper on our car this evening. On our
back platform has been riding one of the Russian railway
employees. He has seven children, the oldest being a son 30
years of age. He (the son) was in the war on the Roumanian
front and came back with consumption. The youngest boy is
working in Vladivostok. None of the children are married.
He lived with his family in the Ukraine, being a Ukrainian,
but he moved out here twelve years ago because he thought
living would be better. He has been with the railroad two
years. He doesn't care to bother his head about politics. He
wishes all people would be just people and not Bolsheviki, or
Horvats, or monarchists, or Germans. Why can't everybody
do his work and live peaceably, he asks.

Harbin
November 22

We arrived here about two o'clock this morning after a bucking
bronco ride across the Manchurian plains that reminded me
of the Amur River line with you last March. I had to give
up writing annual reports or figuring except at station stops.
The leg of the table was yanked off by the motion.

While at the Consulate, I saw Bob Gailey of Peking who
had just arrived. He reports that China raised over a million
dollars on the United War Drive. The President subscribed fifty
thousand. The country simply went wild with enthusiasm for
the Allies and America, and the money poured into their
campaign headquarters at Peking so they had to cart it away
by the wagon load. It was primarily a movement of the Chinese
businessmen. Foreigners played but a small part in it.

The Russian businessmen here in Harbin got in the same
drive in a remarkable way—raising 270,000 rubles. Consul

Moser regards it as the crowning success of his career. A whole
new world has opened to me with these revelations. Vladivostok
must have been about the quietest city on the map when it
came to peace demonstrations, as there seemed not the slightest
interest by the inhabitants either in the peace demonstration
or the war drive. I would not have known that a war drive
was on there.

Harbin

November 23

I'll be glad to shake the dust of this roaming, rambling place.
It was attractive in the summertime when there was a bit
of green about, and I suppose there would be something attractive about it if there were snow on the ground, but in this
halfway stage, when there is nothing but dust and cold wind,
it is not attractive.

Beath, who acts as advance agent for Professor Robertson's
lectures, is now added to the party in our *sluzhebny*. He goes
as far as Irkutsk where he will set up the campaign for Professor
Robertson. Professor Robertson's lectures seem to be regarded
even more than last year as a part of a capitalistic program
by the working people.* He was with us a few minutes ago and
considers the situation anything but encouraging. He agrees
that we do have a clear piece of service with the Czechs,
however, no matter what happens in other directions.

November 24

Courier Holenja, who came through from the west, says that
the center of Siberia is extremely cold now. It is about ten
degrees above zero here, but no snow. There was hardly any
snow even in the mountains on the way from Vladivostok.
Holenja says it is not so cold again at Cheliabinsk and Ekaterinburg. The coldest stretch is from Irkutsk to Omsk. He stayed
in the cars all the time; was afraid to venture out.

* The professor's lectures dealt with such things as wireless telegraphy and
  the gyroscope.

Colonel Emerson says that the Russians have been cutting down on the American telegraph privilege until they have only one wire two hours a day. That is why they have had to cut the Y.M.C.A. out. The Japanese have exclusive use of three Russian wires and two of their own through Manchuria. Colonel Emerson says the Americans expect to lose even the two hours; then they will move out.

En Route Harbin to Manchuria Station,
Between Tsitsicar and Boochedoo
November 26

Yesterday I had the great privilege of a half-hour's talk with Madame Breshkovskaya, the Grandmother of the Russian Revolution, "Babushka" as she is fondly called by the Russians. She was on the same train from Harbin to Vladivostok that Gailey took; in fact it was owing to her kind offices that he got a coupe adjoining hers after two days of unsuccessful efforts to get a seat reserved.

She is going to America to ask for aid for her beloved Russians.

I remember when I was in Petrograd how much excitement there was when she returned from exile in Siberia. At that time the Czar's box in the theaters used to be reserved for returned exiles, and great enthusiasm greeted her as she appeared in the Czar's box surrounded by a large group of others who had returned. Those were in the days of the Kerensky regime, when she was popular with the government. For the kind of revolution she wanted was one for political democratic liberty such as we have in the United States, where she has spent several years, and not this Bolshevism. Bolshevism has not been kind to her. She has spent many months in prison under Bolshevik rule. It is marvelous how young and hearty she looked. "Why, I am not old, I am only seventy-six," she replied when I remarked on her vitality.

We were lucky to get permission to attach our car to the train of General Chechek, a Czech general, who arrived at Harbin from Vladivostok with a small Czech military train of

only seven cars, Sunday, the 24th. This means that we ought
to get through quicker than by post train, or by the long military train that has already gone ahead. We left Harbin last
evening.

En route between Boochedoo and
Hailar, Manchuria
November 26

Dear Goodsell:

At the last large station the Death Car filled with Bolshevik
prisoners of war under mixed Russian and Czech guard stood
on a siding. Russian railroad workers at the station asked
me why the Americans allowed such a crime, for these prisoners
were starving to death and no one was feeding them bread.
"Why don't the Russians feed them?" I asked. "They are under
Russian guard and are outside the jurisdiction of the Americans." "Nobody allows us to feed them," was the reply. "Who
prevents you?" I asked. "Semyenov," he answered. "Why do the
Russians allow Semyenov to do this?" I asked again. The reply
was a shrug of the shoulders while they pointed in the direction
of the Japanese soldiers standing on guard at the station. "The
army of salvation (the Russian cynical name for the Japanese
army) prevents it," they said. "Let the Allies get out of Russia
and then we'll fix things soon enough," was the further comment. "Why did the Allies come in and overthrow the Bolsheviki?" Czechs tell me that the railroad workers are purposely
causing many wrecks on the Omsk division out of spite for the
government.

November 27

Dearest Emily:

We woke up this morning on the Manchurian plains where
the railroad begins its ascent of the mountains of northwestern
Manchuria. There was just enough snow to give a general white
effect. The sunrise was beautiful, the sky clear and yellow
white in the east, and pink over the snow hills to the west. We
have been traveling through good game country all morning;

have seen several flocks of grouse and in several places bear tracks
and pheasants. Bread is already twice as high as in Harbin.

The last station was Boochedoo, which reminds me of
letters received from our secretaries last August and September
when the Czechs were encamped in barracks here waiting to
be outfitted before advancing on their campaign into the
interior. It was about the first of September when the road was
opened through to Irkutsk and then the movement began from
this point. There is still a Red Cross hospital car left on the
siding, a reminder of the time when they had a flourishing
hospital here, all of which has been moved further west to Omsk.
The weather is colder, zero at the last point, and the railroad
men say that fifty miles further on, where we cross the divide, it
will be forty below. We have just gone through the long tunnel which pierces the range dividing these two provinces of
Manchuria. Now we shall be going down hill all the way
to Manchuria station, following down the Argun River whose
tributaries rise in these mountains. I have a fine large scale
map of Manchuria which gives a splendid idea of the lay of
the land. Practically the only population in this part of
Manchuria lies along the railroad.

En route between Karimskaya and Chita
November 27

We have been making good time today, beating over 50 versts
an hour for the past four or five hours. In another hour's
time we ought to reach Chita.

Today we crossed the barren desert plains between Manchuria and the main Siberian road. It is snow-covered and
beautiful for all its desolation. Many cattle feed on the grass
which is pretty general. At one place we passed droves of camels
which were roaming at large. It has been cold all day, down to
18 below zero last night, but our car has been warm as toast,
in fact overly warm.

The car of General Chechek, who commands the First
Division of the Czechs, adjoins our car. I showed him the
pictures I have taken of the Czech work, and he returned the

compliment by showing me the pictures which his regimental
photographer has taken during all their experiences around
Samara and the Urals. One historical picture was that on May
27 showing General Chechek reading the telegram to the Czech
troops in which Trotsky gave orders that the Czechs should
not go on to Vladivostok, and the general told how the soldiers
responded when he said they would go on. He invited me to
lunch, and I must say we are living higher than he. I have all
the more respect for the Czechs for their simplicity of living.

At noon today we arrived at Olovyannaya where the big
bridge over the River Onon was wrecked by the Bolsheviki.
They are repairing it now, but we had to go over a temporary
wooden structure. The river is, of course, frozen, though its
current is so swift here that all this zero weather has not frozen
it entirely across. At the station we saw another train of Bolshevik prisoners of war in a terrible condition. They looked more
like animals than any group of human beings I ever saw. They
fought with each other for the pieces of bread which some of
them were able to buy. Their clothes were not fit to protect them
from the intense cold. When I asked where they were going, the
reply was "back and forth." The attitude of their captors,
both Russians and Czechs, seemed to be that they were suffering
just punishment for the cruelties they had perpetrated, and
that to keep running them around the country would have a
salutary effect of fear of the population. My observation,
however, was that instead of scaring people out of Bolshevism
it was creating Bolsheviki.

We are now traveling over country which you and I traveled last March. Transportation and order are much better
now than then in spite of all the defects of the present time.
Between here and Irkutsk is the most congested part of the trip.
In the stations along here there are large crowds of people
waiting to travel, the trains not being plentiful enough to take
care of them. Through Manchuria the stations had no crowds.

En route Chita to Irkutsk

Thanksgiving, November 28

We have made better time than anticipated today. It isn't often
one beats schedule in Russia, but we have been doing it right
along the past two days. Irkutsk is the last point that belongs to
the Eastern Division of our work. My territory begins west
of Irkutsk.

We are missing the views of Lake Baikal again, passing it
by night. We are passing along its edge now, but there is no
moon; it is dark and we shall see nothing but the swirling snow
which is thicker here than at any spot thus far. It is also cold
again. Last night at Chita it was 25 below zero, but it was
milder this noon and afternoon until we dropped down near
Lake Baikal. We covered today a distance greater than we
covered in two days last spring. All is covered with snow as
then. I asked at one station how many trains a day passed that
point, and the reply was three daily passengers in each direction
besides two others five days a week, and three freight trains in
each direction daily. Sixteen trains a day isn't so bad.

We celebrated Thanksgiving by inviting General Chechek
and his adjutant to partake of tea with us this evening. With
our tea we had cheese, jam, apricots, chicken, sardines, dough-
nuts, candy, chocolate, and raisins. He told us of some of his
experiences during the war. He was in the Austrian Army in
1905 and 1906. After that he came to Russia and lived in Moscow until the war broke out. He received a telegram from
Austria to report for mobilization on July 30. The telegram
was sent from Austria July 29. Russian mobilization was
declared the next day in answer to the Austrian. Germany followed two days later. He stayed in Russia and volunteered as a
common soldier in the Czech Legion, throwing up the officer's
rank which he enjoyed in Austria. In August he was arrested
by the Russians as a spy and spent seventeen days in prison.
After his release he settled his business affairs in Moscow, where
he had charge of the automobile department of a big concern,
and returned as a private to the legion. Later he became captain. He told me of one time on Christmas morning when with

seven men, without any rifles but simply with sticks, they
captured 230 Austrians and with this stunt enabled the Russians, almost without firing a shot, to capture 1,500 more with a
large number of cannon, machine guns, and other munitions.
The Austrian government placed a price of 5,000 rubles on
any Czech who could be captured dead or alive who was with
the Russian forces. Up until the Brest-Litovsk peace practically
all the Czech higher officers, such as generals, were Russian
because there were not among the Czech troops leaders old and
experienced enough to attain to these positions. But after the
Brest-Litovsk Peace most of the Russians decided to drop their
military duties with the Czechs, and it became necessary to
raise the Czechs themselves to the higher positions. He had
already earned the colonelcy for action in battle and was
advanced to general when the Czechs united for their overland
trek this spring. The qualities that seem to characterize him
are promptness, decision, and courage.

He says that the commercial and industrial development in
Bohemia after the war will be simply enormous. Plans are
teeming in every Czech mind. Before the war over half of all
the income from commerce and industry in Bohemia was mort-
gaged to the Austrian militaristic machine. Now all of it will
stay in Bohemia, and the country will boom. But the Czechs will
not all stay at home, he says. Great numbers will go to America
to learn. Twenty-five years from now there will be no train
anywhere in the world that will not be bearing two or three or
more Czechs, he says. It was a great treat to have this friendly
chat. I acted as translator for the other three American members
of our party.

En route Irkutsk to Krasnoyarsk near Nijni-Udinsk
November 29

When General Chechek's aide came into our car at Irkutsk this
morning and asked if our party was all present and ready to
start, Keeny smiled after the aide had departed and said, "Well,
this is something new in Y.M.C.A. circles for the general to
come around and ask the Y.M.C.A. secretaries if they are ready

for his train to start. That is different from the way we ran things down in Mesopotamia." Keeny was a Rhodes scholar at Oxford when the war broke out. That is how he came to go with the British *Y* to Mesopotamia.

We arrived at Irkutsk about eight o'clock this morning and left before ten o'clock. My telegram to Scherer had not been delivered, and he was not at the train so I got an *izvoschik* and went over to the house where he is staying. Bill Francis opened the door. Both of them drove back to the station with me and visited at the car until time for the train to go. Bill is doing athletic work among the Czechs and Russians in barracks at Irkutsk but will come on west to rejoin his beloved Czechs as soon as another man arrives from Vladivostok to relieve him of his present work. I handed him a pile of letters from home which put him into raptures. Beath, who had been with us from Harbin, stayed at Irkutsk to work up Professor Robertson's lectures.

My trip to Scherer's rooms gave me my only glimpse of Irkutsk. Streets were crowded with innumerable frost-covered horses rapidly pulling rough wooden sleighs of peasants, the latter bundled up in big furs and fur hats to keep out the 25 below zero cold; school children on the way to school, also bundled to the nose tips. Great banks of fog rose from the water that still ran free in part of the Angara River, the current being so swift that even a month of continuous zero weather has not frozen the river over. It was the nearest to arctic life that I have seen, and much livelier and full of business than I had expected. I looked for everybody to have practically all skin spots completely concealed, but many were working or walking around without overcoats or even ear caps, and apparently not suffering.

Just passed Krasnoyarsk
November 30

We made remarkable time from Irkutsk to Kransnoyarsk. General Stefanik's train—the big military train—left Irkutsk 12 hours ahead of us and we caught up with it at Krasnoyarsk, thus exceeding its speed by 12 hours in a period of 32 hours. General

Stefanik's train has 14 cars as compared with 7 on ours, hence the difference in speed. This speed, however, is hard on one's health in these bouncing cars, and I had a headache most of the day from it.

It is much milder today in spite of the fact that we are the furthest north that the road goes, and we were told that the coldest stretch would be between Irkutsk and Omsk. There is still snow all along the way but not much; enough, however, to make a picturesque scene with the green pines and white birch trees which we have been passing all day. The sunset this evening reminded me of a Levitan painting with the dark pines and snowy ground showing sombrely under a melancholy clouded sky all except an open streak where the sun was setting.

We passed many refugees today, all living on trains, and many begging from us as our train went by. They seem to be well bundled in warm clothing. It was out near this region where Alpin and Humphreys worked with the Siberian refugees several months.

En route between Novo-Nikolaievsk and Omsk
December 1

Last night after I finished my letter, a Czech engineer who is accompanying the general's train got caught on our car before he had time to get to his, the train started up so unexpectedly. He has plans for electrifying all Siberia. All he needs is capital. Czechs everywhere have plans for developing Siberia.

The more I think of it the more I am convinced that the region of the world's greatest material development during the next generation will be Siberia. There is already a sense of coming big development among all classes of the population. I rode on the locomotive today and talked with the engineer and firemen. They only get 350 and 290 rubles respectively monthly. Their wages have only doubled the past two years at a time when prices and most wages have advanced four to ten times. The above salaries represent decidedly less purchasing power here than $35 and $29. Yet they hang on and keep their job going in a truly heroic manner. They pointed out coal mines along the way. "Those on that side belong to the railroad, and those on that side to private people," they said. "That is the best coal in Siberia. Only four percent less than anthracite grade. This whole region is very rich. All of Siberia is very rich. All that is needed is head," he concluded pointing to his own head. He was using telegraph blanks as wrapping paper for the cheap cigarette tobacco, not being able to afford the regular wrapping paper.

Today has been milder, only 18 above zero, but snowier. As we passed the forests laden with snow the engineer gave expression to his Russian sense of beauty, saying "Such beauty." He said the woods had big bear in them and that it was a favorite region for hunters.

When I was back at Vladivostok and Harbin, I heard nothing but melancholy rumors about the disorders, bad communications, intrigues, wrecks, etc. out in this part of the world. I find to the contrary that there seems to be healthy, independent industry, progress, and good order out here. The two parties, democratic and monarchistic, are well defined, and both have their able press organs. The emphasis has changed from the Bolshevik-capitalistic issue which was prevailing when you and I came out, to the democratic-monarchistic issue, though there is still fighting going on at the Ural front with the Bolsheviki.

Omsk

December 3

We arrived here yesterday afternoon at 2:30 beating schedules all the way. Noyes had just arrived though he left Vladivostok twelve days before me. He sprained his ankle at Harbin, and in the mail I brought him was news of his brother's death and his mother's need for him at home. He will have to go at once. We are mighty sorry. His going will be a big loss. It is remarkable how some of the rougher spirits admire and respect him.

Found the office arrangements here impossible. A space 4 by 6 feet on one of the cars serves as the office for a work directing twenty-five men and handling business amounting to over two million rubles ($200,000) monthly. One third-class car is serving as living quarters and office for all the secretaries in Omsk and

six helpers besides. We are transferring the bunks to another
car and converting one car into an office temporarily until we
can find quarters in town.

Went over to the city yesterday and visited the American
Consul, Mr. Harris. Omsk is a well laid out city, of generous
proportions, with big business blocks reminding me of Petrograd
more than any other city I have seen in Russia; but the spirit
of the city is entirely unlike Petrograd, more like Moscow. The
sleighs are more numerous and finer than in other cities and
speed along at a great rate. The prices are not so dear as I
imagined from all reports. Got a good beefsteak dinner last night
for 7.50 rubles ($.75) including soup and fried potatoes. Butter
is only 3 rubles per pound as compared with 12 to 15 in Vladivostok. Cheese is also plentiful and fine. This is, of course, the
center of the great dairy business of Siberia. Omsk is a center
for many great Siberian cooperatives, such as meat, butter, and
dairy. These cooperatives, managed by long-whiskered peasants,
are thriving uninterruptedly in these revolutionary times when
private stores are mostly out of business. Step into the office of
one of these cooperatives where 40 typewriters are clicking away,
and you can imagine yourself in an office on Broadway.

I like the breadth, sweep, and western spirit of Omsk. The
inhabitants are remarkably well dressed. I am almost reminded
of Nevsky Prospect. Most of the people are big, healthy, splendid-
looking specimens physically, with little of the spoiled feminism
of the capital. Winter is on in real earnest, below zero every day.
It has been as much as 40 below, and this will keep up without
a let-up for about four months more.

I had lunch with the Carl Comptons yesterday. They were
in relief work in the Caucasus last year. They have been roving
up and down Siberia in refugee work, going down as far as the
Altai mountains south of Novo-Nikolaievsk last summer.

En route Omsk to Ekaterinburg
December 6

We are pounding along on the branch of the Siberian road that
veers northwest from Omsk. It is the line which the Siberian
Express takes to Petrograd, but this is my first time over it. I

suppose you came this way when you went to Petrograd. Our train is a special train of Consul General Harris. There are four Y.M.C.A. *teplushkas* loaded with supplies for the front, our third-class car, and four coaches of the consulate party. We left Omsk yesterday noon and expect to reach Ekaterinburg tomorrow morning.

Just before getting on the train at Omsk a letter came in by courier from Chez who was only a few versts out of the city with his Tenth Regiment of the Czechs. They were coming back from the front for a rest. They had been through a period of stiff fighting on the northern front before being shifted to Samara, where they found the cold very severe, more so than further north. Our train stopped at the siding where Chez was located. He and Captain Badura were there, and I had a short chat with them, handing Chez a good bunch of home mail.

I interviewed Consul Harris regarding the letter which I received that morning from the Minister of Foreign Affairs of the Omsk government. It was an appeal to the Red Cross and the Young Men's Christian Association to extend the same service to the Russian army which we have been rendering the Czechs and other Allies. I sent a wire to the Vladivostok office after receipt of this letter recommending doubling the scale of our service.

I have received a new conception of the Kolchak Government, and a favorable one in comparison with former ones. Until I reached Omsk I had classed the Horvat, Semyenov, and Kolchak groups as all of the same stripe, and one and the same thing. Now it seems that Kolchak is not Czarist, not autocrat, not playing with Bolshevik leaders, but an able man who is trying to restore sufficient order so that the Russians can say what kind of a government they want. He and his colleagues are friendly to America and anxious for our cooperation. He has at the heads of his departments of Foreign Affairs, Ways and Communication, War and Finance, probably the ablest and best fitted men that Russia can offer for those positions at the present time. Minister of Foreign Affairs Kliuchnikov, with whom we dealt concerning the relations of the Y.M.C.A., impressed me as a capable, efficient man with a pleasant personality.

We are passing through a pretty region of white birch trees,

with a good sprinkling of evergreens, making an attractive background to the snow-covered ground and the leaden sky. The
day that we came into Omsk was the most magnificent I have
ever seen. All the trees and shrubs were covered with a coating
of ice, the sun was shining, and we were traveling through an
ever-changing fairyland all day.

Ekaterinburg

December 7

We arrived here at two o'clock yesterday, only 24 hours from
Omsk instead of the scheduled 36. I met Alpin in the station.
He looked much older than last year, and pale, as if not healthy.
Riley had gone to town, and I didn't meet him for a couple of
hours. Our telegram had not been received and my arrival was a
perfect surprise, as he did not know I had even left Vladivostok.

Before Riley and I connected, I met Svanda, an American
Czech, who is secretary with one of the Czech cavalry groups;
Alexander, who was with Noyes in Odessa, and who is doing a
splendid work in the city, especially popular with the railroad
and working men; and Shindilkah, the kino operator. I went to
the Czech staff to deliver a package to a Russian officer related
to Madame Maslinakova, at whose apartments we stayed at Dom
Brynner. The officer invited me to visit him and his wife at the
train, where they, like many others these days, are living.

The sleigh ride to the Staff headquarters, taken just as the
early evening dark was settling, gave a little glimpse of this most
fascinating summer resort of some 60,000 population.

When Riley arrived here as district secretary, he found that
Alpin had organized a big and flourishing Y.M.C.A. work with
the best club quarters in the Ural region. In the evening Riley
and I called on him and his Russian wife at their apartments in
a well appointed house. She is the charming White Russian girl
you and I knew at Kiev. They seem to be very happy.

Alpin has the reputation of being the best connoisseur of
Ural stones of any of the Americans in this region. He has
resisted the attractions of the precious stone business as a commercial opportunity but helps his friends get good bargains. He

buys the stones from the miners, and has them cut by a jewel cutter in the city, and sells them to his friends at cost.

This noon being clear for the first time for many days at Ekaterinburg, Riley and I picked up our cameras and strolled over town. It is the most fascinating city I have seen in Russia, a Ural gem. Its situation is picturesque, the center of the city rising to some height, on the highest point of which stands a Russian church with a high tower. The city slopes off in all directions, with patches of pine forest on the rising heights opposite all about. It is full of beautiful churches. The broad avenues and prospects are lined with splendid substantial stone buildings, and an air of Petrograd at its best greets one at many corners.*

The new National Army of Russia is much in evidence here, and it gives a favorable impression with its stalwart marching columns and the ringing singing of troops. The Russian troops are really distinguishing themselves on the northern front against the Bolsheviki. One of the soldiers who lives where the Alpins do returned from the front today. They had captured nine villages, one after the other, in a few hours. The Magyars and Germans have withdrawn from the Bolshevik front.

This evening I went to the Russian church and the Russian Club with Riley, Keeny, Tinkham, and Woodberry. The club was an eye opener and a monument to Alpin's ability. It is run entirely by Russian secretaries. The head secretary, Poisty, formerly a Methodist preacher, has preached in the Swedish church in Finland and gives religious lectures to the soldiers with audiences running 4,500 to 5,000. There are no places vacant when he lectures. His subject tomorrow will be: "Why the Young Man Needs Christ." He lectures in such a non-partisan and non-sectarian manner that the priests express themselves as sympathetic and congratulate him on how good his lectures are. There is a social program every night with kino pictures, buffet in operation, music, barber shop, library, magazines, and news-

---

* Heald's enthusiasm for Ekaterinburg might have been less had he known of the murder of the Czar and his entire family which took place there the preceding July.

papers. There were 50 in the class for illiterates. The whole club
was entirely self-supporting under Alpin's direction, the buffet
paying for itself and all the other expenses of the institution,
and yet the buffet prices were below city prices. The buffet is
always jammed with great lines of soldiers. I regard this club as
the most significant thing our army work has yet produced in
Russia, showing how admirably the Russians themselves can
develop such work.

En route Ekaterinburg to Cheliabinsk

December 9

We are passing through the picturesque pine forests that line
the railroad most of the way between Ekaterinburg and Cheliabinsk. It is before sunrise of another clear day, the third in
succession, very unusual here. The ground is covered with snow
but not so deep as I expected as this line is reputed to be snowbound part of the winter.

Yesterday morning Mrs. Alpin guided us around to the
Monastery Church at Ekaterinburg beyond the Czar's Bridge.
The archbishop took part in the service, and there was special
choir music, as fine as the Kiev choirs. The interior of the church
was very bright, and the walls decorated with copies of paintings that appear on the Kiev churches, all in light ethereal blue
colors that give a pure uplifting atmosphere. The trip out to
the church took one through the city, and the charms of Ekaterinburg grow upon one the more one sees of it. There are many
tasteful homes of Russia's wealthy people.

The Y.M.C.A. Czech Club at Ekaterinburg opened yesterday afternoon. They have fine large rooms covering the top floor
of the Art School. The rooms are rent free, as is also the theater
in which the big Russian Club is located. Ekaterinburg is not so
overcrowded as most other cities in Siberia, and the Y.M.C.A.
has better accommodations than in any other city.

General Stefanik arrived at Ekaterinburg yesterday. The
train was late and the Russian and Czech soldiers stood lined up
along the street from the depot to the city about five hours.
They got so cold that they had to take to the restaurants, coffee

houses, and Y.M.C.A. club rooms to warm up. Suddenly the alarm was sounded that the general was coming. Before the soldiers could get to their stacked arms the auto carrying the general whizzed by. The delay upset the opening program for the club and the orchestras, bands, etc. who were engaged for the reception. Both Czech and Russian soldiers look well equipped and clothed.

We have been witnessing a wonderful sunrise. The forests of silver birches sprinkled with evergreens first caught snatches of the pink light on the tops of the trees, a picture that Kuindji would have delighted to paint. The lower parts of the trees looked like a gray mist, everything all coated with ice. The gray mist grew lighter and lighter, until all at once the flood of pink light burst out everywhere. We have now run out from the hills on to the plain on which Cheliabinsk stands.

Ekaterinburg won my heart. What a different idea you would have always had of Russia if you had gone there instead of to Minsk.

Duncan had another close call at the front a couple of weeks ago. He was on his car which was attached to a Czech train when all at once machine gun fire began. He thought at first it was practice. The bullets began whistling about his car. He doused the lights and looked out the door. It was dark, but he could tell that the Czechs had left the train. He took to the woods. After a while he ran upon his cook who was trying to get away on a horse. The horse had gotten caught by a big log, with its two forefeet over the log on one side and the hind legs behind on the other. It couldn't budge either way. Voices and shooting could be heard all around. It was cold and swampy. Duncan was wading in water up to his armpits most of the night. The next day he heard that the whole train had been captured by the Bolsheviki. On the third day he got back and found the train back in the hands of the Czechs. One of his helpers was lying in the car dead and another seriously wounded. There were bullet holes through his frying pan, and many other evidences of battle in the car.

Cheliabinsk

December 10

This is an age of car homes in these refugee-crowded cities of
Siberia. The use of cars for homes and offices cripples the passenger and freight service. On the train we came down on from
Ekaterinburg last night, there was only one passenger coach beside our own, as no others were to be found.

Miller has a wonderful piece of work going here. We visited
his bakery which turns out 8,000 rolls of bread daily which are
sold within an hour after they are placed on his store car. The
bakery is run with two shifts of men and is going day and night.
They make rolls such as the Czechs make in Bohemia, and they
sell very cheap, for 10 kopeks or one cent each. This and his
other factories produce for the Czech army only.

The sausage factory is another big concern. We saw the
process from the dog to the smoked product. Miller said he could
no longer look a dog in the face. He has his purchasers after
meat, flour, and butter all over this end of Siberia. They purchase in lots as high as 25,000 rubles at a time. His business last
month amounted to over 300,000 rubles. All his managers are
Czechs, and he has the work so highly organized now that he has
largely freed himself from the business details. The sausage factory is the biggest one in the city. He says they have to work to
avoid making profits; they try to keep it at cost.

Miller told about the history of Cheliabinsk since he arrived
with the Czechs April 29. They were then still at peace with
the Soviet. It was here that the trouble started that ignited the
whole Czech-Soviet conflict. According to his story, it arose over
a Hungarian who was killed. The Bolsheviki arrested Czechs
charged with the killing. The Czechs appointed witnesses, and
the Bolsheviki arrested the witnesses. The Czechs sent a delegation to remonstrate, and the Bolsheviki arrested the delegation. Then the Czechs seized guns and released delegation,
witnesses, and those charged with the killing. This was the action
which gave rise to the famous telegram of Trotsky ordering that
the Czechs be disarmed and prevented from proceeding on their
way, and that is what caused the Czechs to begin their campaign
against the Bolsheviki. At the beginning they had five fronts

out from Cheliabinsk. Miller said it was a joke how the Czechs would send a company out here to take a regiment of Bolsheviki, and a battalion here to take a city, always against great odds, and they always walked away with whatever they had to do. They took Cheliabinsk by surprise.

Cheliabinsk is a city with a normal population of 50,000 and a present population of 100,000. It is chiefly important as a big railroad center. It stretches in straggling fashion over a large territory and is unattractive and dirty. Typhus has broken out, and the overcrowded condition of the refugees adds to the danger. Schools have been closed and the work of the Y.M.C.A. clubs is endangered. The American Red Cross is working at the problem and cleaning up some of the worst spots. One spot called The Vulcan is frightfully crowded with refugees, a number of whom have typhus. The Red Cross has requisitioned a big building 20 versts out to which 100 of this group will be moved. The other 400 will be spread around in the building after it has been disinfected.

And now come the Siberian prisoners who have been in Austria and Germany. They are being allowed to come through the Bolshevik lines. It is hard to understand why, as they are always rabidly anti-Bolshevik. Probably there are such crowds of them that the Bolsheviki cannot help themselves. They are arriving in terrible condition, many without shoes, and with tatters that hardly cling to them.

En route Cheliabinsk to Ufa
December 11

We are passing through the most scenic part of the Urals today. The last station was Zlatoust, meaning Gold Mouth, and Miller and I got off and purchased a few stones. The sidings along here are full of scores of locomotives that are out of commission. I believe we have passed over a hundred this morning. Zlatoust is probably the biggest precious stone center in the Urals.

Keeny, Heinz, and Tinkham are along with Miller and myself. Ufa is the end of passenger service and the last large station before the Bolshevik lines. The Czechs have withdrawn from the front all along the Ural region, giving the Russians a chance to show what they can do. At first the Russians on this front started to fall back, and we considered evacuating Ufa, but the last few days the Russians have been holding. On the northern front the Russians have been advancing right ahead.

Miller and I had a two hour hunt for our home last night in the Cheliabinsk railroad yards. We stood in the 25 below zero weather for half an hour waiting. We stood opposite the entrance to a big waiting-room, in front of which there was an icy spot. Half of the people who came out stepped on this icy spot and fell. No matter how badly they were hurt they got up, made a few remarks that sounded better in Russian than in their English equivalents, then proceeded on. No one made any attempt to have the spot thawed out, and no one cared what would happen to others following. At least twenty, including children, fell while we were there. This study of Russian character helped pass the time. Finally Miller's feet got too cold, so he started off hunting the car while I stood guard over the baggage. No luck. The switchmen and conductors all knew ours would be switched on, but no one knew where it was. Finally at 1:15 a.m., an engine came pulling it along and we clambered on, eighteen hours behind time.

En route Ufa to Cheliabinsk
December 13

Yesterday we spent in Ufa. Greiner, a Baltic Russian, is our secretary there. He and his wife are living on a car in the Ufa station yards. His wife is a Russian girl from Moscow. They were married five days before war was declared. He was called with the first mobilization, wounded in September, returned to the front in November 1914, taken prisoner under the Carpathians in April 1915, and spent two years in the prison camps of Austria, much of the time at Spratzern. As he was an officer he had easy conditions in the prison camp and was in communication with his wife and got food parcels through Copenhagen. Finally he was brought to Copenhagen as an invalid, and after a year there, exchanged and returned to Russia a year ago. He

connected up with the Y.M.C.A. soon after his return and worked
at Moscow and Samara.

He is a live wire. He has organized work at the front from
Ufa, running supply cars out to club cars on the front. He has
established excellent relations with the officials at Ufa. From
the town mayor he has obtained, rent free as long as the Y.M.C.A.
wants it, a theater with a big hall for shows of kino pictures,
another that will serve as a gym, and about twenty other rooms
for offices, living quarters, educational rooms, club rooms, etc.
The whole city knows and wants the Y.M.C.A. The securing of
this building is really a big stroke and indicative of how we
are developing a Russian staff that can do things. There are now
three Russians associated with our secretaries in this region
who are of the calibre of American secretaries—Greiner at Ufa,
Dr. Liperovsky at Cheliabinsk, and Poisty at Ekaterinburg.

Ufa is a city of about 50,000 population, standing on high
bluffs above the Byelaya (White) River. The sleighs charge
thirty rubles for taking you up to the city one way and forty for
the round trip. We decided to walk and save the money, but it
was like climbing Cheyenne Mountain at Colorado Springs, and
we were ready to agree with Greiner, by the time we reached
the top, that to walk was impossible and that the sleigh charges
were impossible. His solution had been to get a horse and sleigh
as Y.M.C.A. property. The horse was requisitioned free to him
by the Russian military officials. That is the difference between
requisitioning out here and in Eastern Siberia. In Western
Siberia they requisition things free; in Eastern Siberia requisitioning simply means paying an enormous rent.

We visited the commander of this front, General Voitsikovsky, a Pole. He is commander of both the Czechs and Russians. He is the successor of General Chechek, with whom we
rode on the train from Harbin to Omsk. General Voitsikovsky is
an approachable, direct, forceful, cleancut, young man of something like 35 years. He is much in sympathy with the *Y* work
and thinks much of Miller. He is another sample of the better
day that is dawning in Russia. The last five or six days have seen
a big change in the atmosphere on the southwestern Ufa front;
the Russians are holding and beginning to advance and the

most critical time seems to have passed. The new Siberian troops make a fine-looking army; husky, healthy young peasants, who put some spirit into their step and do not have the leaden, dull face of the peasant soldiers of the old regime.

Ufa itself is three-fourths Mohammedan. There are also many Bashkirs.* The Bashkirs are excellent soldiers. The Mohammedans are more of a problem. They visited the Y.M.C.A. quarters the other day and took possession saying they needed some warm rooms. When they left, most of the Y.M.C.A. furnishings disappeared with them.

The Siberian prisoners of war returning from Germany are pouring into Ufa almost a thousand a day. They are passing through into Siberia. They are mostly without hats, shoes, or ear covers in this sub-zero weather. It is a pitiful sight, and yet they are happy to be getting home. Our train was passing one of them this morning. He was walking briskly along the road smiling happily while he was rubbing his bare hands and trying to keep his ears warmed with his hands. It was about 25 below zero. The train to which our car is attached is filled exclusively with returning prisoners of war. At the last station, one of the prisoners met his sister. There was a shout of joy, which was joined in by crowds of the passengers.

At Ufa I received a telegram forwarded from Banton to the effect that Peters had not yet been able to leave Vladivostok with his train of 32 cars. He has been standing there three weeks. Traffic is hopelessly tied up. They are putting it up to me to try to get orders through from this end. We hoped to have that train out before Christmas, but now it is impossible.

Cheliabinsk

December 14

We arrived here last night after making the trip to Ufa and back in the short space of three days. Yesterday was a quiet day spent in enjoying the beauties of the Urals with the trees all ice-

---

* Heald was inadequately informed. The Bashkirs whom he admired were just as Moslem or "Mohammedan" as those, presumably Tatars, whom he disliked.

covered. Especially beautiful was the night view under the bright moon. Just at the top of the Urals where the downhill grade begins, the mountains and valleys covered with the snow and ice-laden birches and evergreens presented a scene of marvelous glory.

The switchman has just been in to announce that our train will leave at eight o'clock in the morning. He said it would have gone out this evening only there didn't happen to be a spare locomotive. Thanks to the lack of the locomotive, my car didn't start off for Omsk taking all my belongings and 50,000 rubles in cash after which I would have had a merry chase. I made it clear to the switchman that I did not want to go until tomorrow night.

December 16

Yesterday was spent investigating the needs of the Siberian prisoners of war who are returning from Germany. They are coming through with a speed and unexpectedness that surprise us all. Four thousand have already passed through Cheliabinsk. From what they say we can expect forty thousand through here. This will be the most important point for meeting their needs as all will pass through here. They are coming through by train. Between Samara and Ufa they have to walk for one hundred versts (about 65 miles) between fronts. There are between seven and eight thousand of them in Samara without enough clothing to proceed further. They received food only at two points through Bolshevik Russia, at Smolensk and at Tula. The rest of the time they had to exist on the scanty supply provided them when they left Germany. Every one who arrives here is a rabid anti-Bolshevik. They say conditions in Bolshevik Russia are terrible, that the Red Army is all that is keeping the Bolsheviki in power. A peasant invites you into his "four walls" instead of his home as nothing else is left. The Bolsheviki are carrying off everything else. Conditions in the city are just as bad, they say.

The Kolchak Government here is acting effectively to meet the prisoners as they arrive at Ufa. They are given trains and locomotives and carried free. They receive four rubles at Ufa. They were given instructions to pay for their food along the way with this four rubles but that is evidently an oversight as that amount (about 40 cents) does well to last a day. They are all out of money by the time they reach here. The government is furthermore providing feeding points about every 250 versts along the railroad where the prisoners receive soup, bread and kasha, and yesterday was added tea and sugar though the latter was only enough for two days. The food is good as Russian food goes. Their great need is clothing. They are a pitiful sight in their rags that hardly hang on them and feet done up in old rags and bare hands and bare ears. The American Red Cross has some cloth for garments at Omsk, and we have agreed to cooperate in finding machines to make them into garments if they furnish the cloth. We are also organizing with the assistance of Dr. Posdnikov here a canvass of the city for second-hand clothing either to be given or sold cheaply to us. We will give it to the prisoners, none of whom have money. Keeny plans to organize the Boy Scouts of the city for this purpose. We plan to conduct similar canvasses in other cities along the line where we have secretaries. We will also give big wooden spoons and teapots, one teapot to each ten men, and be ready for sugar and tea, if necessary.

The Russian Red Cross has no organization here. Doctor Posdnikov, their only accredited representative, says there is no organization in the other cities along the line. He has a sum of 20,000 rubles advanced him by the Omsk Government.

En route between Cheliabinsk and Omsk, just past Kurgan
December 17

Keeny made a survey of Cheliabinsk with reference to plans for returning prisoners of war with some interesting results. In this city of 70,000 population, there were 5,000 Singer sewing machines, which were on the list of the office of that company. There is a tailor's union in which there are at present a dozen unoccupied tailors, though in tailor shops that are open you have to wait three months for a suit to be made. The head of the tailor union is a Jew who has spent several years in London, a socialist, and "agin all government." When it came to getting

something done, our good Dr. Posdnikov of the Russian Red
Cross proved to be absolutely without resources and threw up
his hands and said go ahead and run the show. The mayor had
gotten further, and plans were being made to arrange for sewing
machines to prepare garments for the prisoners.

The winter here is beautiful. The glory of snow-covered
and frost- and ice-covered trees, which is a thing of hours in
America, is the normal thing here, lasting day after day and week
after week. We had something approaching it in the Ukraine,
but it is still more wonderful here. The plains and the Urals
alike are one continuous stretch of fairy land. Whether cloudy
or clear, there is equal enchantment. By day or by moonlight,
it is hard to tell which is the more splendid. It is only 2:45
in the afternoon but already getting dark.

There was a sudden change of the situation after we left
Ufa. We arrived at Cheliabinsk to find a wire from Greiner
announcing that they were beginning to evacuate the Ufa
railroad yards. Last night Greiner reported that he was sending
three cars of Y.M.C.A. property and two secretaries to
Cheliabinsk while he and Mrs. Greiner are staying at Ufa
with the other secretaries to the last.

Omsk

December 18

We arrived here at two o'clock this afternoon, the coldest
day I have yet known, 32 below zero. We passed a train of
800 Russian prisoners returning from Germany and Austria,
fifty versts out of Omsk. The train was stalled, no wood for the
stoves, and the men were freezing. Four of them clambered
on to our car, and I invited them to ride on to Omsk with me.
They had nothing to eat since the preceding morning. I gave
them all the bread I had, opened up a can of bully beef, which
was all the meat I had with me, and wound up with some tea
and sugar to each man and a teapot for the party. They sure
did get away with the food, but not until after they had
finished a cigarette apiece. They hardly knew what to make
of their luck. Two of them were from Austria and two from

Germany. The two from Austria were in worse rags but had fared better with food. The two from Germany were distinguished with brown-colored arm bands and uniforms looking like these the Russian railroad workers wear. They said prisoner's food had been mighty scarce. They estimated that seven hundred thousand prisoners had died in Germany according to the Berlin papers they read. Two years ago there were 2,000,000 Russian prisoners in Germany, now only a million and a quarter, the others having died. On one camp where one of these prisoners was, the prisoners had died at the rate of 500 daily when the typhus struck them. The bodies were buried in the cemeteries three deep. They all left Germany on the same date, November 11.

They gave a new picture of the German revolution, a real Bolshevik revolution. The Soldiers' and Workingmen's Soviets were running everything. They came to the prison camps, told them they had the power, the war was over, opened the gates and told them they were free and to go home. Through Bolshevik Russia they were offered three hundred rubles per month, food and room and clothing if they would join the Red Army. Very few joined. They were rabidly against them, *saying the Bolsheviki were all Jews and they showed their permissions which had been signed at the front, to show that the signers were Jews.** One of the prisoners was going clear to Vladivostok where his home was. He was an intelligent artisan, and I gave him a note to Goodsell.

Had an interview with Mr. Thompson of the American Red Cross this evening. He has charge of the relief work for the refugees, is an excellent businessman, and shows a fine spirit. We discussed caring for these Russian prisoners of war. The problem is to locate the clothing. The forty thousand suits which the Red Cross had on the way never got beyond Vladivostok.

* Italicized words were censored.

December 20

Yesterday was a real Siberian day, 47 below zero. Until the temperature gets to 40 degrees below the natives always laugh at the cold and say "Wait until January," but when it passes the 40 mark they are ready to admit it is winter. I made good use of the knit helmet yesterday. Had two long sleigh rides over to town and back. The thing that surprised me was how many people remained at outdoor work at such a temperature. All sorts of hauling was going on, mostly wood, and some English soldiers who were hauling wood looked the coldest of all. They are less well clothed to meet such weather than the Russians. The latter are eternally bundled up, especially the women who waddle around like animated rag mountains. Men were working on the telegraph wires high overhead. I was freezing enough in my sleigh but the thought of getting up without an overcoat in those wires and trying to do anything with tools was no joyful thought. Then came along a bunch of soldiers marching without any nose covers, and I felt sure mine would be frozen in two minutes if I didn't have it covered. Next came a soldiers' band, with their instruments, but they didn't play. And the newsboys selling papers and having to take off their mitts continually to fish out change. It has not gotten above 25 degrees below zero any time during the day for the past five days. Yesterday the warmest it got was 29 degrees below, and such will be our winter here for three months to come.

Such weather brings the Siberian prisoner-of-war situation home to one terrifically. Those fellows have no warm place to stay, their cars are cold most of the time. It is incredible that they live at all. One meal a day scheduled and much of the time missing that. No one else is doing anything for them except the meal a day that the government provides. We arranged yesterday to serve them tea and sugar free, and we are turning over big cartwheel hard-tack biscuits to them which were intended for the army but which the army is too well fed to care for. In fact the refugees and German and Austrian prisoners of war are living in luxury compared with these Siberian prisoners who are returning from the Central Powers.

December 22

The city is under martial law this morning. The first word we
got was that all the thieves and criminals in the jail had gotten
out at night. The next was that there was a general uprising of
Bolsheviki. The next that certain companies of the younger
Russians had mutinied. We are cut off from railroad communication with the west, the front being only about five miles west
of here, just beyond the big bridge. The way is open east but
no trains running. Things seem to be moving about the same as
usual about the station yards for Sunday, but of course most
of our plans are held up now. Professor Robertson is about a
day's journey east of here bound this way. There are a couple
of trains of Russian war prisoners held up between here and
Petropavlovsk, the last feeding point west of here, and they
are probably freezing and starving to death. We have plans
ready to rush hard-tack biscuits, sugar, and tea to the Russian
war prisoners as soon as the way is open.

Turovsky, the Russian interpreter with a sort of hatchet
face whom you met at Vladivostok, arrived here from Novo-
Nikolaievsk last night. He has been handling Red Cross work
there for the past six weeks. He has handled two hundred
thousand rubles, and eight hundred thousand rubles worth of
supplies in six weeks time. He was loaned to the Red Cross by
us for this work. We are now calling him back to help us
with the Russian war prisoner work.

He says there are seven hundred Russian war prisoners at
Novo-Nikolaievsk without shoes, overcoats, socks, gloves,
or ear covers, and so far unprovided with food. All that they
have received they have gotten by begging. The reason the
Russians were unprepared for these was that they came
through not in large organized parties but in driblets without
previous notice. There are similar groups of Russian war
prisoners at Barnaul and Taiga in as bad condition; some of
them almost naked in this 30 below zero weather.

December 22, Evening

It was dark as I returned to our railroad home from the city. After I arrived here, I learned that the city was under martial law with orders to shoot any one on sight after eight o'clock. I came through the main street at exactly eight and was struck by the absence of everybody, the fact that there was only one light the whole way; theaters, restaurants, hotels, kinos all dark. Luck was evidently with me as no one took a shot at me. Here in the yards we are only under military law which isn't so strict. The Bolsheviki west of town were put down and the affair "liquidated" this afternoon, the Czechs coming across and saving the day. The Czechs say that they lost one killed and two wounded; the Bolsheviki, 80 killed, 400 wounded, and 1,500 prisoners.

Christmas Eve

I got back to the railroad town at 3:30 after my day's work in the main city. My first job was to see whether the train of the Red Cross left for Vladivostok at three o'clock according to schedule. It did not, but was still standing at the military platform a half mile down the tracks. That gave me time to prepare more mail for it. The next thing was to see whether Professor Robertson's car was properly ordered for the six o'clock train to Ekaterinburg. It was.

While I am dictating further correspondence, Peterka, Noyes' old Czech helper, comes in and wants to go back to Vladivostok. As we need men out here ten times worse than in Vladivostok, I talk with him and he agrees to stay in the west and to take a holiday until the day after New Year's. Gelka, another Czech from the Reserve Regiment, who is on special sentinel duty around the station, comes in to get fifty cigarettes for the Czechs who are guarding with him. I give him the order to get them from Bixby at the warehouse. I also arrange with Gelka, who speaks English, to come around the next morning to get a paper requesting that he be transferred to the Y.M.C.A. as interpreter as we are very short of every kind of help. Three more Czech officers appear in the meantime from the staff of the Reserve Regiment, to see whether they can get some cigarettes for the staff, and I promise that there will be some around Christmas morning.

By this time Professor Robertson has shown up for his appointment. We go back to my car where we will not be pestered with *trebovanias* for cigarettes, and there he lays out his plans for the future of the lecture department.

We now go to his car, which we find properly attached to the Ekaterinburg train. Beath, his promoter, is also there, and we have a little visit all together, winding up with prayers in which we remember the folks at home who are at that moment perhaps exchanging their Christmas gifts and opening the Christmas stockings.

I then go back to our office car, collect the mail for Vladivostock, and go with Jack Turletz down to the Red Cross train. I take along some Bull Durham and Fatimas for a consular representative who is on his way to Tomsk, and who fears that he will not be able to find any smokes to purchase for months to come.

Jack and I return to our freight-car home. One end of it has the appearance of a country grocery store, with its shelves filled with chocolate, candies, tobacco, cigarettes, soap, toilet articles of various kinds, candles, and various other things that are found in these parts only on Y.M.C.A. cars. An unpainted partition separates this part of the car from the other part which is used as bedroom, living room, and dining room by the American secretaries. Between the store and the partition are the cupboards with provisions, dishes, and sundry houskeeping utensils. Standing with an absent-minded gaze in apparent search for something is the "Professor." We call him Professor because he speaks some English. That is probably the closest to any accomplishment he ever had, though I hear he speaks some French too. He is a German prisoner of war, a mild-tempered, harmless, willing, slow, dirty, inefficient individual, who at present is filling the functions of cook, dishwasher, water carrier, coal scuttler, and general housekeeper in our model "home." His duties are so "heavy" that he has not had time to shave or wash for some weeks past and the evidence of that neglect accumulates every day.

We sit down to our Christmas eve repast. We are six in

number: Bixby, our warehouse man, a businessman who has a wife and child in New York; Hooper, stenographer, who has a Japanese wife in Japan where he has taught English for twenty-eight years (he himself is an Englishman); Bennison, auditor and accountant, also an Englishman, who is the only secretary in the party aside from myself who can speak Russian; Jack Turletz, Russian interpreter who was through the Kiev bombardment; and Rhone, another Russian interpreter who is laid up as an invalid with sciatic rheumatism. This is our national force for Western Siberia—except Banton, who left the night before for Novo-Nikolaievsk to organize work for the war prisoners returning from Germany and Austria.

As there is not place at our two by three foot table for all of us at once, Bixby keeps on writing, Jack goes down to the Red Cross car to say good-by to some lady friends who are leaving, and I stand while I eat. Our repast is bread, tea, and jam. We are lucky to have the jam. There are not enough spoons to go around so we all use the same spoon. Likewise with the butter knife. The Professor, as usual, has not laid the table, and doesn't know where the knives, forks, spoons, and dishes have been mislaid, so we have to hunt around to locate them for him. The fire in the stove won't burn because the Professor has put in too much wet coal dust. The room is getting cold, and the coffee and tea and Rhone's supper won't heat up on top of the stove. But *nichevo*. We're in Siberia, as Consul General Harris would say.

In the midst of our festivities, there is a rap on the door and the faithful Czech woodheaver asks if we want more wood and coal. He evidently has an eye for the extra cigarettes which such extra fuel signifies. Of course we want the wood and coal. So all hands lay off from supper and help heave the coal and wood into the coal bin and wood box. The open door lets in plenty of the 25 below zero air that thoroughly ventilates and cools off the car, down to the freezing point. After which coal and wood heaving we, of course, must wash our hands. Only there isn't any water. And it is no easy thing to get water. Professor must go and stand in line where some hundreds of other German and Austrian prisoners are likewise standing

for water for their respective proprietors who are living on
these thousands of cars in the Omsk railroad yards. He may be
back in half an hour, perhaps not for an hour and a half,
if he gets held up by long trains between us and the station,
as we are on the fifth track from the station, and it is impossible
to get through a moving train with a full pail of water. We
can get the worst coal dust off by rinsing our hands with the
tea in our glass, which has cooled off sufficiently by this time to
be used thus. After which we can proceed to pour out more tea.

Bennison isn't feeling well. He took a lady to the theater a
couple of nights previously, and when they returned the train
on the branch wasn't running. Martial law had been declared as
a result of the inmates being let out of jail. He and his lady had
to stand in the cold until 3 a.m. before they could get a sleigh
to take them home. He caught a bad cold. Hooper has a racking
cough which he has not gotten rid of since before he left Vladivostock. Rhone is moping around with his sciatica as usual. We
had been planning a big celebration for Christmas dinner at
the car with the ladies from the Red Cross Hospital as our guests.
Then came the Russian prisoners of war pouring through from
Germany and Austria. We had as many as 1,100 through here
in one day. It was absorbing all our energies to give them the
service of tea, sugar, biscuits, and some clothing. Then Banton
had to go to Novo-Nick to organize the tea room there, which
would take him away from here Christmas. So the dinner was
converted into a stag affair and the invitations were cancelled.

And now things begin to look up. We all have invitations
out to a dance at the Red Cross Hospital tomorrow night.
So we have another chance to blow in 60 rubles for a sleigh and
as at least one member of our party dances, it is sure to be a
success. Spice is added by the fact that the city and surrounding
country are still under martial law after 9 p.m. so that we
stand the chance of being shot as outlaws coming back across
the prairies after midnight.

That cigarettes and tobacco are no scarcer locally than
most other things was borne in on me today when I tried to
do some Christmas shopping. Bookstores empty, jewelry stores
empty except for some Ural stones. No toy shops anywhere.

No embroidery work. No calendars or writing materials of any kind, not even pens and pencils. Buying Christmas presents is no easy task under such circumstances. I finally picked up a soup spoon, not even silver, for 52 rubles. There were no knives, nor forks, nor carving sets, nor dishes of any kind in the city.

Oh yes, and our office manager, a Czech, wounded himself accidentally last night at the Czech banquet, shooting himself through the abdomen. He was operated on yesterday, but is not expected to live. This is tough. A Russian prisoner is in "our home" now warming his frozen legs and arms. He has too much fever too eat. This is our Christmas 1918—Omsk, Siberia.

December 29

We are getting down to our last sheet of writing paper, our last envelope, our last pin, and a good many last things. Nothing can be bought here. We must simply wait for the Vladivostok train. The affair at the Red Cross Hospital on the evening of the 26th was very pleasant. They had the Virginia reel at one time so I got in the game there, and enjoyed all the good cakes, cookies, and candies that the tables were laden with about midnight. The only drawback is that it uses up most of a month's salary to go out and back that fifteen versts in a sleigh. It cost 80 rubles for the sleigh Bixby and I came back in.

Colonel Teussler, Consul General Harris, and other notables were present in addition to the Y.M.C.A. secretaries and consular staff. The one cloud on the affair was the news of the death of one of the Red Cross nurses at Tyumen from typhus the preceding day.

We reached home at two o'clock. The consular party found their station car in a bonfire when they got home. Luckily one of the men had stayed home from the party and saved the papers.

A new spirit is abroad in the land; a spirit of faith and confidence in army and government. It is the most hopeful atmosphere since the first days of the revolution. The working-men at Ekaterinburg have sent greetings from their convention

to Admiral Kolchak expressing their confidence in his arms and
in the new government. At the restaurant this afternoon in came
a committee to raise funds for the army. They had musicians
and actors along who mixed entertainment with their appeal for
funds and then went after the money with a pep and vim that
I haven't seen in that sort of work since June 1917. And they got
fives and tens of rubles instead of the customary kopeks.

The cathedral this morning was crowded to the limit. It
was much like the crowds I saw in the Russian churches in
Petrograd before the revolution. The music in this cathedral is
very fine. The walls are decorated with copies of Nesterov's
religious painting, many of Vasnyetsov's also; quite a reminder
of old days at Kiev. And then there was that wonderful chant
which you remember the whole audience joined in at St. Sophia's
at Kiev. It was not so powerfully done here, but done well
enough to bring back the Kiev picture. And following the main
service came the modern product of the revolution; the preacher
delivered a powerful sermon. It would have been right to the
point in an American pulpit. He told the people what was
needed in Russia was real Christianity. Let the people show it
in their lives. Let them show it in the way they gave to public
and charitable causes, to the army, the prisoners, the poor. Let
Christian principles lie at the bottom of the new Russia. Germany is an example, he said, of the fate of a country which
thinks Christian principles unnecessary. A country that had the
last word in technical and scientific progress, but ruined because
she sought to impose her will on the whole world. The speaker
did not have the long hair of the ordinary Russian priest, and
I was curious to meet him. He had gone before the service was
over so I missed him, but learned that he was Fominsky from
Petrograd, not a regular member of the local clergy. He had
been abroad and was now connected with the Department for
Foreign Affairs. My informant, incidentally, was a Russian
from Moscow, who was a department head in the Post and
Telegraph Ministry of the new government.

A courier has just come in bringing a batch of mail from
Miller. There has been a big change in the lineup at Cheliabinsk
since I was there, short time though it is. He says the work

for the returning Russian prisoners is the big piece of work they now have on hand. The Russian end of the work keeps looming up as the big job here, even to the secretaries who came out attached to the Czech regiments and are still with them heart and soul. Miller has received his official appointment from Vladivostok as head of the Czech Y.M.C.A. expedition, and they have authorized three other secretaries to accompany him.

The Comptons have certainly had a checkered career in Russia. They came over with a relief mission for Armenia. They spent three months in Japan. Then three months in the Caucasus. Bolshevik battles drove them to Baku. They stayed there another three months when the Bolshevik capture of that city drove them to Astrakhan. They stayed there during April waiting for the Volga to open, then went up to Samara, arriving there May first. That was when he went over to the Y.M.C.A. work. They were in Samara when it was captured by the Czechs. They then came out as far as Irkutsk, then back to Barnaul where they spent another three months. From there they came to Omsk. Quite an experience for a frail little lady like Mrs. Compton, but she seems to have thrived on it.

December 31

Last night the Comptons, Mr. Cherrington, and I went to the theater and saw *Dvoryanskoe Gnyezdo* (Turgeniev's *Nest of Gentle Folk*). This theater is not up to the Petrograd, nor even the Kiev theaters. It is provincial. The crowd is provincial. The scenery is provincial, very provincial. And the actors are provincial, at least most of them. The grandmother was an exception. I am convinced she is a refugee from Petrograd, and that I saw her in the theaters once there. They say she has been living in the hotel here for a half year or more. And the old tutor musician was good. But I was much disappointed in Lisa and her lover, and could hardly believe for some time that this was the play I had read. The Comptons, however, said that the acting was much better than in another play they attended here some time back. The prices are low enough, only three rubles and three fifty ($.30 and $.35) for the best seats.

January 5, 1919

Yesterday brought your letter of November 7 in which you said they had turned back your Christmas package for me and that your dander was up and you were going to find some way of sending it. I got your letter at the consulate in the morning. In the evening, your package came by Czech post, with the fudge, stuffed dates, cookies, can of cocoa, and cake all intact and GOOD, Oh ye Gods, how good! We American secretaries, Bixby, Bennison, and Hooper, were eating our usual frugal evening repast of bread and tea when the Czech appeared at our freight-car palace and shoved in the packages. Believe me those sweets went a long way. I haven't seen any other packages from America out this far yet.

The same mail from America brought a letter from Mrs. Chez to me stating that she was sending a package to Mr. Chez, and she, supposing me to be in Vladivostok and Chez in the interior, was asking me to give the package special attention and see that it got out to Chez. She had not heard from him since he wrote from Boochedoo in Manchuria in September, and he was heading west at that time. Her letter was dated Morgantown, West Virginia, November 4. She will be surprised to learn that when I received her letter I was only a few hours' run from Chez's station, and that that very same night he arrived in Omsk for supplies and hospital treatment, so that he was able to read the letter almost as soon as I received it. The package, however, has not yet come through.

The people out here have the objection to the new style calendar that it was promulgated by the Bolsheviki. The government decreed that the Russian New Year this year should be the same as the western New Year, but the Russians celebrated it very little aside from taking a day off from work. The big celebration will be according to the old date as in the past. They call the new style New Year "the Bolshevik New Year."

I haven't told you yet how I celebrated New Year's eve. The Comptons invited us up to see the old year out. Bixby was sick, Hooper was sleepy, Bennison had another date, and Banton was in Novo-Nick, so I was the only representative

left. Bixby took a long time to decide that he was too sick and
that held me until 8:45 at the station yards waiting for him
to decide. At last I started out with Jack Turletz. The *vyetka*
(branch line) railroad train was standing on the track
evidently ready to make the trip to the city, so we thought we
would save our ten rubles, the cost of a cab, and take the train
which is only 30 kopeks. We got on. It was full. The people
said they had been waiting a long time; there was something
the matter with the engine. So Jack gets off and asks the
engineer what the trouble is. A pipe has burst, but it will be
ready in ten minutes. Although we have our doubts about
the length of ten minutes in Russia, we decide that there is no
special rush, and that we will still save those ten rubles. We
wait 30 minutes. Jack makes another investigation. The pipe is
fixed, but the road is not open to the city yet. It soon will be.
We wait some more. The Russian peasant woman next to us
keeps exclaiming continually, "*Pryamy scandal! Uzhasny scandal!*" (A plain scandal, an awful scandal.) Her head is aching.
Jack makes another investigation. The road is open, but for
some unknown reason the signal is not given for the train to
move forward.

Finally at ten o'clock we decide to take a sleigh after all.
We go over where the sleighs are lined up. They all demand
20 to 25 rubles in honor of New Year's eve, except one old
peasant who offers to take us for 15. Only after we are seated
in his sleigh, do we realize that he is dead drunk, so drunk
that he can't talk straight and can hardly keep his seat.
The rest of the drivers all give him a good cussing for under-
bidding them and then wind up with a wild torrent of
joshing. We get along all right until we hit the railroad track.
The snow is scraped off the tracks and the sleigh bumps on
to the rails and one of the runner supports breaks and holds
the sleigh tight on the tracks. As our weight is too much, we
all get out to examine the damage and shove the sleigh over
the tracks. Suddenly the horse gives a lurch and goes darting
off down the road with no one in the sleigh or holding the
reins. The driver is too drunk to run. My hat, which is never
solid when I have my knit helmet on, comes off when I start

to run. But Jack Turletz saves the day. He runs and manages to jump into the sleigh while it is tearing along, catches up the reins and stops the runaway horse. The driver agrees to take us on as far as the end of the *vyetka* in his broken sleigh and there turn us over to another driver. He wanders all over the fields getting to the *vyetka;* we get safely transferred and with no further adventures I arrive at 10:45 at the home of the Comptons.

Mrs. Compton was in bed and Carl taking a bath when I arrived at their room. They had given us all up. Their room adjoined that of one of the consular men, Mr. Cherrington, and Mrs. Compton asked me to make myself at home in his room until she got dressed. Cherrington's room has the reputation of being the coldest room any of the Americans have discovered in Omsk yet. It was not much above zero. The electricity, as usual, wasn't working, and I couldn't locate any matches for the candles. By energetic efforts with the maid I was finally able to get lighted up enough to admire Cherrington's Chinese ornaments which he had hanging on the wall and resting on the window sill, and to look through his photo album while the Comptons prepared. About 11:30 we were all together and ready to celebrate. I came prepared to stay the night with Cherrington, not fancying the return trip to the station with the *vyetka* not running. But Cherrington was off with the consular crowd celebrating New Year's eve at a circus and hundred ruble-per-plate dinner at the Hotel Europe, and didn't get home until 1:15 a.m. We all waited until he got home, then I wrapped myself up in my bath robe, covered myself with the overcoats and occupied his divan until 10 a.m.

There is now a new Minister of Foreign Affairs, Mr. Sukin, the third since I have been here. Mr. Sukin is a young man who has been connected with the Russian Embassy in Washington. He speaks English perfectly and seems to be imbued with much regard for America. I believe he is a capable, energetic, and rising young man. I met him yesterday in his apartments. He is living in beautiful rooms, far removed from Bolshevistic atmosphere—rich rugs, beautiful pictures on the walls, great plants and ferns about the room, and a complete equipment of type-

writers, dictaphone, and the other conveniences of a modern
business man.

The prisoners keep rolling through steadily in great numbers from Germany and Austria. I spent two hours last evening
at the feeding point where we give out our tea, sugar, and
biscuits free of charge and, where the need is greatest, sweaters
and boots. It is a great sight as the men line up and pass by,
getting their biscuits from our Serb helper, Alexander, their
cigarettes from me, and their tea and sugar, done up in neat
paper packages, from Jack Turletz. Jack is on to his job. He
keeps his eyes open for the prisoners' clothing condition. When
he spies a man who looks as if he has too little around his body,
he feels his clothes, and if he is plainly too thinly clad, stands
him aside, and tells our other helper Ozersky to give him
a sweater, issuing the same on the prisoner's document. In case
the prisoner is quite without covering for his feet, he is stood
aside for a pair of boots. Most of the prisoners are wearing *laptia*,
a straw covering over their cloth bindings, which they have
received from the Russian peasants as they came through Russia.
Others have the much prized felt boots called *valenki*, quite a
number having received these from the Bolsheviki at Moscow.
When they left Germany, they all had wooden shoes. As soon as
it gets noised along that some are getting boots or sweaters, of
course, all want them. Jack or Ozersky carefully examines each
one who requests them and settles each case. Only those in
extreme need get any, for if we started to give in questionable
cases, we would be swamped.

January 11

While one department of the government is asking us to extend
our services through the army, another department is closing
our club for the Russians at one city, another department is
issuing orders to the effect that our work is temporarily not so
much needed as other things at the front, another department
calls on us to extend our work throughout the Cossack Army
offering every sort of cooperation and assistance, and thus it
goes. The great development of the past week is the wonderful

opportunity that has opened up with the Cossack Army. It is the most promising romantic opportunity we have had in Russia. The Cossacks, as you remember, are far from being the wild and woolly cowboy sort that they are still often pictured in America. They are the most cultured, most democratic, most liberty-loving, best educated group in the Russian body politic. They are very enthusiastic about things American. It promises to be similar to our service for the Czechs. Head Ataman Dutoff has made formal request for Association service. General Choroshkin, who was acquainted with our work in Samara, is taking an active interest in it here. And the officers and members of the Cossack council are all showing a wideawake interest. I am asking Banton to head up this special work.

I went up to see Mr. Rassuschin Christmas day. He is here with the Japanese Diplomatic Mission and living on one of their cars. When I found him at noon Christmas day, the car was freezing cold and deserted. The *provodniks* (guides) had all gone on a grand carouse the preceding eve and let the fires go out. There was no fuel on the cars, and none to get until the holidays were over, the pipes were frozen, the Japanese members of the party had all fled to the town to find warmer quarters, and Mr. Rassuschin was left alone shivering in his big overcoat on this first-class car with its temperature near the zero mark. He knew no one in the city and was having anything but a Merry Christmas. I invited him down to share our life on our cheaper but better heated freight, third- and fourth-class cars. He has been living with us ever since. He had been expecting to have conferences with some of the ministers, but they are all off on holidays, and instead of finishing up his business in a couple of days, it will take him a couple of weeks. He is sending his engineer over to America to buy machinery for his coal mines. He is getting the papers and documents from the government here allowing him to do so. He was asking me where to go and who to buy from in the States.

These holidays in Russia always fill me with foreboding. The country never seems to be able to recover from them before some great wind blows. The present is a time of great strain and uncertainty here. The splendid victory on the

Perm front a few days ago has been offset by a correspondingly great retreat on the Ufa front before a thrust of the Bolsheviki with greatly superior forces that threatens the center of the Russian front.

It seems to me that Bolshevism has entered on a new phase. My impression is that it has gained immense strength from the German revolution. Its army must have gained greatly in numbers and in confidence. Bolshevism has overflowed from Russia into the center of Europe. It is no longer purely a Russian civil war. It is a world civil war. What the Versailles conference will decide about it seems to me one of the most important questions before that conference.

The opportunities before the Y.M.C.A. here are wonderful, or would be if it were not for the sheer physical difficulties of getting things transported and work done, and the most elemental ABC's of existence provided for. It is the same story that we have been up against ever since the disorganization that followed the revolution, and will continue for an indefinite time ahead. Go into the beautiful stone blocks of business buildings here, handsome, solid, columned structures that would be a credit to Chicago or New York, and what do you see? Empty rooms where formerly were busy counters and throngs of purchasers and clerks. Great tiers of empty shelves greet you instead of the well filled shelves of two or three years ago. The cotton and wool that used to come from Turkestan and the provinces no longer find transport. The factories stand idle, and the great wholesale and retail houses which used to handle these goods have had to close their doors. They now house investigation committees, government offices, consular offices, generals and their staffs, or refugees or soldiers. It is an oppressive sensation that one feels as he goes into one of these former stores. Our Y.M.C.A. office will be in such a place. Plenty of shelf space for a dozen Y.M.C.A.s. Talk with the owners. No hope for trade for a year anyway. They do not hesitate to sign up contracts for a year's lease of their office quarters.

The Comptons have been invited by the British Consul to occupy the consul's home while he is away for the next five or

six months. They have two bedrooms and have invited Banton
and me to occupy one of them. I have not seen the house yet
but there are also living rooms and reception rooms. Altogether
it is a very pleasant place. They are moving in tomorrow, and
I shall move in as soon as I return from Cheliabinsk. Mrs. Compton has offered to board all of us secretaries which, of course,
has been accepted with glee. We also had luck this morning by
getting good office quarters requisitioned to us in the center of
the city. There will be plenty of room. Soldiers have been quartered there, but they are moving out. The procuring of these
offices is the end of a long tedious hunt and removes a load from
my mind.

En route Cheliabinsk to Ekaterinburg

January 18

We waited all day last Sunday for the train to leave Omsk.
It finally left, fifteen hours late. We were traveling 51 hours
from Omsk to Cheliabinsk. The last day we covered only
117 versts, less than 90 miles. Outside of Cheliabinsk stand great
rows of broken-down locomotives on the sidings. During the
month since I made my last trip, the operation of the railroad has
suffered a terrible slump and one now feels that the last movement may occur any time, much as we felt coming from Kiev
to Moscow a year ago. The express train to Vladivostok which
has gone once a week for the past month did not go last week
owing to lack of engines and first-class cars. A ticket one way
now costs 1,500 rubles ($150) from Omsk to Vladivostok.
Military men and government officials have first claim to a place.

Before we left Omsk, Dr. Newman of the Red Cross arrived
at the station bound for Petropavlovsk, where typhus has broken
out and men are dying at the rate of twenty a day. When we
got out to Cheliabinsk, we found that typhus had also broken out
in the Red Cross Hospital there in spite of the greatest precau-
tions against it.

At Petropavlovsk, Secretary Viles met us at the train at
6 a.m. with his Czech interpreter, Valish. Professor Robertson
was pulling into the station from Cheliabinsk just as we were

pulling out. I had had no word about Professor Robertson's plans since his leaving Ekaterinburg for Cheliabinsk. He has quite an organization with him including his advance agent Beath, but he is so fearful that if any of his organization gets separated they may never get together again that his advance agent never advances, but arrives at each new point in company with the Professor, unheralded by their telegrams which usually reach there some days after their arrival. Greiner calls his advance agent his rear guard. Of course, the Professor is always astonished that his campaign has not been all set up and going by the local secretaries. I didn't get a chance to see him but learned from Ken Miller that he is headed east as fast as he can get there. Just my luck to be out at Cheliabinsk when he should arrive at Omsk, and no way of heading off his departure except the same uncertain telegraph service.

I found Miller, Keeny, Heinz, Wheeler, and Irons all at Cheliabinsk. Greiner, whom we had left at Ufa, was at Zlatoust, and Tinkham, whom we left with Greiner, was at the very front with a tea car. When he evacuated Ufa, his baggage got left behind, but he is an even-tempered fellow and just said *"nichevo."*

We are rolling into Ekaterinburg. It is fine to be here again for Sunday with the inspiring services that characterize the beautiful Russian churches here. The day is cloudy, but it is nevertheless beautiful amidst these fascinating pine forests. There is a great difference between the weather here and at Omsk. It is quite mild today; would be pleasant with a light overcoat. In Omsk it is always cold, with that kind of cold that brings the cold haze up. When the temperature falls below 25 or 30 below zero, it nearly always becomes hazy, and people who have seen it 80 and even 90 below state that the haze becomes very dense then.

We have come into the second station at Ekaterinburg and must wait here a Russian half hour, which will more likely be two hours, in order to attach two cars to our train. There is only one droshky at the station; it is busy, and to ride by cab from here to the main station, three miles away, would require a half hour and twenty rubles, so we have decided to stay with the train.

The prisoners who came through have quite changed their attitude towards the Bolsheviki lately. The Bolsheviki have evidently organized to meet this emergency considerably faster than the Russians on this side. The prisoners are now getting substantial supplies of clothing from the Bolsheviki, and at two points they received money, forty rubles at one place and twenty-five at another. These sums were strategically given just before they passed out of Bolshevik Russia and, of course, left a favorable impression. Many of the prisoners say the only bright spot in their entering Siberia is the *Amerikanskaya Missya* (Y.M.C.A.).

Bolshevik papers that come through the lines with the prisoners have a victorious tone that was absent some time ago. They are singing "To the Hour" with apparent conviction that the world revolution is at hand. This in spite of the fact that Bolshevik Russia is suffering the most terrible hunger and starvation, and that she is surrounded on every side by a ring of foes. Her newspapers have to devote several columns to the news from the multitude of fronts. It is quite evident that there has been a great development of discipline and order in their ranks.

One of the problems which we are facing now is the meeting of the food situation in the interior of Russia as the way is opened up. Bread which sells for 30 and 40 kopeks a pound through here costs 15 rubles a pound in Moscow. The trouble is that the speculators, who will probably be the most active in getting the first food supplies in, will be more interested in keeping the prices up than in relieving the food needs. We have an example of that here in Cheliabinsk. Cheliabinsk is only 250 versts west of Kurgan, the dairy center. At Kurgan you can buy butter for 2.20 rubles per pound. At Cheliabinsk it sells for 8.50 rubles per pound in the open market at so-called officially controlled prices. Miller's enterprises have made it possible to supply the Czech soldiers with bread, sausage, butter, etc. at the lowest prices that can be obtained within a radius of a thousand versts from Cheliabinsk plus only transportation and help. The same thing ought to be planned on a big scale for the interior. But no one seems to realize the need for it. The War Trade Board is more concerned with manufactured articles and machinery from abroad. We realize that the thing is too big for anything except government backing, but Keeny has worked out an excellent plan which we are submitting to the government, proposing that certain phases of it be worked out with the Red Cross, other phases with the Y.M.C.A., and others with the Russian organizations.

January 20

We are still standing in the yards at Ekaterinburg waiting for an engine to take us back to Omsk. We have been standing here since 9 p.m. last night, the time the train was scheduled to go. It is now 10:30 the next morning. Bids fair to equal the 15 hour wait we had at Omsk.

The greatest dairy and grain market of the world lies right here in Western Siberia next to the greatest hunger zone, and nothing is being done to provision the starving people. Americans are extending their Hoover food programs, denying themselves food, and sending their surplus across the ocean to relieve the suffering that is next door to us, whereas the Russians here are doing nothing to set in motion the surplus that lies at hand. So far as public and private life goes on in Western Siberia you would not imagine that these people have an army at the front; there seems to be no sacrifice or thought of the army or of the starving population beyond.

Outside of a few public-spirited officials and citizens whose efforts seem to drop unnoticed into a chasm of public indifference, there seems to be no public spirit or organization. And any person or organization that comes with a program of unselfish service or aid immediately becomes an object of suspicion with little chance of getting cooperation or even recognition. It is the logical result of the circumstances that have overtaken Russia. All her best people are continually lamenting the situation. They say: "You see Russia is ill"; "No one has any hope"; "Everyone feels that there is no use trying to do anything." And so with every ten pounds of lament there is scarce an ounce of the one thing that will cure the situation—effort.

The morale of the social organizations seems to have had

a great slump during the past month. It is noticeable in our work. Thefts of our property keep increasing in number and size, and we are powerless to get anything done to prevent it, even to get guards to stand watch. In many ways I am reminded of the situation in western Russia and in the Ukraine a year ago.

Well it is now twelve o'clock. We are still standing, after fifteen hours of waiting, and are informed that it will be another two hours before there is an engine.

It is interesting to notice in some Samara Bolshevik papers that the returning Russian prisoners have brought through that the Bolsheviki have copied the Y.M.C.A., calling it the Young Men's Communistic Association (same initials in English, and just one change in Russian.) They have evidently got it highly and effectively organized. It is organized with every Bolshevik army regiment. It has the same general program as ours except that communist activity takes the place of Christian activity. The Samara papers carry ads almost daily of the lectures which are conducted under the auspices of the organization.

Omsk

January 26

It took three days and four nights to get back to Omsk from Ekaterinburg. At Ishin Chez came to the car. He has a thriving club and brought down some of the local newspapers that contained articles praising his work. He started to write a letter to Mrs. Chez, but the train started up before he finished, and I had to enclose it along with a note explaining why he didn't finish it. I was glad of the chance to get acquainted with Greiner and his wife. They are among the finest Russians I have met. He is a musician, and she is also very musical. He learned to speak English in the Y.M.C.A. prison camp in Austria, and is about the best interpreter I have known in Russia. Professor Robertson, who is now lecturing in Omsk, was delighted with him and said it was like getting out of prison to get hold of such an interpreter. Greiner, who has been with the Y.M.C.A. about a year now, is to be associated with me in Omsk, and I believe he will be a great addition to the work. I feel that I can counsel with him fully.

On getting back to Omsk I find British troops, mostly Canadians. They are everywhere and, I believe, add a healthy tone to the atmosphere. The Canadians are taken for English rather than for Americans, though they are much more like Americans than English.

January 31

The express train is announced to leave this afternoon. It has been announced to leave weekly for the past three weeks and daily for the past six days, and I have already written a number of last letters. But it might leave, in spite of all, so I'll write another.

The Comptons have not been able to move yet, and accordingly I have been unable to move because British Consul Jordan has been unable to leave the city because the express has not left because the first express trains did not return from Vladivostok and there were no other sleeping and dining cars available because they are all used up for various Allied Generals and High Commissions and Russian General Staffs, etc.

Yesterday I visited the Czech factories in the prisoner-of-war camps. They were an eye-opener. They are turning out 8,000 pairs of pants monthly, 1,500 overcoats weekly, a ton of candles daily, a ton of roasted coffee daily, 30,000 cigars daily, 120 pairs of shoes daily, and buttons, shaving brushes, and all other toilet articles. All for the Czech army. And all built up out of nothing the past half year. They started in with six tailors last summer, with no machines or tools. Now they have discovered a Czech-made electric generator somewhere and have inaugurated their own electric plant which means they can work ten or twelve hours a day instead of five or six. And the prisoners are cheerful and happy. They are getting soldiers' food, clothing, half soldiers' rations of sugar and tea, they get tobacco, and they are warm and comfortable. In contrast the lot of other German and Austrian prisoners in Western Siberia, where they have not come under such happy circumstances, is wretched.

It is a striking commentary that the Czechs have accomplished such a feat as this in a region where no other power has been able to organize any industry to speak of.

The recent proposal of President Wilson and Lloyd George that the various Russian governments including the Bolshevists send delegates down to Dog Island near Constantinople to settle their disputes has raised quite a furor in political and military circles here. An explosion of popular indignation was exhibited in one of the cafes here the other evening by some Russian officers who were more or less vodkaized, towards some Canadian officers. It has made it necessary to postpone Professor Robertson's lectures on the wireless telegraph until things cool off a little.

The weather continues at about 20 to 25 below zero right along.

February 9

I have gotten settled in the former British Consul's home with the Comptons and am now cosily fixed. I spent five nights at the office here waiting for the express to take the British Consul so that there would be room for me at the house. I have a little room, a sort of den, all to myself, sharing the big living room, dining room, and kitchen with the Comptons.

The last few mornings I have gotten up early, chopped wood, and built the morning fires. The first night we were alone in the house after Mr. Jordan left, Mrs. Compton fired the Russian maid because she was entertaining too much company, and causing supplies to disappear too rapidly, but chiefly because she was entertaining a second husband nights at the house. Her first husband, she said, was wounded in the war and had disappeared two years ago so she felt freed from him. This second man she wasn't legally married to, but she said she loved him very much and wouldn't leave him. She would seek another place. She couldn't understand why there could be any objection. She said Mr. Jordan knew about it and didn't object. She further declared that no maid would stay with Mrs. Compton because they would all have as many friends as she and would all boycott Mrs. Compton because they were unionized and wouldn't go to any place where one of their number was

unfairly treated. She said that one of the Russian ladies she had
worked for, who was a very respectable, nice lady, not only
hadn't told her not to have any men spend the night with her,
but had invited her to have that privilege as one of the special
inducements of working at that place. I could call her up on
the telephone and verify it if I wanted to. (I conducted the final
delicate conversation having a slightly larger Russian vocabulary
than Mrs. Compton). She had the telephone number ready to
give me. As to the food which she had used when guests were
present, it was all her own food. She had her own stores of
sugar, tea, etc. which she got as pension for her first husband
who had been wounded.

As in most Siberian cities, there is no city water system in
Omsk. Men bring the water around in barrels. You can have
it brought once a week for twenty rubles monthly, and twenty
additional for each additional time. Mrs. Compton is teaching
English at school and was away when they brought the water,
so we were down to our last drop when we were able to
steer a candidate for the servant job into the house long
enough to get the water while Mrs. Compton was at school.
The servant left as soon as Mrs. Compton got back from school
because the house was too cold. Carl had broken the axe handle
while cutting some wood the preceding day, and as no axes are
to be bought in this part of the world, we had to get a new
handle for the old one, which will require three days. Meanwhile
we have located a small axe with a neighboring Englishman
who was on the point of borrowing ours, as his was so small
and dull.

February 14

A terrible blizzard has been raging here all day. It is the worst
I ever saw. People cannot walk against it. It blows them against
walls and railings. More snow has fallen the past twenty-four
hours than all the rest of the winter. The wires of the great
French wireless station have been blown down. To face the wind
gives your face a lashing of sleet that is unbearable. The street
is lined with people who have given up the struggle and have

sought nooks at building corners until the storm spends itself.
It has increased in fury all day. It is now 7:30 p.m. but wilder
than ever. Professor Robertson and I ate lunch together this
noon, and he said it reminded him of blizzards in Dakota where
he grew up. Well, I at last have the old storybook pictures of
Siberia verified. Up until now the winter has been a tame affair,
pretty cold but nothing much to talk about. Such storms as we
are now having are rare, about one each year. Last night it got
warm, the temperature passing above zero in cloudy weather this
morning. Then came the blizzard.

We planned a Valentine party at the house this evening
but had to call it off. Professor Robertson's party is booked to
leave for Tomsk tomorrow, but railroad and telegraph service are
probably at an end for some time. We shall probably feel
isolated without the wireless. It is a tremendous station, the
poles about 250 feet high and the wires between the receiving
and sending stations 750 feet long.

February 16

The blizzard of day before yesterday kept increasing in intensity
well into the night. Storm warnings were sent out to the offices
about town in the middle of the afternoon, and all the help and
the other secretaries at our office went home, leaving me alone
until I started out to walk home about 8:30. It took me an
hour to cover a distance usually requiring twenty minutes. I
didn't meet a cab the whole way, except one that was stalled.
Two horses were being led along by one man walking. I only
passed two pedestrians the length of the main street. When
I crossed the bridge in the howling swirling storm, I could feel
the truth of the report that two people had been blown off the
bridge during the day. I had to cross over to the windward
side and hang on to the railing facing the storm as I inched
across. My face kept icing up, but I found that it was warmer
to leave the ice on than to remove it and kept punching holes
over my eyes so that I could see out. When I got home, my
whole face was covered with an ice mask half an inch thick,
which I removed entire and passed around for inspection.

I never knew when I crossed a street intersection whether I was continuing in the same direction when I got across or not. Our Czech purchasing agent spent four hours trying to get from the *vyetka* station to the Czech club, and when he finally reached there, dropped down almost lifeless. Eighty people are reported to have fallen by the wayside and frozen to death between the *vyetka* and the main station. A big sign fell down killing three more. As I walked along the main street, these big store signs, which hang across the fronts of the buildings supported by iron hooks on each end, were swinging back and forth with a slamming that sounded like a bombardment. Realizing that it was unsafe to walk along the sidewalk under them, I kept to the middle of the street.

Telegraph communications are still open, but the French wireless is a wreck, and trains were at a standstill yesterday.

Yesterday we were notified of the appointment of a Y.M.C.A. representative on the Russian General Staff, same being Admiral Kolchak's representative and arrangement. This is what we have been waiting for so long and gives us the opportunity to improve our service rapidly.

February 22

Thursday evening we had dinner in a peasant's home where an English lady, Miss Brown, is staying. These peasants moved into Siberia out of Russia and have become quite well to do. They have a saw mill and flour mill operating in their back yard —an industrious oasis in this chaotic time. Their house is nicely furnished with more than the usual number of art works, books, and magazines. It is lighted with electricity from their own power plant, which also runs their factories. The master of the household wore a long peasant beard. There were two other peasant-looking men members of the household—guests. The mother looked like a well educated, well dressed farmer's wife. The older daughter is a college graduate, plays the piano, has history and literature as her hobby and has taught. The younger daughters, bright children, remind you of children in a typical American family. The younger one took her first English lesson from a couple of British officers who visited the home the same evening we were there. Miss Brown herself is a former estate owner of 9,000 acres in the Samara region, which is now held by the Bolsheviki. A British major and the British chaplain were guests with us, and all these different people felt perfectly at home and on an equality with these emerged-from-the-peasant-class Russians. Russia will develop wonderful power from her peasant class when they become educated, given an opportunity.

The long heralded Vladivostok train arrived at the edge of town today. It has been snowbound within forty versts of the city for three days. Over three months since I left it standing on the tracks at Vladivostok all loaded for the interior. We learn that 150 tons of club equipment, kino outfits, canteen supplies, etc., which Story and I ordered last May and June from New York, are at last at Vladivostok and being sent out on another train.

The most frequent question in Omsk society these days is, "When will Moscow, or Petrograd, or Samara be taken again?" The great mass of the society people here are from the cities of European Russia and their one big object in life is to get back to their homes.

February 26

Such a flood of things have descended all at once. Within three days, eight of your letters reached me, dated November 9, 16, 21, December 6, 23, 26, and January 3 and 7. It is now just midnight, but the only times I find for writing letters is after 11 p.m. and before 9 a.m. Kenneth Miller is here en route to Vladivostok, and I want to finish so he can take this along tomorrow.

Sundays we always have a gathering of the secretaries and assistants for religious service and tea and a social time afterward, and there are usually a dozen to a dozen and a half people here. Miss Brown and the Desels, Baltic Province Russian Germans, are regular attendants at these meetings also. Wednesday afternoons are our five o'clock teas for all comers. Only tonight the five o'clock bunch had no sooner left than the

Y bunch from the railroad station and some Red Cross men
and an American lieutenant arrived, along with Riley and
Miller, and we had to get up an extra supper at which thirteen
people sat down. Monday we had all the secretaries for supper,
twelve on that occasion. Mrs. Compton is having her hands full,
but is naturally gifted for such entertaining. Your maple sugar has
been used in various ways but the best is with the pancakes in
the morning. Yes, we have pancakes out here in Western Siberia.

March 2

I have just come back from the Russian church service. Nothing
thrills me like the Russian church music. They had two chants
in which the whole congregation joined. The church was packed
with several thousand people, the great majority of whom were
men.

This is the coldest March day I ever knew, 34 degrees below
zero, sunshiny but with a sharp wind. The few springlike days
which occurred two or three weeks back have been followed
by the worst blizzards and sharpest, if not coldest weather, of
the winter.

Friday night was the Maslinitza masked ball. The American
Red Cross and Y.M.C.A. joined in fitting up one of the rooms
as an American corner where we served tea and showed cowboy
pictures. The tea was popular early in the evening, but became
less in demand as the evening wore on and real drinks took
its place. The affair was really less turbulent and more proper
than I had expected—up to 2 a.m. when we left. At that time the
electric lights went out, and I won't guarantee for the order
that followed. It was the first Russian masked ball I had
attended. Between 300 and 400 people were there. The British
sold cigarettes which went rapidly at five rubles per package
as the prevailing price for the same kind of packages was
fifteen rubles. Even at that price the British cleared a thousand
percent or so, giving the proceeds to the Petrograd colony for
whose benefit the masked ball was advertised. We dished the
tea and cakes free but took collections at the door, amounting
to 777 rubles, and also turned this over. The Kirghiz erected a

dome-like wigwam and served refreshments inside. The Tatars also served Tatar dishes, and a Tatar chorus sang Tatar songs.

I rather suspect that the expenses of the affair were about as great as the receipts, and the vast expenditure of individual effort and expense out of all proportion to the benefits. Even the Russian press came out with comments before the affair, calling it "a feast in time of plague," and scoring the promoters for such extravagance and the offering of prizes for pretty feet (the Russian word means legs also), when all around was need and suffering. If we could have withdrawn in good grace, we should probably have done so, but the fact that the English were taking part and that withdrawing would have been more conspicuous than staying in, persuaded us to remain.

The three of us overturned in the sleigh with all our dishes returning from the masked ball. We were strewn around considerably, but no dishes or bones broken.

Our supply train is acting like a magnet and drawing in the Czech secretaries from all over the country for their share of the supplies.

March 7

I had my first view of Admiral Kolchak at the entertainment which the British soldiers gave last night in his honor. He was standing in the first row in front of the orchestra, facing the audience with many other officers and officials during the intermission. I had expected to see someone more haughty and reserved in manner. He was much simpler and more approachable than I had anticipated. Again this morning Riley and I went out to see the review of the Czechs in honor of Professor Masaryk's 69th birthday. Admiral Kolchak was there with General Janin and others. Riley and I took pictures of him about ten feet distant. Then this afternoon I attended the Czech banquet in honor of Professor Masaryk which Admiral Kolchak also attended as guest of honor. The best of spirit between the Russians and Czechs was evidenced in this meeting in the after dinner speeches where all spoke for the brotherhood of the Slav peoples.

March 8

Dear Mr. Phelps:*

Your telegram of March 5 from Vladivostok to Captain Schuyler for me arrived yesterday, being delivered to me last night. It was something of a bomb as it was the first intimation that I had received that there was objection to or criticism of our work by the Minister of Foreign Affairs. The rumor that we refused to permit Russian officers to enter entertainments given for Russian soldiers was without foundation.

Captain Schuyler advised me to go straight to Minister Sukin and have a frank talk with him which I did. The minister stated that he had received official information that we had given orders that officers were not to attend our entertainments for the Russian soldiers. He, however, did not or could not say who had reported it or upon what foundation. He further said that it had been reported to him that we had been engaging in much political propaganda, had employed many Jews in our organization, and had asked to have officers released from military service in order to serve as Association secretaries. All of this had aroused great criticism. He said that the unfortunate political policy which America was pursuing had increased the sentiment against the Y.M.C.A., especially for the front work. They didn't mind so much about the work for the army in the rear.

I said that we had no desire to continue our work on the front or anywhere else unless it met with the wholehearted and sympathetic support of the Russians and their government. We were over here not to secure favors or privileges but simply to serve when and where our service was desired. I said that the train of supplies which had been received from Vladivostok with goods for the benefit of the soldiers on the front was still standing at Cheliabinsk while our secretaries still waited for the papers which were promised three weeks ago.

He replied that we must realize that the Russians are sick. "You cannot understand," he said, "how bad the situation really is with Russia. They don't know what to do or how to save

* Heald's superior in Vladivostok.

themselves or help themselves. You must be patient and bear with us and excuse our apparent failures and delays and the inconveniences and difficulties we suffer." He would do everything he could to hasten the matter of the official papers and put in a favorable word regarding the *pomeschenie* (hut).

March 16

Dearest Emily:

My diary which I have faithfully kept the past year is nearing the end of the blank pages, and none are to be bought in the local market.

Last night I attended a swell affair, a charity concert and supper, the proceeds of which are to go to the Russian soldiers on the front. The price of admission to the concert proper was 200 rubles ($20). After the concert came a supper at which you paid 50 rubles for a seat and then so much extra for each thing you ate. The whole affair was gotten up by the ministers' wives who were there with their husbands.

You would be interested in the menu prices: ham with tomato dressing, 30 rubles ($3); partridge, 35 rubles; ice cream, 80 rubles; an apple, 40 rubles; and a collection was taken up besides. Total cost of supper, 185 rubles. Of course, these prices were a trifle high even for Omsk and the occasion to be counted as charity.

March 17

Yesterday I took Filipi, our American Czech secretary, from the Czech club out to the American hospital. The Czech doctor thought that he had typhus. He still has a bad fever today, the fourth day. They usually have fever badly for about six days before the typhus breaks out. There is considerable danger from typhus in a busy crowded club like the Czech place. We are fortunate to have a good American hospital here. The Red Cross has done much splendid work in Western Siberia fighting the typhus.

One of the favorite recreational pastimes for the Comptons and myself after the strenuous Sunday program is, about ten o'clock in the evening, to walk down to the Irtish river, which is a short two blocks from the house, and walk out over the ice (for it is still frozen solid) and get the view back towards the city. These moonlight nights, it is magnificent. The wide, sweeping, snow-covered prairie spreads out to the west. Beyond the edge of the city to the north and the grove of birches and evergreens that surround the city in that direction is the Agricultural College, now occupied by the American hospital, which is beautifully lighted up with electricity at night. Before us lies the city. At the other end of the city is the high-span bridge over which the Siberian Railroad crosses.

March 20

We are temporarily withdrawing all our secretaries and closing all our work west of Omsk. We will center all our efforts in the rear, especially in the larger cities. We shall promote chiefly kino entertainments, sports, scientific lectures, canteen service in connection with our clubs, and the teaching of the English language. These are the activities that meet with the heartiest approval from the authorities. The general attitude towards the Association work seems to be increasingly friendly. I had a good interview with Minister Sukin today. He has been friendly to the Association right along, as have practically all who have been abroad and familiar with it in other countries. We will hereafter confine our canteen articles to things we bring in from the outside and not deal with the local supplies.

March 23

I was struck at the students' concert by the little change there seems to be between the students now and before the revolution. They dress much the same and seem to have much the same interests. Only before the revolution the students were reckoned as the most revolutionary influence in Russia, outside of the definite revolutionary organizations, while now they are among the conservative forces. They have remained about the same, but their position with relation to the rest of society has reversed. Schools and universities are closing now so that the students can be enrolled in mobilization.

Filipi, our Czech-American secretary, has the typhus and quite seriously. Yesterday he was reported to be dangerously ill. The crisis has not yet been reached. He is a Presbyterian pastor from Wisconsin and has a wife and two children at home.

March 27

I saw Filipi at the hospital last night. He has failed rapidly during the ten days since I took him out, and I fear he is a dying man. He has been in a stupor the past two days, fever high.

The Orenburg cadets arrived here day before yesterday. We are distributing some of our chocolate, biscuits, and cigarettes among them. There are two trains, about 600 in all, besides a couple of hundred sisters, mothers, and fathers. They all walked 600 versts across country in the dead of winter from Orenburg to the railroad between Ufa and Cheliabinsk. The leader of the expedition was in our office yesterday. He said there had been little sickness going across the country, but now there was more. They are on the way to Irkutsk. They were very enthusiastic over the supplies they received from the "*Amerikanskaya Missya*," and Heinz got tossed in the air as a sign of their enthusiasm at Cheliabinsk. Only about 100 out of the 600 are old enough to smoke. The non-smokers get biscuits instead.

March 29

Last night the Comptons and I and most of the rest of the American colony, Red Cross and Y.M.C.A., were at an international concert given at the City Theater in honor of the Supreme Ruler (Kolchak). The Czech orchestra from the Sixth Regiment was there and played among other things, selections from Tchaikovsky's opera, *Evgeni Onyegin*, which you and I saw at Kiev. The Russian orchestra played two new compositions, one a proposed new Russian national anthem. At the present an old Russian hymn is used in place of *God Save the Czar*.

They also played a new march in honor of Admiral Kolchak
who sat in the box throughout the program. The composers
of each piece directed the orchestra during the execution
of their pieces.

The English put on a pantomine which had a Russian
plot and was good. They also sang American ragtime, and
wound up with a clownish satire on *Alexander's Ragtime Band*,
which the Russian audience did not consider in good taste. A
Russian woman sitting next to me kept saying, *uzhasny* (awful),
while I felt as if my sides would split with laughter. The Russian
stage is always dignified. The program was not over until 12:30.

The Russian troops are now coming out in British uniforms.
It seems to have a peppy effect upon their bearing and also
seems to furnish a comradely feeling between them and the
British soldiers. They go along the sidewalks saluting each
other with a new sort of recognition.

In the afternoon I went out to the hospital and saw Filipi.
He had passed out of danger with the typhus. He has nearly
lost his English speech; the German keeps coming to him first
all the time, and he can talk only with difficulty. He is looking
better, however.

April 6

The office is again my bachelor's hall. Music is furnished free
at night by the rats. It takes two or three nights to get used to
them. They are healthy. Rat poison from the American
Red Cross doesn't seem to feaze them. My mattress is spread on
a high table. After the lights are out, I feel the rats approach
from all angles, level with my head on the shelves, under me by
the floor, over me by the projections. It gives the sensation of
the incoming tide, and I wonder when the waves will touch me.
And then I remember shoes and puttees and other "eatables"
which I left on stools and I wonder whether the stools are high
enough to keep those things above the rats' reach.

But our office is infested with but a few of a mild breed
compared with the one next door which we have been trying
to get for our city office for the past month and a half. Yesterday

came the end of our hopes in that direction, however. One of the pretenders came around early in the morning flashing an order on the office, and the order bore a later date than the order which we had on the same place. The reason we had not moved in earlier was that about forty typesetters had been rooming there since they had failed to get the space we and the Red Cross now occupy. The last of them moved out yesterday. Later on yesterday, the same party, who came for the key in the morning, came around with an order from the requisition quarters for me to deliver the key over to the bearer. I did so. An hour later the agent of the owner came around and demanded the key. I showed him the order on which I had passed the key over. He said that I had no right to hand it over but should have returned it to the owner.

The British Consul, Mr. Hodgson, arrived yesterday. He expected to get the entire cottage that the Comptons are living in. But he had no paper from the British Consul, Jordan, who owns the house. Compton, on the other hand, has the paper from Consul Jordan, authorizing him to occupy the house, and only to set aside one room in it (the one I have been occupying) in case the British Consul arrived. This doesn't meet the needs of Mr. Hodgson at all. He has three servants and another man in his party and needs the whole house or none. As he was planning to be here only a month and a half or two, and as the Comptons are planning to leave in less than a month, they don't know where they are. For the present the Comptons are remaining in the house. The British Consul says he wouldn't have come out here at all if he had known that the house was occupied.

My new room with the Simeonovs was to have been ready today. My room at the Comptons may be available again, but I have decided to let one of the other secretaries who does not speak Russian occupy it, if it is free. The Simeonovs' room would not be open to any of the other secretaries, and rooms are so scarce that we cannot afford to pass up any.

The Alpins arrived from Ekaterinburg yesterday morning. He is not well. I went down to their car in the evening and spent the evening with them. They had quite a time getting away from Ekaterinburg. It became known that he had a large

sum of money as a result of closing up the work, and he learned
of a plot to rob him. An auto came up about three o'clock in
the morning with the prospective robbers. They were arrested.
The chauffeur was the detective. They turned out to be the same
party which had murdered the war prisoner, Kuhn, expecting
to find a lot of Y.M.C.A. money with him as he had charge
of the Y.M.C.A. warehouse. They only found 1,200 rubles of
Kuhn's personal funds. The guard stayed with Alpin to Omsk.
In spite of his bad health, he wants to be right on his way to
Krasnoyarsk where we have assigned him for his next work.

Filipi is much better. He has quite recovered his memory
and will probably be out in a week or ten days. One of the Red
Cross military commission, Major Allen, came down with
typhus while on his trip to the front. He is in the Red Cross
typhus hospital at Petropavlovsk now.

Our Cabinet decided at yesterday's conference to move
the headquarters to Irkutsk immediately, completing everything
by May 1, if possible. I expect to make one trip to Novo-Nick,
Tomsk, and possibly Krasnoyarsk before that.

I wired again yesterday repeating requests for passage for
the Comptons and myself on the first sailing date after June 1,
preferably from Shanghai.

It will be quite an experience to make this 12,000 mile
trip out of the most isolated region of the world back into the
Orient and then to America. I have been in Russia and Siberia
continuously longer than any other secretary now in the country.

April 9

Spring has come. The sleighs are singing their swan songs
through the slushy streets and sinking snows of Omsk. Only here
and there is a peasant sled left. The country roads are still
possible for sleds, but there is nothing but mud in town. And
such slush and mud. It freezes by night and melts by day. And
the thaw hasn't really started. Snow still lies packed three and
four feet deep in drifts along the streets. All of the weeks of
carrying off snow on sleds to the river during the past two
months seem to have made little impression on the total amount,

and we shall now have its ooze with us for some weeks to come. You cannot go out walking without getting in mud over your rubber tops. You can't go in a cab without getting mud splashed all over you. The recent arrival of a bunch of new autos in town adds to this splatter. An auto would be the one pleasant and clean way of travelling, but even autos have their calamities. Last night Dr. Dilley,* head of the American Red Cross here, was at the Comptons' house with a party of Red Cross nurses. They had to get out every now and then and push the auto over a critical spot. The roads are spotted with big melt holes where you can sink in up to your knees, and it is ruinous for autos and passengers alike. Peasants succeed in getting their sleds full of wood drawn to the edge of town and then as the pulling gets too hard, the wood is dumped out in the middle of the muddy road, carts are called for, the wood is picked up out of the mud and reloaded on to the carts, and then hauled to its destination in town.

Cab fares have gone out of sight. And one couldn't blame them for charging high with such roads, if it were not made the excuse for a permanent new level of charge. When I came here in December, I could get a cab from the town station to the consulate for six rubles. The same ride now costs fifteen to twenty rubles. The new Siberian currency is only in denominations of five, ten, twenty-five, fifty, one hundred and two hundred fifty and higher denominations of rubles. There are no longer kopeks, or rubles, or half rubles, or three rubles in circulation, unless some uninitiated from Vladivostok pulls out some change he got there. Everything is by five-ruble denominations. Your cab must cost you five or a multiple of five. I went to the main station from the town station yesterday bargaining for fifteen rubles. I only had a twenty-five in my pocket. The cab driver only had a coupon for 12:50, freakish accident. I said, well, let it go at that. So he handed over his 12:50 and accepted the 25. I don't know whether the 12:50 is

---

* Frederick A. Dilley, an American medical missionary in China, who headed the Red Cross operations in Siberia.

in circulation as it is the 1917 Loan of Freedom, but I can probably work it off on another cab.

All this slush and mud have caught us before the boots and rubbers have arrived from Vladivostok. Our winter overcoats and mittens reached us the first of March, after winter was almost over. Our spring wading apparatus will probably reach us after we are suffering from summer heat and dust.

April 15

We are now ending the second day of maneuvers to get out of Omsk on the Siberian Railroad. I moved down night before last with bag and baggage. I put in my declaration with the station agent the next morning that we wanted our car to go out on the first train. Our car is the one the Greiners had. We saw them off on the express Sunday night. The Comptons moved down to the car Monday. We were informed that we would go out with the sanitary train Tuesday. This morning we put in a request to be attached to the post train which goes through quicker than the sanitary train. It takes more red tape, which we went through with, and we were assured that we would be attached. The train was then announced as due at 2 p.m. Later it was announced for four o'clock. It arrived at 5:30. It was then stated that it would leave in three hours. It is now 10 p.m. and our train is not made up yet. I have just been out to see what the prospects are. A returning Russian prisoner said that they were maneuvering to get our passenger cars in front of the *teplushkas* which were standing beside us.

We have a pleasant car to live on and are enjoying life. In fact I think this is the nearest to a real vacation that is possible in Siberia now—traveling in your own railroad car, which serves as dining room, living room, and kitchen. When one gets on the railroad, he forgets all about time and schedules and keeping appointments as completely as a person off on a fishing trip. All cares and business worries roll off his shoulders; he leans back and thinks only of taking things easy. Riding on one of these cars is much pleasanter than on a Pullman or even one of the Siberian express trains, which are much more comfortable than Pullmans. There is enough room to change around and do different things here. It is a regular Harlem flat, with kitchenette, beds, and everything all complete except that we have to be satisfied with a gramophone instead of a piano. And it is real cooking we get. Just finished a supper of ham, sweet potatoes, peaches, and cake.

Heinz arrived from Cheliabinsk this morning, enthusiastic over the Russian army. He had just come from the front. Every one of our secretaries who visits the front comes back with great enthusiasm for Russia and the new Russian army, and are stunned when they learn that the government has not yet been recognized by America or the Allies. Duncan arrived yesterday and will stay at Omsk.

Spring has come with a rush the past few days. It is warm enough during the day now to go without overcoats, and it is not even freezing at ten o'clock at night. The days lengthen rapidly. It is light until 8:30 in the evening and by 4:30 in the morning it is so light that it is hard to sleep in the car where we have no blinds or curtains and where the shades fail to keep out the light.

A train is just pulling out for the front loaded with Russian soldiers who are shouting and singing enthusiastically. Victory is in the air these days. New towns are reported captured every day. Today newspapers report the destruction of a Bolshevik army in the Caucasus with the capture of 50,000 prisoners, 13 armored trains, and 200 big guns, and the driving out of the Bolsheviki from all the northern Caucasus.

Barabinsk, en route Omsk to Novo-Nikolaievsk
April 16

We finally pulled out of Omsk after midnight last night and have been rolling along at a fair rate all day. The ordinary run from Omsk to Novo-Nick is 24 hours now, but this will take us 36 hours.

I have been surprised at the amount of snow that still covers the ground. It is drifted up in great piles along the snow fences, sometimes ten or twelve feet deep. Much melting has been going on, and the roads along the side of the railroad disappear in lakes in many places. We saw a man this morning whose cart had toppled over in the middle of such a lake, probably due to a hidden hole, and the load of barrels, probably full of butter, had been dumped out into the water where they were rolling around while the driver was trying to manage his startled horse and capture the barrels at the same time.

I have yet to see Central Siberia with the snow off the ground.

At Tatarskaya I visited with the engine crew. Their wages have been raised over what they were when I came out in December, though the difference in prices makes it practically no better for them. The head machinist now received 516 rubles per month, his assistant 400, and the cleaner 350. Their faces lighted up when I left a few Kingfisher cigarettes with each. I snapped their picture with the Comptons standing beside them. Also I snapped three little refugee children who refused to pose until we whispered the charm, "chocolate." Then they stood with broad smiles despite their pitiful rags and pinched faces. They had lived at Tatarskaya over four years; had fled from Russia near the beginning of the war. Their mother lived in Tatarskaya but their father was from old Russia. The oldest child was not old enough to remember anything about Russia, or even what part of Russia they came from. Most of the refugees in Siberia have no idea of geography. They simply crowd on to a train and let it take them wherever it goes.

Tatarskaya station presented a dismal picture with the former station burned to the ground by a fire last winter. The station has been transferred to a row of half a dozen big American freight cars standing back of the former station site. One car is the freight station, another the hall for the third-class passengers, another the hall for the first-and second-class passengers, another is the baggage room, etc.

I chatted with a Russion soldier who was going home for a vacation. He had been stationed at Tomsk. His home was about 200 versts south of Tatarskaya, of which distance he could go about half way on a little branch line and the remaining distance on foot, or if lucky, catch a peasant's cart or sled. He said Russia is having a hard time, but it wasn't so bad in the country He asked whether it was like this in America? He was what would be called half illiterate in Russia, but showed an intelligent interest in America.

At Barabinsk I met Madame Lofitchky, the French wife of the Russian colonel who was at the head of the Czech Second Division when I was in Vladivostok last summer. She was riding on the same train with us to Krasnoyarsk where her sanitary train was standing. She had been riding five days from Cheliabinsk and had not been able to get a meal or wash all that time, it was so crowded in the second-class car in which she was traveling. We invited her to come back and visit with us, which she promised to do.

The last little station gave another illustration of how the work we did in Vladivostok last summer is scattered abroad over the whole of Siberia now. A Czech soldier met me on the platform and asked whether I had any English reading material. I brought out an armful of the *Japanese Advertiser* and the *New York Times* for him, and though they were back in January and February, he was happy to get them. He said that he had learned English under Secretary Noyes in Vladivostok last summer. He belongs to the Fifth Regiment which was located up the valley where the Sokol was held. There are eleven Czechs stationed at this little isolated point, an officer and ten men. We will find similar groups of men at every station all the way from here to Novo-Nikolaievsk, all from this same regiment, in which we conducted several English classes last May and June in Vladivostok, in which some two hundred men got their start in English.

The Czechs who guard the railroad from Omsk to this last station belong to another regiment with whom the *Y* has had Duncan as its representative ever since a year ago. The Tomsk region is guarded by another Czech regiment with whom Riley started work at Vladivostok last summer and with whom he is again at work at Tomsk, happy to be with his old friends again. The Krasnoyarsk region is guarded by another regiment of Czechs with whom the *Y* has been represented by Chez since

July. The men Bunker is with extend part of the way between Novo-Nick and Krasnoyarsk. The Irkutsk region has several other regiments with whom Ken Miller and other secretaries have been associated for a year and a half. Thus the personal contacts of the Association secretaries stretch from one end of Siberia to the other.

As I sit here looking out of the windows on this evening, the sixteenth of April, it has the appearance of a January night as the sun sinks in the west and throws a pink glow over the clear sky and the snow-covered expanse broken only here and there with clusters of white birch. The temperature is now freezing and will probably drop to fifteen above zero tonight.

April 18

Madame Lofitchky did not return for three hours. When she came she apologized, saying she had fallen asleep on returning to her car owing to a loss of sleep the preceding nights. Her story since leaving Vladivostok was short. She had been with the American Red Cross all of the time. She had been assigned to one of the Red Cross sanitary trains, had accompanied it to the front where it had assembled invalid Czechs, carried them back to Vladivostok, then come out with supplies, gotten more invalids, and gone back to Vladivostok again. She was on her third trip. She said she had traveled 43,000 versts the past year. She knew the exact distance between every station on the Trans-Siberian.

We arrived in Novo-Nick yesterday morning. This is a rambling sort of city stretching along the banks of the Ob River which the railroad crossed on a large bridge, the beautiful cathedral facing the bridge and forming a conspicuous landmark for a long distance. Unlike most Siberian cities, instead of having to travel two to four versts from the railroad station to reach your city, it begins right at the station, reminding me in this respect of Cheliabinsk. But it is a larger place than Cheliabinsk, and the central business district is more built up with many more imposing buildings. There is a splendid Commercial Club building, earlier occupied by the Polish troops, now by the American Red Cross Hospital with an American flag flying over it. There is a splendid high school building, an imposing town hall with the most crowded market behind it I have seen in Russia. Novo-Nikolaievsky Prospect is a boulevard with a park down the center planted with trees; I understand that in summertime this is a regular Nevsky for promenading. Across a deep gully from the main part of the city is the *voenny gorodok* (army encampment).

I suppose our impression of Novo-Nick is spoiled by the season of the year in which we see it. I had thought that Omsk mud was the limit, but it was like a Paris pavement compared with Novo-Nick. There was evidently more snow here than at Omsk and the thaw is not so far along. In fact only one or two cabs have ventured out yet—sleighs are still the rule. After trying both I decided the drivers were wise in not venturing out with cabs yet. Nelson and I tried it in a cab to the *voenny gorodok* this morning. We thought we were going out into the mud a dozen times. It was nerve-wracking. How the wheels stood those ice gullies and holes is a marvel to me yet. The bottoms of the streets are still covered with thick ice so capped with dirt and manure that you don't realize it is ice until you take a slide and spoil your suit or dress. The streets are full of rushing torrents which plow along in deep gullies sometimes two or three feet deep, through solid ice, and your sled takes flying leaps over these if they are narrow enough or you get jolted if they are wider.

Secretaries Nelson and Cattron had arrived at Novo-Nick a day ahead of us. Secretary Convise has been here about three weeks, working with the Polish troops, of whom there are a large number, this being their headquarters. They have taken him into their family in much the same fashion the Czechs welcomed our work a year ago at Vladivostok. He is a live, energetic, bright little man of about forty years of age, who was a pastor in Chicago, a worker in the Division Street Y.M.C.A. there, in a Polish district, and who has made the Poles his specialty for the past ten years. He had already started to study the Polish language in Chicago. He is intensely enthusiastic over his work with them, and believes in them strongly. He says he is going to stick with them until they get to Warsaw.

The American Red Cross has been doing good work here.

They are looking after about 8,000 refugees; they have excellent quarters for sewing rooms, a hospital, and care for all typhus cases in the city. The latter are already decreasing with the approach of spring.

Tomsk

Easter night, April 20

Our train stood at Novo-Nikolaievsk all Friday night and Saturday leaving at seven o'clock Saturday night. The secretaries, Convise, Nelson, and Cattron, were in Friday night, and we talked and conferred until eleven o'clock. Then Cattron got out his scissors and gave Carl and me haircuts. Cattron never did any haircutting before he came to Novo-Nick, but just undertook the job with some of the Y.M.C.A. fellows en route from Vladivostok. When some British officers blew in and asked where they could get a haircut, some of the Y secretaries laughingly said Cattron could give it. So they went to Cattron and he performed the job with all the flourish of a professional in spite of the fact that he only had scissors. Carl has given him a pair of clippers, so now he is becoming equipped as a Y.M.C.A. barber.

The trip Saturday was through the beautiful wooded country between Novo-Nick and Taiga, the latter place so named from the forests. The snow was drifted along the road, more so than when you and I went through in early March a year ago. We reached Taiga at two o'clock in the afternoon. I expected to find Bunker and his club there, but the kino building which he had used as a club was closed and the club and Bunker had transferred to Marinsk. We found Woodberry there, however, and his Czech club was going in full swing on the tea cars.

I decided to stick with this car with the Comptons to Irkutsk as I have come to the conclusion that to try to get back to Omsk without one's own car is a risky thing to do. It will also be worthwhile to see what arrangements are being made to take care of our people when they transfer.

We caught the train to Tomsk leaving Taiga about eight o'clock and reaching Tomsk at midnight. We had planned to get

there for the Easter service which begins at midnight. When we
reached Tomsk we found that there were two stations, First
and Second, each about five versts from the center of the city.
So we walked over to the nearest church from the Second station instead of going into the city. This was a little wooden
church with the letters X.B.—*Christos Voskres* (Christ Is Risen)
in Russian—at the top formed with electric lights which glowed
with pink and blue colors a long distance. Around the church
were long benches loaded with hundreds of cakes waiting to be
blessed. Peasants were standing by, from all over the countryside.
The cakes were wrapped in cloth, a candle stuck in the top, and
also a little cross. It is the first time that the Comptons or I had
seen this at the Easter service. The interior of the church was
so crowded that we could not get in.

There are many tales about disturbances along the line but
we have seen nothing that wasn't peaceful. The disturbance
always seems to be just "over there." The reports are always
worse at a distance than right at hand. We are going through
territory about which we heard alarming reports, when we
were in Omsk, but which seems quite normal now we are in it.

This morning we found ourselves attached to a line of cars
on the eighth track of the Tomsk yards, where at least a dozen
other Y.M.C.A. cars are stationed, most of them being club and
store cars. After inspecting the cars we started over to town with
Bixby to get a view of the city. It stretches for a long distance
along the Ob River. It slopes down from the station to the central part of the city which lies close to the river. The Easter
church bells were ringing continually.

In the center of the city we met Riley and Meredith who
were just starting to the railroad station to meet us. Meredith,
whose special mission here is in connection with our relations
with the Russian Church, had been at the Russian Church
service from eight o'clock until four a.m. the preceding night.
Under his guidance we proceeded through the main part of the
city to the cathedral. The city is attractive and substantial. It
is not laid out in the deadly Chicago checkerboard regularity
of Omsk, but twists and winds around to suit the curves of the
river and the hills. The Europe Hotel occupies a fine building

and a commanding position in the center of the city, facing the little river that joins the Ob at this point. A block back of the Europe Hotel, at the end of a short street, is the old cathedral, a yellow building 150 years old. Tomsk gives an impression of substantial well-settled middle age. There are balconies hanging over the sidewalks that recall Petrograd and Moscow. There is more of style and art and culture. It is a city one likes at once. A beautiful castle standing out against the evergreen forest on the opposite side of the Ob River, plainly seen from all parts of the city, adds an artistic touch.

We went on to the new cathedral, which is about eighty years old. It stands in a large open space between the business part of the city and the university buildings and, with its greyish finish and four-square high-lifting style, reminded me of the Church of the Saviour in Moscow on a smaller scale. The dome is a beautiful landmark that attracts the eye from every quarter of the city. There were no services when we went inside. The iconostas and screen are richly decorated in subdued gold, and while the painting is the conventional kind in vogue eighty years ago, it is finely done. It is the finest cathedral I have seen in Siberia.

Meredith is an enthusiast on the Russian Church. He is rector of the Episcopal Church in Japan. He was for three years a missionary with the Moros in the Philippines. He is a great believer in the worshipful value of ritual and ceremony. He says the world has much to learn from the Russian Church and the wonderful service of worship which it has preserved. Especially has the Anglo-Saxon Church much to learn from it. If the Protestant churches in America think they are commissioned to convert the Russians and adopt the attitude of reforming the Russian Church they will make a mistake, in his opinion. He has been received by the bishop and priests with every courtesy and attention.

The streets here are much as we left them in Omsk, not so much snow and ice as at Novo-Nikolaievsk, and sleighs have disappeared. It is still cold nights—last night 19 above zero, and a cold wind for Easter day.

April 21

I think my impression of Tomsk will be one continuous Sunday. These Easter holidays, with all work at a standstill, stores and restaurants closed, everybody out promenading, and church bells constantly ringing, no newspapers, hardly any trains running, certainly join with the general spring air to steal away the sense of work pressure.

This afternoon we visited the university grounds. We had heard much of the size and fineness of Tomsk University, but what we saw exceeded our expectations and greatly impressed us. There are two institutions, Tomsk University proper, which is between the cathedral and the crown of the hill south, and the Polytechnic Institute, which crowns the hill. The latter is larger and has even more imposing buildings than the university. Last year there were 5,500 students in the two institutions, of whom 3,000 were women. A larger attendance is expected this year. The Russian universities will hardly be opened up for another year, and there will be many refugee students here from Russia proper.

En route near Bogotol
April 23

A more beautiful day could not be imagined. A cloudless, smoke-less blue sky over a snow-covered hilly evergreen-forested land-scape. We are nearing the picturesque hill and forest region which stretches from here most of the way to Irkutsk. This is still about a day's run west of Krasnoyarsk. The temperature is about 55 degrees Fahrenheit and invites us to get out to walk or play ball at the station stops.

We left Tomsk yesterday afternoon at 3:30, ahead of schedule, and had a pleasant daylight ride down to Taiga. The railroad approach to Tomsk is certainly puzzling. The train arrives at station number one, which is four or five miles from the center of the city. Then it runs off down into a valley, circles around a range of hills, never giving you a peep of habitation, for another ten miles, winding up at the highest elevation in the region, as far the other side of Tomsk as the

first station is this side. None of us can puzzle out any
reason for the course it takes.

We attended an entertainment at the Czech club, which
Woodberry and the Czechs had arranged, that evening at Taiga.
It was at the town schoolhouse. Czech soldiers, officers, and
townspeople, men, women, and youngsters, were out in force.
The first part of the program was music, then a stereopticon lecture with pictures of the Czechs in Eastern Siberia, most of which
I had snapped with my camera and saw on the screen for the
first time. Then the floor was cleared, the band struck up the
music, and the dance was on. The first dance number brought not
a couple on to the floor; the Russians do not know the Czech
dances. The second number was a Russian waltz and the floor was
instantly jammed with waltzing couples. The town dancing-
master was there, with white collar and the artist's shock of bushy
hair. The mayor, the chairman of the Board of Education, and
other town notables were also there, with their wives and friends
occupying the front seats. It was as typical a provincial gathering as I have seen anywhere in Russia—genuinely democratic.

Then there was the business of catching the train. As soon as
our train rolled in to Taiga from Tomsk, I went to the commandant of the station and requested him to attach our car to the
daily passenger train when it came through that night. It was
expected about midnight. It was then seven o'clock. In order to
make sure of no oversight, I wrote out the request formally asking that this be done. The commandant assured that it would be
O.K. When we went over to the schoolhouse, which was near
the tracks, to see the entertainment, we left word with our *pro-
vodnik* to come and notify us if by chance the train should pull
in before we were back. During one of the intermissions, feeling
uneasy about the train, I looked out and there was a big train
at the station. I plowed through the mud only to find that it was
a long sanitary train which would take no extra cars.

After the entertainment, I went back to the station again
to make sure that the order had been given to attach our car.
The commandant said that it had been ordered. I returned and
wrote letters until one o'clock for Woodberry to despatch back
to Omsk and Tomsk. By that time, the passenger train had

arrived. I went out to get hold of the train assembler, and he had the order for attaching our car and assured us that there could be no slip-up on the matter. I lay down to snatch a nap, keeping my clothes on, however, to be ready to go to the car door if someone knocked. There is usually a big crowd of people who try to get on our car at these larger stations. Meanwhile our car was being switched around. I made one more trip out about 1:30 a.m., made sure that the switchman had gotten his orders from the train assembler all right, chatted with him, remembered him with a couple of packages of Kingfisher cigarettes, then retired feeling that all was well.

I dropped to sleep. An hour later Carl came out to my part of the car saying he thought the train had gone out without our car. We opened the door, and the guard on the tracks said, "Yes, the passenger has gone without you." So I dressed again, hunted up the switchman and asked him why this had happened. "Got new orders," he said. "We had you attached, then someone came along with another car, and they took yours off and put his on." He had received his orders from the train assembler. The latter I hunted up, and he said he had received orders from the commandant and that we were going to be attached to a military train which was going soon. I walked back to the station and found the commandant. He was sorry that circumstances had arisen which made it necessary to change orders and take our car off even after it was attached, but it couldn't be helped—ours was a service car and the other a regular passenger car, and there was too heavy a train for both, so we were being put on the military train which was leaving in an hour. There was nothing to do but to accept the situation. I went back to the car, and turned in after 3:30. It had been light since three o'clock, and by the time I got to sleep the sun was almost shining. After all, we were lucky to get out in seven hours rather than thirty-seven after arriving at Taiga.

We are reminded the last couple of days of the shortness of spring. Yesterday it was uncomfortably warm at Tomsk. The weather jumps from winter into summer. Before the snow is off we will be sweltering in Siberian heat, which is as bad as the cold. Only the cold lasts longer. There is snow and ice between seven and eight months of the year here.

Taiga is a reminder of Russian graft. The story is that under the old regime in the days when the Siberian Railroad was being built, a committee went ahead to determine how near the cities the railroad should run. If a city came across with a handsome amount of graft, the railroad would run close to that city. If the graft was not sufficient, the railroad would give the city a wide berth. When the committee came to Tomsk, the Tomskis were so certain that the railroad would go through their city, on account of their size and prestige, that they turned the committee down. As a result the nearest the Trans-Siberian comes to Tomsk is the junction point of Taiga, 40 miles from Tomsk. A branch railway had to be built to connect this cultural capital of Siberia with the main line.

Krasnoyarsk

April 25

We arrived here a couple of hours ago, five o'clock in the morning. It is a cold, cloudy, windy April morning, and the snow-covered mountains that lie east of the city make it feel wintry.

Yesterday we spent all day at the little station of Chernoretchenskaya, 38 versts east of Achinsk. I think the name means Black Little River. They had received orders not to let any trains through to Krasnoyarsk, and the train we were on was the first to be held up by the order. Trains kept coming from the west all day so that the yards were soon jammed full. It was thought that the fighting that has occurred lately with some marauding bands west of Krasnoyarsk, who call themselves Bolsheviki, was perhaps holding up communication east of Krasnoyarsk. But as usual rumors at a distance are worse than facts close at hand. When we arrived here this morning, we found trains going through as usual.

Last night a Polish officer rode with us from Chernoretchenskaya to Krasnoyarsk. He lives in Cracow. He was a professor before the war and, as such, was free from military duty. He volunteered, however, for the Polish legion which was a part of the Austrian army. The frank aim of the Polish legion in those days was to help destroy Russia. There were about 30,000 troops in this legion. When the Russian revolution occurred, however, they felt that they must cast their lot with the Allies rather than with the Central Powers and accordingly went over in a body to Russia. There are now something like sixty thousand in the Polish legion in Russia, the larger part of which is in the Don Basin.

En route Krasnoyarsk to Irkutsk

April 26

We had a day and a half at Krasnoyarsk, glorious, sunshiny, rare spring days. Krasnoyarsk is beautifully situated in the valley of the broad Yenesei River which the railroad crosses on a handsome bridge. The city itself lies for the most part on a perfectly level stretch between the Yenesei and a smaller stream which flows into it at this point. East of the city, beyond the Yenesei, are high picturesque mountains. West, beyond the smaller stream, rise barren hills. South is a suburb now known as Bolshevik Hill where poor people and masses of children live. I climbed this hill last evening. A fire tower stands near the top, which I secured permission to climb. The sun was still shining, and I took pictures over the city which stretched straight ahead to the junction of the rivers. Broad Bolshoy Prospect ran straight through the length of the city, the big yellow cathedral shone in the declining sun, while other smaller White Russian churches stood out here and there. Nearer were the railroad yards, the dark brick Russian railroad church, and clear around to the right the big bridge. The Russian who stood in the tower keeping watch said that there were not many fires now; people had so little wood and were so careful with it that the fires were fewer than they used to be.

The center of the city contains some fine, stone business blocks, as substantial as any I have seen in Siberia. There seems to be more room even than in other Siberian cities, in the streets, on the sidewalks, and in the numerous squares. At the center of the city around the cathedral is a large square.

Heinz and I visited the Italian army headquarters yesterday morning. These are Italians who were in Italian Austria and forced to fight in the Austrian army at the outbreak of the war. Like the Czechs, Poles, and Roumanians, who suffered similar fates, they organized troops out of their war prisoners, and this is the army now in Siberia; not large, but full of pep and ginger, with a splendid band which was practicing when we visited the barracks.

We visited Lieutenant Pokrovsky, who is much interested in the *Y* work for the Russian troops, and who was acquainted with our work in Vladivostok. He is one of the younger generation. When we called first this morning, he was not ready to receive visitors, so we climbed the hill west of town until the appointed time. The top of the hill gave a splendid view over the city, the Yenesei River, the mountains east of the river, the prairie west and northwest of town, and the *voenny gorodok*, some distance from the city, where the war prisoners are located. Just as we reached the top of the hill, we saw our train pulling into the station. Our first temptation was to rush back to the station, passing up our appointment with the lieutenant. On second thought we returned, had our visit with him, caught a slow cab to the station, and still had an hour and a half before the train left.

Krasnoyarsk is the camp for the German and Austrian prisoners of war, who are on the streets all the time. The stores are full of the art work and toys, which they make. Many of them speak English well and give lessons to the people in the city. Until recently their orchestras were constantly in demand, but now there are restrictions. Most of the prisoners are well dressed, and all salute all other people in uniform, according to regulations.

The Comptons were out at their camp this morning and bought some articles, which can be bought cheaper at the camp than in the city. They happened to be a day too late, however, as practically the entire store of things on hand had been sent into the city for sale the day before. The prisoner of war who showed them around said that they all wanted to work in the city, as there was such an atmosphere of grumbling and

complaint in the camp all the time. He said that these prisoners
had been released by the Bolsheviki, when they had been in
power, and told they could go home. They sold everything
they had, and set out for Germany last May. When they had
gone about a thousand versts, however, the Czechs overthrew the
Bolshevik regime and compelled the prisoners to return to their
camps. It was a great blow to them.

In the evening we had tea with the American Red Cross
dentists on their Czech train which is located here temporarily.
Dr. Marquis and Dr. Puterbaugh are stationed here. They are
both from Los Angeles, and we had known them at Omsk.
Dr. Marquis is extracting teeth at the rate of 90 daily, besides
many fillings and some cleanings. He doesn't have time to use
anesthetics at such a rate. His pulling hours are five hours daily.
There is a big line of patients constantly waiting for him. The
dental profession is not much developed in Russia and Siberia,
but Russians have less trouble with their teeth than Americans
because of the black bread and kasha which constitute
their main foods.

This is the first time that I have left Krasnoyarsk in the
daytime and seen the fine mountain scenery which lies east
of the city. The hills are white with snow, though the
streams are now free of ice. The Yenesei River is still frozen
and people still walk and ride across it on the ice. We saw the
river boats at the docks, still locked in the ice. We were told
that they can only make one round trip a year to the mouth of
the Yenesei, at the Arctic ocean, 2,000 miles away, and there
they transfer their loads to British boats which carry them on
to the British Isles. The Russian boats just have time to get back
to Krasnoyarsk before the river freezes over again. Spring is
further along, however, at Krasnoyarsk than at any city we have
visited yet. The streets are entirely free from snow and ice,
and even dried off, so that the dust is beginning to be bothersome.

The Czechs are at every station. I meet many of my old
friends of Vladivostok days. At the last station I met the man
who was Czech station commandant at Vladivostok when I was
there last summer. He is the one who helped us get the big
American freight cars for the tea cars which are doing service

all through Siberia now. He seemed glad to meet an old
acquaintance in such an out-of-the-way place.

We are now traveling through the most dangerous part
of the trip. There is no danger during the day, but at night
things happen. We have just passed a bridge which was damaged
yesterday, and the tracks torn up near it. It happens that we
are all unarmed on our car. Compton, Gilbert, and I are the
only men on the car besides our war prisoner. Meredith says
that he never carried a gun when he was working with the
Moro headhunters in the Philippines, but that he always carries
one in Siberia. The other cars on our train are mail coaches,
one car of officers behind us, and the rest *teplushkas* filled with
ordinary passengers, for this is supposed to be the one daily
passenger train.

Of all the cities of Siberia and the Urals which I have seen
to this time, I think Ekaterinburg the most charming, Tomsk
the most attractive for home and work, Krasnoyarsk the
most finely situated, and Omsk—well, our favorite saying is
"See Omsk and die." There is something about the atmosphere
of Omsk that depresses—something intangible that prevents
people from liking the place. It is hard to lay a finger on the
cause of this. The only specific things one can mention are mud,
dust, distance. As for architecture, Omsk can boast as good as
any other Siberian city, in churches, business blocks, and public
buildings. In situation, the view over the Irtish and the prairie
behind compares with the charm of the Western prairies.
And yet something seems to spoil the effect. It is like Chicago
with the greatness left out. It is like a big crude rough boy whom
you feel like spanking. Perhaps it is the absence of culture and
refinement which you find in nearly every other Siberian city.

En route Krasnoyarsk to Irkutsk near Nizhni Udinsk
April 28

Most of last night and today we have been traveling through
what is known as the Bolshevik danger zone. Early this morning
we saw two dead Bolsheviks, hanging to the trees near the
railroad tracks. We were told afterwards that there was another

body there—a woman lying on the ground. We have passed
a number of armored cars and trains, but all has been quiet
with us. From the point where the bodies were hanging, there
was a village some twenty-five versts from the railroad which
was the Bolshevik center where their staff was located. There
are Czech guards all along at the different stations, but quite
small compared with the number of Bolsheviki who are reported.
One of the Czechs who was traveling with us this morning was
reporting an interview with a peasant woman at the last station.
She was from the Bolshevik village. The Bolsheviki at the village
had asked her who were on guard at the station. When she
replied "Czechs," the Bolsheviki said, "Well, we don't want
them. We're after Cossacks." The snow is deep between the
railroad and the village and makes an expedition impossible now.

Today is the first day that we have come out of the snow
zone. I have seen central Siberia without snow for the first
time. When we rolled into Nizhni Udinsk, it was dry and
dusty, and the train rolled up a trail of dust as it pulled past
the railroad roundhouse.

Irkutsk
April 29

We arrived at Irkutsk yesterday noon, making excellent time
the last five hundred versts from Nizhni Udinsk on. Snow
is all gone. The ice was out of the gorge of the glorious Angara
River over a week ago. I am sorry to have missed the grand
sight of that ice break-up. Viles, one of our Czech secretaries,
who was here then, says that people could not get from one
side of the river to the other for almost a week preceding the
break-up. It was too dangerous to cross on the ice and the
pontoon bridge was not ready. People simply had to stay on
whichever side of the town they happened to be caught on. The
railroad station is on the other side from the main part of the
city, but few trains happened to be running then, owing to the
Easter holidays and the Bolshevik troubles up the line. Yesterday
was the first day that the bridge was opened.

This is the first time I have stopped in Irkutsk long

enough to get any idea of the place. It strikes me as the largest and most substantial city of Siberia. Yesterday was a poor day to get an idea of it as the wind was blowing a gale, the dust was everywhere, and this is not typical of Irkutsk. The main street, Bolshaya, is quite a business thoroughfare. The Y.M.C.A. has excellent quarters in what is normally a fine residence near the university grounds, which are at the end of the main street where it meets the river. We went to a modern restaurant yesterday, where there are plants, singing birds, mustard on the tables, and many other rarities which we have not seen in a restaurant for many a moon. The prices were not so bad either, only 15 rubles each for a decent dinner including chocolate ice cream sundae! On the other hand a pair of black shoe strings costs 3 rubles and a pair of brown, 8 rubles. Hardly the place to do much shopping. And what a spiral the ruble is taking. It has gone down to 30 to 1 at Vladivostok and 40 rubles to the dollar at Harbin.

I visited the Rassuschins yesterday, and they welcomed me with open arms. They are the people with whom we stayed at Dom Brynner, you will remember. Their home is a regular mansion. The Japanese Consulate occupies the lower floor. But they have extra room upstairs. They invited me to live with them while I am here and have offered me a cozy corner room. There are a couple of divans, and they said any time I had any visitors who wanted to stay overnight, they could use the divans. Our assistance to Mr. Rassuschin at Omsk was much appreciated. He is in Japan now, visiting the daughter who is in the same English school as the Phelps children.

Was out at the opening of Viles' club at the Czech First Regiment quarters last night. Gilbert became quite enthusiastic and said they had no club like it around Vladivostok. Viles is quite a wonder. He is a young fellow, only 25 years old, but has had a successful business career already and lived long enough in Japan and China to know both languages fairly well. He is always helping somebody out. The soldiers and officers all love him, and he has some handsome swords as souvenirs which they have presented him. One is a beautiful Toledo blade of 1688.

The Association and the individual secretaries have splendid quarters here in contrast with the accommodations which we have at Omsk and other points. That is partly because of the long period of work which the Association has had in Irkutsk, this being the third year.

The sharp April winds and the sparkling blue sky keep reminding me of Colorado. Only the Angara River is a phenomenon all by itself; deep, clear, cold, beautiful, it swings on its swift course of 2,200 miles to the Arctic. From the banks of the river in Irkutsk can be seen the snow-clad mountains around Lake Baikal and in the same view the city, stretching before one with its many churches like a bright mosaic, behind the blue Angara. They say that the Angara is too cold to swim in even in the middle of summer; and that they catch trout off the end of the main bridge.

May 3

The Rassuschin home, the biggest and finest in Irkutsk, was bombarded for nine days when the Bolsheviki seized Irkutsk in December 1917 and January 1918. Shells pierced the roof and walls in many places tearing up the beautiful furnishings. The family lived downstairs and no one was injured. After the battle, all fled to Vladivostok except the sister who remained behind and lived at the house during the troublous times that followed. While the Rassuschins were away, the Japanese Consulate occupied their home and is still in it. The Rassuschins feel that they owe the preservation of the house to the Japanese, as bandits came around seeking Rassuschin just after the Japanese had occupied the house. The Japanese Consul said that he could not turn the house over to the Bolsheviki, as he was responsible to the owner, and could not do so without the permission of the owner.

Gardens surround the house on every side. Just across the garden in the same block is the university and its grounds. My room is richly furnished, a Gobelin tapestry decorating one wall. The bed has rich silken coverlets, with fine linen sheets. And then I can have a hot bath at any time by giving a half hour's warning. I had one yesterday morning, with the

water up to the top of the tub, the best bath I have had since
I left Japan a year ago, and the only tub bath I have had in
Siberia. And a big bath towel, as big as my army blanket, to wrap
up in and dry off with.

The home has the atmosphere of culture, refinement,
luxury, and good taste, such as you would expect to find in
some New England city. The high-ceilinged rooms, the paintings,
the libraries, beautiful vases, stuffed animals and birds, and rich
furniture are all so different from what you would look for in
this isolated place. And yet it is not an exception. The American
Consulate is located in a millionaire's residence, and there are
many fine homes here.

I have hardly ever been in a home which seemed to have
a more stimulating atmosphere culturally and intellectually
than this one. French, English, and Russian are spoken at the
table with almost equal ease and frequency. It is evident that
German could be, if it were good taste. This household gives
me a new conception and regard for the Russian home. The
table is the great family gathering place. The informality of the
Russian table is conducive to sociability, a conversational
atmosphere, and a give and take. The home is as free and easy
in its democracy and comfort and lack of restraint as it is
dignified and stimulating culturally.

The eldest son is in military service, an interpreter with
the French Mission. The next son is in high school. He was one
of the organizers of the Irkutsk Boy Scouts, of whom there
are now 800. It was interesting that in the first interview which
the scoutmasters had with Mr. Ross, the Y.M.C.A. Scout secretary, the Russian scouts said that what they wanted chiefly was
the spiritual and ideal side of the Boy Scout movement. This
seventeen-year-old boy, for the scouts are older here than at
home, said last night that he would soon have to cut out smoking
as he would be in scout work again and smoking was forbidden
the scouts. It is a revelation to see how widely the boy scout
movement has spread in this country.

May 4

We are having a snow storm today. It is melting as soon as it falls. The past two days have been mild, summer weather, but one can count on snow any time during May here and even in June.

This morning I went to the cathedral. It is the largest church I have seen in Siberia, a big brown building, with a long low approach between the outer entrance tower and the main body of the cathedral. The service was not so fully attended as in Omsk, but then church attendance has been high during the Easter services, and most people feel like taking a little rest. The choir in the cathedral is splendid, the deep bass voices being very strong and beautiful. The decorations are simple, almost lacking, though there is plenty of gold on the iconostas and a few big icons on the pillars. The Royal gates are unusually low and heavy.

Secretary Ostergren has done a splendid piece of Red Cross work here this winter with the Bolsheviki prisoners, from the Death Train. They were in terrible shape when he took hold of their case, had been shunted from one end of Siberia to the other, and were dying from starvation and cold. Ostergren got them back into health, saving hundreds of lives, and now the bulk of them have gone back voluntarily into the Russian army to fight Bolshevism. Another illustration of the probable truth that the best way to cure Bolshevism is to cure the wretched conditions that call it forth.

May 7

Two days ago the long-expected blow came. An American engineer called on us at the office and pleasantly announced that we were requested to vacate all cars, particularly passenger cars within forty-eight hours. That meant that the Alpins, who had just settled down comfortably in the car on which the Comptons and I came from Omsk, had to vacate just before taking the car to Krasnoyarsk. That put them on the hunt for rooms, and the net result of a two-day hunt has been to get a hotel room promised for next Saturday. Meanwhile we have turned over one of the rooms of our office to the Alpins until Saturday. Five hundreds rubles monthly is asked for the poorest rooms.

The Alpins have had to change their plans further as a result of losing the car; she will stay here, as it seems best not to run the gauntlet of the danger zone again, only to arrive at Krasnoyarsk without a room. She will work on our staff at Irkutsk. We lose another passenger car on which we calculated to transfer some people to Manchuria, but now they will have to take their chance on the express.

The trouble with the express is that you never know when it is coming; it sometimes arrives a day ahead of announcement, more often a day behind. You have to live at the station for a day or two before it arrives to make sure of it, as it usually proceeds on its way within an hour. And then you can't reserve seats in any way. You just have to take your chance with fifteen to fifty other people on what places will be vacated when the train arrives. As to post trains, they are still out of the question for women to travel in; they are made up mostly of *teplushkas* which are all right for men traveling singly. On the train we came on from Krasnoyarsk, aside from our car and *teplushkas*, there was only one car, called an officer's car. It was fourth-class, small, and between fifty and sixty people were constantly traveling on it.

The good old days of living, working, and having our being on the railroad have gone. No longer can individuals drop in on the officials and solicit locomotives, cars, or trains for their private or commercial convenience. A little courteous attention with cigarettes or tobacco or sugar will no longer work such wondrous results. Temporarily, it is inconvenient but is for the gain of all in the long run.

The history of the Rassuschins is certainly interesting. They seemed more American than any Russian family I had met. I learned that he is of Siberian stock, himself, not an emigrant from Russia. His forebears have lived around Irkutsk for three hundred years. Mrs. Rassuschin was only two years old when her father died, and four when her mother died. She remembers nothing about them, but knows that her father was a Cossack from Poland. Why he came to Siberia she doesn't know. She knows nothing further about her people. But the fact of her father being Cossack allows the son to be a Cossack, and he says when he is twenty-one years old he will enlist with the Cossacks.

Mr. Rassuschin, in spite of his present wealth and possession of the finest home and property in Irkutsk, was a poor boy. He worked hard, long hours and finally scraped enough together to go to Petrograd and get an engineer's education. He came back and built the pontoon bridge over the Angara River. He also discovered and opened up coal mines, and these were the chief source of his wealth. He has a reputation for absolute honesty and fair dealing. When the government recently purchased mining interests, they paid him the full price that he asked, twelve million rubles. He was the only mine owner who received all he asked for. Of course, with the violent fluctuations of the ruble Mr. Rassuschin stands to lose a lot. He gets it converted into foreign investments as speedily as possible.

The Rassuschins showed me last night the track of one of the shells that came through the walls into their home. It pierced four walls, and in the last room wound up with glancing around the walls, lodging finally in the wall next to one of the members of the family, after just missing her as she sat at the desk. The room I am staying in has a dozen holes made by machine gun fire. The same block in which we are living has two large two-story buildings with the roofs, the windows, every bit of woodwork gone, and nothing but the brick walls standing. The same is true in several other parts of the city. Irkutsk got the Bolshevik revolution good and hard, but not so much as Kiev did.

May 10

I am learning some of the differences between Russian and Siberian life. The kissing of the lady's hand is not a Siberian custom. It is perfectly proper for Siberian ladies of the best families to do their housework and work in the garden. When finishing a meal with a Siberian family, the guests and members of the family do not go around and shake hands with the lady of the household, but simply express their thanks across the table before they get up to leave. The Siberian standards are much more like the American. There is another interesting resemblance. They chew gum in Siberia. The gum comes from trees, and peasants bring it to town. The Siberian upper classes are quite apologetic about it, thinking it a rather boorish custom to chew. They were immensely surprised to know that Americans chew. They said that they supposed they were the only people in the world that had such a horrid custom. They could not understand the extent, popularity, and respectability of gum chewing in the States.

The name Siberians is given to those Russians who came to Siberia before the advent of the railroad. They are supposed to have more of an independent and enterprising character than those who have come out since, under government encouragement. I had supposed that there was a native race like our American Indians but resembling the European Russians, to whom the name was applied, but I learn that this is a mistake. The present Siberians bear much the same relation to the Russians that the early English settlers in America bore to the English in England.

If rooms are easy for Americans to find in Irkutsk, they are not easy for the Russians themselves. There is a woman with four children who is living at our office address. Now she must find a room elsewhere. We wrote a letter to the town council asking them to assist her to find a room. They wrote on the back of the request: "No rooms at present. Your turn is number 467."

We learned of one room this morning which we can rent for 250 rubles monthly, but only on condition that we buy the furniture. The furniture consists of one plain small table, and a few plain chairs. They ask 5,500 rubles. We pass.

The weather continues cold again. The snow Sunday covered the ground white. There was some snow again last night.

May 11

I have just returned with some of the other secretaries from attending a Protestant church service for the Czechs. The attendance was about two hundred. This is the third Czech service which has been held the past three weeks in the beautiful little German Lutheran church in Irkutsk. The first meeting was held by one of the new Czech secretaries who had just come over from America and who was a Methodist pastor in America, Vancura by name. The interest was great and came just at the time when the Y.M.C.A. was given official recognition by the Czech government, and when Professor Masaryk founded the new Protestant Theological Faculty in Prague University.

This is a time of readjustment for the Czech army. Until the war was won and the independence of Czechoslovakia established, the Czech army was not only a military body but a political body, the body politic of the Czechoslovak revolutionary movement. Consequently, the movement to the rear this spring has given the Czechs the first opportunity to put their army on a purely military basis. Furthermore, the establishment of the Czechoslovak government naturally means that the political functions of the Czech soldier cease automatically, and he becomes just a soldier and the army just an army, with the same relations to its lawful government as any other army. These two facts coming into conjunction and at a time when the men are tired and homesick, have caused widespread dissatisfaction and discontent. The men are finding it hard to adapt themselves to army life in Siberia when all that they want to do is to get home to Bohemia. Undoubtedly, too, there has been some Bolshevik propaganda amongst them, though not very much.

I came across the Angara River on the boat this noon. The water is so clear that you can see the pebbles on the bottom all the way across. This is one Russian city where water does not have to be boiled. It is even clearer at other times of the year— now it has some of the dirt caused by floods from the melting snows.

Yesterday afternoon Scherer, Captain Katterfield, and I went over to the Czech club on the other side of the river.

It was the first Czech club here. There are now three others in the city. On the way the captain expressed himself about the present situation. He feels that Bolshevism cannot be defeated simply by force of arms. Other means must be employed. He laments the lack of union among the anti-Bolshevik forces. And Bolshevism cannot be dealt with simply by calling it robbery and pillage, he says. It could not have been so strong and stood so long if that was all there was to it. Its leader is one of the noblemen of Russia. One of Katterfield's friends was acquainted with Lenin as a boy and young man. They grew up together. And he says Lenin was thinking and talking about the economic betterment of people even in those days. He has given his whole life to that cause. The educated and well-to-do classes must remedy the evils which produce Bolshevism and get acquainted personally with the poor people, take a real interest in them and their welfare, and help them to better living conditions. Above all must speculation be stopped. It is the continuance of such speculative evils that produces discontent among the masses as much as anything else, according to the captain.

We had an interesting talk with Colonel L. of the American Railway Service Corps yesterday. He gave us the most intelligent view of the railroad situation we had yet heard. He said that it was hard to get people out of the cars. The trouble was that they had gotten the habit of living on cars, and it is hard to change a nation's habits. He himself hoped that they could get the road into good enough order this summer so that he could return home. He had seen all he wanted of Siberia. He didn't think the Siberian road could ever be worked on American standards. In the first place it wasn't built to make money but for military purposes. It wasn't expected to make money any more than the American army or navy were expected to make money. Take the matter of officials living on cars. In America they would not tolerate it because the stockholders always had to be remembered, and for officials to live on private cars hits the stockholders' pocketbooks. But here there were no stockholders to think about. The Russians can run the road all right themselves, according to their way and for their own purposes. They object to foreign help, naturally, though the officials have been courteous and helpful. The Russian railroad is very well built. Few roads in America are so well built, though the American roads usually try to avoid curves, whereas the Russian roads seem to create them.

The express service is the least adequate in proportion to the demand of any service now. There are only two express trains and at Irkutsk there are usually forty to fifty people waiting to catch it, and usually only ten or twelve available seats. There are plans for adding another two express trains from Irkutsk to Vladivostok, making twice-a-week service from Irkutsk and once-a-week from Omsk. The post train has daily service from here to Vladivostok, but takes six days as compared with the express, which takes three days and a half. The post train is cleaning up all passenger traffic daily. Freight service is improving right along, though its effects are not much felt this far out as yet. They are sending a train and a half of merchandise out from Vladivostok daily now, part going Harbin way and part Amur way.

The Russians like their own short spring. The Rassuschins used to go to France every spring for their vacation. But they said the spring there was not so nice as the Russian spring. It came on too slowly so that you hardly noticed it in France. Here it came with a rush, so fast that the buds and leaves seemed to break out with a click. Then there was a wonderful atmosphere here which one never got with the spring air anywhere else.

En route Irkutsk to Vladivostok, nearing Chita
May 17

Mr. Phelps arrived finally Tuesday evening at six o'clock. All of the secretaries joined him at dinner. In the conversation an interesting sidelight was thrown on the conflicting points of view of the American as contrasted with the British and French representatives in Siberia. The British and French representatives now in Siberia were picked because of their knowledge of the Russian language. Where did they learn the language? In Russia before the revolution. How did they happen to be in Russia then? Largely as political and military representatives who were personae gratae to the Czar's government then in power. That is how it happens that they seem so generally to represent a monarchical and reactionary point of view. The Americans, on the other hand, have practically no representatives who learned the language under the old regime.

Light was also thrown on the contradictory political policies of Vladivostok and Omsk, and their influence on Association viewpoints in Eastern and Western Siberia. The Omsk Y.M.C.A. policy followed the lead of the American Consul General there. Depending on Chinese communications, he was wholeheartedly sympathetic with the Kolchak government. The Vladivostok Y.M.C.A. policy, following the lead of consular and military representatives at Vladivostok whose communications with America lay through Japan, formed unfavorable impressions of the Kolchak government. The Japanese, supporting and utilizing Semyenov, have thwarted Kolchak. It is all a part of the baffling difficulties that one faces in trying to formulate any policies that can cover this enormous extent of territory, with the complex and varied political and social phenomena which exist.

Our train made up at Irkutsk last night with greater despatch and order than anything I have seen on the Russian railroad since Petrograd before the revolution. When we stopped at Verkhni Udinsk yesterday, one of the railroad officials was saying to the other with a smile, "Well, we're traveling right along, *po-Amerikansky*."

For the third time, my trip around the tunnel section of Lake Baikal has been at night. We left Irkutsk at ten o'clock and ran through the tunnels between midnight and four o'clock. The moon was full, however, and we had a wonderful picture of the region—more wonderful than if it had been daytime. The lake is still covered with an unbroken surface of ice. It has melted a little on top and has a sort of mushy appearance. The old wagon roads across the ice are now lanes of water, just freezing at night. The moon was chasing through fleecy clouds. Now it would come out bright and clear straight over the lake from us, lighting up the ice with a great yellow glare. Then all would change to inky blackness. Now we would be coasting along sidewise headed for one of the rocky bends, and the moon would be straight ahead of us. Then we would be swallowed up in one of the sixty-three, solid rock tunnels. The next instant we would be coasting in the reverse direction with the moon behind us. We could just make out the eastern mountains across the lake and the range of mountains back of us for a long way back. For an hour I stood on the platform where we could get the entire view.

As Scherer said, this would probably be our last chance to see Lake Baikal, while we had six or seven days ahead of us on the train when we could sleep. By a quarter to three o'clock daylight was beginning to break. By four o'clock day had fully dawned and the eastern sky was all aglow. The snow-capped mountain range loomed up in glory. We had practically finished the tunnel section and reached the easternmost point of the lake, where the railroad swings around sharply to the northwest and begins to wind along the eastern shore. We could look back across the lake to the rock hills and tunnels we had left behind along the southern shore. As the sun rose we had revelation after revelation of Baikal glory. Now we had a study in blue. Across the lake the mountains were capped with snow blue-tinted, the hills were clothed with forests of pines, blue-frosted. The shore was lined with rocky cliffs blue-dark. Then came the great stretch of bluish ice over the blue Baikal water, which broke into sparkling view along the ice edges next to the railroad embankment along which our train was running. Here the ice was slick and smooth, greyish blue; here it was snowy and flaky, whitish blue; here it was soft and mushy, brownish blue. And over the whole scene stretched the great canopy of Siberian blue, a wonderful soft blue as dainty as a Japanese cherry blossom, with fluffs of blue-tinted white cloud floating across.

Then all at once the sun touched one of the fluffs of cloud and the whole marvel of blue changed into a miracle of green, with every imaginable tint and shade of green replacing the previous panorama of blue.

I stood on the platform a long time watching the changing glories come and go and the inspiration was such as I had seldom experienced. It was typical of the greatness of Russia. Here was a feat of engineering rivaling anything that America could boast. Here was a stretch of scenery as exquisite as the rarest scenic gem in Japan, and yet as vast as the Rockies. Lake Baikal is the fifth largest fresh-water lake in the world, larger than Lake Erie. We traveled along its shores continuously for over twelve hours.

We are on a third-class car. Scherer, Beath, and I are sharing a compartment with a Canadian from Toronto by the name of Fried. We call him Fried Salmon because he is in the salmon business. He has lived in Siberia fifteen years. He has a large salmon fishing plant at Nikolaievsk near the mouth of the Amur River. At this point, a Japanese fellow traveler has sat down to observe the operations of this Corona. He can read English and is reading this. He is a comical fellow, can talk Russian exceedingly well, and loves his vodka dearly and his capacity for it seems unlimited. We had a compartment reserved for us on the officers' car. He came in posing as an American and secured permission from the commandant to travel with us, though he is a civilian. He explained that he was an interpreter. His wit with the Russian language is as quick as his wit with the English, and he is quite a mixer, getting acquainted with everybody on the car as well as with the Canadian and British soldiers on a couple of cars which are attached to ours.

Our car has two compartments full of Russian soldiers and officers, two other compartments full of Russian officers and relatives, and the rest of the car full of a mixed assemblage of Russian civilian population, Chinese, Mongolian, Korean, and Jewish commercial people. The Rassuschins were saying the other day that one reason why it is impossible to find house servants or day laborers now is that they are all traveling from one city to another engaged in the business of speculation. The quickest way to force people back into labor will be to send so many wares into the interior that people will no longer find it profitable to carry parcels about with them on passenger trains.

Between Chita and Manchuria
May 18

We arrived in Chita yesterday afternoon. Chita is the famous capital of Semyenov's Mongolian Republic. It is in the section of the Siberian line guarded by the Japanese army. The station platform was bright with the various reds, browns, yellows, and greens of the Japanese and Cossack troops. Japanese influence, wares, and currency are evident on every hand. Russian counterfeit rubles, made in Japan, flood the markets. In the station newsstand the only picture postal cards are Japanese make, two different kinds of local Chita views.

We are traveling through a part of the country where the atmosphere is different than any I have been in for a long time, an atmosphere of terrorism and outlawry, where one feels like keeping as quiet and making himself as inconspicuous as possible. We meet *broneviki* (armored trains) at various stations with one big word "Merciless" in Russian on each car. You are not allowed to take pictures. A pretty-looking miss looking out from one of the windows of the parlor car of the armored train attracted the attention of Scherer who started to snap her picture but was stopped by the Russian guard just as he pointed his vest pocket camera.

A village is pointed out as the place where one of the local rebels against the Semyenov rule had his staff. At another place a hill is pointed out as the place where political offenders are executed. At every station are one to a half dozen *arrestantsky* (jail) cars, well filled with offenders awaiting trial. On our car there was a quarrel last night between a Cossack officer and a non-Cossack which reached such a high tension that we expected the guns to let fire any moment. The ladies in the adjoining compartment, where the quarrel was in progress, took refuge in our compartment scared to death. Our Canadian friend warned us to lie low and keep quiet as the situation was very dangerous. As soon as we came to the first stop, one of the Russian girls, our student medical friend, ran out to the commandant and asked his help. The quarreling parties were called outside and we were informed that one had been placed in the *arrestantsky* car and the other had apologized. They were both back in the car a little later but quiet for the rest of the evening. The excitement had one advantage of clearing the car of half its occupants, who took refuge in quieter cars. We appreciated this as the car had been getting overcrowded.

A few minutes ago another quarrel seemed brewing. The same Cossack who started the trouble last night was asking our Canadian friend to leave the car as he was not a military man. The Canadian objected. The Cossack ordered his soldier to put our friend out, but the soldier refused to obey. Now the officer has gone into another car, the soldier has come to us and told us not to be worried, that the officer is crazy with drink, and he (the soldier) has his gun ready loaded to protect us if needed. Meanwhile our Canadian friend has ascended to the upper berth to be less conspicuous and developments are awaited with interest. This is a part of the world and time when the fact of being an American or Canadian gets scant consideration. Americans are particularly unpopular officially.

To add fuel to the flames of our Cossack officer, at the last station the Canadian boys were passing the ball between the platforms of the cars just as the Cossack appeared and caught a blow from the ball. He took it as anything but a joke.

We met many Mongolians who are in the Semyenov army.

Two stations back, the express from Omsk overtook us. We had hoped to make it at Manchuria or Harbin. While we are disappointed to miss the one or two days which we would have had extra, the tickets for the three of us to Vladivostok from Irkutsk cost 470 rubles third-class, whereas they would have amounted to about 5,000 rubles on the express (nearly 1,800 each). So we feel we are saving the Association a tidy sum, which, however, will be reduced when we transfer to a higher class at Manchuria. By the time we have put in another day with these toilet arrangements and spent the night on the floor of the station at Manchuria, we will be ready to pay extra from there on. There is a second-class car for officers which had been added to this train, but it has been filled up with Russians and we couldn't get a place on it.

Our fellow travelers have greatly changed since leaving Irkutsk. There they were practically all officers or middle class civilians. Here there is a great mongrel breed, mostly soldiers, much roughness and dirt everywhere. There is one Dane left who got on at Irkutsk who was in the telegraphic service there. He is much disgusted with the conditions. Our girl medic friend and all of the other young ladies who are left on the train, except one, have left this car for the second-class car. We all look forward to reaching Manchuria Station this afternoon as the first opportunity to improve our conditions. It is about as dirty as the trip you and I took from Kiev to Moscow, though not so crowded. Scherer has had none of this kind of traveling before and keeps remarking how glad he will be when we get out of this mess. He is sorry to leave Irkutsk; it was so pleasant and quiet there.

Leaving Manchuria Station en route Vladivostok
May 19

The ride all day yesterday lay through the barren treeless Mongolian steppe land between Olovyannaya and Manchuria Station. We passed Olovyannaya at four o'clock in the morning with the sun already up. The high bridge which was destroyed by the Bolsheviki last spring has been repaired so that we crossed on it instead of on the temporary bridge which we had to use when we went out in November.

At Manchuria Station we met Beyers, the American rail-road service man, the only American stationed there. He seems to know every man, woman, and child in Manchuria, and they to know him. Going along the street he has a word with every-body he meets. On the station platform a big circle of admiring Chinese were jabbering with him, and he knows enough Chinese to jolly with them. He is democracy personified, and likes Russia and the Russians immensely. Says he is willing to continue in the service over here after peace is signed. We found some Americans with an American Red Cross train which was stand-ing in the yards ready to be forwarded to Omsk. A number of nurses' voices and one or two men were heard starting some hymns for a Sunday evening service on one of the Red Cross cars.

Beyers went with us to the Russian railroad club restaurant, which was recommended as the best in town. It promised to be our last and only meal between Irkutsk and Vladivostok where we could sit down for more than the usual twenty minutes. Beyers says he is quite isolated here, but he doesn't mind it because he has become enough of a Russky to say *nichevo* and carry on.

The Czech commandant at Manchuria Station was one of my old acquaintances from the Fifth Regiment at Vladivostok, and he helped in getting places on the train this morning. We have first-class tickets on a car which will go right through to Vladivostok.

The British commandant has also been kind to us and gave us a coupe on his station car to sleep in last night. I had to be up at a quarter after four this morning to cinch matters about a place on the train. When I arrived at the station at five o'clock, the platform was already crowded with passengers and Chinese lining up for places on the train.

Manchuria Station is a dust-swept town of fifteen thousand inhabitants of whom two-third are Chinese and the other third Russians and various others. The Russian side of the city is on one side of the railroad, the Chinese on the other. The Chinese quarter is a bit of China. The main streets are lined with peddlers and little bazaar shops. Gin, whisky, sake, and vodka bottles beckon to the passing travelers from half the windows, and judging from the number of "stormy seas" we passed, the advertisement is not in vain. The Danish telegrapher who came on the same train with us from Irkutsk was waltzing up the street in tow of a couple of Canadian pals as happy as could be. I met him this morning a few minutes before the train left. He was without a seat, he had been robbed, he didn't know exactly where his baggage was, and he was exhibiting the usual appearance of the morning after, but he beamed as he said, "I'll never forget those Canadians as long as I live." He is sharing our double coupe with Scherer, Beath, and myself. Most of our other companions to Manchuria Station are on the second-class section of the car.

There is no better way to learn and study Russia and Russians than riding third- or fourth-class, though the latter should be restricted to the shorter runs. On the third-class car all is open between coupes and everybody gets acquainted with everybody else. On the first-and second-class coupes, partitions close you off and you get little acquainted. Then on the third-class car you find the common people who are more communicative and really represent the greater mass of the population. We learned the story of nearly everybody on our car. It was a laboratory of contemporary Russian social, moral, and economic life. People who travel on express or first-class miss all this.

I feel like recommending that every Y.M.C.A. secretary who comes to Russia should proceed to his field from Vladivostok on a third-class car. He will get more education and understanding of the Russian people in a few days that way than in months without it. He will undoubtedly find several people who can speak enough English so that he can make himself understood, as most of the people who travel third-class are of the intelligentsia, though there are also peasants, the latter usually standing in the aisles or on the platform. There are also students, priests, teachers, and professional people.

You get a vivid picture of the social disruption that the revolution has aggravated if not caused. On our car was a young lady out to see the "big white world." She was twenty years old. Her mother died two months ago, her father four years ago. She was going to Vladivostok first, then to Japan just to see what could be seen there. Then on to America where she said she had been invited by an American to come and live with his family. This American she had met on the train between Irkutsk and Vladivostok last January. He had shown her pictures of his wife and children. She herself was married to a Czech officer now stationed at Krasnoyarsk.

Another young lady on the car was evidently looking for company. On the morning of the third day she was the "wife" of one of the officers riding on the same car, and is now riding with him in one of the coupes on this car. Another lady boarded the train near Chita. Her home was Harbin where her husband, a commercial man, was located. She left Harbin five months before to visit friends in Siberia and had not heard from her husband since she left Harbin.

In spite of the great tragedy of the revolution with all of the pressing problems that call for seriousness, sacrifice, and work, it seems as if the new "young woman" of Russia is bent on one object in life—a good time, and as much of it as quick as possible. There are apparently few standards left to prompt her conscience in another direction. There is no force of public opinion, no press, no organized effort on the part of the church or any other institutions with any practical appeals or programs to direct the revolutionary energies into any other direction except war.

The recent collapse of the ruble has been a crash, a debacle, a wreck of unbelievable dimensions. Salaries that were sufficient two months ago now have a half to a third of their purchasing power. Whatever rubles I will have left when I reach Vladivostok will not be worth half what the same rubles were when I left Omsk.

We have just passed Hailar and seen the first trees in the landscape since yesterday morning. The hills around Manchuria Station are the bleakest-looking brown hills you can imagine, much like the dry lands of eastern Colorado. We are on the uphill now until we reach the top of the Hingan range where the railroad doubles upon itself, crossing itself at a higher elevation.

Nearing Harbin
May 20

We are traversing the rich Manchurian plains between Tsitsicar and Harbin. I have seen trees leaved out this morning for the first time this year. It is like a day in May at home, much warmer than any time yet. Yesterday I had the first apple since I left Vladivostok last November, and today we can buy oranges.

The finest scenery between Manchuria Station and Harbin is where the railroad goes over the Hingan Range. It takes about three and a half minutes to go through the tunnel. On the Harbin side of the range is a great loop-the-loop where the course of the train can be seen for a distance of two stations as it winds down the valley towards Boochedoo.

A young Russian has come to visit us in our coupe. He is a student eighteen years old. Scherer got acquainted with him last summer when he used to take athletic supplies out to the American railroad service men who were stationed at these Manchurian points. He expects soon to go to the front to fight with the Kolchak forces. Students eighteen years and over are being drafted from Eastern Siberia as well as from Western Siberia.

One of the ladies who is on our car traveling to Vladivostok knows a few English words, the first ones Russian young women usually learn: "I love you. Kiss me quick. Please take me to America."

One of the things that will make Russia a different country after this upheaval is the better knowledge they will have of their own land and people. Half of the people you meet in Siberia seem to be refugees from Russia. They have been thrown upon the hospitality of Siberia. Siberia has always been much separated from Russia in the past. Siberians have had the attitude that they are virtually an independent country. After going through all these experiences together, there should be a closer tie between the Russians and Siberians.

Travel out of the western part of Siberia to Vladivostok on a regular post train this year under non-Bolshevik administration is a much different thing than it was a year and a quarter ago when you and I came out under the Bolshevik regime. To have come on anything except a special car then, or with a military train, was a longer, dirtier, and more hazardous trip than it is now. I am impressed with how much the service has improved within the last couple of months. There is a snap and a go all along the line. Instead of reaching Harbin fifteen to twenty-four hours late, which used to be a common occurrence, we are arriving within a few minutes of schedule time. No one is kept waiting at the stations on account of lack of room on the trains. Every passenger is moved out of every station every day. The morale of the railroad workers seems to be gaining constantly. And all of this gain has occurred at a time when the road is taxed with military operations. A constantly increasing stream of military supplies is being sent out to the western front from Vladivostok.

En route Vladivostok to Harbin

May 25

We arrived in Vladivostok Wednesday night, and I have spent three busy days there settling accounts and making preparations for return to America. A main feature of my visit was seeing Rodney again. We had supper at the Zolotoy Rog Thursday evening and were together Saturday afternoon and evening. He is looking in fine health and apparently good spirits. I introduced him to Miss Breck and the Y.M.C.A. Home, and we enjoyed the home meals there a couple of times.

I decided to leave this morning (Sunday) by train via Harbin and Korea to catch the *Empress of Russia* from Yokohama June 21. Beath is traveling with me to Changchun. They were so slow in getting our transportation ready at Vladivostok this morning that we didn't have time to check our trunks, but I got an order from the commandant to let our trunks come by the express train to Harbin. The express leaves tonight from Vladivostok and reaches Harbin almost as soon as we do.

This is a beautiful day for the trip to Nikolsk. We are now near Razdolnoye, in the region where the American troops are fighting the Bolsheviki. The latter have recently attacked the railroad, even attacking the passenger trains. The Americans up to the present time have refused to mix up in the fighting in Siberia any further than to defend the railroad in case of attack. A couple of our secretaries are along with the American troops on the new "front."

We have passed the station where the Americans are fully equipped and ready for instant action against the Bolsheviki.

There have been alarms every night along the main line, but most of the fighting has been on the branch line to Suchan Mines. The boys have entrenchments thrown up and constantly occupied. One of the fellows got on our train at the last station and is going up the line to another detachment. He is from Peoria, his father is Czech and his mother Slovene. This probably explains why he is already an interpreter though he knew no Russian when he came here last summer.

The Russian soldiers through here wear Japanese uniforms, as contrasted with the English uniforms which they are wearing further west.

En route Harbin to Changchun, Manchuria
May 27

We are speeding along over the broad Manchurian plains south
of Harbin. They remind me much of Iowa, Illinois, and
Kansas prairie lands. They are well tilled, and the soy bean crop
will evidently be as good as ever this year. This is the center
of the great soy bean region. Everything is fresh after a rain,
which came as a welcome relief after the worst sand and dust
hurricane I ever knew. I thought Kansas had the last word in
dust storms, but the worst I ever saw there was like a gentle
zephyr compared to this hurricane we have just been through.
It held the train up until it could hardly move; you could see
only a few feet from the car window; it sifted in everywhere;
and among other things spoiled my camera. I was rash enough
to want a snapshot of the storm and went on the back platform
to take it. After nearly smothering, I returned having taken
the snap, but only to find the sliding part which pulls the shutter
back and forth clogged up with dust and sand, and myself a
mess. The train is pulling hard now, and every time it starts and
stops you hear the crunching of the sand and dust in the axles
and bearings. It probably means that we shall miss our connections at Changchun and have to stay there overnight.

We are rapidly losing the Russian influences. The station
platforms are lined with Chinese and Chinese soldiers, but there
are a few Russian railway officials.

Yesterday was a glorious day coming across the Manchurian
ranges between Pogranitchnaya and Harbin. I slept at Pogranitchnaya so as to be ready for the express which arrived at 5:45.
I found our baggage aboard all right, checked it, and got on
myself. There were no free places, but Mr. Rassuschin happened
to be on, en route to Irkutsk, and kindly invited me to share
his coupe with him for the day.

Including the range that Pogranitchnaya is on, the railroad
crossed four ranges between the boundary and Harbin. Each
of these has a sizeable stream which the railroad crosses, dropping
down and ascending by branch streams. Two engines have to
be used on every grade. The serpentine curves of the railroad,

especially as it nears the top in each instance, are remarkable. We got many a view looking back down the valley for miles, with sometimes five or six zigzag levels of the road in one view. The first three ranges are almost barren, the last one towards Harbin, the famous Handaohedzie, is well wooded and much wilder. The latter we reached just at sunset, and it reminded me of the upper Hudson and the Lake George region.

I thought I had mastered the subject of Russian and Siberian distances, but after meeting a Russian gentleman from Yakutsk yesterday, I must confess that new vistas were opened to me. This man was going home by way of Irkutsk, four days by the express train we were on from Vladivostok. Then he could take either horses or steamer. If horses, it would take him twenty-five days longer, twenty-nine hundred versts, roughly two thousand miles. If by boat, he must take horses the first four hundred versts, roughly three hundred miles, from Irkutsk to the Lena River, and then the steamer twenty-five hundred versts, roughly sixteen hundred miles, on the Lena to Yakutsk. If he wanted to go on to the mouth of the Lena River, he had before him another trip of twenty-five hundred versts. Thus there is a river trip of five thousand versts, or nearly thirty-four hundred miles, which one can make on the Lena River if my informant was correct, or a distance about equal to that from San Francisco to New York.

My informant said that traveling used to be pleasant, but now it is dangerous. Yakutsk was for some time the Bolshevik center after the Czechs drove them back from the Siberian railroad, but now they are driven out of Yakutsk. He said that the town of Yakutsk had a population of ten thousand and the district of three hundred thousand. Most of the trip from Irkutsk to Yakutsk lies through virgin forests. Most of the gold fields are south and east of Yakutsk. It is exceedingly cold in winter and hot in summer, but their springs come on almost as early as at Irkutsk and along the Siberian railroad. Cattle raising, fishing, and fur trading are the main occupations. He himself was a well-educated, well-dressed man. I asked him if it wasn't lonely so far away from the main trade routes. He said no, that he liked that country probably as much as I liked the

U.S. They had good telegraph communication with the outside world. There is a shorter route to the outside world going east of Yakutsk to the Sea of Okhotsk, but it is more unsettled now, and the safest routes are the most popular these days.

I met an interesting Ural Cossack on the train. He was on his way home from France. He had served in the Russian army early in the war, then returned home, fought against the Bolsheviki to save his home possessions, then gone to the French front. He was proud of being a Cossack, and the Ural Cossacks were the best of all. He said every Ural Cossack had the right to 33 dessiatins of land (about 100 acres), 100 head of cattle, and 100 horses. No Cossack ever worked for any one else, he said. And as for the Bolsheviki, the Cossacks would fight them to the last drop of blood before recognizing or succumbing to them. And with a regular Fourth of July peroration he said, "Come to our country. We have a rich country. We have fertile land and big crops. We have wonderful cattle and horses. And the rivers abound in the most tasteful fish, which have no bones. And watermelons that weigh from forty to eighty pounds, not like the little Petrograd melons which really aren't melons; everything that the heart can desire, except forests. For we live in the steppes, the broad level glorious steppes. But the crowning creation of all are the Ural Cossacks. We're the flower of creation. We have souls, and we fight, live, love, and die for glory, for freedom, for honor, for our rights. I love nature," he continued. "See that beauty," and he pointed to a picturesque view in the Manchurian range through which we were passing. "Though I cannot paint, I see that with the eye of an artist. Beautiful nature inspires and intoxicates me. We live only once, and I believe in seizing all the joy and happiness possible from the present moment. See those wretched mud houses of these hardworking Manchurian natives. They scrape and toil and suffer, but the rest of us benefit by their toil. Why are we able to enjoy this ride on this wonderful railroad today? Because of the labor of thousands of hardworking natives who toiled and suffered for the benefit of others. It is a principle of nature. Out in our country the Russian muzhiks toil on the poorer soil while we live on the best land. Why? Because we are strong,

because we are powerful, because we are gifted with courage
and readiness to fight. My father is President of the Ural
Cossacks. The Bolsheviki demanded that the Cossacks give up
their officers. My father refused. We are not afraid of the
Bolsheviki. Therefore we will keep what we have."

"The Russians are much like the Chinese," he continued.
"They are impracticable, they are good-natured, and they
cannot direct their own affairs. The leaders who have done most
for Russia were not Russians. Catherine II was German. Peter
the Great was only half Russian."

I jot this down because it is typical of the Cossack spirit
and is the first time that I have had a Cossack open up to me
so freely.

En route Changchun to Mukden
May 28

When we pulled into Changchun last evening and saw the
beautiful Japanese train of the South Manchurian Railroad
standing there with its American-style Pullman cars, all elec-
trically lighted, its clean windows, and cleanly dressed men and
women comfortably seated in the plush seats, we just stood on
the platform and gazed with rapture as if we had suddenly
been dropped into a new world. And then when the train
began to move with no warning three bells, with no trainmen's
whistles, and exactly on the second, and the beautiful lighted
palace silently glided out of the station, we felt that we were
home again. It was like watching the New York Central pull
out. I felt more homesick all at once than all the time I had
been in Russia.

There, on the track we had just come in on, stood our
Russian train, the best to be found now in Russia, and which
had satisfied Beath and me in comparison with most of our
Russian traveling. But after seeing the South Manchurian train,
the Russian train stood there like a gloomy, dirty, sorrowful
funeral, a symbol of the land it came from and into which it
was soon to return. And the difference in the order and system
of operation was the same. We had a half hour to catch the

Manchurian train, but we couldn't do so because we couldn't get our baggage off the Russian train until they opened the baggage car, and they couldn't do that until the baggage master came. I went after the baggage master, but he was busy getting baggage on another train going to Harbin. Finally he finished that and came to open the car. Meanwhile the car had wandered off down the track switching, and by the time the car returned it was too late to check onto the Manchurian train. Then we had to be careful to get our trunks into the Japanese baggage room or we would come around for the seven o'clock train in the morning and find it locked up in the Russian baggage room, the office closed, and no one due to report for work until nine o'clock. And the difference in the appearance of the Russian and Japanese sides of the station. The Russian side was dirty and crowded with Chinese and luggage and packs of all kinds over which you constantly stumbled if you tried to walk around. The Japanese side was spick and span; no one was waiting for a train. All who wanted to travel were taken care of promptly.

After three years in Russia, there are three things that I want in Paradise: cleanliness, order, and industry.

Changchun is the point where you change from the Chinese Eastern of Northern Manchuria to the Japanese South Manchurian Railroad. It is the boundary between the Russian and Japanese spheres of influence, as agreed upon in the Portsmouth Treaty of 1905.* There is no question of the use Japan has made of her opportunity. Beautifully laid out streets, parks, and cement and brick structures greet you in the new Changchun which Japan has built up in recent years. The Japanese have shown their shrewdness in running their railroad three or four miles from the old Chinese cities and building up brand new cities around the station and near the railroad where values have skyrocketed, leaving the Chinese cities stranded and stagnating from the lack of railroad facilities.

We stayed overnight in the Yamato Hotel, a splendid artistic building within a block of the station, in front of which

---

* Negotiated under the eye of an American president, the treaty made no reference to "spheres of influence," but only to railway concessions.

is a tasteful square with green trees, lawn, and shrubs. And joy of joys, a clean room with sheets to crawl between, a bathroom with hot water, and boys to wait on you when you ring the bell and to clean your shoes if you leave them in the corridor, and soap and toilet paper and mirrors. Although we only had six hours before the train left, we could not sleep until we had tried these various novelties. The troubles of traveling were ending, the joys of travel beginning.

For a traveler coming into Russia for the first time from the south, the shock at Changchun must be great as he turns from the brilliant comfort and luxury of his South Manchurian accommodations to the bleak prospect of the Chinese Eastern. Somehow the contrast between Russia and Japan impressed me even more vividly here in Manchuria than when we went from Vladivostok to Japan last year. Perhaps an added year of Russian revolutionary conditions prepared me for a keener reaction. Perhaps it is the impressive contrast afforded of the different use made of the same sort of land, the same physical conditions, the same climate, the same commercial opportunities, in a contiguous stretch of territory, by the two different races. It is easy to understand Japan's point of view of the reasonableness of her desires to extend her sphere of influence. It almost seemed as if the Russian officials who came on our car at Changchun to examine our passports were conscious of failure in the presence of the physical evidences of Japan's success, a success which is reflected in the attitude and bearing of the Japanese officials.

En route Southern Manchuria to Korea
May 28

All through Manchuria, the station platforms are crowded with Chinese. There are Chinese who come simply to watch, others to sell to passengers, some to travel, others to beg. I have seen more beggars in twenty-four hours than I have seen in beggar-famous Russia in twenty-four days. In Northern Manchuria, besides the Chinese civilians, there are the Chinese troops on guard and the Russian railway officials. The restaurants are conducted by Russians, and the ruble is the ordinary currency.

In Southern Manchuria, the Chinese crowds continue with a constantly increasing number of Japanese civilians, men, women, and children. Besides the civilians are Japanese troops on guard and Japanese railway officials. The restaurants are conducted by Japanese, and the yen is the regular currency.

We must comment that the Russian restaurants are more to our taste than the Japanese. Beath and I came nearer to starving this morning than any time in Siberia. It was too early for breakfast at the hotel before we left. It was too early for service at the railway restaurant at Changchun. There was no diner on the train. The train doesn't make the long stops at stations which it does in Russian territory, and there isn't time to buy anything. It no more stops than it begins to start again. I suppose it is no speedier than American trains, but it seems so after the leisurely saunter of the Siberian trains. We finally stopped at a large station where we bought a can of pineapple, a can of ham, and a couple of bottles of citron. We were giving the bread up in despair when we unearthed some among the passengers in the third-class cars.

This Corona is a regular three-ringed circus on this car. I guess most of the people have never seen a typewriter in action, at least on a car. As soon as I begin to hit the keys the long-dressed natives in front of me turn around and get up on their seats on their knees or stand up to get a better view. And if I turn around the man in the seat back of me is peering over my shoulder, and there is a line of faces all directed my way from the seats back of him. The Japanese train boys come running to our seat and sit down beside us trying to make out the English words. If at any time Beath and I want any service from the train boys, and they are not at hand, I pick up my Corona and begin typing and the boys flock around.

It is a new sensation to be riding on a car with vacant seats. Half of the seats on this second-class coach are unoccupied, and there is hardly anybody on the first-class coach.

There is one glory that we have left behind, the blue of the Siberian sky. It is cloudy today, with rainy stretches here and there, and Beath says we can expect to find the rainy season on in China, Korea, and Japan. But it is a comfortable time of the year to travel. I donned my BVD's at Harbin and was comfortable without an overcoat last night, the first time at night since last September.

We are now in the region where the Russo-Japanese War was fought. At the last station, Szu-ping-chieh, was held the first conference between the Russians and Japanese after the war. As one passes the various monuments that mark the ruin of Russian imperialism, it is interesting to speculate whether that ruin will spread further or whether there lies in the Russians a genius that the present chaos will call forth to reassert her power and prestige.

On board Ferry en route Fusan to Shimonoseki
May 31

We arrived at Mukden Wednesday afternoon, at five o'clock, after passing through the rich fields of Southern Manchuria which kept reminding me of the prairies of the Middle West. As we neared Mukden, there was another big dust storm but not as bad as the one we had leaving Harbin. Harbin will always live in my memory as a mass of swirling dust, wind, and gravel.

As soon as we got to Mukden, Beath and I went over to the old city, or Chinese city; it promised to be the best chance I would have to see a Chinese city. Of course this is not China proper, but it is the center of the Manchu region. The city serves as a good sample of the structure and appearance of a typical Chinese city. The old city is a long distance from the station. To get to it, we took a rickshaw through the leased Japanese section which is built up with fine new buildings and reminds one more of an American than of a Japanese city.

When we got to the high wall of the Chinese city, a wall that can be seen a long distance away and looks something like a big black screen afar off, we asked a Chinese policeman whether we could go to the top and take a look. (All through the Japanese section were Japanese policemen). The policeman at first said it was impossible, but after Beath jollied him a little in Chinese, he said we might try it. So we went up and had a good view over the city. The inner wall, on which we stood, was higher than most of the buildings of the city. The palace was before us in the center of the city. We stood at the western gate. The wall is about five miles around, almost square, a little over a mile in each direction. We stayed up some ten minutes taking it all in and were just starting down when we ran into the policeman, who evidently had begun to wonder how long we were going to stay up there and was coming up to see.

Mukden was where Beath and I separated. He was taking the train to Peking the next day. I left for Seoul at ten o'clock that evening. Thursday morning I woke up just before we reached the end of Manchuria. It already seemed like Korea. In fact all the preceding day the mountains which we skirted, lying to the east of us, reminded me of the pictures I had seen of Korea. The Korean natives, who are rather numerous in Vladivostok, which is really not far from Korea, are little in evidence through most of Manchuria, but were numerous in this southern stretch. At Antung we had a baggage examination and then passed over the long bridge of the Yalu River into Korea. All day Thursday we were passing through Korea's beautiful scenery. It resembles Japan, though the fields are not ridged into so many tiny plots as in Japan.

One of the American Korean missionaries boarded our train after we had gone a little way. He was much stirred up about the recent inhumanities which he said the Koreans were suffering in the Japanese effort to put down their revolution. He pointed out spots where churches had been burned down. At one place he said twenty-seven Koreans had been gathered into a church, where all were killed without warning, and then the church building had been burned down over them. He had pictures of the way some of the natives had been mutilated. He himself came from the northern interior. He said that many of his students and friends had suffered lashings and imprisonment for three months. When given a choice, they usually chose the lashings because that allowed them to go out and till their fields and also they did not suffer the political disability that they did if they were imprisoned.

The revolution seems to have been effectually squelched; the disorders have all been put down. But, of course, there is a deep inner resentment ready to blaze forth at the least encouragement.

This morning we arrived early at Fusan, where we took the ferry for Shimonoseki. It is an eleven-hour boat trip, and we ought to be in Shimonoseki in two hours and a half. This trip is usually rough, but it is pleasant and smooth today. I am on the second-class side where most of the people are Japanese. There are also some Russian Jews. I expect to take the express tonight and be in Yokohama tomorrow evening.

This trip through Korea has afforded an interesting study of the Japanese problem in the Far East. Korea, China, and Siberia provide a magnificent setting for the Far Eastern Prussianism, which is far-reaching and penetrating, even if less powerful than the European Prussianism. It is doubtful whether the Far Eastern Prussianism will listen to anything except force any sooner than German Prussianism did. One thing is sure, the Far Eastern Question will not be settled until Far Eastern Prussianism is settled.

Yokohama
June 20, 1919

Dear Rodney:

I am still on deck, in Japan, but have my ticket for the *Empress of Asia* for tomorrow. One of Emily's last letters, dated May 19, said that they had word that you had received your discharge, but you seem to have heard nothing of it.

The past week I have been up at Karuizawa, the famous summer resort of the foreigners in Japan. Among other stunts I climbed Mt. Asama, one of Japan's active volcanos, and the highest mountain in the empire after Fuji. I went up without a guide and was enjoying the view of the crater and Fuji and other parts of Japan in the distance when the wind suddenly veered, blew down a thick fog, and almost suffocated me with sulphurous steam. I beat it quick, believe me, only to run onto a narrow path between the precipices of the new and the old craters. I suddenly remembered that the guidebook warned travelers with weak heads to beware of this trail on the east side of the crater. I reckon the heads didn't need to be very weak either. Well, I couldn't find the trail as the fog prevented me from seeing more than a few feet in front of me. I decided to keep going down until I struck bottom anyway, and after a momentary scare when I thought I was going down the live crater instead of the old one, I found myself in the old lava bed. Some bed, believe me. Took me two hours and twenty-five minutes to get through this bed, with darkness coming on and my muscles tied up after walking constantly for thirty miles. But I got down, and out, and back to the hotel at ten p.m. having left at nine a.m. They were just getting ready to send search parties out after me. Felt none the worse the next day except for some sore muscles.

Well, this is my last farewell, I guess. I am sure glad I don't have to mail another wail to Emily about watching the boat go out without me.

Hope that your luck will come soon and that you will be on the way back.

After landing at Shimonoseki, Heald spent nearly a month in Japan awaiting transportation to the United States. Most of this period was less exciting than the descent from Mt. Asama, and he must have suffered boredom as well as impatience. Ironically, the admirable equanimity with which he had faced the hardships and delays of his three chaotic years in Russia deserted him temporarily, and he ended his tour of duty with an outburst of petulance against the Japanese. He besieged the steamship office in an effort to advance his sailing date but without success although, according to his account, other Americans were being accommodated in that way. Heald was convinced he was a victim of discrimination because of his connection with the Y.M.C.A. He charged that the Japanese had always opposed the Association and had hampered its work in Siberia. To one who remembers the throngs of Japanese who happily frequented the Tokyo Y only seventeen years later, it is hard to know what to make of this accusation. Perhaps Japan had seen the Y.M.C.A. in Siberia as an agent of American interests.

In spite of the delay, Heald was home before the end of the summer, helping his family, visiting old friends, and generally picking up the threads of peacetime life. In 1922 he left the Middle West to become secretary of the Y.M.C.A. in Troy, New York. The love of natural beauty and outdoor life which appears so vividly in his Russian and Siberian experiences led him to organize the Hikers Club and roam the mountains along the Massachusetts border. In 1929 he published an account of these rambles under the title "Taconic Trails."

In the same year the Healds moved to Canton, Ohio, where they were to spend the remaining years of their lives. (That Canton was less than one hundred miles from Oberlin may have influenced their choice.) There Edward Heald resuscitated an earlier Y.M.C.A.—William McKinley had been one of its presidents—and headed it until 1945. His taste for the out-of-doors remained with him; he roved the woods and fields around Canton as he had done at Colorado Springs, at Troy, at Pavlovsk.

Retiring from the Y at the age of sixty, Heald began his career as a historian, helping to organize a historical society, writing his six-volume county history, taking the lead in planning the Stark County Historical Center, and becoming its director. This remarkable library-museum houses exhibits of old autos, fire engines, and furniture in addition to printed and manuscript historical materials. It is adjacent to the McKinley Monument and is visited by many thousands of people every year as well as being used by students of history.

In 1964, at the age of seventy-nine, Heald resigned as director to devote all of his effort to a pictorial history of William McKinley and his times. At his death, three years later, he left twelve bound volumes of typescript, totaling almost 5000 pages as well as an extensive collection of photographs and cartoons. It is to be hoped that some of this material will eventually take its place in published form on the shelf beside Heald's other historical work.

Index